1789

no subj.

IGNATIUS LOYOLA

IGNATIUS LOYOLA.

An Attempt at an Impartial Biography

BY

HENRY DWIGHT SEDGWICK

"Biography, the most interesting perhaps of every species of composition, loses all its interest with me, when the shades and lights of the principal character are not accurately and faithfully detailed; . . . I can no more sympathize with a mere eulogist, than I can with a ranting hero upon the stage."

WALTER SCOTT.

MACMILLAN AND CO., LIMITED
ST. MARTIN'S STREET, LONDON
1924

52/89

TABLE OF CONTENTS

PREFACE

ANOTHER biography of Ignatius Loyola requires, perhaps, an apology or justification; if so, there is one, as it seems to me, ready to hand. In the fewest possible words it is this: The Society of Jesus has played an extraordinary rôle in the world during the last four centuries, and still plays an important one; that Society cannot be judged with fairness apart from a knowledge of its founder; and there is not, at present, any adequate biography of Loyola in English; therefore, an attempt, in the light of recent scholarship, to tell the story of his life as it is presented in the original sources, is neither superfluous nor presumptuous. But as this compendious apology cannot embrace all the respects that make Loyola a great figure, I must ask leave to enlarge upon it, and that in a more or less roundabout fashion.

During two centuries Spain was in the race for the foremost position in Europe, and in her days of high prosperity led all competitors. If one were to make a list of the half dozen men that gave to Spain her strength and swiftness in the race for glory, there would be no very great divergence of opinion, except in so far as the chooser's taste might lead him to rank war, adventure, art, literature, or religion as the matter of chief interest. But at the head of every discriminating list three names would stand—Cervantes, Velasquez, and Ignatius Loyola. *Don Quixote* is read wherever European books are read. The paintings of Velasquez make the Prado one of the chief shrines of art, and pictures, over which critics dispute whether they may be his or not, are treasured by the great galleries in Europe and America. Nevertheless, lovers of art who make a pilgrimage to see the *Surrender of Breda, Las Meninas,* or the listless face of Philip IV, are to be reckoned by hundreds only, and readers of *Don Quixote* by thousands at the most, but hundreds of thousands of men and women, not only of almost every nation in Europe, but also of every race and every class from Paraguay to Ethiopia, from Ethiopia to Japan, have had their lives influenced by what Ignatius Loyola did.

In the year 1538 this little Spaniard—he stood not quite five feet one and three-quarter inches—with deep-set, deep-seeing eyes, and high, smooth brow, trudged barefoot, slightly limping, from Venice to Rome, and petitioned the Pope to bestow upon him and nine other soldiers of Christ leave to serve their God and their neighbor under the name of the Company of Jesus. When he died some fifteen years later, these soldiers were a thousand strong, and their houses and colleges, like *castra Romana,* held fast against the Protestant aggression in Europe, won lost provinces back, and were spreading the Roman Catholic faith far and wide in Asia and America. Two generations later this little Spaniard was proclaimed by the Roman Catholic Church to have been one of that small band of holy men, called Saints, through whom the Spirit of God has wrought marvelous things for their fellows. At that time the Jesuit army numbered over 13,000, and an enumeration of its provinces maps out great regions of the world—Lombardy, Tuscany, Rome, Sicily, Aragon, Castile, Andalusia, Portugal, Lithuania and Poland, Austria, Germany, Bohemia, Belgium, Mexico, Philippine Islands, Peru, Paraguay, and so on, to the number of thirty-two. And as generations rolled by, through the pulpit, the confessional, and the schools, the Jesuits came near to dominate secular society. They directed the education of the upper classes, and held in subjection, so Protestants thought, the consciences of kings. Lord Macaulay's rhetorical passage concerning them is but a sober and moderate statement: "With what vehemence, with what policy, with what exact discipline, with what dauntless courage, with what self-denial, with what forgetfulness of the dearest private ties, with what intense and stubborn devotion to a single end, with what unscrupulous laxity and versatility in the choice of means, the Jesuits fought the battle of their Church, is written in

every page of the annals of Europe during several
generations." And Guizot in his *History of Civilization*
says: "Ils ont eu la grandeur de la pensée et la grandeur de
la volonté—Greatness of thought and greatness of will has
been theirs."

The greatness of the Order is plainly measured by the
host of enemies that banded together to pull it down. And
yet, in spite of all its enemies, it rose again, and to-day its
colleges and schools continue to maintain and propagate the
Holy Catholic Faith, Apostolic and Roman, in every quarter
of the globe. This is Ignatius's doing. You may run over
the whole list of famous Spaniards—whether warriors,
Charles V, Gonsalvo de Córdova, Cortez, Pizarro, Alva; or
adventurers, Vasco Nuñez de Balboa, Ponce de León,
Hernando de Soto; or men of letters, Lope de Vega,
Calderón, Quevedo; or painters, El Greco, Ribera, Murillo,
Zurbaran, Goya; or saints, Dominic, Theresa, John of the
Cross, Louis of Granada—and you will find that none have
left a monument comparable to the Society of Jesus.

Lord Acton calls him "that extraordinary man in whom
the Spirit of the Catholic Reaction is incorporated," and the
most eminent of modern Spanish scholars, Menendez y
Pelayo, says, "Ignatius more than any other man is the
living embodiment of the Spanish spirit in its golden age."
In this aspect, then, as the representative of Spain at the
time of her glory, Loyola has a claim on our general interest.

Second: the great heritage that our world of to-day has
received from Spain, or, perhaps I should say—though it is
all one so far as the Jesuits are concerned—from the Iberian
peninsula, is the civilization of South America; and in that
civilization, as I am told, the Order of Jesus has been the
chief individual factor. I quote from a very recent book
by a French scholar: "The greater part of whatever was
good and useful that had been accomplished for the civilization of South America [he is speaking with reference to the
date of its independence]—the development of education,
both primary and higher, the progress in agriculture—was
their doing. In a word, the material and moral wellbeing
of South America had been wrought by the Jesuits."

And, again, there are the feats of the Jesuits in North America. Readers of Parkman know what they did for the civilization of Canada; and if any one is curious as to the place that the Society occupies in the United States to-day, he has but to visit the colleges of the Jesuits in New York, Boston, Washington, Worcester, and many another city, or, if he prefer, their schools and churches, scattered all over. The originator of this stupendous achievement offers an interest that transcends the boundaries of kingdom or church.

And one word here as to his personality. Some sentences in Lord Rosebery's estimate of Oliver Cromwell seem to me applicable to Ignatius Loyola: "He was a practical mystic, the most formidable and terrible of all combinations. A man who combines inspiration apparently derived . . . from close communion with the supernatural and the celestial, a man who has that inspiration and adds to it the energy of a mighty man of action, such a man as that lives in communion on a Sinai of his own, and when he pleases to come down to this world below seems armed with no less than the terrors and decrees of the Almighty Himself."

Having such a character and such an achievement to deal with, it was to be expected that the biographies of Loyola should be marked either with the stamp of approbation or with that of disapprobation, and, as far as I can find out, they are in fact so marked. There are said to have been written more than two hundred biographies, but if indeed there ever were so many, scarce a dozen are of any account, and such as there are, whether of account or not, may be divided into three categories. In the first come the biographies written by Loyola's personal disciples, Polanco, Ribadeneira, Lainez, and by their immediate successors who had original documents under their eyes, such as Orlandini and Maffei, with whom Bartoli may be included, although he wrote much later. These lives are good, but hardly sufficient to satisfy modern taste in biography.

In the second category I include all the subsequent books on Ignatius written during some three hundred years, a long period in which passion and prejudice

prevented men from writing fairly. Every one was
a partisan either on one side or the other. By the
act of canonization Catholics were committed to eulogy;
since that event adverse criticism has meant disrespect
to the Pope, and perhaps to higher authority. Moreover, during the proceedings of canonization reports
were forthcoming of over two hundred miracles wrought
by Loyola's intercession; and, also, memories of what
had happened seventy or eighty years before were fished
up out of many pools of local tradition. From that
time until the present generation few if any Catholics have
ventured to disregard these miracles and these pious traditions. On the other hand, Protestants, and Catholic
partisans of the forces that ultimately caused the temporary
suppression of the Jesuits, included Loyola in the belligerent
dislike which they felt towards the Order as it became a
hundred or two hundred years after his death. To show
their state of mind, I will cite two random instances, come
upon in picking up various books on the subject. In a
French book of the eighteenth century occurs the following
passage, "This Society has a plan, framed at its very birth,
to do away entirely with the teachings of Jesus Christ, to
destroy His religion, and overturn crowns and kingdoms, in
order to build up on their ruins an absolute despotism";
and a Spanish book, written as late as 1880, has this title,
"The Jesuits—their mode of life, their habits, adulteries,
assassinations, regicides, poisonings, and other peccadillos
committed by that celebrated Society." In short, from 1595
to near 1900, I repeat, those who in any way concerned
themselves with the founder of the Society of Jesus were
not able to see clearly on account of passion and prejudice.

Besides this, during that long period, there was more or
less difficulty of access to the original sources. Therefore,
from the time of the first disciples down to the present,
owing to bias and to ignorance, it was difficult, or rather
virtually impossible, to write a fair and accurate biography
of Loyola.

Since 1900 the situation has completely changed. The
odium theologicum has died away; if there are Catholics

who are opposed to the Society of Jesus, they are temperate
in words, or mean to be, and Protestants have attained to
justice and to appreciation, or nearly so. Fiery partisan-
ship no longer distorts this ancient history. And also there
is now no excuse left for ignorance of the sources; most of
these—biographies, memoirs, records, letters, and so forth,
in Latin, Spanish, Italian, and Portuguese—have been published in fifty large volumes; moreover, two accomplished
scholars in the Society, Father Astrain in Spain, and Father
Tacchi Venturi in Italy, are publishing long histories of the
Society in their respective countries, and each has recounted
at considerable length the life of the founder, adhering
closely to the original sources already known, and supple-
menting them by very varied information which they have
gathered together from unprinted documents stored in
various archives in Spain and Italy. These two biographies, imbedded in the history of the Order, may serve to
represent the third category, that of fairness and modern
scholarship. A French biography also has been announced,
and may be out already. And a German Protestant, Dr.
Heinrich Böhmer, has published *Studien zur Geshichte der
Gesellschaft Jesu.* European scholarship has prepared the
way, and the time has come, therefore, when a faithful
biography of St. Ignatius can be written in English without
a controversial spirit, and at no greater cost than a certain
amount of study.

None of the books that fall in this third category have
been rendered into English. Not counting translations of
some books that belong in the second category, and brief
sketches in encyclopedias and such, there is, I believe, but
one original biography in English, and that is *Ignatius
Loyola* by Catherine Stewart Erskine, Lady Buchan
(writing under the name of Stewart Rose), published in
1870. This biographer encountered both difficulties heretofore mentioned—for they existed, although in diminished
force, at the time she wrote—a bias to eulogy and lack of
complete access to original sources. I say hers is the only
English biography, because that by Francis Thompson, the
poet—Pegasus hitched to the plow—is scarcely more than

an abridgement, a briefer retelling in his own sonorous
prose, of Lady Buchan's book, and the short lives, such as
Father J. H. Pollen's, are rather biographical essays than
full biographies.

My endeavor has been to narrate Loyola's life as, aided
by the works of the scholars to whom I have referred, I
find it in the original sources, although not without comment or criticism, nor without my own interpretation upon
such episodes as seem to me in need of interpretation. I
have also tried to do what neither Tacchi Venturi nor
Astrain has done—for it lay quite outside their purposes—
and that is, to provide a frame of contemporaneous history
in which to set the picture. I believe that I am fairly
free from religious bias—although no one knows his own
deep prejudices—and in telling Loyola's story, I shall be as
strictly impartial as a profound admiration for this heroic
soldier of Jesus will permit.

Cambridge, Massachusetts, May, 1923.   H. D. S.

IGNATIUS LOYOLA

IGNATIUS LOYOLA

CHAPTER I

BOYHOOD AND YOUTH (1495-1521)

IGNATIUS LOYOLA was born in the Basque province of Guipuscoa, at the castle of Loyola, not far from the little town of
Azpeitia. This province lies between the Bay of Biscay and
what was at that time the Spanish portion of the Kingdom
of Navarre. His father, Don Beltran Yáñez de Oñaz y
Loyola, belonged to the principal nobility of the province,
and was of kin in some degree to a great nobleman, Don
Alonso Manrique, duke of Najera. Don Beltran had eight
sons, of whom Ignatius was the youngest, and five daughters.
The date of Loyola's birth is usually given as 1491; however, for reasons set forth in the appendix, I incline to think
that 1495 is the true year. He was baptized Iñigo but in
manhood took the name Ignacio, or in its Latin form Ignatius, for the reason that it was more generally known, and
for some years used one or the other indiscriminately, and
then finally dropped Iñigo entirely.

Of his doings during boyhood and youth few facts are
known, and those vaguely. On the other hand, of his disposition and general behaviour the evidence is definite
enough. Late in life he dictated to one of his disciples,
Father Luis Gonzalez de Camara, a brief memoir of his
career, in which all he says concerning his youth is, that it
was given over to vanity, adding, in explanation, that he
entertained a "love of martial exercises and a vainglorious
desire for fame." His earliest biographer, Father Polanco,
another of his disciples, says: "Like other young men bred
in court to a military life" he was keenly interested in sports

1

and contests. Father Nadal, also a disciple, records that
Ignatius "took no thought of religion or piety," and Polanco
adds that "he was free in making love to women," an accusation that is fully borne out by his own acknowledgment after
conversion. The morals of the time were not puritanical,
and, except by the religious-minded, sins of the flesh were
deemed very venial. The gist of the evidence is that Loyola
lightly adopted the contemporary standards of young gentlemen who were quite free from any thought of becoming
saints.

As to the events of his early years these disciples seem to
have been as much in the dark as we are; but certain details
have been brought to light. While still a young boy, he left
his father's castle and went to live in the town of Arevalo in
Old Castile, not very far from Salamanca. An important
personage, at one time governor of Arevalo, Don Juan Velazquez de Cuellar, for some motive that is not apparent, invited his friend Don Beltran to send him one of his sons that
he might bring him up in his house like a child of his own,
proposing to procure for him by and by a place in the king's
household. The offer was accepted; Ignatius was selected
and sent. He lived with this nobleman, as it seems, until
the latter's death, though perhaps with interruptions and
not all the time at Arevalo. There is no satisfactory evidence that Ignatius was ever attendant upon the king's
court, although he may have visited it in the train of Don
Juan.

It has been repeated often that Ignatius in his youth was
very wild, and it is true, as I have said, that according to his
own confession, his personal morals were loose, but there is
no evidence of this beyond what he himself told his disciples; and one must remember that it is customary for great
saints, who in their serious years set a very high standard
of human perfection, to see the irregularities of their youth
in colors far blacker than they look to less scrupulous eyes.
There is, in addition to his self-accusation, one other bit of
evidence of wild oats. This evidence is found in some documents of an incomplete judicial record of the year 1515,
when, as I think, Ignatius was in his twentieth year. Only

the accusation is given; the documents on behalf of the defendant were either destroyed or lost. What is left of the record suggests some carnival frolic, an escapade such as Prince Hal and Poins might have engaged in without the least smirch upon their reputations, certainly no worse than the foolish frolic of many a young soldier. As there is so little information concerning his youth, I will quote this record.

It appears that at Azpeitia, there was a dispute over an ecclesiastical benefice, or something of the sort, in which the Loyola family took part. On Shrove Tuesday a fracas occurred. Nothing is known of the affair beyond the accusation that Ignatius and his elder brother, Pedro Lopez de Loyola, who was in clerical orders, had committed, in the language of the prosecuting attorney, some offense "by night, on purpose, with fraud, guile, and malice prepense (*sobre habla é consejo*)." These vituperative epithets were no doubt used in order to bring the misdemeanor within the language of some criminal statute. Nothing further may be reasonably inferred than that the brothers had perhaps carried the license of carnival too far, and that in consequence some indignant citizen lodged a complaint against them.[1] Pedro and Ignatius returned, or fled, from Azpeitia to Navarre. Thereupon the Corregidor of Guipuscoa, a sort of high sheriff, demanded of the authorities in Navarre that the two should be delivered up to him. The brothers obtained an order from the episcopal court in Pamplona enjoining the execution of the Corregidor's writ of arrest, on the ground that they were both clerks and not subject to secular jurisdiction. A hearing was had before the ecclesiastical judge and a brief submitted on behalf of the Corregidor. The case against Pedro Lopez stood on a different footing from that against Ignatius; the elder brother was admittedly in clerical orders, and therefore some offense sufficiently heinous to deprive the ecclesiastical court of jurisdiction had to be alleged; for this reason, I surmise,

---

[1] Possibly a story, told years afterwards, how Ignatius had drawn his sword on a peaceable citizen may represent the view of the other party to the quarrel.

the pleader inserted those vituperative words, "with fraud, guile, and malice prepense." As to Ignatius, it was only necessary to show that he was not in orders, or else, for some reason, was not in a position to claim benefit of clergy. The Corregidor's position was this: Two bulls of Pope Alexander VI provided that no clerk should be entitled to claim benefit of clergy unless he had worn a tonsure and a recognized clerical garb for the period of four months prior to the commission of the offense. A local synod had gone further and required a clerk to be duly registered, and had enacted that the tonsure must be at least the size of a penny (*una tarja*), that the clerk's hair must be cut so that his ears or a part of them showed, that his cloak should be of a sober hue, free from ornament, and reach to within about six inches from the ground, that his cap should not be dyed, etc., etc. Ignatius, the Corregidor alleged, did not come within these provisions. His name was not on the register; he had no tonsure; his hair hung down thick about his shoulders; his cap was of a gay color; he wore no cassock, but went about with corselet, gorget, crossbow, arrows, and all sorts of weapons; in short, "he displayed the insignia, not of celestial, but of earthly soldiery." And all this he had done continuously for years. The record terminates abruptly at this point. There can be no doubt that Ignatius, though he may have received the tonsure when a child, was a soldier and not a clerk; but as no enemy has ever unearthed any further evidence of the alleged offense, and no friend has ever thought it worth while to suppress these documents, one may fairly conclude that ill will between factions in Azpeitia or jealousy between the secular and ecclesiastical tribunals lay at the bottom of the prosecution.

The record, however, establishes the fact that Ignatius began his military life probably as early as 1511 or 1512, when he was sixteen or seventeen years old, and further, since the scene of the episode is laid in Azpeitia and Pamplona, that he was no longer a resident member of Don Juan Velazquez's household, for that nobleman was in those years royal governor of Arevalo. Nevertheless, some tie

must have continued to exist between them, ior upon Don
Juan's death in 1517, at which time it became necessary for
Ignatius to shift for himself, his widow, evidently in fulfillment of her husband's promise to Don Beltran to bring
up Ignatius as if he were his own child, fitted the young
man out with two horses and a purse of five hundred crowns.
So provided for, Ignatius went to Pamplona and took service with the duke of Najera, his kinsman, who had recently
been appointed viceroy of Navarre. In the duke's service
Ignatius seems to have showed character and spirit, not
only willingness to undertake a difficult task, but also both
good sense in laying plans and perseverance in execution,
and, in spite of little experience, to have given proof, even
then, of his rare skill in handling men. On one occasion
he was despatched to settle some quarrels in Guipuscoa;
this task he accomplished to the satisfaction of both parties
and thereby won special approbation. On another, he
showed disinterestedness. The duke's soldiers captured
the city of Najera, which had revolted; Ignatius was among
the foremost in the fight, but refused to accept any share
of the booty.

So much for the facts of Loyola's life prior to his conversion that have any trustworthy historical support.

As we have now come to the time when both Ignatius
begins his great career and Spain hers, it may not be inap-
propriate to see how the nation, entering into European
affairs, like an athlete on his mark starting to run a race,
was judged by contemporaries. I will quote from some
distinguished Italian observers, and first Lucio Marineo, a
lover of learning (about 1535):

The Spaniards delight greatly in the use of weapons, and
the blast of trumpets in battle stirs them to the quick. It
is my opinion, and that of many others, that they surpass
all other nations in the art of war, not only by reason of
bodily strength and agility, and heroism, and endurance of
work, hunger and other necessary toils, but also because,
besides that, they have great good sense. Their behaviour
is excellent, and their temperance most praiseworthy, in

eating, drinking, and other respects. I have lived in Spain for fifty years, and in all that time I have not seen a man drunk, and I have known many who only drink water, and the women, too, for the most part, abstain from wine.

The majority of the men are very particular with their dress, and spend more on their clothes and personal ornaments than on food and lodging, or any other necessaries. Some austere persons may not approve of this; nevertheless I applaud it, especially for those who can afford it without hurt to anybody, and without putting on airs, but from a regard for their own dignity and to show their liberality. I like their ways of living and have always adopted them. They concern themselves about religious matters and the salvation of their souls with quite as much diligence and care as about the riches and amusements of the world. Indeed the Spaniards of the present day are very religious, and display great reverence for the worship of God; the priests are very solicitous for the spiritual welfare of the people, over and above celebrating mass and observing the canonical hours, and instruct their flocks with sermons and good example. And laymen,—not only noblemen and educated men, but also the common people and the uneducated, —are very obedient to the commandments of Christ and the Church. While some go to confession at least once a year, others three times, and many four times; and others, not only old men but even young fellows, confess ten times a year, or every month, to the curate or some other priest, I do not think any nation in the world today is as Christian as the Spanish.

I now quote Gaspar Contarini, the Venetian ambassador (1525), whom we shall meet hereafter, as cardinal and patron of the first Jesuits:

The Spaniards are inclined to melancholy: they are all physically fit for martial exercises and fighting; they are intelligent and make a cult of honor, which they think usually obliges them to a military career; and by natural bent they excel all other nations in whatever pertains to war. They are reserved of speech, very proud and haughty in their manners and carriage, with little love toward their neighbors, and of an envious disposition.

Other Italians, believing in their own intellectual super-iority and the greater civilization of their own country, were more critical. Francesco Guicciardini, of Florence, looked severely out of his cold, shrewd, distrustful eyes (1513). He reports to his government:

Spaniards are saturnine in disposition, of swarthy complexion, and small of stature; proud, and full of the conviction that no nation equals theirs. They are boastful in speech, and take pains to make all the impression they can. . . . They are much inclined to arms, more perhaps than any other nation in Chris-tendom, and well fitted so to do, for they are very dexterous, agile and quick of limb. They make a great point of honor, and had rather die than suffer a stain. . . . They are considered intelligent and shrewd, and yet they are not good in liberal arts or mechanical matters; almost all the artists and artisans at the king's court are French-men, or from some other country. They think it beneath them to become merchants, for they all affect the humours of persons of quality, and would rather go soldiering even with poor prospects, or take service with some great noble and put up with a thousand discomforts, or (in earlier days) betake themselves to the road as highwaymen. There are of course certain manufactures that they take up, but as a rule they are averse to such things. . . . In public worship they affect great religious behaviour, but they are not so in reality. They are very formal in their manners, and cere-monious, and make a fine display of obeisance, with hand-kissings and expatiation of titles, "Sir, I am yours to com-mand"; however, it is better to fight shy and trust them but little. They are great dissemblers, in every rank you will find past masters; it is this quality—Punic ingenuity—that has got them their reputation of smartness and ability; it underlies their ceremonious ways and make-believe.

The Flemings, who came to line their pockets in the train of Charles V, also recorded various impressions. The Spaniards were poor. In Asturias for instance, most of them went barelegged and the young women, on workdays, barefoot; and in some places the poverty was so great that villages were underground, the dwellings, on account of the scarcity of timber, were mere cellars or caves dug in the earth, like a rabbit warren. And to this day (it may be said) lack of energy has left a small region of Spain, occupied by people called Jurdes, in a very similar plight. Laurent Vital, whom I am quoting, attributes their poverty to pride and laziness. If the men chose to work they might be rich and have well-appointed houses; but they esteemed themselves all noble, and were above unnecessary industry. Perhaps it was their pride that rendered them, as he thought, ill bred. (But it must be remembered that there was much bad feeling between the Flemings and the Spaniards.) Vital gives this instance of what he means: When the king went to Valladolid, although it was the custom, sanctioned by law, that his retinue should be billeted about in houses, occupying if need were half the rooms, some ecclesiasts refused to grant admittance. When the magistrates forced the doors open, the priests retorted by excommunications and by refusal to conduct divine service in the churches.

Possibly Vital was one of those to whom admittance was refused. At any rate, he noticed—*horrescit referens*—other fallings below the standards of the Low Countries. Babies were left out of doors, to die of exposure, or be eaten by wild beasts. And in Valladolid, even while royalty was there, robbers and robberies abounded. And, what shocked him even more, housewives and chambermaids made a practice of emptying slops from upper windows into the streets. He introduces his description of what takes place, which reads like a passage from Rabelais, with a careful *"sauf vos révérences,"* and protests that at least a warning cry should be given. He also draws a comparison between the treatment of servants and horses in Germany and that in Castile, greatly to the advantage of the Germans, in spite of the fact that they are *"ruides et rebelles"* and the Castilians *"assez courtois"*; for both man and beast are well cared for in Germany, while in Castile servants are obliged to run on foot after their mounted masters in the country as well as in town, and at night, tired, hungry, thirsty, and often wet, get poor fare, being lucky to find a bench or table to lie upon, and their wages are paltry. The horses are treated in like fashion, and become lean, weak, and emaciated, and at that they are belabored with blows. But in spite of these shortcomings Monsieur Vital asserts that in other respects—with his mind on the gentry and prosperous merchants—he much prefers the ways of the Castilians to those of the Germans, for the former accept with good grace what God sends them, and make good cheer without wassailing, wastefulness, or gluttony, as people do in Germany and the Low Countries, *"de quoy Dieu est souvent grandement offensé."*

To dwell further on this subject would take us too far out of our way. Enough has been quoted to show that Spaniards were proud, sober, observant of Christian ritual, and poor—neglecting, as they have done ever since, the economic development of the country, in their quest of glory and empire.

CHAPTER II

CONVERSION (1521)

THE year 1521 is the turning point, the master year, in Loyola's life. Up to that time he had followed the common road of common men; but in that year there befell him the mysterious religious experience which men call conversion, and he surrendered himself to a dominating influence that led him all his life. From that time he could well say, "I go to prove my soul"; and he proved it heroic.

His conversion was not of the kind that can point back to one overwhelming moment, such as St. Paul experienced on the road to Damascus, or St. Augustine under the fig tree, when he heard the voice say *Tolle lege;* nevertheless, Loyola's turn-about was as complete as theirs. From a self-indulgent boy seeking his own pleasure, he became an austere and steadfast man, following the gleam that lighted up the path of grievous self-denial. The child of the world became a child of the spirit. The cause of his conversion is ascribed by Catholic tradition to the grace of God. So be it; but without derogation to the explanation, we may look about to find what educational influences were at work to prepare the ground in which divine seeds might lodge and germinate.

In his youth Loyola did not go to college, and had, as it will appear hereafter, but scanty schooling; he lived the life of a young gentleman, doing his duty while in service, and amusing himself with escapades and women in times of leisure, and, so far as he had any use for books, in reading tales of knights errant, especially the very popular *Amadis of Gaul.* These occupations would make unlikely conduits for the flow of spiritual grace. But an educational force was abroad of great potency, a moral tonic was in the air, that affected young men of finer sensibilities, and educated them as the universities of Salamanca or Alcalá de Henares could not do. During the formative years in Loyola's life, the tide of Spanish fortune was mounting to the flood; the spirits of young men were swept up on the crest of an exultant wave of national pride and self-confidence. So it had been in the Athenian democracy under Pericles, and was to be in Elizabethan England. This was the beginning of what the Spanish call *El siglo de Oro*. Let me remind the reader of what happened then.

Some twenty years before Ignatius was born, Aragon and Castile had been united by the marriage of Ferdinand and Isabella. These *Reyes Católicos,* as they are called, were able rulers; and from their marriage and the consequent virtual administrative union, great advantages, economic, political, and social, accrued to their kingdoms. Stirring events soon followed hard on one another's heels. The national crusade against the Moors, which after seven hundred years of dispossession, liberated the last plot of Spanish soil from the shame of Mohammedan dominion, ended in a desperate campaign for the capture of Granada; that campaign lasted ten long years, and was more memorable for its fierce and chivalric episodes than any struggle for a city since the fall of Troy. The Spaniards did not rest content with driving out the Moors. The primate of Spain, Cardinal Ximenes, equipped an expedition out of his ecclesiastical revenues, transported his army to Morocco, and blessed it as it rushed to its victorious onslaught upon Oran. Gonsalvo de Cordoba, *el gran capitán,* fought the French for the possession of southern Italy, won battle after battle, and added the kingdom of Naples to the Spanish dominions. Two of Loyola's brothers were killed in these wars. The duke of Alva wrested the southern portion of Navarre from its native sovereign and ran the northern boundary of Spain along the Pyrenees. Ignatius was just seventeen at the time and may possibly have taken some part in the campaign.

But stirring as were these events in Spain and across the waters of the Mediterranean, far more adventurous and romantic success befell the bold spirits that sailed out over

the Atlantic Ocean. Spanish and Portuguese discoveries,
like beacon fires, one kindled from the next, lit up the great
darkness that had hung over the globe, and revealed unknown islands and continents to an astonished Europe.
Columbus and his followers brought back marvellous tales
of mysterious shores, and cosmographers began to set down
on their charts fanciful outlines of a western world. Ponce
de León landed in Florida; Balboa "stared at the Pacific";
one ship followed in another's wake and nosed its way, past
strange beach and headland, into new creeks and rivers. A
third brother of Ignatius perished on one of these expeditions. And while Spaniards were sailing westward, the
Portuguese sailed to the east, each nation inciting the other
to fresh rivalry. Vasco da Gama doubled the Cape of
Good Hope; other mariners and buccaneers, emulating his
example, cruised along the east coast of Africa, past the
shores of Arabia, across to India, and on to Ceylon, Sumatra
and Java. Never had there been such a time in Europe;
high romance on canvas wings skimmed the oceans, as
swallows skim a pond. And human pulses beat strongest
in Spain. Even in remote Navarre, these tidings must have
passed from mouth to mouth, exciting young men with
thoughts of adventure and conquest. Every soldier's mess
in Pamplona discussed adventure in some form. It could
not have been otherwise; the famous pass of Roncevalles,
where Charlemagne's retreating rearguard had been routed,
and, according to Spanish tradition, Roland himself had
been slain by Bernardo del Carpio, lay not a day's ride dis-
tant. His horn, the trophy of victory, still hung in the
chapel there.

The romance of discovery and adventure was, as I say,
in the air, but the austere Spanish character, which love of
romance heated to action, had been forged and tempered
by seven centuries of warfare with misbelievers. While the
Cross was struggling with the Crescent, the Roman Catholic
creed was being bred in Spanish bones, as integral a part
of each man's personality as his dark eyes and swarthy skin.
Religion was one with patriotism, one with self-preservation, one with the lust of battle and the joy of triumph. So

strong was their devotion to their faith that all pure-blooded Spaniards welcomed the Inquisition (1478) with joy, and felt a sense of personal purification at the expulsion of the unbelieving Jews (1492). Spaniards looked upon themselves not only as the chief men of Europe, "of earth's first blood," but as special champions of the Cross. To be a Christian was to be a soldier, and to be a soldier was to dedicate oneself to the service of the God of Battles. Such thoughts, like chemical fluids, lay in solution in Loyola's mind, awaiting the sudden troubling of the soul that should crystallize them into a definite form of devotion, self-consecration and service; and underneath, in those deep regions of self where the issues of character are decided, lay a sense of repentance and regret for fruitless years and trivial acts, and deeper still the consciousness of power that goes with genius and the desire to put it to use. Be that as it may, on a sudden Loyola's soul came to birth.

To return to the year 1521, when Ignatius was a young officer in the garrison of Pamplona. In the month of May, a French army marched up against the city. The invasion came about in this way. For a generation and more there had been disputes over dynastic rights to the kingdom of Navarre; France supported one claim and Spain another, but the real issue was whether France should control the passes of the Pyrenees and have a foothold south of the mountains, or Spain establish her northern boundary along the mountain tops. Previous campaigns do not concern us; but I may recall the fact that Cæsar Borgia, after strutting in his brilliant braggadocio rôle upon the center of the world's stage, perished in this out of the way corner, unnoticed, in some chance raid, a luckless soldier of fortune. Ferdinand played the game better than the French and, as I have said, annexed that portion of the little kingdom that lay south of the Pyrenees to the crown of Castile. The French bided their time. In 1521 a revolt of various Spanish cities, *las comunidades,* seemed to offer them their opportunity, for Navarre was stripped of troops. The French army crossed the mountains, meeting virtually no resistance, and advanced on Pamplona.

A letter by some partisan of the older régime, dated May 17, 1521, says:

The French are coming down the Roncal Valley in such numbers that they can't be counted. The towns round-about rose yesterday for King Don Enrique [the claimant supported by France]; Pedro of Navarre, with the Marshal's son, is at their head. The duke of Najera has hurried from Pamplona. The city is left to itself. The French army will be there tomorrow, and it is said that they need not unbuckle their spurs before taking the citadel; it's a sure thing. The whole kingdom is up for King Don Enrique, and the duke of Najera may thank God if he gets safe into Castile.

And, on the 21st:

You will have heard how the Spanish, shut up in the citadel at Pamplona, started to train their artillery on the city; the French set up their cannon against the barbican of the citadel, and, can you believe it—it seems incredible—after a siege of six hours by the clock, the Spanish surrendered, asking for quarter. The French wished to refuse; the Marshal's son was obliged to intercede in order to save them.

These letters appear somewhat biassed; at any rate, after the French had entered the city and opened fire on the citadel, it became plainly impossible for the garrison to maintain itself, and all the officers, except Ignatius, advised immediate surrender; but he persuaded the commandant to hold out as long as possible. After a cannonade lasting some six or eight hours at most, a breach was made in the wall, the French rushed in, and the garrison lowered its flag.

Just before the last assault, on May 20th, a cannon ball broke the bone of Loyola's right leg and inflicted a flesh wound on the left. The victors treated him with much consideration, tended his wounds, and at the end of a fortnight sent him home to the castle of Loyola on a stretcher.

For some reason, the bone of the right leg had to be broken again and reset. Ignatius was very ill, and the pain very severe, but he bore his suffering with extreme pluck. His condition grew steadily worse, until on June 28th, the vigil of the feast of St. Peter and St. Paul, the crisis came. Ignatius had always entertained a peculiar reverence for St. Peter, and he ascribed his recovery to the apostle's interposition. The bone, however, had been badly set, and an ugly protuberance showed itself near the knee, and as he had not yet resolved to abandon the world, and was still far from indifferent to his personal appearance, he insisted upon a further operation, although the surgeons warned him of the suffering. In addition to the surgical operation, the leg had to be stretched by means of a weight, as it was shorter than the other. The pain must have been torture, but the result was successful; Ignatius always limped a little, but so slightly, at least until the last years of his life, as to escape casual observation.

His convalescence was slow. To while away the time he asked for books of knight errantry, the only novels existing in those days. There happened to be none in the house, so they gave him a Spanish version of the *Legenda Aurea*, by Jacopo da Voragine, and a *Life of Christ* by Ludolf of Saxony, a pious and learned Carthusian monk, who had lived about two hundred years before; as it is evident that the latter book exercised a great influence upon Ignatius, during these critical weeks, it will be best to say something of it. Ignatius's copy was in Castilian, but the original work was in Latin. It is long, longer I think, for instance, than *Guy Mannering* or *David Copperfield,* and could well occupy a man during several hours a day for a month in the careful reading of it. It is a didactic treatise, written from a devout zeal to help other men to a knowledge and love of Christ. It treats of all the important episodes in Christ's life and interprets their significance, confirming the author's comments and exhortations with many passages from St. Augustine, St. Chrysostom, and other Fathers. It begins with a Procemium that sets forth the basis of Christian belief.

Christ Is the Foundation of Salvation.

For other foundation can no man lay than that is laid (as the Apostle saith) which is Jesus Christ. St. Augustine says that God is wholly sufficient and man wholly deficient, and God is so supremely good that it cannot be well with any one who turns away from Him. Therefore whoso wishes to escape the damnation due his sins and to be amended in spirit, must not forsake that foundation, because there he shall find remedies for all his needs.

The Sinner is Invited to the Mercy and to the Imitation of Christ.

First, therefore, let the sinner who desires to lay aside the burthen of his sins and attain peace of mind, listen to God inviting sinners to His mercy, saying, "Come unto me all ye that labor (that is with frailties) and are heavy laden (that is with the burthen of sins), and I will give you rest (that is by healing and comforting you) and ye shall find rest unto your souls." Therefore let the sick listen to the tender and compassionate physician, and go to Him in deep contrition and with zealous purpose to turn from evil forever and be good.

Second: let the sinner, now that he is become a faithful disciple of Christ, being reconciled to Him through penitence, strive with all diligence to abide with his physician and become acquainted with Him, pondering with all possible devotion over His most holy life xx. Let him read the life of Christ in such manner that he shall strive with all his might to imitate Christ's behaviour. xx

Third: as to the third point in the imitation of Christ, you must know that to imitate Christ is to follow in His footsteps, and to conform to His ways. We must imitate Him in the threefold way He trod—the way of poverty, humility, and hardship.

The whole book, in short, is a summary of the beliefs and ideals of mediæval Christianity. It is not to be wondered at that a young man, back from the brink of death, suddenly thrown in upon himself, facing the chance of being maimed for life, and suffering intense physical pain, should be touched to the quick by what he read. Many passages, if one may judge from his after life, sunk deep into his memory. Much that he did and various precepts and counsels in his book of *Spiritual Exercises* sound almost like echoes of Ludolf's book; as, for instance, where Ludolf says that death to self is attained by five steps: "First, from a sense of humility a man shall deem himself the meanest of men; second, he shall say so in words; third, he shall bear patiently hearing it said by others; fourth, he shall bear patiently being treated with contempt by others; fifth, he shall not only not grieve, but even be glad that he is scorned by other men." And Ludolf's precept, *Pone ante oculos gesta præterita tanquam præsentia, et sic magis sapida senties et jucunda*—Conjure up before your eyes the past as if it were present, for so doing you will find them [he is speaking of Christ's actions] more savory and pleasant—is a direct precedent for Loyola's precepts upon contemplation. And the passage in the *Spiritual Exercises* which bids the novice contemplate hell in "its height, depth and breadth," putting his five senses to the service of his imagination, seems traceable to Ludolf's description of hell:

Ibi erit calor ignis, rigor frigoris, tenebræ, fumus, lacrymæ interiores, aspectus dæmonum, clamor, improperium, mallei percutientium, serpentes et dracones, ariditas sitis, fetor sulphuris, vermis conscientiæ, vincula, carcer, timor, dolor, pudor, et confusio peccatorum omnibus patientium, invidia, rancor, tristitia, ablatio spes omnis salutis. (There shall be the heat of fire, the cold of ice, darkness, smoke, tears that cannot be shed, demoniacal appearances, uproar, reproaches, hammers pounding, serpents, dragons, drought, thirst, smell of sulphur, the worm of conscience, chains, dungeons, fear, torture, shame, and the hurly-burly of sinners suffering from all these, and envy, malice, sorrow, and the loss of all hope of salvation.)

We read this description, cold and incredulous; but suppose a man, who has just felt the finger of death touch his forehead, should believe, and believe intensely, that such would be his fate, and the fate of all men, for everlasting, if he and they should die in mortal sin, would he not engrave the terrible rede on the tablets of his memory? And Loyola, who was not intellectual, not interested in things of the mind, not metaphysical nor curious concerning speculations, not poetical, not a man of imagination or many ideas, had one faculty, in which so far as I know he has only been excelled by Dante, that of an intense vividness of conceiving imaginings, as corporeal things, in definite, concrete forms. This faculty was, in great part, the source of his extraordinary power over men.

To return to Loyola's sick bed. In these books he took much pleasure and satisfaction, nevertheless his thoughts, still tinged by *Amadis of Gaul,* did not concern themselves all the time with saints and salvation; they often wandered off on the wings of day dreams to regions of romance. One fancy, indulged in for hours at a time, which he recalled vividly more than thirty years afterwards, was to imagine a lovely lady, the Queen or Empress of some far country, himself devoted to her service, what feats he would perform for her sake, what device he should wear, and so forth. Much ingenuity has been spent in surmises as to who this great lady was. My own notion is that she was inconstant in form. In his period of worldly thoughts, I think she resembled Don Quixote's Princess Micomicona, and in his religious moods the holy Queen of Heaven. At times also he made vague plans of a pilgrimage to Jerusalem, barefoot, living upon herbs; he meditated upon the lives of early saints, their privations, flagellations, temptations, sufferings, their triumphant self-mastery at the end, and their knowledge and love of God; and also upon St. Francis of Assisi and St. Dominic, and would say to himself: these two did thus and so, why should not Iñigo de Loyola do the like? In this fashion, as he lay upon his couch, his vagabond fancies wandered to and fro between vanity and religion.

Ignatius's own narrative of what went on within him at

this crisis of his spiritual development is meager; but there is one article of his doctrine that can be assigned to this time, and both because it is the most direct evidence of what was going on in his mind then, and because he regarded it as of great help in solving a perplexing and dangerous point in spiritual regeneration, I will say something about it. His psychological analysis is sometimes a little difficult to accept at first sight, because the mediæval terms in which it is couched tend to conceal from the modern reader the truth and reasonableness of his conclusions. Appetites, impulses, inclinations, yearnings, are to him incorporeal spirits from heaven or hell. And, where we, for instance, adopting a system of material localization, speak of nerves and so forth, he speaks of angelical comfortings or of the artifices of Lucifer: a habit, indeed, that continued even in Protestant theology, down to the days of our fathers. In the passage to which I refer, he concerns himself with the proper interpretation of the differences between states of contentment and exaltation on the one hand, and states of depression and melancholy on the other. The difference is all too vivid; the difficulty lies in referring each to its proper source. Do they, whichever they may be, come "on airs from Heaven or blasts from Hell"? At first we are likely to ascribe consolation to good angels, and desolation to bad, but "It is possible," he says, in his *Spiritual Exercises*, "for the good as well as for the bad angel to afford consolation; the good angel does so for the advantage of the soul, that it may progress from good to better, but the other in order that he may bring the soul to yield to his wicked and malicious designs. The bad angel, transfiguring himself into an angel of light, sometimes begins by inspiring good and holy thoughts in conformity with the dispositions of a just soul, and afterwards endeavors to draw the soul into his secret snares."

This question as to the source of inclinations, joys, consolations, hopes, apprehensions and alarms, was not new. From the very beginning of Christian history, spirits of evil had disguised themselves as spirits from heaven in order to cajole timid and troubled souls. St. John the Evangelist

warned his flock: "Beloved, believe not every spirit, but
try the spirits whether they are of God." (I John, IV, 1.)
And St. Anthony of the Desert says: "We must pray for
the gift of discerning spirits, because as it is written, we may
not believe every spirit." And not only the Christians but
the pagans knew the difficulty, too. "Often one who zealously pushes toward some excellence, xxx is really being
led utterly astray by the will of some Power, which makes
those things that are evil seem good and those things seem
to him evil that are for his advantage." And that the difficulty continued to give anxiety to spiritual directors for
several generations after Loyola's time, is confirmed by such
a play as *El Condenado por desconfiado* which turns on this
very point. An unfortunate man is persuaded by a demon
in the shape of an angel to doubt of God's infinite mercy,
and, in despair of salvation, gives himself up to sin; while,
on the other hand, he fails to pierce the disguise of an angel
who appears to him in the likeness of a shepherd lad and
drops holy hints in vain. The consequence is that the
man's soul is damned forever. Or, to take an instance from
Ignatius's own experience: On several occasions he perceived a strange, monstrous, yet beautiful thing, that bore a
resemblance to a serpent, all studded with what looked like
innumerable eyes, but were not really eyes, and this vision
brought him great consolation; nevertheless, as he afterwards discovered, it was an emanation from the Devil, or the
Devil himself. It might prove, therefore, of infinite consequence, rightly to determine what spirits were of God and
what of Satan. All that the *Memoirs* say, however, is this:

There was always this difference [between worldly things
and divine]: when I thought of the world, I experienced
great pleasure, but when I grew fatigued and dropped the
thought, I felt arid and discontented; and when I thought
upon going to Jerusalem barefoot, with no food but herbs,
doing the most grievous penances that ever the saints
had done, I not only found comfort in these thoughts but
after I had dropped them, I was contented and happy. But
I did not keep my attention on this distinction, nor did I

stop to think about it, until on one occasion I opened my eyes a little and began to wonder at it and reflect upon it, and then I perceived from my experience that after some thoughts I remained sad, and after others happy, and little by little I came to recognize the difference between the spirits that influenced me, one was from the Devil, the other was of God.

This power of discrimination is of the first importance in the spiritual direction of souls, and it is in his character as director of souls that Ignatius, while dictating his *Memoirs* was thinking of the subject; and he is so brief, because he assumes a general knowledge of his teaching, both in its fundamental principles and in its amplifications, on the part of those for whom he is writing. It would take me too far afield to go further into the subject here. In the crude, obvious distinctions between right and wrong, he agrees with our modern ethical teaching, that the persistent instincts which postpone the reward of obedience till the morrow or beyond, are, under a rough and ready classification, virtuous, while those more imperious, that bestow pleasure at the moment of indulgence, where enjoyment passes as the cup is quaffed, and is followed by discontent, or some ill consequence, are vicious. Abiding satisfaction must, it would seem, be the ultimate test. But he has in mind more delicate distinctions than that,—scruples that trouble a tender conscience, perplexities that obsess a penitent, who perhaps from fasting, from sleeplessness, from remorse, has become hypersensitive, uncertainties that must always obscure the road to perfection, embarrassments that arise from the conflict between social duties and the biblical counsels of perfection, and other such causes of ambiguity. At any rate, during his convalescence he was busy with the great question of right and wrong, of what he ought to do.

One can but guess at the turmoil in his conscience. His bodily ills, the teaching of tradition, the over-refinements of theological thought, were at work, and nobler agencies as well. In times of pain and weakness when idleness is

enforced upon the body, there rise up, from some mysterious
region, influences that penetrate and subdue the waking
consciousness, thoughts and beliefs that have been sown
unnoticed, subtle experiences that have left no trace in the
work-a-day memory, and these, under the heat of emotion,
germinate and grow, and become the guides and masters
of conduct and theory. Many good spirits crowded to his
bedside; the strength that had come to him in youth when
he lifted up his eyes to the Pyrenees and saw their tops
flattered by the morning sun or consecrated by the deepen-
ing hues of evening; the lesson of chivalry, that a man of
honor must enlist in the service of what to him is the noblest
and most beautiful; the simple words of some good priest;
his mother's smile, his father's expectations. And with
Ignatius the good spirits prevailed, and marked him for
their own.

In this state of mind his sensibility became so delicate,
his power of imaginative concentration so vivid, that the
objects of his thought seemed to appear in bodily presence
before his corporeal eyes. One night as he lay awake, he
beheld Our Lady with her Child in her arms. This vision
gave him great consolation, that is, it "increased his hope,
faith and charity, and called him to heavenly things and
the salvation of his soul." The old Adam was cast out.
He conceived so great a loathing for the lusts of the flesh
that all the voluptuous images that had been wont to rise
up and disturb his mind, departed from him forever. Never
once again, so he told Father Gonzalez in 1555, had he
known the temptations of the flesh. He surrendered completely to these religious impulses. Much of the time he
spent in prayer. And he seems to have become for the time
being as a little child, and did childish acts of devotion.
For instance, he took the two books I have mentioned, the
Life of Christ and the *Anthology of Saints,* and made a
compendium of their contents, writing the words of Christ
in vermilion, and those of Our Lady in blue, all in most
careful calligraphy, an art in which he excelled. It was the
childhood of his new life. That was but one aspect of his
condition. At night he loved to look up at the starry sky,

for while gazing he felt within him a mighty power to serve the Lord. This lifting up his eyes to the stars was a practice all his life.

I have often seen him, in his old age [says Father Ribandeneira], standing out on the balcony, or on some place of vantage where he could look at the sky, fix his gaze upward, and remain motionless, lost in thought, for a long time, and then, overcome by emotion, shed tears of joy. And I have often heard him say: "How contemptible the world seems when I look up at the sky."

Besides his prayers and his gazings at the heavens, he sought for strength in the Bible, and would quote to himself: "I can do all things through Christ which strengtheneth me." (Phil. IV, 13.)

CHAPTER III

In some such manner Loyola's conversion took place; and the first fruits were plans for his new life. According to tradition and authority there were two ways of purifying oneself from past sins. One of these was to make a pilgrimage to Jerusalem, and many did so, for instance among Spaniards of note, Juan de la Enzina, the earliest of Spanish playwrights, who had gone but two years before. The other way was to practise vigils, fasts, flagellations and whatever other acts of penance the example of ascetics might suggest, or ingenuity devise. Ignatius proposed to take both ways, and he became impatient to set about them.

Toward the end of February, 1522, his health was pretty well re-established, and he decided that the time had come to go. His elder brother, Martin Garcia, who had become the head of the family on their father's death, suspected something, and, being quite out of sympathy with this renunciation of the world, spoke out his mind to Ignatius. From worldly considerations he was right. The times were full of promise for a soldier; Spanish influence was spreading over the world and Spanish opportunity travelled in its wake; the young King had been elected Emperor of the Holy Roman Empire, and ruled over more lands than Charlemagne had done; the regent of Spain, Charles's old tutor, who was at Vittoria, a scant day's ride from the castle of Loyola, had just received news that he had been chosen Pope; the struggle with France for Milan and domination in Italy was on; the reputation of Spanish infantry was at its height; a military career offered a straight road to honor. Ignatius, however, was not to be diverted from his purpose, and fearing hindrance gave an evasive answer.

24

His biographer says that "he did not depart from the truth as to which he was very scrupulous," but the answer did not contain the whole truth. Let me say here that, in view of the opinion popular among Protestants that Jesuits are inclined to equivocate, I shall set forth in full any equivocation, dissimulation or subterfuge, or suspicion thereof, that may appear in any of the sources of his biography; at this moment I recall no other. He said: "Sir, as you know, the duke of Najera is aware that I am well again. It will be no more than my duty for me to go to Navarrete where he is." So he went; but once there, having paid his respects to the duke, he dismissed his brother's servants, turned his back on Azpeitia, and took the road to Montserrat, the seat of an ancient and far-famed Benedictine monastery.

At this period of his life, Ignatius was wholly dominated by mediæval ideas. He had probably never been outside the little district between Azpeitia, Arevalo and Pamplona. Stories of Spanish prowess had reached him no doubt, but he knew nothing of the great intellectual stirrings which had set a new glory on Italy, as resplendent as the crown of the Cæsars or the tiara of the Popes, and was affecting peoples north of the Alps like new wine. He had lived in the mental atmosphere of an earlier century, and in many ways he always remained an intellectual contemporary of St. Francis and St. Dominic; the singularity of his career lies in this, that, in spite of these mediæval ideas, he was destined to divine with clearer eye than any other supporter of the Roman Church just what was necessary to be done in his and in succeeding generations in order to rally the forces of conservatism to the support of the ancient ecclesiastical order.

After leaving Navarrete, he began a course of penitential discipline such as the anchorites of the Thebaid had practised, without regard, as he himself avows, to discretion, patience or humility, or any notion of proportioning the discipline to his sins, out of a desire to undergo all that the saints he had read of had undergone for the glory of God. I will give a specific instance of this mediæval state

of mind. On the road a Moor chanced to ride alongside;
the two fell into conversation, and talked about Our Lady.
The Moor was willing to admit that she was still a virgin
after she had conceived, but averred that he could not
understand how her virginity continued after the birth of
her child. Nothing Ignatius said could shake him; and the
Moor, weary perhaps of his fellow traveller's persistency,
rode ahead and was lost to sight. As Ignatius reflected over
this blasphemy, he thought he had done wrong to let the
infidel go unpunished, and was nearly carried away by a
sudden impulse to gallop after and stab him. Should he
or should he not? He hesitated. The Moor had told him
just where he would turn off from the highway, by a side
path on his way to a village in the neighborhood. When
Loyola reached this fork in the road he was still in doubt
as to what he ought to do. Stories were rife of vengeance
inflicted by indignant Spanish gentlemen upon Mohammedan dogs for just such blasphemy. Ignatius dropped the
reins on his mule's neck; he would appeal to the judgment
of God. If the mule turned and followed the Moor, he
would run him through; otherwise not. The mule, in
brutal indifference to theological errors, kept to the main
high road. The incident not only reveals the literal simplicity of Loyola's piety, but also, I think, judging by the
usual behaviour of Spaniards at that time towards the
Moors, rather a high standard of self-restraint.

The mountain of Montserrat lies in Aragon, a day's ride
to the west of Barcelona. There is no place similar to it
anywhere. It rises abruptly out of the plain above the river
Llobregat, like a mad fancy of Doré's pencil, to a height,
at its topmost peak, of twelve thousand feet, one great mass
of fantastic shapes, pillars, pinnacles, pyramids, in a savage
heap, *"ad nubes quasi elevatus."* The Benedictine monastery stood on a sort of table-land about two-thirds of the
way up, and scattered about in wild places higher still were
hermitages—for as a traveller justly noticed *"elegantissimus
locus est pro heremitis"*—hardly to be reached except by
climbing on all fours. The way to the monastery was very
long, narrow and rugged. James Howell, the English letter

writer, who went there in the reign of Philip III before any changes had been made, says:

It is a stupendous monastery, built on the top of a huge land rock, whither it is impossible to go up, or come down by a direct way, but a Path is cut out full of Windings and Turnings; and on the Crown of this Craggy-hill there is a Flat, upon which the Monastery and Pilgrimage place is founded, where there is a picture of the Virgin Mary Sunburnt, and tann'd, it seems, when she went to Egypt.

Ignatius had no sooner arrived than he sought out a venerable monk, to whom he might at once make a confession of his whole past life. He could brook no delay in unburdening himself of his sins. In order to obtain a scrupulous accuracy, he spent three days writing out the narrative at great length. One of his chief temptations had been sins of the flesh; so he resolutely made a vow to the Virgin of perpetual chastity. Another had been ambition of worldly honor; so he stripped off his cavalier's clothes and took the pilgrim's dress of sackcloth, with staff, and gourd. He also dedicated himself to a life of poverty, and gave his mule, all that he had left, to the monastery. Thus prepared, on the eve of the feast of the Annunciation, March 24, 1522, he went into the monastery church of the Blessed Virgin. He had heard how gentlemen of old, that were received into the order of chivalry, kept watch throughout the night preceding the ceremony, and deemed it appropriate to follow these precedents. He hung up within the church his sword and dagger as an offering, and, accoutred in the pilgrim's panoply of spiritual warfare, held the vigil. In this manner the new soldier of Christ entered into the service of his Master.

This first stage of Loyola's conversion, from the defence of Pamplona to the vigil in the church at Montserrat, is the tale of how a sensitive being, calm in exterior, yet passionate within, his imagination peopled by figures of knights errant and ascetic saints, out of a chaos of discontents, sufferings and yearnings, fashioned, still rudely and imperfectly—as an artist makes his first sketch, to be

changed and improved, yet nevertheless through all changes
and improvements maintaining its identity—the first design
of a consecrated purpose. That purpose may be described
as an ambition—for all life long, though he triumphed over
the meaner forms of vainglory, he was a very ambitious
man—to lead the life of St. Francis or St. Dominic, as he
understood their lives. The fantastic literalness of his purpose to live according to a mode of life that had passed away
three hundred years before, cannot but suggest to a modern
reader, however full of admiration and sympathy he may
be, some resemblance to the noble, chivalric Don Quixote,
in his purpose to lead, amid an alien generation, the life
of Amadis of Gaul. This resemblance was recognized by the
English controversialist, Bishop Stillingfleet, more than two
hundred years ago, but it was not accounted as a compliment, for the Protestant critic fixed his eyes on Don
Quixote's valiant disregard of common sense, and deemed
the comparison a happy form of vituperation. Those, however, who admire Don Quixote and judge that heroism is
of necessity a disregard of many maxims of common sense,
and see in Loyola a hero, dominated indeed by alien, mediæval notions with which they are out of sympathy, will find
much in his conduct paralleled by the high-flown idiosyn-
crasies of Cervantes's hero. Both Loyola and Don Quixote
were heroic figures, both were Spanish through and through,
and both, to our way of thinking, fantastic; certainly to
modern minds, especially those educated in a Protestant
community, the ideas and purposes which Ignatius entertained are no more in accord with work-a-day reason than
the ideas and purposes that haunted Don Quixote's
romantic brain. There is more than one passage in the
novel where Don Quixote pledges his loyalty to a most
beautiful lady whom he has never seen, that might without the least infringement upon veneration, if taken seriously, be transposed to Loyola's devotion to the Virgin
Mary; and his self-dedication to the rigorous career of
knight errantry, in the purpose to overthrow injustice, right
wrongs, and succour widows and orphans, needs but to be
raised from a corporal to a spiritual plane, in order to serve

as a description of Loyola's heroic purposes. There is, making allowance for the needs of comedy, no more gallant gentleman in literature than Don Quixote, and, making allowance for his mediæval inheritance, there is no more gallant or passionate lover of souls in Christian history than Ignatius Loyola.

We—that is most of us—live in a world alien to Loyola's; we have been bred upon ideas and dogmas very different to his, and we necessarily find it at first a little difficult to step across the chasm, and give him the sympathy that is necessary to any just judgment. We must make use of what some writers call the historical imagination. In the hope that it may help the reader to understand what Spanish sentiment and Spanish religion were in Loyola's time, in *el siglo de oro,* I will quote Menendez y Pelayo again:

In that society, higher than the idea of monarchy or of aristocracy, high above any earthly consideration and all worldly greatness, rose pure and spotless the idea of religion, free from all taint of heresy and novel notions. That idea of religion, that ardent Catholicism, which at the close of the middle ages had driven out the Jews and dyed itself in Moorish blood, was the unitive force that held together peoples diverse in race, language, laws and customs. And when the Teutonic spirit rose, in pseudo reform and horrid protest, against the Latin principle of unity, Spain put herself at the head of Southern Europe and fought,—not on behalf of temporal gain but against it—in Flanders, in Germany, on the English seas, with fortune sometimes prosperous, sometimes adverse, but always holding back the Northern flood within those dykes that it has never since passed, and she saved herself, and Italy and France as well, from the Lutheran infection. I cannot deny that we were left poor, spent, almost defenseless; but only a criticism that is meanly utilitarian will judge of great historic feats by the issue; and it is true that there has never been an example of greater self-abnegation or of more heroic self-sacrifice for an idea, than that which our forefathers then showed. Let politicians and political economists laugh their fill, but if we are to choose between the maritime greatness of England under her Virgin Queen, and the slow martyrdom and impoverishment of our own nation, which during two centuries was the unselfish arm of the Church, every heart that beats with enthusiasm for the noble and the beautiful, will not hesitate to bestow the palm on us. I grant that in all these epic feats of knightly prowess there was some mixture of blind, narrow, national pride; but that, too, had a noble origin, for we did not look upon ourselves as a nation born to command and other nations as destined to obey, but we ascribed our feats to God as their source and origin, narrowing all our vainglory to the belief that God, in reward of our faith, had chosen us, as once He chose the people of Israel, to be His sword in battle, the instrument of His justice and His vengeance upon apostates and sacrilegious men, and therefore every man among our soldiers, from the mere fact that he was a Catholic and a Spaniard, believed himself a Judas Maccabæus.

If the most distinguished Spanish scholar of our own times, feels in this way of those heroic days, we may imagine what the patriotic Spaniards who lived in those days must have felt. But, in speaking of this ardent struggle to maintain Catholicism against Protestant dissenters, I anticipate later years—as there was as yet no Protestant schism—and I do so in order to make Loyola's knightly self-dedication of himself to the service of his God more intelligible to readers who take religion placidly.

CHAPTER IV

MANRESA (1522-1523)

WE have now come to the second phase of Loyola's new life, a period of mystical and emotional experiences, and as a knowledge of these experiences is essential to an understanding of his temperament and character, I shall describe them in some detail.

The morning after his vigil, Ignatius set off on foot for Manresa, a town lying a few miles to the north. On the way he fell in with a lady, Doña Inés Pascual, who from this chance meeting became a lifelong friend. Ignatius would not tell his name or station, but the discrepancy between his clothes and his demeanour aroused the lady's interest; she guided him to a hospital or house of mercy in the town, where he found a lodging.

At Manresa Ignatius put into practice the habits of asceticism and prayer that he had read of in the lives of ancient saints. What those ways were I need not expatiate upon. St. Basil tells of the anchorites in his days, "whose abstinence and endurance I admired, and whose constancy in prayer I was amazed at; how they overcame sleep, in spite of the necessity of nature, bearing ever a high and free spirit in hunger and thirst, in cold and nakedness, not regarding the body, nor enduring to spend any thought upon it, but living as if in flesh not their own." The whole ascetic tradition was very rigorous. St. Augustine says: "By fastings and watchings, and all chastisement of the body, prayer is especially aided." Ignatius regularly attended mass and vespers, passed seven hours upon his knees, and flogged himself three times every day. Tradition points out the chapels he prayed in and a cave where he retired for meditation. He let his hair grow unkempt, and

31

forbore to cut his nails. He begged his food, and would eat no meat and drink no wine, except a little on Sundays and feast days. These bodily privations disturbed his mental equilibrium, and distressful thoughts tormented him. At one time, he was troubled by fears lest he should be unable to endure for long this mode of life that led, as he believed, to holiness; at another, he felt no joy in prayer or in the office of the mass; and then, on a sudden, "as if he had dropped his cloak," his heart felt light again. But more often deep depression prevailed. His heart dried up; bitterness and tedium lodged in it. Then, after a time, like a flood of sunshine, joy would spread over his soul, but only to subside again in darkness. Gladness and grief alternated like day and night. His mind teemed with doubts and scruples. Had he really, in that long confession before his vigil, recounted every sin and fault, or had he held something back? If his sins had been absolved why was he so troubled? At times he would weep for hours, and cry to God for mercy, and repeat over and over St. Paul's words: "O wretched man that I am! who shall deliver me from the body of this death?" Suicide flashed across his mind.

In his castings about for relief, he remembered to have read how some saint, in order to obtain a favor from God, had fasted until the favor had been granted, and he determined to do the same. He went out of town privily to a chapel dedicated to Our Lady and spent a week without a mouthful of food, still keeping to his three flagellations a day and seven hours of prayer. His absence was discovered, and pious ladies of the town, among whom he had many friends, went forth in search and brought him back. His fast had lasted from Sunday to Sunday, and he would have still persisted, but that his confessor, under penalty of refusing absolution, commanded him to eat. So he ate, and for two days felt much better; on the third day, however, a relapse came and the black thoughts rushed back. But now his mind was clear enough to perceive that all these perturbations had been the Devil's doing in order to turn him from his purpose, and at this discovery peace and consolation descended upon him in wonderful abundance.

Nevertheless, scruples still dogged him. For instance, when he went to bed, spiritual joy gushed up within him, and was so grateful and comforting that he lay awake with the pleasure of it, and had little time left for sleep; but without sleep he found himself ill prepared next day for his duties, and, therefore, he denied himself his spiritual reveries. Years afterwards, at the university, he learned a similar lesson, that he must not let meditation or prayer cut into the time that should be spent in preparation for lectures; for a man's business is to do his allotted task and he must not permit even the highest spiritual joy to hinder him. At length he passed into a season of peace and happiness; he felt that God was dealing with him, as a schoolmaster deals with a little child, proceeding step by step, always proportioning the child's task to his strength, and not passing on to the next lesson until the last had been mastered.

Writers on mysticism, familiar with the recorded experiences of saints and visionaries, usually describe the course of their singular psychical phenomena as taking place very much in the same general way. First comes conversion, that is complete surrender to an imperious impulse to abandon the world. Next follows the purgative way, in which purification is partly voluntary and partly not. The repentant man by means of prayer, meditation, scourging and privation, strives to wash from his soul the stains of sin; and, as if physical pain were not enough, black thoughts not of his willing crowd upon his spirit. But after repentance, discipline and mental torment have cleansed the soul, then the grace of God descends upon her in blessings,

> A thousand liveried angels lackey her
> And in clear dream and solemn vision
> Tell her of things that no gross ear can hear.

This stage is called the illuminative way. Loyola trod it; so did the two famous figures in Spanish religious history who came after him, St. Theresa and St. John of the Cross. They have left of their spiritual experiences a far fuller

record than any that we possess from him. What they tell
at great length enables us to fill in and round out the con-
densed narrative of Loyola's mystical experiences. And
if in these three saints we find the language that they speak,
their symbols, their emblems and their imagery, alien to
our thought, or outside the pale of our sympathy, hard even
to understand, then we must translate their visions and
ecstasies, as we do their Spanish words, into such figures and
symbols as shall represent for us, with our different education, this trudging up the purgatorial hill by passionate
souls, and their solemn delight at beholding gleams of divine
splendor on the summit far above them.

Cardinal Newman in hitting off three types of spiritual
life, says that St. Benedict represents the poetical, St.
Dominic the scientific, and St. Ignatius Loyola the practical. And Loyola was practical, very practical, in that
he set before himself a definite plan for the salvation of men,
and in order to execute that plan busied himself with social,
political and ecclesiastical forces, and studied his disciples
as an artisan studies his tools, so that he was able to use
them with nice discrimination, setting each to the particular
task for which his character or talents fitted him. That,
however, is but one side of the man; the other is this passionate, mystical side, upturned to God, losing itself in
visions beatific. Supernormal sights appeared to Loyola
all his life, but it was at this time that they played their
formative part in his spiritual education. Some of them I
shall describe. They were all fashioned out of images and
ideas familiar to Catholic teaching, set forth, that is, in the
pictorial language with which he was familiar, hieroglyphics
of mediæval spiritual life.

Once, while on his knees in prayer to the Virgin, his
soul was lifted up, and he beheld, as if with his corporal
eyes, an image of the Trinity. He was so moved by this
that even after he had gone to table he could not keep back
the tears; he talked of nothing else, and expounded the
blessed mystery with comparisons and instances in so manifold a fashion, that all who heard him were carried away
by admiration. Not satisfied with telling of it, he com-

posed a little book of eighty pages about it; and all his life
the vision endured fresh and vivid in his memory.   And
whenever he prayed to the Trinity, he was conscious of a
singular sweetness.   In another vision he grasped intellectu-
ally how and in what manner God had created the world;
but this he could not recount in words.   As Dante says—

il mio veder fu maggio
che il parlar nostro ch'a tal vista cede.

My vision was greater than our speech
Which quails before such seeing.

And again, during mass, with the eyes of the spirit he beheld
the Lord Jesus Christ, very God and very man, present in
the host.   Often—and this happened to him also later, at
Jerusalem, Padua, and various places—he saw a vague
shape without members in a luminous body (so he described
it) our humanity in the divine person of God the Son.
Visions of the Blessed Virgin were also vouchsafed to him.
These divine revelations filled his soul with celestial light,
and established his faith in such certitude that he was ready
to die for it; and, as he used to say, if the Bible were to be
lost, he could teach the divine mysteries from his knowledge
of them got in this vision, so deeply engraven were they
on his heart.

But of all these experiences the most memorable was that
which occurred while he was walking along the bank of
the river Cardona on his way to a chapel, a mile out of
the town.   He had sat down looking toward the water.
While he sat there, the eyes of his understanding were
opened.   It was not a visual experience, but he was conscious of a comprehension, an intellectual revelation, concerning spiritual matters that touch faith and Holy Writ,
vivid beyond all comparison with what he had known or
understood before, so that it all seemed quite new.   His
mind was so illuminated thereby that he seemed to himself to have become another man and to possess another
understanding.   He was never able to recount this revelation with any particularity; all he could say (as he did late

in life) was that his understanding had received a great
light, and that if he were to take and put together all other
gifts of help and succour that he had received from God
in all his years, their total sum would not make up the
equivalent of what he had received in that one experience.

One other psychical experience remains to be told.　It
rests upon good evidence although Ignatius himself never
mentioned it.　He was naturally reserved.　Father Polanco,
the earliest disciple to write his life, says: *"Erat in suis
rebus communicandis difficilis";* the reason was that his
modesty forbade him to reveal many strange happenings
which he believed were special favors from God.　I quote
Father Ribadeneira:

One Saturday at the hour of compline Ignatius fell down
in a trance.　A great number of men and women beheld
him, and were about to make preparations for disposing of
his dead body, when one of them noticed that his heart
was still beating, though faintly.　This extraordinary condition lasted until the next Saturday at the same hour.
Then, in the presence of several people who were keeping
watch, Ignatius opened his eyes, and, as if awakening from
a sweet sleep, said with love in his voice: "Ah! Jesus." This
I had from persons present; for the blessed father never
spoke of it to my knowledge, hiding in silent humility this
great act of God's grace.

Doña Isabel Roser, a lady of Barcelona who knew
Ignatius well afterwards, also told Father Ribadeneira that
eye witnesses had recounted the same story to her; and
Juan Pascual, son of Inés Pascual, also told Ribadeneira
that he was present, being then sixteen or seventeen years
old, and that when he saw Ignatius in this state he ran to
his mother calling out, "Mother! the saint is dead."

These ecstasies, visions and other emotional experiences
were primarily due, unless we accept a mystical or supernatural explanation, to the weakness of his poor, ill-treated,
underfed body; but that they dealt with heaven and things

divine, and not with worldly honors or bedizened courtesans, was wholly due to the habit of his thoughts.

At Manresa Ignatius made the first draft (though I should not speak positively in a matter concerning which we have little definite to go upon) of his *Spiritual Exercises,* or at least of the earlier chapters. These *Exercises* were the fruit of his own experience; they are a carefully arranged exposition of the practices which had enabled him to triumph over temptation, or rather a syllabus of such practices, since they are meant for use in the guidance of souls by spiritual directors, and not for the disciple or novice himself. I shall speak of them more fully hereafter. They are intended to rouse the soul to repentance and effort by means of prayer, of meditation both on the mysteries of religion and the consequences of sin, and to instil into the penitent a feeling that it is his duty to enroll himself as a soldier under the banner of Christ. No doubt, as time went on, and his experience of life broadened and his knowledge of men increased, he altered and added; but probably the *Exercises* remained in essentials as he first conceived them. The book had an extraordinary influence, supported, as it was, by the potent personality and passionate purpose of the teacher. He believed that he had composed this treatise not without divine guidance and help.

Ignatius stayed at Manresa about a year; it was a year of spiritual labor as well as of spiritual experiences. He began to gather disciples about him. Perhaps I should not use so strong an expression, but limit myself to saying that he got into the way of sharing with his neighbors the light, which, as he believed, he had received from God. He gave spiritual counsels to all that would hearken to him; and, as he was gifted with the eloquence that comes from conviction and from the passionate desire to save souls, he had a number of listeners. In this occupation he spent several hours every day. He prayed with them and exhorted them, taking care not to assume the tone of a teacher, as if he were better or wiser than they. He gives an instance of his behaviour. Usually he lived upon the food begged from charitable persons, but if any one invited him to dine, he would accept. During dinner he did not speak, unless asked a question; in that case his custom was to stop eating and answer. Observing this his host usually forbore to ask questions until they had left the table. After dinner he would take his cue (though not always) from something that had been said at table, and enter upon a spiritual discourse, according as God prompted him, for he used not to think beforehand about what he should say; if he did he spoke poorly. These talks, it is said, were very edifying; and in part owing to them but chiefly to the *Spiritual Exercises*, which were already spread abroad in the town, many persons mended their ways of life and made noteworthy progress on the spiritual path.

During the winter he fell ill of a serious fever, probably in consequence of his austerities. He recovered, but returning to his privations and discipline, fell ill again; the same thing happened a third time, and his friends in alarm now took care of him. The magistrates provided a lodging and what things were necessary, and honorable ladies took turns in watching by his bedside through the night. Upon convalescence he was induced to wear warmer clothes, and a cap, as well. He also abandoned the exaggerated asceticism of not cutting his hair and nails. From these illnesses he learned the lesson for himself,—he always was profiting by his experiences—and in later years taught it as a precept to his disciples, that in times of sickness a man should abate the fervour of devotional practices, until bodily strength has returned, and in the meantime, so far as his condition will permit, cultivate patience and concern himself with the edification of others. As Father Polanco says: "God had indeed given him a remarkable talent for unmasking temptations and for directing those who were deeply concerned with spiritual things."

During his stay in Manresa he had mastered the first lesson in his spiritual education, and, as he believed, God, the divine schoolmaster, now summoned him to another. It was time to go to Jerusalem, so he bade goodbye to his friends and betook himself to the port of Barcelona. Here we get our first understanding of how wholly he was absorbed by his inner vision. Every other visitor was enchanted by Barcelona. Set on little hills in the midst of its gardens of oranges, lemons and cypresses, guarded by its turreted walls and watched over by its stately cathedral —*fabrica exquisitissima*—no town could be more picturesque and charming. In this pleasant region Loyola came upon all the beauty of the south, with its luxuriant herbage, its pomegranates, medlars and pineapples, its vines heavy with grapes, all ripe (as it seemed to travellers from the north) before their time, and the tropical palms standing like sentries here and there. But he noticed these things no more than the Prince in the story galloping to his Princess notices the road of gold beneath his horse's hoofs.

CHAPTER V

ALL that we know of these travels of Ignatius through Italy to Jerusalem is what he himself has said in his *Memoirs*. Probably even at the time he dictated them, in his old age, he did not appreciate the immense influence these experiences had had upon him. In Italy he learned, all unwittingly, of the Renaissance, already past its meridian, and of the dawning Reformation, and in Jerusalem how mistaken his conception of the true danger to Christianity had been. I mean that he became aware of facts and circumstances from which his sagacious reason, working in some subconscious part of his mind, slowly fashioned the policy for saving and strengthening the Holy Roman Church that he finally matured and put into effect.

His plan of going single-handed to convert the Turks to Christianity sounds, in modern ears, most Quixotic. Loyola's sagacity, however, as I see things, was as sound at that time as in his later years; even this wild plan is evidence of it. His creed was simple; Christianity was set over against Mohammedanism, and as a faithful soldier of Christ it was his business not to balk at any forlorn hope. The boldest strategy was to strike at the very center of the enemy's position; it was also the wisest. Had not David overcome Goliath? This belief that Mohammedanism was the most dangerous enemy of the Holy Roman Catholic Church was purely mediæval. It is evident that Ignatius knew nothing of the great intellectual awakening that had swept over Italy and from Italy northward, and had affected Christianity so powerfully; nothing of the recent Lutheran revolt. Intellectual doubts and disobedience within the body of the Church constituted its danger, not the followers of an alien creed. Loyola's complete ignorance of the state of religion in Europe outside of Spain prevented him from understanding this; but with regard to political matters, he was not far wrong. Islam was at the height of its power and full of aggression. The Ottoman Turks had overrun Syria and Egypt, they were already in Belgrade and drawing nearer to Vienna; they had possession of Rhodes and disputed the supremacy of the Mediterranean; they threatened Italy, even Rome itself. Suleiman the Magnificent seemed certain of Mohammed's Paradise, if conquest could make sure of it. The gentle, Christian, meek Pope Adrian was doing all he could to equip an army, and to induce Charles and Francis to make peace and turn their arms against the common enemy. Alone of Europeans Loyola put his faith in the teaching of Jesus: "I say unto you, love your enemies" and wished to obey that teaching. Erasmus, it is true, had written:

We are not, I presume, to kill all the Turks. The survivors are to be made Christians. . . . While our lives and manners remain as depraved as they now are the Turks will see in us but so many rapacious and licentious vermin. How are we to make the Turks believe in Christ till we show that we believe in Him ourselves? . . . Show them that Christ's yoke is easy, that we are shepherds and not robbers, and do not mean to oppress them. Send them messengers such as these instead of making war, and then we may effect some good. . . . Christians ought to show their faith in their works, and convert Turks by the beauty of their lives.

But Erasmus was not in earnest, he was indulging himself in irony at the expense of current Christianity. So was his Spanish disciple, Juan Valdés, who already betrays his Protestant leanings in his *Colloquy* between Charon and the soul of a King who has come to the fatal ferry:

CHARON. Did you do aught for the love of God?
SOUL. What a question! Of course I did.

CHARON. What?

SOUL. I made war against the Turks.

CHARON. How?

SOUL. I did them all the harm I could.

CHARON. And how did you come to think that you were rendering God a service by so doing? Don't you see that the more harm you did to the Turks, the more they hated Jesus Christ, and became more obstinate in their opinions?

SOUL. Well, in what way would you have us make Christians of them?

CHARON. After you had governed your own subjects well, in peace and prosperity, and you and they were leading good Christian lives, then it would have been soon enough to try to convert the Turks. The first thing would be to use them with great kindness, in order to win them to our faith by means of love, as the Apostles did when they preached the gospel of Jesus Christ; and afterwards, if they could not be converted by means of love, and there was no other way to safeguard the honor of Jesus Christ, then you might proceed to convert them by force, but you should act with such great moderation that the Turks would know that you were not making war for conquest, or for robbery, but solely for the salvation of their souls. Tell me, then, is that the way you went about it?

SOUL. Of course I didn't act in that way; nobody ever advised me that such was the way to do.

CHARON. Then you may take it from me that before you shall turn Turks into Christians you will have turned your subjects into worse than Turks.

This is a satire. Valdés no more than Erasmus, would have dreamed that preaching the gospel was a practicable means of converting the Turks; but Ignatius did. St. Francis had gone to Egypt and tried to convert the Soldan by preaching; why should he not at least try to convert infidelity in the most sacred of cities, and thereby bring all the world into one fold, under one shepherd? His ambition was very great, he was confident in what Father Gonzalez calls "la voluntad que el mismo Diós le avia dado por *servirlo*—the steadfast will that God Himself had given him for His service," and up to this visit to Italy he had lived in a world of mediæval thought. Infidels were the enemies of God, whether they were Moors, Arabs or Ottoman Turks. All Spaniards had been taught this from infancy. Might it not be that he was God's chosen instrument to accomplish by humility and love, what force and arms had failed to achieve? I think it will help to explain his state of mind if I quote what a recent historian writes of Christopher Columbus, himself the best exponent of ideas that helped shape Ignatius's character in his youth:

Christopher Columbus was wedded to an ultimate purpose, one which dominated his life and which in dying he bequeathed as a legacy to his heirs,—the institution of a new Crusade and the recovery of the Holy Sepulchre. All else that he proposed or accomplished was subordinate and subsidiary to this absorbing project. This was his mission. He believed that to effect this he had been brought into the world, a predestined agent of God to restore to the Christian world the birth-place of the Saviour. He believed himself a messenger of the Most High charged with the deliverance of Jerusalem. . . . We can comprehend him only when we see him as he saw himself, when we realize that he held himself a Divine agent selected to execute a grand design, the accomplishment of which he believed would close perhaps the last chapter of the world's history and introduce the thousand years of peace.

But Columbus meant to conquer Jerusalem and put down infidelity by force, while Loyola proposed to follow the example of St. Francis. So strongly did this idea dominate him, that even fifteen years later, after he had seen much of the world, he remained outwardly at least, faithful to it, and proposed to lead his little band of disciples to Palestine. I do not mean to deny that Loyola wished to benefit his own soul by undertaking the holy pilgrimage to Jerusalem, by no means: he always held to the double purpose of saving his own soul and the souls of others. But I

cannot but feel—though I must admit that the scanty
words of his *Memoirs,* our only direct evidence, do not
justify it—that he hoped to convert the Turks and win
Jerusalem single-handed; I think that he had infinite confidence in the power of the Christian God and felt that
prayer, preaching and example were the right methods to
overcome an enemy.

Loyola had two sides, of so different an aspect that it
seems almost incredible that they belonged to one man,
the mystical Loyola, who fixed his eyes on heaven, beheld
visions, dreamt dreams, was subject to ecstasy, and the
intensely practical Loyola, who kept his eye on the earth,
estimated human capacities and weaknesses with the nicety
of a diamond cutter, knew how to play upon hope, ambition, desire and fear, was patient, laborious, contriving, and
full of resources. And strangely enough, if this be
psychologically possible, while his waking consciousness was
lost in dreams, down in the depths of his nature his practical genius was considering how to put those dreams to use;
and, vice versa, while his senses were busy with the actual
his mind's eye gazed into the far future. For instance, in
the midst of his spiritual devotions something within him
brooded over the plan of a society; and, again (so at least
it seems to me), while he was teaching some young novice
the elementary rules of self-discipline, primarily for the purpose of saving his soul, his visionary eye already beheld the
boy, a grown man, master of himself, preaching the true
faith to the weak, the deluded and the tempted, or risking
corporal life in order to save the souls of savages in Ceylon
or Brazil. Perhaps I am mistaken, but I cannot but suspect
that the practical Loyola, as soon as he got to Rome and
learned a little of the real state of things, down in subconscious depths became aware that this plan of converting Turks was, to say the least, by no means possible, and
that this subconscious knowledge was the real cause why
when he actually got to Jerusalem he did not stay.

With this digression I return to my story, and give his
narrative, somewhat abbreviated. He reached Barcelona
in the end of February, 1523, and set about finding passage

by sea to Italy, the first stage of his pilgrimage. Friends wished to go with him, but he refused. He said that he desired no companions but Faith, Hope and Charity. In order to have his companion Faith without flaw, he proposed to take absolutely nothing except gown and staff. But the captain of the ship, who was ready to give him a passage gratis, put his foot down and said that he must take his own food. Ignatius hesitated. However, compelled by his confessor, he acquiesced, but the coins which were given him while begging, he left on the beach. This spirit of ascetic piety was personal to Ignatius, not a mere appurtenance of the times. Records show that pilgrims to the Holy Land took good care of the body, making provident bargains for its keep; "for breakfast three rolls and a brimming glass of Malvoisie; for dinner, soup, two kinds of boiled meats, cheese, and wine; for supper, a roast, two dishes again of boiled meats, and cheese; and two hours later a cup of wine."

The voyage to Gaeta lasted five days. In company with several fellow travellers, including a mother and daughter, Ignatius started on foot for Rome. They begged their way. The first night they lodged at a farm, the women in the house, Ignatius in the stable. At midnight he was roused by cries of the women that they were assaulted. He rushed to their rescue, shouting, "Shall we submit to this?" frightened off the assailants and got the women away. The pilgrims took to the road in the dark. They reached some town, but finding the gates locked, slept in a church. The next morning they had nothing to eat and were still excluded from the town for fear of the pest which at that time ravaged the country. Ignatius was exhausted and could not walk, the others went on. By good luck a great lady passed that way, and procured his admission to the town, where alms were given him; and after two days' rest, he was able to proceed to Rome. He arrived there on Palm Sunday, and stayed about a fortnight; he visited the seven churches, saw Pope Adrian officiate, and then started on for Venice, where he intended to take ship for Jaffa. At Rome he must have heard the alarming news that the Turks had captured the island of Rhodes, that they were shouting "Italy! Italy! On to Rome!" that their spies had just been caught in the city, that some of the rich inhabitants frightened out of their wits were preparing to leave, and how the Pope had levied taxes for a crusade and was trying to rouse Europe to the common peril. Naturally enough people sought to persuade him to abandon so foolhardy a pilgrimage. Nothing, however, but a direct command from some ecclesiastical authority ever deterred Ignatius from his purpose. He yielded, however, to friendly apprehension so far as to accept some money for his journey, but soon felt ashamed of this lack of faith in Providence and gave it away. St. Francis had been wedded to Lady Poverty, and why not he?

The journey to Venice was hard. He was feeble and ill; he could speak neither Italian nor Latin; he could not keep the pace of his fellow pedestrians; his purse was quite empty; shut out of towns from fear of the pest, he slept in the open, or at best in the portico of some church. At the boundaries of the Venetian state he had his reward, for Christ appeared to him in a vision, to his great consolation; and when he reached Padua, he was permitted to enter (through divine interposition, as he believed) without a health certificate, and again at Venice, although other travellers were obliged to present theirs. At Venice, he slept on the piazza of St. Mark's, continued his practice of begging his food, and did nothing towards finding a way to make the voyage to Jaffa. Was not his life of more value than many sparrows? His faith was his fortune; he felt an inward certitude that God would provide, and his faith was justified. One day a rich Spaniard accosted him, asked what he was doing, what he wanted, and took him to his own house.

In Venice, as in Rome, people tried to persuade him to forego his dangerous pilgrimage, but he said that if a single plank should cross the sea to the Holy Land he would go upon it. And his host, who had taken a great liking to him, just as both men and women had done at Manresa and Barcelona, for there was something very attractive in this little Spaniard with his mixture of humility and authority, dignity and graciousness, kept him in his house and procured for him an audience with the Doge, so that he might obtain permission for the voyage. The sea was dangerous, Turkish corsairs were abroad, and space on shipboard was very scarce. The Doge, however, granted him passage on a government ship bound for Cyprus. On the day of sailing, July 14, 1523, Ignatius was ill and miserable, and the physicians bade him go aboard if he wished his body to be buried. He went, however; and, lo and behold, a fit of seasickness made him feel much better. In these unexpected deliverances Ignatius perceived the providence of God.

Four Spaniards, three Switzers and a Tyrolese were fellow pilgrims with him. On board ship certain vile doings came to light, and Ignatius rebuked the evil doers. The Spaniards on board begged him to hold his tongue, but he spoke out roundly. The sailors said that they would put him ashore at the first land sighted; but by God's grace the first land was Cyprus. Here he was transferred to a pilgrim's ship for the rest of the voyage. All this time visions of Christ kept appearing to him. The ship reached Jaffa on September 4th. The pilgrims procured donkeys and rode to Jerusalem. As they drew near, a Spaniard in the company called out: "Soon we shall see the Holy City; it will be well to prepare our hearts." They dismounted, and gave themselves to solemn thought, and, when the towers of Zion appeared, they felt a consoling happiness that seemed beyond the power of nature to confer.

In Jerusalem he put up at the Franciscan monastery. Ignatius had meant, as he believed, to stay and save the souls of infidels, but whether his zeal betrayed itself too openly, and excited apprehensions that he would get himself and others into trouble, or whether Providence was directing his life on another path, the prior of the monastery refused him permission, representing the danger to his liberty or even to his life. Ignatius protested, said he would be no burden, that he would beg his food, all he asked was a roof. The prior was inexorable; he stated that his ecclesiastical authority was absolute, and that he was ready

to produce the official documents conferring it. Ignatius
replied humbly that that was not necessary, he would obey.
So he returned to Jaffa and took ship by way of Cyprus
for Venice.

One anecdote of his stay in Jerusalem displays again the
mediæval character of his religion. Before leaving for good
he wished to make one last visit to the Mount of Olives,
and see once more the marks of his Saviour's feet imprinted
upon the stone from which He ascended into Heaven. He
went privily, without guide or permit. This was contrary
to the Turkish rules; he ran the risk of arrest as a spy. He
had no money, but the gift of his pocket knife bribed the
guard to let him in, but after coming out he could not
remember which way the imprints pointed. His scissors
procured him readmission. As he started homeward, a
man, sent after him by the alarmed friars, hurried up in
hot haste, scowling and brandishing his stick, caught him
rudely by the arm and led him back to the convent. Nothing mattered to Ignatius, for on the way back he beheld a
vision of Christ hovering above him.

This devotion to physical objects consecrated by association with religion—whether places or things, whether
reminiscent of Christ or of the saints—seems to be derived
from primitive beliefs in magic and fetiches. Of course,
a belief may spring from an unreasonable origin, and yet
be justified by reason. Physical sensibilities were originally
fashioned upon the concrete, and things perceptible dominated the animal mind for ages before the abstract began
to exercise sway over habits of thought. We cannot cut
loose from the inheritance of that long domination. A god
endowed with abstract qualities only, who never reveals
himself, who leaves no divine fragrance clinging to some
physical object, soon ceases to be a god. Abstract truth,
abstract beauty, affect only the trained philosopher. Sight,
sound or touch are necessary to conjure those divine essences
down into the world of daily life. An image, an idol, a
shrine, helps the sluggish imagination to a more vivid conception of spiritual things. For this reason, statues, relics,
pictures—half symbols, half memorials—have ethical and

spiritual values. A photograph will stiffen a man's upper lip. Primitive men were comforted and strengthened by stocks and stones; we look to the mountains or lift up our eyes to the stars. Human experiences remain constant; the interpretation varies. In all such experiences of help and strength, the influence exerted lies somewhere between sentiment at one extreme and magic at the other. At the extreme of magic, it is necessary to go through the right motions, repeat the right formula, and the gift is granted. The door will open only at the cry "Open Sesame." This, after all, is the law in the physical world; no piety influences nature, but at the magical act, performed by a Morse, an Edison, a Marconi, spirits of the air and the earth become obedient servants to the will of man. At the other end of the scale, the passion of a contrite heart generates ethical or spiritual energy within. In most people of religious desires, spiritual yearning blends with a half confidence in magic, or, at least, with a blind hope that from behind the veil of that which seems will start up a sudden power to demolish whatever troubles them, and in its place set up a new order that shall comfort and satisfy. Such notions are far older than Christianity; the Greeks had their sacramental rites, their mysteries which, rightly performed, would ease the blows of fate or give immortal life. In Loyola's case there can be no doubt of his passionate yearning for spiritual communion with his God, and yet I cannot help thinking that he believed that his spiritual salvation would be far better assured if he knew the right formula. This seems to be the teaching of the Catholic Church; perhaps, as men are not creatures of reason, it is a wise, a necessary, teaching; possibly, it is true. Our ordinary conception of spiritual progress postulates pain, repentance and good resolutions, but perhaps the mere expectation of being lifted up to that higher ethical or spiritual state by the power of the true formula, may have an equal efficacy.

Loyola believed, I think, that his vision of Christ on the way back from the Mount of Olives was not only a mark of Christ's sympathy and approbation, but a sort of necessary consequence from his solicitude to see exactly how the

imprints of Christ's feet were engraven in the rock. Nevertheless (I had better say it here), our lack of sympathy
with Loyola's devotional practices, is not due to his reliance
on magical formulæ, but to a certain baldness and aridity
that comes from the lack of poetry. The defect lay in him,
and not in his creed. The grace of poetry may attend upon
a belief in formulæ as well as upon a passionate emotion.
In the case of St. Francis of Assisi, as the shadows of
bracken fall on the turf beneath and give an added grace
to the shafts of light that have made their way between
its fronds, so Francis's belief in miracles serves but to
heighten the beauty of his passionate yearning to imitate
his Master and live the life of the spirit. With Ignatius
it is not so, and the Jesuit biographers, in order to supply
this absence of poetry, lay too heavy a stress, according to
my way of thinking, upon the reports of miraculous occur-
rences and the contortions of his spirit in travail with
penitence and aspiration.

To return to Loyola's narrative. At Jaffa, he was refused
passage on two ships, and went aboard a third that appeared
the least staunch of the three; but Providence kept watch
over it, whereas the other two perished on the homeward
way. His ship reached Venice in January, 1524. The
Memoirs say nothing of his stay there at this time. On
his way from Venice to Genoa, he met with sundry adventures, which he tells, as an old man will, because he remembered of what great moment they were to him at the time,
and therefore, out of indulgent sympathy for his inexperi-
enced youth, interested him still, rather than that he
attached importance to them. In the cathedral at Ferrara
he distributed among a crowd of beggars all the alms that
had been given him in Venice for his journey. And, further
on his way, he fell in with the Imperial army and then
with the French, in the midst of their tedious and inter-
minable wars for the duchy of Milan, and ran a fair chance
of being hanged as a spy. At one place he was let go because the commander thought him underwitted; and somewhere the soldiers mocked and buffeted him, but the
thought that he, even in humblest measure, had been

judged worthy to experience maltreatment similar to Christ's, gave him great consolation. At last he reached Genoa, and embarked for Barcelona, but even then his dangers were not over, for Andrea Doria, the famous Genoese admiral, for the nonce fighting on the French side, pursued his ship. The importance of these adventures lies in the impression made upon his mind by his escapes, leading him to believe that God was guiding and protecting him. Perhaps, a voice angelical sounded in his ear:

Se tu segui tua stella,
Non puoi fallire a glorioso porto,

Following thy star
Thou canst not fail of haven glorious.

CHAPTER VI

THE REFORMATION AND RENAISSANCE

IGNATIUS had been away from Spain for about twelve months. This *Wanderjahr* proved to be a revolutionary education. He turned his back on an apostolic life, and started on the long road to a university degree. It is true that for fifteen years, on the surface at least, he adhered to his early project of going to Jerusalem, and laid that project down as the basis for the permanent association of his disciples; and yet, it is very difficult to understand why he should think that, in order to convert the Turk, an elaborate instruction in the humanities, in philosophy and theology, would be of advantage. There was nothing in his experience in Jerusalem to lead him to infer that the infidels would yield to a scholastic exposition of Christian dogma, when they were deaf to the simple beauty and pathos of Christ's own teaching. The end and the preparation seem to be at odds. I think that the man's extraordinary tenacity of purpose held tight hold of his conscious intentions, but that underneath, in that psychical laboratory that evades the waking consciousness, in the *arrière-boutique* of his mind, the experiences of his foreign travels were gradually shaping a conception of the policy that he finally in fact did pursue. This complete rearrangement of his plan, the putting aside of St. Francis's example, of the joyful preaching of the gospel out of a passionate heart, and the substitution of Thomas Aquinas and conventional education, grammar school, colleges in Spain, the University of Paris, twelve years in all, was due to his new knowledge of the world, or, to be more precise, of the two great movements that affected educated men, the Renaissance and the Reformation.

It is appropriate here to make some reference to both those movements, for it will appear, I think, that the formative influence acting upon ,Ignatius at this time, persuading him to the course he took, was repugnance to the spirit of the Renaissance far more than opposition to the Reformation. He saw the effects of the Renaissance in Italy, whereas of Germany and German affairs he was wholly ignorant. I lay stress upon this, for we are apt to think of the Society of Jesus as one of the main factors, perhaps the most influential, in that revival of vigor within the Roman Catholic Church, usually known as the Counter Reformation, which displayed itself in all Latin countries, but chiefly in Italy, after the Protestant secession had roused the Catholic world. The instinct of self-preservation, loyalty to the unity of Christendom, devotion to what the Church held to be the truth, wounded pride and the mere joy of combat, brought to the front able and high-minded Catholics, who in the earlier period of self-indulgence and Roman riot, had been pushed aside or left unregarded, and enabled adherents of the old order, under the lead of Spain, "to keep back," in the words of Menendez y Pelayo, "the northern flood within the dykes it has never since passed, and to save Spain, Italy and France from the Lutheran infection." During this struggle of self-defense and counter attack the Jesuit Fathers furnished the vanguard, often the forlorn hope. But one must not carry back the situation of 1556, the date of Loyola's death, when his Society was an active power, north, south, east and west, to this present year 1524, when he returned to Barcelona. To make this clear, and for the sake of bringing the general situation before our minds, I will refer briefly to the religious movement in Germany and then to the intellectual condition of Italy.

It is convenient and reasonably accurate to ascribe the first beginning of the Protestant schism to the sharp issue raised by the sale of indulgences. Underneath, larger causes of disruption had been at work, national sentiment indignant at foreign ecclesiastical tyranny, as the discontented termed it, moral revolt at the vicious lives of prelates,

priests and monks, democratical dissatisfaction that the
bishoprics should be but chattels of the great nobility, unwillingness to pay taxes to the Roman curia, anger at the
papal judicial system, and so forth; and, long before this,
frequent protests, not without ample justification, had made
themselves heard in Germany and elsewhere, against the
doings of the Church. The danger of schism had been
threatening enough, but until this time, when the humanists, with their pagan interests, their speculations and their
indifference to Christianity had prepared the way for a
rending asunder, the unity of the Church had managed to
maintain itself. The doctrine of indulgences had not up till
then been the point of danger; it had been generally, if not
universally, believed in and accepted. The doctrine is this:
The merits of Christ more than suffice to redeem the sin of
Adam, and this superfluity constitutes a great treasure ready
to be applied to the needs of sinners. The saints also have
contributed their extra sum to the general store. In its
essence the doctrine is true. Christ's goodness still serves
to wash away the sins of men, and the virtues of saints support waverers and raise up many that fall. It is the
property of one man's goodness to help and strengthen his
neighbor. Because my friend forbears, I am enabled to
forbear; because he turns his back on temptation my feet
are brave to keep the narrow way. Take St. Ignatius himself. It is not a mere allegory to say, that his doings have
heaped up stores in a treasure house, that are lent to the
poor without usury. His example is like the grasp of a
helping hand, his *Spiritual Exercises* enable many to unbar
the door that shuts them from a love of God. The Church,
however, went further than this doctrine, and ascribed to
the successors of St. Peter the power of giving or withhold-
ing the alms of superabundant righteousness. Such an
addition may be, perhaps, open to question. Anyhow, the
Church took that position. But the Church did not profess
to give these alms except to the penitent. A contrite heart
was an indispensable prerequisite; and good works were,
naturally enough, the best evidence of repentance and a
resolution to do better. Unfortunately in practice the pre-

requisite good deeds shrunk and shrivelled into the mere payment of money. Buying and selling polluted the temple of the Lord.

Perhaps the Papacy had an itching palm. At any rate Leo X, who, quite apart from the expenses incident to maintaining the papal dominion over sundry Italian cities, was put to considerable outlay in paying for his hunting lodge at La Magliana, for Latin and Greek manuscripts, for jewels, and for the encouragement of art, needed large sums of money for the construction of the new basilica of St. Peter's, on which Bramante, Raphael and others had spent and were to spend their genius. In order to procure money for this purpose he issued indulgences. The details of the story need not be retold here. I will confine myself to one quotation from a proclamation hawked about by pardoners: "Whoever puts into the box a tester for a soul in Purgatory, at once sets that soul free, and the soul infallibly goes to Paradise; so, by putting in 2 testers for 2 souls, or 1000 for a 1000 souls, they go forthwith to Paradise." These indulgences were hawked about Germany, as a mountebank might sell lottery tickets at a county fair. All persons of religious mind were of one accord on this practice; and Luther became their spokesman. Satirists joined in the attack. A passage from a Spanish classic of Loyola's time, *Lazarillo de Tormes*, may serve to indicate the popular opinion in Spain.

Lazarillo is a poor little boy cast on the world for a living. He takes service with an itinerant friar who travels about selling indulgences. This friar made a practice, on entering a village, of giving little presents to the priests so that they should commend him to their parishioners. If he thought the priests knew Latin he spoke to them in Spanish, but if they were *reverendos,* that is, better furnished with money than with scholarship, he discoursed for hours in what he called Latin. Nevertheless, in a certain town, he had no luck at all, not a soul would buy. Not discouraged, he arranged to be present at service in church on Sunday. Saturday evening he and the alguazil dined together at the inn. At dessert, all of a sudden, they fell into a quarrel, called one another names, shouted curses, snatched weapons, and made such an uproar that all the town-folk gathered about them. The two were parted with difficulty, the alguazil bellowing that the friar was a fraud. The next day the church was crowded. The friar got up in the pulpit and exhorted the people to buy indulgences and shorten the torments which their relations and friends were suffering in Purgatory. In the midst of his passionate exposition, the alguazil entered with great bustle, and bawled out loud that the friar was a cheat, a scurvy knave, and that his bulls were bogus. Some pious folk started to put the calumniator out, but the friar raised his hand, bidding no man touch him, and then fell on his knees and, rolling his eyes to heaven, entreated God to judge between them; if he were a cheat let the ground open and swallow him up, but if the bulls were genuine let it so appear by a miracle. Hardly had he spoken, when the alguazil fell down with a bang, foamed at the mouth, writhed and wriggled in a frenzy. The crowd tried to seize him but he kicked and struggled like one possessed. The friar remained kneeling, lost in divine contemplation. Several people ran up and besought him to save the poor sinner who was dying, since it was plain that he was a liar, that the friar was innocent and that the bulls were full of salvation. This brought the friar back to earth, and he prayed aloud for the sinner. The alguazil slowly came to his senses, crawled to the altar, and asked forgiveness, pleading that he had been possessed by a devil, who was trying to forestall the immense good that the bulls would do. And so on. The bulls were bought like hot cakes. Of course the pair were in collusion.

If this was the way in which orthodox, pious Spaniards spoke of indulgences, it is easy to imagine that Germans might pass from speech to action. So they did. When Tetzel, the Dominican friar, came peddling indulgences near Wittenberg, Martin Luther posted on the door of the parish church ninety-five heads under which he offered to debate their value. This was the famous year, 1517, when, as Father Ribadeneira says, *Luterus ab obedientia ecclesiæ ad castra diaboli descivit.* A year later came his debate with

Eck. In 1520 Pope Leo issued his bull of condemnation; Luther burned it in the public square at Wittenberg, and the Pope excommunicated him. A month or two later the young Emperor held an Imperial diet at Worms. Luther attended under a safe-conduct and pleaded his cause; the Spaniards present broke into groans and hisses, the Germans into applause. The conclusion was foregone; Luther was put under the ban of the Empire. "This year," as he afterwards said, "by God's grace the holy light of Christian truth, formerly suppressed by the Pope and his followers, has been rekindled, by which their manifold and noxious corruption and tyranny has been laid bare and scotched. So that it looks as if tumults would arise, and parsons, monks, bishops and the whole spiritual estate hunted out and smitten, unless they apply themselves earnestly to their improvement." He spoke sooth. From this time on, the split grew steadily wider; the Protestant doctrines, grace, faith, predestination, were cried up, and old beliefs in priesthood, celibacy, purgatory, transubstantiation, the Virgin, saints and images, were denounced and ridiculed. Insult and injury went hand in hand. The Protestant enthusiasts called the Mother Church all sorts of rude names,—"from the evils of this dragon had been begotten the scum and venom of all sorts of idolatry" and so forth. Christian Europe was rent asunder.

By the time Ignatius travelled through Italy, the Lutheran rebellion was afoot; but except for Luther and his friends, few understood the significance of it. The very name Protestant did not come into being for years. The Italians expected this heresy to die out as so many others had done, and Spaniards were probably more in the dark than the Italians; they were taken up with their own affairs, and had for the most part a simple notion of religion as a war between Christians and Mussulmans. Charles was as yet only King of Spain when Luther nailed up his ninety-five theses, and had enough discontent at home upon his hands without thinking of outside troubles. His imperial election took place while Luther and Eck were debating at Leipzig, and he did not realize the serious character of the heretical movement until the Diet of Worms. The Spaniards in attendance there had an opportunity to learn something of the situation; but at home there was scarce an inkling of what was to happen. It is true that a few weeks before the siege of Pamplona, Leo X had addressed a brief to the authorities in Castile warning them against the introduction of Lutheran books, which, it was feared, had been smuggled into Spain during the preceding twelve months; and Cardinal Adrian, then regent in the King's absence, acting upon the Pope's suggestion, bade the inquisitors lay hold on what books of such character they could. Also, in 1523 it seems that somebody suspected that heresy might filter in from the southwest corner of France, for orders were issued to the Corregidor of Guipuscoa to exercise the greatest vigilance. And in June of the next year, a ship hailing from Flanders, or some port infected with heresy, and bound for Valencia, was wrecked off the north coast of Spain, and two casks filled with Lutheran books were discovered in the cargo; these were seized; and in the official report of the seizure it is said that the whole country-side was talking of the matter. This is virtually all the evidence concerning Spanish interest in Luther at this time. There may have been some curiosity over the new doctrines in Valencia, and perhaps in Barcelona and other ports, but there were no avowed Lutherans, and none were brought before the Inquisition until thirty years afterwards. Erasmus had many followers among the intellectuals; but that was quite a different matter. It is most unlikely that Ignatius, while a soldier in Navarre, ever heard it suggested that Luther was a person of importance. Probably he did not know his name, until he went to Venice. Even then, and after his return to Spain, and I think all his life, he never looked upon Protestantism as a separate issue, certainly not as the special object of the Society's efforts, but rather as an incidental consequence of the principle of disobedience, a disease to be cured by increasing the health of the whole Christian body and not by local treatment, and Protestants as merely one among many classes of the wayward.

The Italian Renaissance, on the other hand, as I think,

appeared to him as an insidious and very dangerous enemy. To us of today the term Italian Renaissance, calls up a prodigal abundance of princely palaces, arched and arcaded churches, frescoed walls, fountains, monuments, galleries of pictures and statues. We think of all the glittering throng that pass over Vasari's pages, from Masaccio, Brunelleschi, Ghiberti, to Leonardo, Bramante, Raphael and Michelangelo, to Sansovino and the Venetian masters; we think of Popes, princes, patrons, told of in Burckhardt, Symonds, Creighton, Pastor, and the thousand modern tellers of that wonderful story, of Nicholas V, Sixtus IV, Julius II, Leo X, of Medicis and Borgias, of Estes, Sforzas, Gonzagas, of poets and men of letters, Lorenzo the Magnificent, Poliziano, Pico della Mirandola, Boiardo, Ariosto, Tasso, Castiglione, Guicciardini, Macchiavelli, and all the rest who set the crown of intellectual supremacy upon Italy. As we look back history is foreshortened, and these men of the *quattro-cento* and *cinquecento* seem to rub elbows, so many were there in so brief a time and so limited a space. We must correct that impression; nevertheless, it is hard to realize that a man could wander among them, could walk through the garden of Italy, as a philosopher might "with unuplifted eyes" pace up and down some gravelled walk in a garden of flowers, and never see or smell a blossom. The French cavaliers who crossed the Alps with Charles VIII burst out with their delight, *"C'est un Paradis terrestre!"* Nothing, however, that Ignatius says, nothing that is said of him, implies the slightest interest in the handiwork of men, none in the creations of nature, unless it were to point a moral.

Rome, at the time of his visit, was a most magnificent city. There was no suspicion of the hordes, crueller than those of Alaric or Attila, that were soon to destroy the full fruitage of that magnificence forever. She was indeed shrunken from the days of her ancient glory; vineyards, olive trees, ivy clothed the slopes where Cæsars and Senators once lived, the forums where the conquerors of the world had taken their ease. She was no more "a princess among provinces," but art was making her all glorious within. Raphael was dead, but the records of his genius

were there in all their grace and loveliness; Bramante was
dead, but the designs for St. Peter's basilica bore witness
that he had not lived in vain; Pinturicchio was dead, and
old Perugino was painting his last frescoes in the Castello di
Fortignano, yet both had left their sign manual in the
Vatican; Michelangelo had gone back to Florence, but the
frescoes in the Sistine Chapel are still the most splendid in
the world; Baldassare Peruzzi, Sebastiano del Piombo,
Sodoma, Giulio Romano, Sangallo, and their fellow artists,
for the moment lacked patronage in Rome, since Pope
Adrian cared for nothing that they could do, but they were
waiting to return when another Medici should ascend the
papal throne.   Bembo was living in Padua, Pietro Aretino
in Mantua or Venice, Macchiavelli in retirement near Florence, Baldassare Castiglione was preparing himself to become papal ambassador to Spain, Sannazaro approaching
the close of a distinguished old age in Naples, Pomponazzi,
the philosopher, after stirring educated society by his doubts
upon the individual existence of the soul after death, was
still lecturing at Bologna.   Influences from all these men
gathered to a focus in Rome.   Ignatius passed them by, as
a man walks, unnoticing, over shadows.   Yet some of these
things might have touched religious sensibilities.   Michelangelo's fresco on the ceiling of the Sistine Chapel, where
God's outstretched forefinger imparts life to the inert form
of man, might well have suggested to him an allegory of
spiritual meaning; the Madonnas of Raphael might have
helped to round out in living loveliness the visions of the
Madonna that had been vouchsafed to him; the construction of the great basilica of St. Peter's might have served
as a symbol that a case may need to be cast away and a
new case put in its stead without hurt to the jewel within
that consecrates the case.   Not so with Ignatius.   He worshipped in the sacred churches, he prayed at the privileged
altars, and confirmed his faith by all that was old, traditional, mediæval, all that had existed before the new spirit
of mental energy and unrest, of intellectual curiosity, of
search and discovery of some new thing, of admiration for
the pagan past, had come like the springtime over Italy, and

thence winged its way northward across the Alps, and westward over the Mare Tyrrhenum to Spain.

It was not the outward splendor of Rome that alienated
Ignatius. He beheld the magnificence of the basilicas,
sumptuous with recent gifts, of the palaces, and rich houses
dedicated to pride and pleasure. He beheld the great prelates with their troops of servants, their banquetings, their
ostentation, their hunting and hawking; but I do not find
that he spoke one word in criticism of this luxury. The
theory that Christianity is a revolt of the proletariat against
the self-indulgence of the rich found no lodgment in his
mind. He was an ascetic of the ascetics, because he believed
that certain services due to God required of the servants
who were to perform them, great self-denial; but he had no
criticism to make of those whose services were of a different
character. His objection to the Renaissance was based on
other grounds. He felt that the spirit which animated it,
the spirit of intellectual curiosity, was an apostate, a
renegade, spirit. What did the Lord God require of a man
but to accept the established creed, to believe in the Three
Divine Persons, in Mary the Mother of Christ, in the angels,
in thaumaturgic saints, and to praise them and pray to
them unceasingly? The duty of man lay in devotion and
unquestioning obedience. He must lay aside his private
judgment and be ready to obey the Spouse of Christ, the
Hierarchical Church, in all things. He must make confession and take the Holy Sacrament once a year; he should do
so every week. He should hear mass, hymns, psalms and
prayers, as ordained by the Church. He must rate celibacy
higher than the married state, he must honor the vows of
obedience, poverty and chastity, venerate the relics of saints,
keep fasts and abstinences, and seek reasons to defend all
the precepts of the Church, never to impugn them. And
"in order to attain the truth in all things, we ought always
to hold that we believe what seems to us white to be black,
if the Hierarchical Church so defines it." All this is the
very antithesis of the spirit of the Renaissance.

Ignatius was right. This exaltation of learning, of literature and art, of the world and ways of Greece and Rome,

of human life on earth in and for itself, depreciated the Christian religion and the Church of Rome, both directly and indirectly. The Lutheran heresy rent the seamless garment of Christ, but the subtle spirit of the Renaissance was poisoning the well of Christian revelation; unless it was strangled, a day would surely come when its disciples would not merely disregard, but also make a mock of, all Christian beliefs. I do not mean that Ignatius would have expressed his ideas in just these phrases, and I may be reading back into those earlier years the lessons that he learned later in life; but what I have said I believe to be correct in substance. This is apparent from the policy he adopted. At Loyola, he had said to himself: "Why should not I do what St. Francis did?" As he knew, St. Francis never studied, and never approved of study; and when he sailed from Barcelona he had received the scantiest schooling. But after his year of travel he turned completely about; when he disembarked in Spain on his return, he started upon a twelve-year course of education, beginning in a grammar school at Barcelona and ending at the University of Paris. His purpose was to fit himself to be the leader of a little band of men, who should devote themselves, body and soul, to combating the pagan spirit of intellectual freedom, by teaching and preaching the traditional dogmas of the Roman Catholic Church. Just why he adhered to the plan of going to Jerusalem, as I say, is a puzzling question. Perhaps his stubborn tenacity of purpose clung to the idea; perhaps he thought that other young men were to be judged by himself, and that this plan would be the best possible to stir their young imaginations and kindle their fervor, as it had done with him; perhaps because it was necessary to have some definite plan, and this was ready to hand. In any case, I think that somewhere in the depths of his soul he must have known that the plan would be but temporary, to be in due time replaced by another.

CHAPTER VII

BARCELONA (1524-1525)

ARRIVED in Barcelona, Loyola, at the age of twenty-nine, as I think, or thirty-four according to the usual reckoning, entered upon the second stage of his spiritual life, as school-boy in a grammar school.

His conversion shows him to have been a man of sensitive imagination, dominated by needs which things of the world could not satisfy. From his book of *Spiritual Exercises* it appears that he possessed remarkable psychological insight, an ability to analyze and understand impulses, needs, habits and aspirations; and this ability to rearrange his whole conception of the world's needs and of his own life's work, displays an extraordinary mental detachment from pre-established opinions, a detachment which is wholly incon-sistent with the mediæval tradition that he represents, and would have been impossible for such a saint as Francis of Assisi, for instance. This volte-face reveals a remarkable side to his personality, and helps one to understand how he was able to acquire his immense influence over disciples of very different temperament, disposition, and intelligence; it indicates that he possessed a power of looking at the oppo-site aspects of a problem that one finds only in men of rare intellectual aloofness, and that one would not have expected to find in him of all men. Up to the time of his visit to Italy, Ignatius was completely a child of the middle ages, his youth might well have been passed in the thirteenth century, and suddenly he has become a man of his own time, a stout conservative indeed, but with a clearer understand-ing of what must be done in order to strengthen the old order within and defend it from enemies without, than any one bred in the Roman curia. Perhaps I ought to add a

qualification to these remarks, if qualification it is, in order
to prevent any misconception. I have spoken of Loyola's
change of plan as revolutionary; so it was, but the change,
after all, was but a change of ways and means, as a navigator
bound for Cathay might abandon his plan of the northwest
passage and, steering south by east, double the Cape of
Good Hope and sail across the Indian seas. Ignatius kept
unchanged his fundamental purpose of serving God and his
neighbor.

It was awkward for a man close upon thirty to go to
school with boys and study the rudiments of Latin; but
Loyola's main difficulty at first lay in his inability to fix
his mind on his book and get the rules of grammar by
heart, because his imagination wandered off to contemplate
celestial things, and his joy therein was so great that he
could not deny it to himself. He recognized his weakness
and, as usual, conceived of it under concrete form as a trick
of Satan's. He went to his schoolmaster and begged him
to go with him to the church of Santa Maria del Mar.
There, under the high aspiring roof this strange pupil fell
on his knees, and, by the religious light that shone through
the great rose window, confessed to his Master that the
Devil was pressing him hard but that he now pledged his
word not to miss a lesson for the space of two years, and
besought his Master to watch over him and treat him like a
little boy and flog him every time that he should be found
listless and inattentive. This exorcism attained its purpose, and he seems from this time on to have pursued his
studies with diligence and fair success.

As usual mundane matters did not come within his field
of vision. In June, 1525, a notable event took place; the
captive king, Francis I, disembarked at Barcelona, and
lodged for three nights in the archiepiscopal palace. An
immense concourse of people thronged to see him, cannon
were fired in his honor, and trumpets, drums and clarions
welcomed his coming. A cavalcade of ladies rendered him
a visit and received his compliments. He attended service
in the cathedral, escorted by a troop of lords and gentlemen,
pikemen and musketeers. Some two or three months later,

his famous sister, usually known as Marguerite of Navarre,
—"*la marguerite des princesses*"—dressed all in white, for
she was in mourning for her late husband, passed through
the town, and hurried on in her litter, being all impatience
to see her beloved brother:

> Le désire du bien que j'attends
> Me donne de travail matière;
> Une heure me dure cents ans,
> Et me semble que ma litière
> Ne bouge ou retourne en arrière.

> My longing for the good that nears
> Is source to me of bitter woe;
> Each hour lasts an hundred years,
> And my slow litter half appears
> To stand stock-still or backward go.

But when she hurried through, and when the captive king
dallied, all the boys of the grammar school must have played
truant on those days; yet Loyola no more heeded these
sights than the "gay motes that people the sunbeams."

During these two years he enjoyed the friendship of
several ladies of the city, in especial, Doña Inés Pascual
whose acquaintance he had made on the day after his vigil
at Montserrat, and Doña Isabel Roser. It is said that for
a time he lived in Doña Isabel's house, nevertheless he continued to beg his food. These compassionate ladies gave
him alms, and tried to persuade him to be less rigorous with
his poor body, to eat more, and wear better clothes. He
consented to put on a black cassock, but continued to sleep
on the floor and, whenever his health permitted, to inflict
upon himself severe acts of penance. Such corporal discipline is in accordance with austere monastic traditions, and
it need not be set down to mere wayward fanaticism. Does
it not quicken the better part in us, to witness the spirit
bully the body, and take revenge for the victories which the
body too often has won over the spirit? But in this tor-
menting of the body there is also the idea of an oblation to
an unappeased God, and this idea takes us back, through
earlier centuries and dark ages, to idolatry and primitive religions. Loyola, I think, always entertained some such

idea. He suggests to me some great fruit-bearing tree, deep-rooted in primitive soil, with bole and branches high in the air, leading as trees seem to do, a sort of double life, drawing their nourishment from the past and giving fruit to the present.

One anecdote told of him while at Barcelona tends to support the notion that thoughts of the pagan Renaissance had a large place in the background of his mind. It concerns his first acquaintance with the writings of Erasmus, and necessitates a digression upon Spanish culture at the time. Of all the humanists of his generation, Erasmus had by far the greatest renown throughout western Europe, in the Low Countries, England, France, Germany, Spain, and even in Italy. His scholarship, both in sacred and secular studies, his editions of the classics, his translation of the New Testament, made his name a household word among scholars; his wit, humor, and elegant Latin, delighted culti-vated society; and his whole-hearted zeal for reform within the Church, his attacks upon monastic corruption, made sometimes with irony, mockery and laughter, sometimes with bitter frankness, won the good will of reformers, both clerics and laymen. The most distinguished men every-where were proud of his acquaintance. Sir Thomas More, Colet, Dean of St. Paul's, Grocyn the elegant scholar, and others among the best in England, were his intimate friends. Charles V favored him, Francis I invited him to Paris, Leo X recommended him for a bishopric. He basked in the sunshine of admiration and applause. His lighter works, *The Praise of Folly,* and *The Colloquies,* were read by everybody, everywhere. He occupied a position in Euro-pean letters such as no man had held since Petrarch, and before Petrarch since Cicero, and no other was destined to take until Voltaire should come with similar powers of wit and raillery. Erasmus imitated the dialogues and disqui-sitions of Lucian and made them the fashion; in particular he fell foul of monks and friars. Reformers and liberal-minded men laughed and rejoiced, but the conservatives took alarm, and when German discontent kindled into re-volt and Luther defied the Pope, they suspected Erasmus of not limiting his sympathy to a mere reformation within the Church. Naturally both parties were eager to bring so powerful a champion to their side; Protestants and Catholics, alike, urged him to step forth and lead their forces. Erasmus was in a difficult position; he agreed to some extent with each side. He went part way with the Reformers. It is said, that when asked to condemn Luther he replied: "Luther is wrong on two points, he has hit at the Pope's crown and the monks' bellies." And certainly his attacks upon the corruptions of the monastic orders were worthy of the most violent reformer. But on the other hand he was a good Catholic in the fundamental matters of the faith, and his sense of propriety, decorum and good breeding, was offended by Luther's rough and rude denunciations of what the Christian world had long held sacred. Certainly it never entered his head to break with the Church. Consequently extremists on both sides belabored him. Luther compared him to Epicurus and Lucian, and charged that he held that God did not bother Himself about mankind, or, that he did not believe in God at all. The orthodox universities of Cambridge and Oxford forbade students to read his writings and booksellers to publish them; the University of Louvain raged against him.

In Spain—to bring the narrative closer to our central interest—Erasmus had a great following, his name was upon everybody's lips. Many of the most distinguished men of letters were avowed disciples, *Erasmistas* as they are called, while others admired his learning and wit, but held a little aloof because of his attacks on church ceremonies, fasts, vigils, invocations of saints and other cherished practises. A number of these *Erasmistas,* using the term in a broad sense, stand high in the ranks of Spanish learning and literature. Luis Vivés (1492-1540) of Valencia, who after studying in Spain and France, became professor at Louvain, is perhaps the most illustrious. His speculations on philosophy have been compared to those of Lord Bacon. Juan Gines de Sepúlveda (1490-1572) who had been educated at the universities of Alcalá de Henares and of Bologna, and had become a distinguished scholar, corresponded with

Erasmus, who praised him highly for his Ciceronian Latin; and the two remained familiar friends until the schism in the Church threatened war, and then Sepúlveda seems to have turned about and cast blame. Alvar Gomez de Ciudad Real (1488-1538), soldier and scholar, was another of them, not indeed well known to the world but with a position of his own in the history of Spanish culture. A fourth, Alonso Fernandez de Madrid (1478-1559), also a man of eminence, translated Erasmus's *Enchiridion Militis Christiani* (The Manual of a Christian Gentleman) a work to which I shall soon refer. A fifth, Alonso de Valdés (1490-1532) served the Emperor in the capacity of secretary, accompanying him to Aachen, for his coronation, and to Worms for the famous diet. Valdés, in spite of his liberal views, like almost all Spanish gentlemen, except his brother Juan, who is to be reckoned as an exception, was a devout Catholic, and found Luther "audacious and shameless." His brother, Juan, (1501-1541) is a recognized master of Spanish prose, the author of the *Dialogue between Mercury and Charon* that I have quoted, and of other satires that show his indebtedness to Erasmus. In later years he lived in Naples, became a half-mystical religious thinker, and teacher, and laid himself open to charges of unorthodoxy. Among those who became his disciples, or perhaps I should say, merely listeners, were two very celebrated ladies of high character, the Lady Julia Gonzaga, and Vittoria Colonna, a poetess herself, but still more renowned because of the sonnets addressed to her by Michelangelo. Besides these men of letters, the list of Erasmus's admirers and supporters included Alonso Fonseca, Archbishop of Toledo, Primate of Spain, Don Alonso Manrique, Archbishop of Seville, all the professors at the University of Alcalá, except one or two, many courtiers in attendance on the Emperor, and so on.

But just as there was an opposing faction in England, the Low Countries, and France, so there was in Spain. Erasmus had denounced and ridiculed the great monastic orders without mercy, and they bitterly resented it. The Franciscan *Osservanti* were the most zealous, but many Dominicans made common cause with them. They rummaged through his books, discovered doubtful words in his translation of the New Testament, and scented traces of agreement with Luther. Putting one thing and another together, they marshalled their charges under twenty-one heads and laid a formal accusation before the Inquisition. The story of this accusation, how it was submitted to the theologians of Salamanca, Valladolid and Alcalá, how it finally went to Pope Clement VII, and how the Emperor used his influence on behalf of Erasmus, belongs to the years subsequent to Loyola's attendance at the grammar school in Barcelona. At that time the enmity to Erasmus had gone no further than indignation among the friars over his attacks upon them.

The incident that has occasioned this digression upon Erasmus concerns his book, the *Enchiridion Militis Christiani*. This had been composed years before, at the special request of a lady in order to arouse her profligate husband to a sense of duty and religion, and had been approved by Adrian, afterwards Pope, who was then, if I remember aright, a professor at Louvain. It was so much liked by Archduke Ferdinand, brother to Charles V, that Erasmus could say "the book is hardly ever out of his hands." When it was subsequently translated into Spanish, in 1526 or 1527, by Alonso Fernandez de Madrid, with a dedication to the Inquisitor General, it was read by everybody in Spain, city folks and country folks, priests, monks, courtiers in the Emperor's palace, wanderers by the wayside, travellers stopping at an inn, and so forth. It is said to be the finest of Erasmus's minor compositions, and, I imagine, would appear extremely pious to anybody at the present day.

Ignatius was advised to read it on the ground that it was not only religious, but also written in elegant Latin. He started to read it, but while he read—this is his own story— he felt a sort of numbness creeping into his soul, so he laid the book down. He took it up again several times, each time with the same experience, and then renounced the reading of it altogether. It is hardly possible that the mere text could have produced this effect; it had been written before Luther was heard of, and except by very wilful or wayward interpretation, no heretical meaning could possibly be read into it. And yet according to Loyola's own story there is no suggestion that he was influenced by anything except the text itself. At Barcelona he may have heard of the feeling against Erasmus among the mendicant orders; but the absence of all reference to this feeling, implies the contrary. It is still less probable that he was aware of Stuñiga's criticisms upon Erasmus's edition of the New Testament, published at Alcalá in 1524.

I dwell upon this incident because I think it sheds light on Loyola's very peculiar psychology. In this rejection of the *Enchiridion*, I do not believe that his mind went through any reasoned sequences. It caught hold of scraps and tags of thought, and by a lightning-like process that we call intuition, started perhaps by Erasmus's turn of phrase, by his choice of words, by the style that betrayed a Laodicean disposition, jumped to the conviction that here was a baleful influence. He was well aware, as I have said, of the fundamental enmity between the spirit of the Renaissance and the Roman Catholic Church; and he knew full well that those who were not with the Church, those that teetered to and fro between her and heresy, were against her. He classed, rightly enough, Mr. Doubtful, Mr. Facing-both-ways, and all such as enemies, and among them Desiderius Erasmus. He never changed his mind. In later years, it is said, he forbade members of the Society to read any book written by Erasmus; but this report is contradicted by the fact that Father Nadal used a treatise on grammar by Erasmus as a text book in the Jesuit School at Messina.

The leaders of the Catholic party subsequently adopted the same notion of the *Enchiridion*. The Sorbonne condemned it, the Parlement of Paris burnt it on the Great Square of Notre Dame. The Spanish Inquisition forbade the Spanish version, and carefully expurgated the Latin. The Society of Jesus held Erasmus up as a heretic, and Father Canisius, one of its early members, declared, *"aut Erasmus lutherizat, aut Lutherus erasmizat."* The "numbness of heart" that Loyola felt while reading bears eloquent testimony to the hypersensitiveness of his catholicity.

CHAPTER VIII

ALCALÁ (1526-1527)

By the end of two years, about the spring of 1526, Ignatius had learned enough Latin in the opinion of his master to commence a course of philosophy at the university of Alcalá de Henares, a town that lies a little distance to the northeast of Madrid. Three friends, who may be accounted his first disciples, though they soon fell by the way, went with him from Barcelona,—Calisto de Sa, Juan de Arteaga and Lope de Caceres.

The university of Alcalá was young. It had been founded about twenty years before by the celebrated Ximenes, who had risen by rapid steps from the position of simple friar and parish priest to be confessor to Queen Isabella, then Archbishop of Toledo, Cardinal and regent of Spain. In Granada, soon after the capture, in the fresh flush of crusading zeal, Ximenes had burned all the Arabic books and manuscripts he could lay hands on, religious or scientific, excepting some treatises on medicine, but he had done this out of devotion to the Christian faith, and not from any ill will to learning. At Alcalá he endowed forty-two chairs, and filled them so worthily that the university sprang into immediate favor; it is said that about Loyola's time there were seven thousand students there. One achievement, the publication of a Polyglot Bible, that is the Hebrew, Greek and Latin versions printed side by side in parallel columns, had made the university famous throughout Europe. Here Ignatius studied three courses, logic, in a treatise by Domingo de Soto, physics, according to Albertus Magnus, and theology, as presented in the books of Peter Lombard, in short the usual beginnings of mediæval scholastic philosophy and theology.

71

Of Loyola's life at the university as a student little is known. He lodged, at first, in a lowly hospice, and begged his livelihood. The warden in charge looked kindly upon him, and transferred him to a better room. A printer, too, Eguia, by name—in those days printers were scholars—befriended him, giving him alms both for himself and for the poor, and for a time took into his own house Loyola's three companions. Loyola, as usual, strove to help his neighbors in religious matters, teaching them to pray, to meditate, to practise a habit of retreat, and instructing them in his *Spiritual Exercises.* His three disciples did very much the same, and also a young Frenchman who had joined them, Jean Reinalde, formerly a page to the viceroy of Navarre. All wore a peculiar garment made of sackcloth. They ministered to many people, most of whom received from their ministrations much spiritual consolation, but several women were affected hysterically. One woman, for instance, when she attempted to lift her left arm to scourge herself, declared that she felt it grasped and held fast. Other episodes of like character occurred. Great talk arose, dubious rumors spread abroad, and reached the ears of the inquisitors at Toledo. A commission of investigation came to Alcalá. Loyola's friendly host warned him of their coming; told him that he and his companions were called *bagmen,* in allusion to their sackcloth garments, and also *illuminati,* and added that the inquisitors would make mince-meat of them. *Bagmen* was an innocent term, but there was danger in the appellation *illuminati,* for this was the name given to persons, considered by the Inquisition to be heretics, who followed inward illumination rather than the teaching of the Church, and indulged not only in extravagant rites and practices of their own devising but, as was generally believed, in very gross vice. The inquisitors turned out to be men of good sense, and did no more than their duty required. The official record of their proceedings gives the only account that there is of Loyola's methods of carrying on what we should call evangelical missions conducted by a street preacher, so I shall quote it in full:

In the city of Alcalá de Henares, on the 19th day of November, 1526, before Dr. Miguel Carrasco, a canon of Santa Justa in the said city, the licentiate Alonso Mexia, canon of Toledo, and before me, Francisco Ximenes, notary: Fray Hernando Rubio, presbyter, of the Order of St. Francis, forty-one years of age, being duly sworn, and asked what he knew concerning certain young men who go about the city, clad in light gray smocks that reach to the feet, some of them barefoot, and say that they live after the manner of the apostles, said—

That what he knew was this: He had seen now and again in the city, four or five such men clad as described, one or two of them went barefoot. And once, about two months before, the witness had started off in company with a boy to fetch a peck of flour that he wanted, and had gone to the house of Isabel, the bedeswoman who lived behind the church of St. Francis; when he got there he opened the door, and saw in the court, carpeted by a grass matting, one of the aforesaid, who went barefoot, a young man, perhaps twenty years old. Two or three women were kneeling round him, their hands folded as if in prayer, and looking at the young man, who was talking. The witness did not hear what was said. One of the women was the said bedeswoman, who exclaimed, when she saw the witness, "Leave us alone, Padre, as we are busy." And that same day, in the afternoon, the bedeswoman came to the witness and said: "Padre, don't be shocked by what you saw today; that man is a saint."

When asked if he knew whether these young men had held other meetings, he answered that he had heard say that they met at a certain hour of the day in the hospice of Our Lady, in Main street, that the young men spoke there, and men and women went to hear them.

Asked if the young men lived together, he said no, each lived alone.

Asked as to their age, whether they were old or young, he said they were all young men, and he thought that the one whom he found with the women in the court yard was the oldest.

Asked whether they were educated or not, he said he did not know; some of them were studying elementary grammar and logic, but that they did not attend other courses in the university.

Asked if he knew where they came from, he said that he did not know, but he had heard say that one of them lived near Najera; and he did not know whether they were new Christians [i. e. persons descended from Jewish ancestry within four generations] or old Christians [persons of pure Christian ancestry].

Asked what he thought of their costume and their way of living, he said that their way of meeting together and discussing, seemed to him very novel.

The witness was bidden not to speak of the matter.

Beatriz Ramires, a resident of the town, etc., testified, that she knew one of these young men [described as before by the examiner] named Iñigo, who she had heard say was a gentleman; he went about barefoot in a sackcloth garment down to his feet. She had also seen four others, who wore the same dress, but did not go barefoot.

She further said that once she was at the house of Andrés Dávila, a baker, and there in a room was the said Iñigo and one of his companions. Various persons were listening to Iñigo, Isabel Sanchez (the bedeswoman) who lived at the back of St. Francis's church, Ana del Vado, house-keeper for Fray Bernardino, the daughter of Juana de Villarejo, a girl of about fourteen, the said Andrés Dávila, and (the witness thought) his wife, and also the wife of Francisco de la Morenna, and another man, a vine-dresser; she thought there were others as well but she did not remember who. Iñigo was instructing them in the two great commandments, that is, Thou shalt love God, etc., etc.; he spoke at great length on this subject; and the witness was vexed to find that while she was there Iñigo said nothing that was new to her, merely all about loving God and your neighbor.

This witness further testified that she had gone there because Iñigo had said, a day or two before, that he was going to speak on the commandments; she did not know of other meetings, but had heard that Iñigo had preached to several persons in the hospital of Antezana in the city. Two of these companions, Caceres and Arteaga, shared a room in the house of Hernando de Parra, Calisto and Juanico de Reinalde lived with Andrés Dávila, and Iñigo lived in the hospital of Antezana, and she had seen some of them together in Iñigo's room. They were all young men. Sometimes they received some little presents, a bunch of grapes, a slice of ham, etc., in return for their teachings, but the presents were thrust upon them, against their will. She herself had persuaded some rich ladies to give Iñigo the cloth for the garment he wore. A mattress also and two coverlets were given, and one mattress lent; and she had given a pillow stuffed with wool to Calisto and Joannes.

The wife of one of the wardens of the hospital also testified. She corroborated what the last witness had said, and gave some further details. Caceres came to the hospital every day for his dinner and supper, and immediately after dinner went off to the university. Sometimes he came to talk to Iñigo, and they would talk together either in Iñigo's room or in the court; she did not know what about. Sometimes, too, before they received the coverlets, one of the companions came and spent the night, but that since then Iñigo always slept alone. She thought Iñigo and Calisto had been in Alcalá about four months. She did not know whether they had induced other persons to wear their dress, but that Juanico, who had been brought to the hospital because of a wound, had at that time worn good clothes, but since then had adopted the same dress as the others. Sometimes women, girls, students, and friars, came to ask for Iñigo, and she had heard him discoursing to them, but she did not know what about. Sometimes her husband scolded the visitors, and bade them let him study; this was because Iñigo had told him not to let them in because they disturbed him.

Visitors usually went to hear him discourse on feast days, and but little on other days; sometimes in the morning, sometimes after dinner, sometimes later in the afternoon, and students at times went in the evening.

The warden was then called. He added little. He thought that some women came every day to see Loyola, sometimes as many as ten or twelve together. Those who came in the morning were veiled. The hospital, he said, provided Iñigo with food and drink, a room and a candle.

This was all the testimony. Two days later the Reverend Licentiate Juan Rodriguez de Figueroa, Vicar General in the court of Alcalá for the Most Illustrious and Right Reverend don Alonso de Fonseca, archbishop of Toledo, issued the decree that, under pain of excommunication, each of the companions [I omit the legal verbiage] should within a week leave off the costume they were wearing and conform to the ordinary dress that clergy or laity were accustomed to wear in the kingdom of Castile.

In view of the troubled time, and the general suspicion attending any lack of religious conventionality, this was a very mild and reasonable decision, and bears honorable witness to the influence of Erasmus and his teachings upon the Archbishop of Toledo, the Inquisitor General, to whom the Spanish translation of the *Enchiridion* was soon to be dedicated.

Ignatius, conscious that he had done nothing that the Church could find fault with, was annoyed by this examination into his life and habits. He said to the Vicar General: "What have you gained by all these questionings? What wrong-doing have you discovered in me?" The Vicar replied: "Nothing; if we had, you would have been punished. You might even have been sent to the stake." Loyola retorted: "You, too, would go to the stake, if you were a heretic." The Vicar General kept his temper, and for a time matters went on as before. Ignatius and his disciples changed the color of their smocks in accordance with the terms of the decree, and continued to teach and preach. Suspicion, however, kept its eye on these serious young men, nominally students, who did not give any great part of their time to their university courses, but went about holding little conventicles and comforting distressed women. In the following March, the Vicar General was again conducting an examination. Perhaps he thought there had been too sharp a tone of defiance in Loyola's retort, or it may be that public opinion in Alcalá demanded further investigation. The *illuminati* had always been objects of suspicion. Moreover, the Lutheran heresy was becoming better known in Spain, and the Inquisition may have felt itself bound to be on the alert. Or, possibly, the Emperor himself may have given some sort of hint to the Archbishop of Toledo that officious piety at home might atone for a little lack of reverence abroad. Only the autumn before, the imperial ambassador, Don Hugo de Moncada, for the purpose of forcing the Emperor's will upon the Pope, Clement VII, had taken part with members of the Colonna family in a raid upon Rome. The raiders had failed to capture the Pope, but their followers rioted through the city. Baldassare Castiglione, the papal ambassador in attendance upon the Emperor, at Granada, wrote home: "All ranks, high and low, are indignant at the raid; the very stones cry out." But whatever the cause, the Vicar General this time conducted the investigation himself. I again quote the record:

Alcalá de Henares, March 6th, 1527. The Rev. Señor Licenciado Juan Rodriguez de Figueroa, vicar general, summoned before him Mencía de Benavente, widow of Juan de Benavente, deceased. She took the oath on the cross.

He asked her if she knew a man by name Iñigo who lived at the Hospital of Mercy, known as the Hospital of Antezana. She said that she knew him and three others who went about with him; she knew Iñigo by sight, by his speech and his manner, and also another man named Calisto; the other two she knew only by sight.

Asked if she knew whether the said Iñigo, or any of his companions collected people together in churches or houses or anywhere, and whether they taught or preached, and what they taught and how, and bidden to tell all she knew, testified as follows: Iñigo had held a reunion in her (the witness's) house, and had talked to several women, to wit: one Maria Dias and her daughter (Maria Dias was the wife of Francisco, a weaver); and a friend who had lived with the wife of Fernando Dias, who had been confined, and was a widow; and the servant of Loranca, chaplain of St. Just; and Inez, servant of Luis Arenes, the witness's sister; and Maria, servant of Luisa Velasquez who lives by the bakery called "of the flowers"; and another Maria, who lived in the house of Anna Dias, a neighbor of the witness; and Maria Dias, of Ocana, a widow, who wished to strangle herself, but the witness had cut the cord on her throat; and other women and girls; and the witness's daughter, Ana; and Leonora, who goes with her (the witness's daughter) to weave. Iñigo talked to these women, telling about the commandments and the mortal sins, and the five senses, and the faculties of the soul; and he explained very well; and made his explanations by means of the gospels, and of St. Paul and other saints; and told them to examine their consciences every day, twice a day, thinking over any sins they had committed, in front of an image, and he advised them to confess every week, and take the sacrament at the same time.

The same day the said Vicar summoned before him Anna, daughter of Juan de Benavente, and of Mencía de Benavente, his wife; administered the oath to her, and asked what Iñigo aforesaid had taught her.

She testified that he had expounded the articles of faith, the mortal sins, the five senses, the three faculties of the soul, and other good things concerning the service of God, and told her things out of the gospels, sometimes when she was in company with other women, and sometimes alone.

Asked where he had taught, she said, sometimes at her house; and sometimes at the hospital, and at such times the witness's mother took her; and at other times she went with some neighbors, who went there; and when they went to the hospital there were many women, and at other times she had seen no women.

Asked how old she was, she said seventeen years old. Iñigo bade her go to confession every week; she had also heard Calisto, who told them in what way they ought to serve God.

And this was all she knew, according to her oath.

The same day the Vicar General summoned before him, Leonora, daughter of Anna de Menna, wife of Andréas Lopez, the witness's father-in-law. She made oath on the cross, etc.

The Vicar asked her whether she had heard Iñigo, and what he had taught. Witness testified that she had heard him explain the commandments of the Church, and the five senses, and other matters that concerned the service of God.

Asked her age, she said sixteen.

Asked where Iñigo had taught, she said in the hospital where there were also other women. And that he had talked to them all together.

Nothing further was done at the time, but two months later the hearing was continued and more witnesses were examined.

May 2, 1527: The said Maria de la Flor, daughter of Fernando de la Flor, an inhabitant of the town, being duly sworn, testified what she knew of Iñigo, as follows: She had seen him often go into the house of Mencía de Benavente, aunt of the deponent; and the two often talked together in private; witness had asked her aunt and cousin what he said to them and to the other women who came in, and they said that he explained how to serve God. They told him their troubles and he comforted them.

The witness told them that she wished to speak to him; so she did, and asked him to teach her how to serve God. And Iñigo told her that the instruction must last a month; and that during the month she must confess and take the eucharist every week; and that the first week she would be very light-hearted and yet not know why, and the second week she would be very sad; but that he trusted in God that she would derive much benefit, and that if at the end of the month she felt in a good state, why, well and good, but if not, to do it all over again. And he told her that he must explain the three faculties of the mind, and so he did, and the merit to be got out of temptation; and how a venial sin became a mortal sin; and the Ten Commandments, and things about them; and the mortal sins; and the five senses; and all such matters.

And he told her that if a woman spoke to any girl of something evil, and the girl refused to listen to her, there was no sin, mortal or venial; but if at any time the girl listened, she committed a venial sin; but if she listened and did what the woman suggested, she committed a mortal sin; and he told her that it was her duty to love God.

He also told her that in entering upon the service of God, temptations would come from the Devil; and he explained to her the examination of the conscience, and that she should examine her conscience twice a day, after dinner, and after supper; and that she should kneel down and say: "O God, my Father and Creator, I thank Thee for all the mercies Thou has shown me, and for those I trust Thou wilt show me. I beseech Thee, by the merits of Thy passion, to give me grace to examine my conscience thoroughly."

And she had related to Iñigo a thought that she had had and that she had confessed to her confessor, and the confessor had told her that it was a mortal sin, and she had confessed and received the holy sacrament the same day. And Iñigo had said to her: "Would to God you had not got up that morning," because the fault she said she had confessed was not a mortal sin nor even a venial one, on the contrary it was a right thought; and he said he would have a talk with Calisto, his companion, and tell him about it and see what he would say. And so he told it to Calisto; and Calisto said just what Iñigo had said. And on another day Calisto bade her tell Leonora, who was learning to weave from the witness's aunt Benavente, that since Leonora told her confessor what he (Calisto) talked about with them, she might go to her confessor for help. And another time he told her that there was no need to repeat to her confessor what she had talked over with him and Iñigo.

And four times it happened that a great sense of sadness came over the witness, so that nothing seemed right, and she could not even lift up her eyes to look at Iñigo; but if in the midst of this sadness she spoke to Iñigo or Calisto, the sadness left her. And her aunt Benavente and her cousin said the same thing, for a very black sadness came upon them. And witness asked Iñigo, what these sad fits were and what they came from; and Iñigo said that when one was entering upon the service of God, the Devil put them in one's path; but that she should stay steadfast in the service of God, and that, through the love of God, they would pass away. And that when she said an *Ave Maria*, she should utter a sigh and fix her mind on the words *Ave Maria*, and then she should say *gratia plena* and fix her mind on those words.

And both Iñigo and Calisto were much pleased when these fits of sadness and faintness came upon her, because they said she was entering on the service of God.

And he told her never to swear or utter an oath, such as "God help me" or, "on my life," but only "certes." And if she saw anybody in the service of God, she was not to feel envy, but encouragement.

And the witness saw Maria (the girl that lived with her aunt Benavente) in a swoon on the ground; and Maria said she had seen the Devil with her eyes. very black and big; so they called Calisto; witness went home, but they told her Calisto had come and lifted Maria up.

And witness had formerly been a bad woman, keeping company with students of the university, and had been ruined. And when she thought of talking to Iñigo, and did not talk to him very soon, a faintness came upon her, and she felt sick at heart till he spoke to her. . . . And once deponent felt a great desire to go to the desert, and she asked Calisto for his opinion, and he said it was a good idea, and to carry it out. . . .

She further declared that they, Iñigo and Calisto, rejoiced

if any woman had a great desire to speak to them, for they said that they should win her soul. . . .

May 14, 1527: Anna de Benavente, was duly sworn, etc. The Vicar General asked her to describe how the fainting fits came on her, and on other women who conversed with Iñigo and Calisto.

Witness said that, according to the best of her recollection, since she began to talk with those two she had been taken by a fainting fit three or four times, and that she was taken in this manner: While she was thinking how she had separated herself from the world, in her way of dressing, and gossiping, and amusing herself, a fit of sadness came upon her and a feeling of faintness, and sometimes fainting fits took her and she lost consciousness. Twice she had been nauseated; and rolled on the ground. Some people seized her but could not quiet her. The fit lasted an hour; at other times, it was longer or shorter. And when Iñigo and Calisto were told what had happened, they said to her that it was nothing, and that she should strengthen herself in God.

Other women, too, had these fainting fits; some in one way, some in another. Leonora, daughter of Anna de Menna, her mother's servant, had these turns oftener than the others, and they lasted an hour; and Leonora said that sometimes she was conscious, and sometimes not. Witness had also seen Maria de la Flor, daughter of Fernando de la Flor, faint away, and Anna Dias, and two other girls who did not live in Alcalá.

When asked what happened when Maria de la Flor wanted to go to the desert and lead the life of Saint Mary of Egypt, witness said that the same thing happened to her. She often wanted to go into the country and lead a solitary life; and in her presence Maria de la Flor consulted Calisto, and Calisto told her to pray to the Virgin Mary to inspire her with what would tend most to the service of God; for it might be sin that prompted the thought. And Maria de la Flor said that she would go with Calisto, and Calisto asked how she dared go with him as she did not know him. Witness did not remember what Maria answered, except that after Calisto had gone, she said she might go and live with him in the same way she would with a woman.

Leonora, aforesaid, daughter of Anna de Menna, a resident of the town, being duly sworn, etc.

Interrogated about the fainting fits which came upon her when conversing with Iñigo and Calisto, she said it was true. Often, when she was thinking how she had abandoned her old ways of laughing and fun, and that she had been better off before, a sadness came upon her, and she lost consciousness, neither heard nor felt, and the sense of oppression brought on nausea, and she rolled on the ground. Iñigo said that the enemy was the cause of it, and bade her think upon God and His passion, and the fit would pass away.

And, besides, the same thing happened to Maria de la Flor, Anna Dias, and the Benavente girl, and other girls, who did not live in the town, but in Murcia.

And Iñigo bade her confess every week, and to receive the sacrament every month.

Mencía de Benavente, being duly sworn, etc.

Being asked about the fainting fits that came upon her and other women who conversed with Iñigo and his companions, and told to tell how often and what they were like, she said that she had hysterics, and also sometimes fainting fits; she thought they were hysterical.

She had seen Leonora, daughter of Anna de Menna, after a conversation with Iñigo, seized by a fainting fit, fall on the ground, be sick at her stomach, and roll round on the ground. And that her (witness') daughter had sweating fits, and she had seen Anna Dias, wife of Alonso de la Cruz, in swoons, and she had also seen Maria from Santorcas (who did not live in Alcalá) in a swoon twice, falling on the ground, and putting her hands to her breast as if she were going to vomit, and also another girl, from Yélamos, who lived in Anna Dias's house, in swoons, and she, too, threw herself on the ground, and vomited, and rolled on the ground. And that is the truth.

Anna Dias, wife of Alonso de la Cruz, being duly sworn, etc., corroborated the last witness as to Maria from Yélamos. Witness had seen her swoon more than twenty times.

The testimony of witnesses ended here.

CHAPTER IX

ALCALÁ AND SALAMANCA (1526-1527)

I HAVE quoted the records of the first two investigations into Loyola's missions and manner of life in full, and I shall also quote the third, for several reasons. One is that these records furnish the only evidence of his life at this time that does not come from himself or his disciples. Another, that they tell something of contemporary life. But my main reason is this: The record shows that Ignatius was beginning his apostolic ministry among the lowest classes of society, simple artisans and ignorant peasants, the basis on which the great edifice of the Roman Church must rest. Other men, in plenty, spoke of needed reforms within the Church, but they were thinking of cardinals and bishops, of friars and monks, and persons in high station; Ignatius alone had the sagacity to see that the Church must be reformed, purified, christianized, from the very bottom. The fate of Christianity does not depend on the priesthood, but on the laity. Tradition says that the great Pope, Innocent III, dreamed that he saw St. Francis holding up the tottering edifice of the Universal Church. Clement VII might well have dreamed a similar dream of Ignatius. Reform, of course, had been talked of long before Luther. In Spain, the great prelate, Cardinal Ximenes, who may be compared to Wolsey in England, or Richelieu in France, had begun the reformation of the monastic orders in the reign of Ferdinand and Isabella. And, at the period we are come to, Clement VII, Charles V, cardinals, bishops, princes, were haranguing and talking of mending and tinkering; they proposed at one time to suppress Luther, at another time to appease him; they equipped galleys and enlisted soldiers to fight the Turk, in the cause, as they said, of religion.

Loyola, alone—for the Italian reformers who founded the Oratory of Divine Love and other such societies, wished to purify themselves, or the priesthood, or some monastic order—recognized that the Church of Christ must strengthen, comfort and ennoble each individual soul, and if it should do so, there need be no further worry over heresy and schism. This was the way to hamstring the wild horse of heresy in Germany, and to loose the cord of the Mohammedan bow. Loyola's instruction of these simple folks in the dogmas of the Church, in the commandments of Christ, in duty and decency, in the primary faculties of the mind and the uses to which they should be put, marks the rudimentary beginning of Jesuit education. This is the germ that grew into the great teaching staff of Europe.

I now return to the official record of the third and last inquisitorial proceeding against Ignatius at Alcalá. This was a matter of greater consequence. Ignatius was arrested, and put in jail, probably on or about April 30th, 1527, rather, from the nature of the complaint, it would seem, or from the importance of the complainants, than because the ecclesiastical authorities were ill disposed toward him. Public opinion of some sort was aroused; one young nobleman, it is reported, declared that Loyola ought to go to the stake. For many days he was not told the nature of his offense, and then he learned that two ladies, mother and daughter, had gone off, on foot, upon a pilgrimage to Jaen, a town two hundred miles to the south, near Granada, in order to see the holy handkerchief of St. Veronica, and that this escapade had caused much scandal and had been laid at his door. The Judge waited until news from the ladies must have made his innocence clear, and then examined him with reference to all the suspicious facts elicited in the testimony that had been taken. I quote the official record:

May 15, 1527, in the city of Alcalá. The said Vicar went to the ecclesiastical jail and had Iñigo brought before him.

First Point: He said that Iñigo well knew that before last Christmas he had commanded him not to hold any meeting in the nature of a conventicle, whether or not under the guise of teaching or instructing—such had been the tenor of his order—and that Ignatius had not obeyed but had done just the contrary, and stood under a charge of disobedience to the commands of our holy mother Church; that if he had any excuse, to plead it, as the Vicar was ready to accept it. Ignatius replied that, there had been no command, not even by way of precept; but that if some reference had been made to this matter, it was a kind of advice, but just what, he did not remember.

Second Point: With reference to the persons with whom Ignatius had been in communication, especially as to the women whom he had taught, the Vicar had been informed that it was usual for them to swoon away after his visit, to lose all consciousness in a sort of ecstacy. Would he please state the cause of these swoons, and what he had to do with them.

To this Ignatius replied, that he had seen five or six women in swoons; that the cause to which he attributed them was that, as these women became of better conduct and refrained from sin, great temptations came upon them, sometimes from the Devil, sometimes from their relations, and caused the swoons. They were a consequence of the loathing they felt for sin. He comforted them when he saw them, bidding them be steadfast under temptations and pains, and telling them that, if they did so, within two months they would not feel such temptations any more. He had said this because, as he thought, he had learned it from his own personal experience of temptation, although he had never swooned.

Third Point: It was alleged that Ignatius had advised some women of Alcalá, or elsewhere, married or maidens, to tell what had passed between them and their confessors in the confessional, and had bidden them to confess certain things and not others, and had advised some of the aforesaid persons, to leave their families, and go roaming on a pilgrimage to places very far away from their homes.

Ignatius answered that some persons had disclosed to him certain conscientious scruples, and as he knew that these were not sinful, he had said not to bother about con-

fessing them; but he had advised them to confess whatever in his judgment were sins. That was all there was
to it. He denied that he had inquired or tried to learn
what had passed between priest and penitent in the
confessional.

Here ended Loyola's examination. As to the evangelical
mission, the religious teachings and so forth, it was plain
enough that everything, however unconventional, was innocent enough, and, more than that, was praiseworthy. The
persons concerned were peasants and they made no complaint. But the accusation that the defendant had advised
ladies to go, without escort, hundreds of miles through a
country where they might be exposed to many dangers,
was another matter. The Vicar General no doubt believed
what Ignatius said, but it was not to be supposed that the
ladies' family would rest content with the defendant's testimony in his own favor. So, on that point of the accusation, further investigation was necessary. I return to the
official record.

May 21, 1527. Luisa Velasquez, a resident of the city,
being duly sworn, in answer to the questions put by the
Vicar as to what she knew, and had seen or heard, of
Iñigo and his friends, and where she had been the days
she was out of the city during Lent, testified as follows:
She had been at Jaen, and to Our Lady of Guadalupe, with
her mother, and her maid, Catalina. Asked by whose
advice she had gone on this pilgrimage, she said, by her
mother's. She had gone in order to accompany her mother,
and also because of her devotion to those shrines. Asked
as to her relations with Iñigo and his companions, she
said that she had known them from before Christmas; she
had met and talked with them in her mother's house twice,
and in the house of Mencía de Benavente, and in the house
of Beatrís Ramires; and twice she had been to the hospital
to speak to Iñigo. Asked in what manner Iñigo taught her,
and what, she answered that first of all he taught the commandments; and afterwards in the house of Mencía de

Benavente, when Mencía and three or four other women were there together, he told them of the life of St. Anne and of Joseph, and of other saints, and said something else that she does not remember. Asked whether she had been seized by any fainting fits, she said no, although in Mencía's house she had seen a daughter of Fernando de la Flor and some other girls faint away. Asked how often Iñigo advised her to confess and take the sacrament, she replied every eight days if she felt so disposed.

Maria del Vado, widow, a resident of the city, being duly sworn, etç. Asked where she had been during the days that she had been absent, answered that she had been to Jaen, she and her daughter Luisa, to see the Veronica, which is at Our Lady of Guadalupe. Asked by whose advice she had gone on that pilgrimage, she answered that she had not done it on anybody's advice, but of her own will; she took her daughter and a maid servant with her. Asked if she had had any communication with Iñigo or Calisto, or any of their companions before going away or afterwards, she said that before she went away she had spoken to Iñigo several times, and considered him a good man and a servant of God, and did so still.

Catalina, wife of Francisco de Trillo, a resident of the city, being sworn as a witness, etc. Asked where she had been while she was away from the city, said that her mistress, Maria del Vado, had gone to Jaen and to Guadalupe, and had taken her and her daughter Luisa. Asked if she had had any communication with Iñigo or any of his companions, she said no.

The Vicar General did not issue his decision in the matter till June 1st. Perhaps the celebrations held in honor of the birth of the royal heir, destined to become Philip II, distracted his attention; or the news of the sack of Rome by the Imperial army (May 6th) which horrified many devout Catholics and set the Emperor's servants to work upon apology and excuse. His order was that Loyola within ten days should take off the costume he wore, which was a sort of loose cassock, and wear what citizens usually wore, either clerical or lay, as he might wish. And further that for the space of three years he should not teach or instruct anybody, man or woman, of whatever rank or condition, in public or in private; he should not hold meetings or meet persons for religious purposes one by one, nor do any such sort of thing; he must not expound the commandments, nor any matter that touched the Holy Catholic Faith. And further, at the end of three years, this injunction should still hold good unless the proper authority should then give him license to teach.

From this decree it appears that the ecclesiastical authorities felt the stiffening of public opinion, or at least greater strictness at the Imperial court. Vagabond and unlicensed preachers were not to be permitted to hold conventicles, or preach or teach as they might choose, nor were unlicensed persons to be allowed to wear clothes that appeared to denote some religious order, but in fact did not. None of these provisions seem unreasonable, but Ignatius was dissatisfied with the prohibition against religious instruction, for that was to be his life work and he would not forego it. He went to the archbishop of Toledo himself, Don Alonso de Fonseca. This prelate having accepted the dedication of the *Enchiridion,* was exercising his ingenuity in protecting Erasmus from the angry friars, and did not wish to embroil himself in other delicate matters. He was politic, suggested that Loyola and his friends should betake themselves to the University of Salamanca, and offered money for the journey. This seemed a happy solution; the young men accepted it, and migrated to Salamanca.

Loyola's studies could not have profited much from his stay at Alcalá. His imprisonment, as well as his missions and evangelical visits, must have interfered seriously with his studies. As he looked back in later years, his comment was that he had tried to do too much, scattering his attention on too many subjects. His comment, as his disciples understood it, is made to refer to too many courses at the university, but that is evidently a mistake; he did too many outside things. The upshot was that he went away

little better furnished with learning than when he came.
Nevertheless, he left a name there as an evangelical mis-
sionary, and either through that reputation, or by personal
meeting, came to be known to various young men, Lainez,
Salmerón, Bobadilla, Jeronimo Nadal, Manuel Miona, and
Martin de Olave, who afterwards became leading disciples.

At Salamanca, however, matters went still worse. To
begin with, clothes had been given them, in order to enable
them to comply with the court's decree, and they were
dressed like students; but Calisto, who was a tall fellow,
had clothes too small for him, a short tunic, a big hat, boots
that came half up his legs, and a pilgrim's staff; he looked
like a guy. Nevertheless, they continued their evangelical
ways. Suspicious reports, of course, spread about. The
consequence was that at the end of ten or twelve days,
Loyola's confessor, a Dominican monk, invited him and
Calisto to come to the monastery for Sunday dinner, saying
that the fathers would like to ask him some questions.
After dinner, the subprior (the prior was absent) took the
two guests into the chapel, and began an examination:

SUBPRIOR *(affecting affability)*. It gives me great inward satisfaction to hear of your saintly way of living, how
you go about like the apostles, and teach men the road
to heaven. All my brethren share my pleasure in this.
Only in order to round out our happiness, we should like
to hear from your own lips things a little more in detail.
Tell us from what University you hold a degree, and what
sort of a degree, and what in particular you have studied.

IGNATIUS. I have studied more than my companions,
but I have little learning. He then explained just how
little.

SUBPRIOR. How does it happen, then, that with so little
learning, no more than the bare rudiments of grammar, you
go about preaching?

IGNATIUS. My comrades and I do not preach, Father,
we merely talk in a familiar way, when occasion serves,
about what we know concerning divine matters; after
dinner, for instance, when we are invited out.

SUBPRIOR. That is just what we want to know; what are these divine matters that you talk about?

IGNATIUS. We talk about the beauty and excellence of virtue, about the shame and ugliness of sin, and try to lead our listeners to good and to turn them from evil. Sometimes we talk of one virtue, sometimes of another, and in like manner, of sins.

SUBPRIOR. But you admit that you are uneducated men; how then can you speak wisely concerning virtues and vices? Those things are to be learned only in one of two ways, either by study or by a revelation from God. Well, now, you have not learned them by study. The only other way is that the Holy Ghost has revealed them to you. We are curious to learn how that happened. Please be kind enough to tell us the revelations you have had.

Ignatius never went off at half cock. He always acted and spoke with deliberation. He paused a moment to reflect; and then said: "That is enough, Father; we will proceed no further in this matter." The subprior insisted, and pressed for an answer. "How is this? Just at this time when so many errors have been taught by Erasmus and by others who have misled numbers of people? And you refuse to speak out?"

IGNATIUS. Father, I shall say no more than I have said, except before my superiors, who have the right to give me orders.

SUBPRIOR. Well and good. Wait a bit, we will compel you to confess the truth.

The case was reported to the Bishop's tribunal, and after three days Ignatius and Calisto were taken to prison. They were lodged in a filthy upper room, with their ankles fettered together by a short stout chain, and left for the night. They could not sleep on account of the *"gran multitud de bestias varias,"* and passed the night in prayer. Their friends, however, were allowed to visit them and bring them necessaries, and Ignatius talked about divine things. His copy of *Spiritual Exercises* was taken for examination, and Caceres and Arteaga were also arrested. A few days later Ignatius was brought up before the judges. Many questions were put to him concerning the *Spiritual Exercises,* about the Trinity, the Incarnation and Transubstantiation. No fault was found with what he said. Then they asked him in what manner he was wont to expound the first great commandment. This too he did without reproof. They laid stress, however, upon one point at the beginning of *Spiritual Exercises,* the distinction between a mortal and a venial sin; they were doubtful whether an unlearned man was capable of making so delicate and important a distinction. Loyola said: "Is it true or not? If it is true, approve it; if it is not true, then condemn it." But the judges would not commit themselves.

Among those who came to see him was a nobleman, afterwards Cardinal Bishop of Burgos, who asked him if confinement was not a great hardship. Loyola said: "I will answer you as I answered a lady today who was loud in her compassion over my imprisonment. I said to her, 'Since this jail seems to you such an evil, it shows that you do not desire imprisonment for the love of God, but I tell you that there are not so many chains and fetters in Salamanca as I desire to wear for love of Him.'"

It happened one day at this time, that all the other prisoners burst open the doors of the jail and escaped, but Loyola and his companions stayed; and that made an excellent impression on the townsfolk. Finally, after twenty-two days of imprisonment, judgment was delivered. They were declared innocent and orthodox, and might continue teaching and discoursing as before, so long as they did not touch the matters of the distinction between mortal and venial sins. Loyola said he would not abide by the sentence; no condemnation whatever had been passed upon him, and yet his mouth was stopped from helping his neighbors where he might.

In consequence he made up his mind to leave Salamanca and continue his education at the University of Paris. Beyond that his plans were indefinite, he might join some religious order, or he might go about as he had been doing, with some companions, exhorting, comforting and helping. He loaded his books on a donkey, bade Calisto and the others wait until they should hear what arrangements he might be able to make for them in Paris, and set off for Barcelona, where he hoped no doubt to get money and provisions for his journey from Doña Inés Pascual and other friends. His stay at Salamanca had lasted about two months.

CHAPTER X

ALONE, and on foot, in the short days of mid-winter, Loyola set out from Barcelona on his way to Paris, a distance of some five hundred miles. The solitary road, the stark defiles of the Pyrenees, the winter snows, the alarms of his friends, the stories told in minute detail of how the French clapped into an oven any Spaniard they caught (for Francis I had broken the oaths he had sworn in captivity and the two countries were again at war), and other bugbears, real or imaginary, had no power to deter him. With a bill of exchange for twenty-five crowns in his pocket, and his staff in his hand, he followed his star. A letter written a month after his arrival in Paris speaks of his journey:

PARIS, March 3, 1528.

To DoñA INÉS PASCUAL:

May the true peace of Our Saviour Christ visit and keep our souls.

Considering the great good will and affection that in God our Saviour you have always had toward me and the deeds by which you have shown it, I have had it in mind to write you this from the time I left you, in order to let you know about my journey. By the grace and goodness of God Our Saviour, I arrived in the city of Paris on February 2d. I had very good weather and I am very well. I mean to stay here and study till the Lord bids me do something else.

Remember me affectionately to Juan [her son]; tell him always to be obedient to his parents, and to observe the religious days; and, if he does his life shall be long in the land of the living, and he will also live in heaven above.

Remember me also affectionately to your neighbor. Her

95

gifts have arrived. Her kindness and good will—for the sake of God Our Saviour—abide with me. May the Lord of the world reward her; and may He of His infinite goodness dwell in our hearts, so that His will shall be accomplished.

Your poor in virtue (*de bondad pobre*)

IÑIGO.

Ignatius may have travelled north by the way by which he had originally come from Navarre, then to Bayonne and up the usual road via Bordeaux, Tours and Orleans, but it seems more likely that he trudged through Catalonia and across the mountains to Perpignan, thence to Narbonne, and to Paris either by Toulouse or along the river Rhone. The Paris to which he came enjoyed the same relative pre-eminence among cities as it does now, or perhaps greater. I quote a description of it made about this time: "The river Seine, forking here, separates this famous city into three parts. The first (on the left bank), is *l'Université;* the second (which is the island made by the fork) is *la Cité;* the third (on the north side of the river) is called *la Ville.* . . . Charlemagne, at the instigation of his counsellor, Alcuin, founded the University . . . which has always been a home of the Muses and of the liberal arts for all the world, the source and fountain of all learning, the mother of scholars, the nursery of knowledge. This University stands on four solid pillars, that is to say, Theology, Medicine, Law and the Faculty of Arts. The first three are subject to a dean and two provosts, while the Faculty of Arts elects a Rector every three months; and all the other faculties obey this Rector as their king. The University is divided into four nations, France, Picardy, Normandy, and Germany with England. It contains 17 churches for the service of God, 14 monasteries, 4 hospitals, 3 chapels, and 30 public colleges. Besides these there are also 30 private colleges where, thanks to the gifts of rich men, students are provided with food and necessaries." There were, so it was said, probably more than doubling the truth, 30,000 students. It was a world in itself.

The part of the city on the *rive gauche*, the Latin quarter as we call it, was girdled in by a wall and moat which started at a point on the river by the Tour de Nesle (near the modern *Institut*) and ran southerly, excluding the Abbey of St. Germain, but swelling out sufficiently to embrace the church of Sainte Geneviève, where the Pantheon now stands, and bending back to reach the Seine again at the Place de Tournelle. The Rue St. Jacques, entering the city from the *faux bourg* St. Jacques by the Porte St. Jacques, and running northward straight to the Petit Pont, as it does today, cut this part of Paris very evenly in two, and then continued, as it still does, across the Pont Notre-Dame and on into *la Ville*, the largest section of the city. Alberti Vignate, an Italian in the employ of Francis I, who visited Paris in 1517, records that the Pont Notre-Dame is flanked on either side with houses and shops, and looks more like a handsome street (*una strada bella*) than a bridge, and that the Petit Pont is occupied by goldsmiths' shops full of silverware and jewels, and is still handsomer (*una bellìssima strada*).

Paris, nevertheless, still wore its mediæval aspect; throughout the Latin quarter at almost every street crossing chains were hung and a portcullis, ready to bar all passage at a moment's notice. And Paris still maintained some of its mediæval customs, for Signor Alberti mentions by the way, that on the return of a royal party from high mass, said in honor of nine knights newly admitted by the King to the Order of St. Michael, while the procession was crossing the Pont St. Michel, Monsieur de la Pellisse, who had not been included in the list, stabbed a high officer, the *Gran Recever de Franza*, because he suspected that he was the cause of the omission.

Ignatius arrived in Paris, as he says in his letter, on February 2, 1528. There were many colleges to choose from, but various considerations restricted his choice. He must enter a college open to the French Nation, in which academic division Spanish students and others from southern Europe were included. And among colleges open to the French Nation he must choose one where he could pursue courses of *gramática*, that is Latin grammar, composition, literature and so forth; and further a college that made special arrangements for poor students also was desirable. As the Collège de Montaigu fulfilled all these requirements, he matriculated there, and stayed for more than a year, until the summer of 1529.

The Collège de Montaigu stood on the hill of Sainte Geneviève, not far from the city wall, about midway between the Porte St. Jacques and the Porte St. Marceau, on a site a little to the left as you face the Pantheon today. It was more than two hundred years old, but it had been reformed once or twice. Its reputation was high. Erasmus had studied there, and Calvin also, probably leaving just about the time that Loyola came. Erasmus did not like the place, he complains of bad eggs and other discomforts, but he had been there long years before and was anticlerically inclined. Rabelais too rails at the college *"pour l'enorme cruaulté et villennie que je y ay congneu. Car trop mieulx sont traictez les forcez entre les Maures et Tartares, les meurtriers en la prison criminelle, voyre certes les chiens en vostre maison, que ne sont les malautruz audict colliege"*; but Rabelais' business was to rail, and he, too, refers to an earlier academic régime. On the other hand, it was said that: "This College enjoys a reputation of great austerity and discipline; behaviour there is as good as in church; for that reason, whenever a boy who lives in Paris is wayward and hard to manage, he is packed off to Montaigu and brought under the rod of humility and obedience." Here was another motive for Loyola's choice. Discipline was not always good in the colleges of the University. For instance, it was not good at the Collège de Sainte-Barbe, just across an alley-way from Montaigu. At this very time, George Buchanan, the famous Scottish scholar—Walter Scott's favorite Latin poet—was teaching grammar and Latin literature there (1529-1531) and his experience might well discourage serious pupils. He says:

While the professor is puffing over his teaching, these lazy boys go to sleep, or into daydreams of play and amusement. One boy stays away and has bribed his neighbor to answer for him; another has lost his stockings; a third is gazing at his foot that peeps out from a hole in his boot; a fourth pretends to be ill; a fifth is writing home. No help but in the rod; then sobbings and tear-stained cheeks for the rest of the day. [These were younger boys, but Buchanan's experience with his older students in philosophy was no better.] Now a troop of loafers from the district across the river tramps in, the clatter of hobnail boots announces their approach. They come in and pay as much intelligent attention as Marsyas did, listening to Apollo. They are ill-humored because they did not notice the announcement of the course, although it is placarded at the street corners, and they are offended because the professor does not read out of an enormous tome scribbled all over with marginal comments. So they all get up and with an infernal hubbub walk across the way to Montaigu, where an odor of soup pervades.

Here the professor complains of his students; but sometimes the students might well turn the tables. Buchanan himself, Dr. Govea, the head-master of Sainte-Barbe, and Juan Peña, also an eminent scholar, were men of character and high respectability, but all the professors were not. Francis Xavier tells that during his first year at Sainte-Barbe, the predecessor of Juan Peña was a debauchee and led his students to the depths of degradation, and that he himself sometimes made one of a rioting party and was only saved from sin by fear of loathsome consequences.

According to the rules of Montaigu College, studies began before daylight and continued until dark, and students, naturally, were expected to be present. At first Ignatius lodged at an inn, and things went well; but unluckily he entrusted the twenty-five crowns, which he received on his bill of exchange, to a fellow countryman who was lodging there also. This man applied the money to his own uses and left Ignatius with none. The sequence to the story of this embezzlement belongs to the following year, but I will relate it here. The embezzler went to Rouen, intending to embark for Spain, but he fell ill. Loyola learned of his illness by a letter—whether written by him to Loyola or to another I cannot make out—and decided at once to go and nurse him, hoping to take advantage of the occasion and persuade the sinner to forsake the world and devote himself wholly to the service of God. Loyola lived in a region of high, mediæval imaginings; he fancied that if he were to walk all the way to Rouen, barefoot, without food or drink, these privations would prove an acceptable sacrifice to the Lord, and bring his enterprise to a happy issue. But he was also apprehensive lest this plan might be presumptuous, as if, I suppose, he were tempting God to perform a miracle through him as intercessor. He prayed over the matter, and decided to carry out his idea. He left Paris before dawn, very fearful, but on reaching the town of Argenteuil, where a garment of Our Lord was said to be, his fear passed off, he felt great consolation, and also spiritual power and joy, and went on his way across the fields shouting and conversing with God. The first night he lodged in a hospital, the second under a haymow, and at last, without tasting food or drink, reached Rouen. He comforted the sick man, helped him aboard a ship bound for Spain, and gave him letters to Calisto and his other comrades there.

But to go back to the date of the breach of trust. Loyola was left without a penny, he could no longer stay at the inn, and whatever beds Montaigu College may have had for charity students had undoubtedly been taken. He was obliged to seek free lodgings elsewhere and went to the hospital of St. Jacques, which was situated across the river, at the other end of Paris, near the Porte St. Denis. Now the college required its students to be in attendance before sunrise and to stay till after dark, and the rules of the hospital forbade its lodgers to leave before sunrise and obliged them to be within doors by sunset; moreover, having no money, Ignatius was obliged to beg his food. Under these circumstances it was next to impossible to make much progress in his studies. He endeavored to obtain the job of servitor to a professor, hoping to receive the privilege of attending the professor's lectures in return for his services, but such positions were few and much sought after, and he had no luck. At the suggestion of a friend, he went to Bruges and Antwerp, and begged enough money of some rich Spanish merchants there to pay his expenses for the coming year. The next year he did the same. On one of these trips he made the acquaintance of Luis Vivés. The third year he crossed the channel and went to London. After that, kind merchants in Flanders and friends in Spain sent him enough money for his needs, and he was able to devote his time to his studies.

In October, 1529, he began a course in philosophy at the College of Sainte-Barbe, which was much frequented by Portuguese students. Its principal, Jacques de Govea, who came of an able and distinguished Portuguese family, had persuaded the King of Portugal to send to Sainte-Barbe all the Portuguese students maintained in Paris at the King's expense. George Buchanan taught Virgil and Latin in general, I believe. Strébée, likewise a distinguished scholar, held the chair in rhetoric, Juan Peña taught philosophy, and Antoine de Govea, a nephew of the principal, and early famous for his Latin poetry, also occupied a chair. At the end of the prescribed period, three years and a half, Ignatius took a master's degree, and then entered upon a course of theology, but never completed it, for he left Paris too soon, in the early spring of 1535. Part of the lectures he attended seem to have been given in the college and part at the Dominican convent on the Rue St. Jacques.

In comparison with his troubles at Alcalá and Salamanca, Loyola's sojourn in Paris was quiet and peaceful. This was probably because he did not conduct missions, or preach in the street. He was too busy with his studies, and Paris was not a good place for an itinerant preacher. *"Car le peuple de Paris est tant sot, tant badault, et tant inepte de nature, qu'un basteleur, un porteur de rogatons, un mulet avecques ses cymbales, un vielleuz au milieu d'un carrefour assemblera plus de gens, que ne feroit un bon prescheur evangelicque."* Twice complaints were laid

before the inquisitors, but both times proved too slight
and unsubstantial to warrant any action; the episodes, in
fact, turned out to the ultimate advantage of Loyola, for
the Dominican friar, Dr. Matthew Ori, who at the time
held the office of inquisitor at Paris, conceived a high
opinion of him, and stood his friend at a time of need,
years afterwards, in Rome. Besides, the book of *Spiritual
Exercises,* which as usual caught the attention of the
inquisitor, on being read testified eloquently to his pure,
religious, and orthodox character and creed. On one occasion, however, the students whom he was drilling in the
Spiritual Exercises got into trouble. This occurred while
he was still at Montaigu College. The three students in
question, Pedro de Peralta, Juan de Castro, Spaniards, and
Amador, a Biscayan, attended Sainte-Barbe, and were,
apparently, young gentlemen of more or less social consideration. These three, carried away by a passion for
privations and ascetic discipline, left the college and went
to live like beggars at the hospital of St. Jacques, where
Loyola had formerly lodged. They gave away everything
they possessed, even their books, and begged alms in the
streets, publicly. Their Spanish fellow students at Saint-
Barbe were scandalized, and, finding the three obdurate
to persuasion, came with swords and staves, dragged them
back to the Latin quarter, and made them swear to conform to the usual ways of students so long as they should
remain in the University. The Principal, Dr. Govea, said
that the first time Loyola appeared at Sainte-Barbe, *on lui
donnerait la selle,* a slang phrase which meant that Loyola,
in the presence of the undergraduates, would run the
gantlet between two rows of masters, armed with rods.
This story, as usually told, represents Dr. Govea suddenly
overcome by Loyola's humility, falling on his knees, begging pardon, and so forth; but as Loyola in his *Memoirs*
says not a word of any such ending, it seems to me an
exaggeration, an embellishment due to a college legend
too readily accepted. Neither Father Astrain nor Father
Tacchi Venturi think it worth repeating.

During his stay in Paris Loyola learned about the government and art of managing a corporation much that was to be of great service to him years later, when he should draw up the Constitution of the Society of Jesus. The rules of the Collège de Montaigu were largely derived from the practices of the Brothers of the Common Life, and so through this channel, as well as by the *Life of Christ* by Ludolf of Saxony, Loyola is connected with the great German mediæval mystical tradition. He also learned much technical matter essential to the teacher's craft, and further, from his own experience, that a student must attend to his studies, and that such time was as truly spent in the service of God as if he were in church on his knees, or going about preaching the gospel, or comforting unhappy women in their distress. But the chief interest attaching to his life in Paris lies outside the University and its courses.

CHAPTER XI

In Paris, as at Salamanca and Alcalá, Loyola held fast
to one great purpose, the service of human souls. But,
though the general direction he should take was plain, the
particular route was much less so. Two considerations
helped mark out his course. On his memorable journey
to Italy he had discovered that the world was far larger
and far less readily intelligible, more stiff-necked and
obdurate, more full of riddles and perplexities, than he had
imagined; that the methods used by St. Francis for the
winning of souls were outworn; that the most burning
conviction of the true faith, would be ineffectual to succour
souls that were wandering in the ways of worldliness and
still more those living in the blindness of disbelief or heresy.
If he would become a light to guide, he must be able to
set forth the truth in the conventional terms of philosophy
and theology; he must be able to combat doubts with the
authority of the Fathers, to refute error with reason, to
confront presumptuous speculations founded upon the
sands of individual experience by arguments built upon
the rock of God's word.

The second consideration sprang, I think, from his perception of his power over other men, his ability to supply
their needs out of the fullness of his spirit, and to impose
his conceptions of truth and duty upon them. Why should
he go forth, single-handed, to serve human souls, if he
could bid others leave their nets and become fellow fishers
of souls with him? He had begun to gather disciples about
him at Barcelona. Three had gone with him to Alcalá and
Salamanca, but they did not have the means to follow him
to Paris, and afterwards went their several ways. In Paris,

also, his teaching had stirred three impetuous young men to sudden heat—some seeds fell upon stony places where there was little earth—but their over ostentatious piety, as I have said, shocked academic sensibilities, and they, too, fell away and did not return. But now, during his residence at Sainte-Barbe he won over to his hopes six disciples who were to stay with him and constitute, under his leadership, the little band that, in their deliberate but passionate zeal for the saving of souls and for the greater gloy of God, would found the Company of Jesus. Loyola's life, however high above the lives of ordinary men, lies for the most part on a level, like a gaunt, stark, table-land; but above this, like peaks, stand out three great happenings: first, his conversion; second, his bidding young masters of philosophy to lay down their private ambitions and worldly ends and follow him; the third will be the formal founding and establishment of the Company of Jesus. The second of these is my immediate subject. Ignatius entered the College of Sainte-Barbe at the beginning of the autumn term, 1529. There, whether by chance or by some law of spiritual gravitation, he made the acquaintance of two remarkable young men, and for a time at least shared a room with them. Of these I shall introduce first Pierre Lefèvre, often called Favre, who is considered the first disciple.

Lefèvre was born in a mountain village near Geneva, in April, 1506. His parents were good, religious peasants in moderate circumstances, unlettered, and, apparently, both loving and reasonable; the son was still more religious minded than they. He was extremely sensitive, and, even at the age of seven, subject to strong devotional impulses. He was expected to tread the path of ordinary peasant life, to become a farmer like his father, and, accordingly, was sent out into the fields to tend sheep, an occupation to which he refers in after life as "worldly"; but he soon evinced a strong desire to go to school. There was some opposition at first, but his tears prevailed, and he went. The schoolmaster was as pious as his pupil; he seems to have seen in Latin poems so many Christian allegories, and to have expounded Virgil, Horace, Seneca and Statius, or whatever poets were the subject of his teaching, as good Catholics in disguise. At any rate he believed that the fear of the Lord is the beginning of wisdom, and instilled into Pierre a religious conception of the meaning of life that abode with him always. One day in vacation, when about twelve years old, Pierre was tending sheep all alone in a pasture, when a wave of religious emotion overwhelmed him with a sudden sense of obligation to dedicate his life to God, and he took upon himself a vow of perpetual chastity. Perhaps he had just waked to a consciousness of those attributes of the flesh which monastic tradition stigmatizes as evil, for during his period of early manhood he was sorely troubled by them, until thanks to Loyola's *Spiritual Exercises* he shook temptation from him. At any rate his vow, the influence of his school, or, as he thought, his love of literature, saved him from sin. He stayed nine years with this good schoolmaster, studying hard; and then, at the age of nineteen, in the year 1525, went to Paris. His memory, however, lingered in his native fields. *La Fontaine du Bienheureux* flows, even (it is said) throughout the hottest period of summer, from the spot where it first gushed forth in answer to the young shepherd's prayers on behalf of his thirsty sheep, and a chapel has been erected thereabouts, and the halt and lame have been known to recover the use of their limbs after praying there.

At Paris Pierre entered the Collège de Sainte-Barbe. Here after a full course of philosophy he took a degree as Bachelor of Arts and a further degree as Licentiate. During these years he lived in close intimacy with a fellow student, Francis Xavier, who entered college and also took his degree at the same time as himself.

In the autumn of 1529 Loyola matriculated at Sainte-Barbe, and the three, as I have said, shared a room together. Loyola was just beginning the course in philosophy, and, following a custom of the University, the professor, Juan Peña, assigned Lefèvre, whose scholarship was excellent, to act as his tutor. The relations between the tutor of twenty-three and the pupil of thirty-four became most familiar and affectionate; they shared one purse, ate together, and Loyola repaid the coaching in philosophy by giving Lefèvre instruction in spiritual matters until at last, as Lefèvre said long afterwards, "we became one in hope, in will, and in our steadfast purpose to choose the life which we now lead."

Poor Pierre's conscience was a troublesome thing. At times he was tempted by pleasures of the palate, at times tormented by carnal desires, and again fearful lest he had omitted some fault in making his confessions. He was caught and entangled in the meshes of fantastic scruples— no real fault was ever laid to his charge—and had no peace; he wanted to go off to the desert and live on roots. Loyola calmed his troubled spirit. He bade him make a full confession, and afterwards to confess every week and partake of the eucharist, and every day to examine his conscience. As Pierre wished for farther discipline, Loyola took him through the *Spiritual Exercises,* proceeding as always with deliberation and refusing to pass on to the next lesson until the preceding had been wholly mastered. By mid-winter Pierre had reached the stage of severe corporal discipline. For six days he neither ate nor drank (a penance that Ignatius had found most helpful in his own case), he slept in his shirt upon logs of wood, and practised meditation in the snow out in the court yard. Loyola, though he had not commanded so much severity, on finding him there, said: "I am sure that you have not done wrong in doing this, on the contrary you have acquired much merit; I shall return within an hour and tell you what to do," and went on to a neighboring church and prayed for guidance. His secret wish was for Pierre to fast one day more, making seven days in all, as he himself had done at Manresa; but after praying, he was convinced that he ought not to counsel such rigor. He went back, made a fire, and bade Pierre take food.

This heroic treatment was in the main successful. Still Pierre was worried in spirit by the faults of others, their suspicions of one another, their unjust judgments, and by scruples lest they, or he himself, might have committed any number of sins, undiscovered, unconfessed and unforgiven. Nevertheless he found spiritual consolation, so that he was afterwards able to say that whenever he had been in distress, anxiety, uncertainty or fear, he had received the cure at God's hands within a few days. And yet, lest he should slip back into lukewarmness, the Lord still left him some nettles. In his *Memoirs* he says:

We spent four years interesting ourselves in religious matters, and talking them over with other students. I made daily progress in the spirit, both as regards myself and in my relations to others, although I was proved in the fires and floods of temptation (for many years, even until I left Paris) and also in vainglory. But in these temptations God revealed to me a great knowledge of myself and of my faults, permitting me to see very deep into them, and, as a cure for vainglory, to suffer deeply. And so, of His grace, He gave me out of all this much peace.

One of his friends, Simon Rodriguez, says of him:

There was a rare and delightful gentleness and grace in his behaviour towards others, which I never found in anybody else. In some way or other, he became their friend, gradually crept into their souls, and by his conduct and his slow pleasant words kindled in them all a violent love of God.

I think that Lefèvre, together with another Frenchman, Jay, was the tenderest of all the disciples. He himself says in his *Memorial,* that a great wave of compassion would sweep over him, and he would pray for "Pope, Emperor, Francis I, Henry VIII, Luther, The Sultan of Turkey, Bucer and Melanchthon. I knew that many people condemned them, and for that very reason a pious feeling of compassion welled up within me." He seems, so far as I have noticed, to have been the only one to keep up a love of the classics. The fact that this innocent, true-hearted man (lately beatified by the Church) was at once drawn to Loyola and remained devoted to him all his life, should remind us, in case we may at times feel Loyola's character overbearing, bordering upon the tyrannical, and his exactions both of himself and others stern and harsh, that those nearest to him found tenderness within as well as a heroic soul.

Loyola's second disciple, François de Jassu et de Xavier, was of the same age as Lefèvre, but from a different social class. An official document declares him to be a *hijodalgo,* a gentleman according to feudal standards. His people dwelt in the kingdom of Navarre, which at that time lay on both sides of the Pyrenees. His father's family had lived to the north of the mountains, his mother's to the south, at Xavier, the family castle and estate, where Francis was born, some twenty-five miles southeast of Pamplona. The parents resided at Xavier, and had been prosperous until King Ferdinand, invaded and annexed southern Navarre in 1512, when they, as partisans of the French claimants, were dispossessed of a portion, at least, of their estates and left comparatively poor. Four years later, on Ferdinand's death, there was a rising on behalf of the old royal house, but this was quickly put down, and Cardinal Ximenes, at that time regent for young King Charles, ordered all the strongholds throughout Spanish Navarre to be destroyed. The castle of Xavier shared the common fate, its towers and fortifications were torn down, leaving it defenseless, almost a ruin. As the duke of Najera, viceroy of Navarre, executed these orders, it may be that Loyola had a hand in the demolition. Besides the injury to the castle, the family were stripped legally and illegally of various rights; their former tenants, finding them outside the pale of royal favor, denied rents and feudal dues; drovers taking cattle across their lands refused to pay toll however long established; and, later on, at the time of the French invasion, neighboring farmers occupied their fields, and lawless peasants cut down their timber. For these latter doings there was some excuse, since Xavier's two elder brothers, Miguel and Juan, were among the inhabitants favorable to the old royal house

who took arms and declared for the former allegiance. So
it came to pass that while Loyola, in the Spanish army, was
fighting to defend the citadel at Pamplona, Xavier's
brothers were serving with the French troops.

The insurrection, if it may be so called, came to an end
in 1524; the two fighting brothers made their peace with
the Spanish government, and returned home to find the
family affairs in pitiable condition. Francis, in the meantime, had stayed with his mother, and had acquired enough
schooling to prepare himself for the course in philosophy
at Sainte-Barbe, and to Paris he went in time for the October term in 1525, where he had the good fortune to fall
in with Pierre Lefèvre. While studying philosophy of the
schools under Juan Peña, he also, so his biographers say,
"was applying himself with great fervor to a better
philosophy of a different kind—the knowledge of self and
the service of God." This better philosophy he owed at
first to Pierre Lefèvre and only afterwards to Loyola; for
it seems that Xavier, in the beginning at least, was less
impressionable than Pierre to Loyola's persuasions. Perhaps the young nobleman entertained more pleasurable
visions of a worldly life than the young peasant, and was
less disposed to renounce them; possibly the fact that
Loyola had served under the Spanish colors in Navarre,
against what Xavier regarded as the patriotic party, may
have put some barrier between them. And, besides, it
seems certain that the new ideas on religious and ecclesiastical matters, that were spreading in Paris, at first possessed
some attraction for Xavier; but all obstacles and causes
of separation, whatever they may have been, were swept
away by Loyola's passionate purpose, and Xavier became
his second disciple. Xavier is the prototype of modern
Christian missionaries, *sans peur et sans reproche*, like
Bayard or Sir Philip Sidney, as renowned for his modesty
as for his dauntless courage; but it must be remembered
that to the clear seeing eyes of Loyola there were other
members of the Company as good as he, for he was not
the first choice for the mission to the heathen of India
and Japan.

The third disciple was Diego Lainez, who finally succeeded Loyola as general of the Company. Lainez was
born in Almazan, Castile, in 1512, and was therefore six
years younger than the two earlier disciples. His parents,
grandparents and great-grandparents were Christians, but
it seems that his ancestors of the generation earlier still
were Jews. He did not fall into the respectable category
of *cristianos viejos,* ancient Christians, *pur sang* as the
Spaniards judged, but to that of *cristianos nuevos,* or new
Christians, which term indicates a failure of four generations of Christian ancestors. Owing to this taint his election to be general of the Company gave great offense to
the Spanish grandees. At the age of twenty he took his
degree as master of arts in the University of Alcalá, where
he and a lad from Toledo, two or three years younger than
himself, Alfonso Salmerón, became great friends. Both
were good at their books then, and in after life became very
eminent theologians. One eulogist says: "As Ignatius
Loyola shone among his first companions, like the sun
among the stars, by the light of holiness and wisdom, so
Xavier and Lefèvre glowed with the glory of extraordinary
piety, and Lainez and Salmerón by the splendor of their
sacred learning." At Alcalá these two heard a great deal
concerning Loyola, and their wish to see him encouraged
them in their purpose of going to Paris to pursue their
studies in theology. By chance Ignatius was the first man
Lainez met in Paris. The two new-comers were soon in-
itiated in the *Spiritual Exercises.*

Lainez, as I have said, became a great theologian; but
history, which has a good deal to say of his prowess at the
Council of Trent and of his work in after years when he
had become general of the Society, says little or nothing
concerning his personality, beyond an enumeration of his
virtues, *"vigilantia, prudentia, charitas, integritas, forti-
tudo"* and so forth. His numerous letters deal with the
affairs of the Society, and afford no self-revelation beyond
an exceeding humility. He returns frequently to this
theme: *"Delicta juventutis meæ et ignorantias meas ne
memineris, Domine."* And when Pope Paul IV was con-

sidering his elevation to the cardinalate he wrote to his
friends to save him from such an honor, *"En Dios y en
mi conscientia io me siento inhábil para lo que de mí se
tratta."* No fair-minded reader will doubt that these early
members of the Society—unless it should be necessary to
make an exception in the case of Rodriguez or of Nicholas
Bobadilla—strove with all their might to attain the virtue
of humility, although the emphasis which they lay upon it
in their letters may, perhaps, in general be better evidence
of their strivings than of their attainments, but no such
doubts, I think, can hang over a letter I am about to quote
written by Lainez to Loyola.

In order to appreciate at its just value the full humility
of this letter, we must remember that before this date
Lainez had received the virtual offer of a cardinal's hat,
that he had been sent to represent the Pope's views on
theology at the Council of Trent, as well as fulfilling other
important offices, and that his reputation stood so high in
the Society that after Loyola's death he was elected general
in his stead. His transgressions were these: Ignatius had
directed a certain prior at Venice to send back one of the
brethren to Rome, and Lainez suggested to the prior to
ask Ignatius's leave to send another brother in place of him
asked for. Second, he had disagreed with Ignatius, as was
evident from his suggestions, as to the wisdom of taking
the brother asked for from Venice, and had let other members of the Society know that he disagreed. Third, he had
sent a student at the University of Padua on to Ignatius
without writing ahead to give him the requisite preliminary
information concerning the student, or some such matter.
To us, an easy-going people, these offenses seem trivial.
To Ignatius they seemed "dissimulations and conceal-
ments," and indeed they were breaches of the vow of absolute obedience *"con ojos cerrados"* taken to the general
"as though he were Christ." But I must not close the incident, which sheds light on the Spartan discipline of the
Society, to which it owed its strength and seemingly miraculous success, without adding that Ignatius was wholly
mollified by the letter.

FLORENCE, November 15, 1552.

To,
THE VERY REVEREND FATHER IN CHRIST, IGNATIUS
LOYOLA, GENERAL OF THE SOCIETY OF JESUS.

JESUS : MARY

May the grace and peace of Our Lord be with us all. Amen.

I have received your letter, that you send to me personally, and I have read it over many times, and by the
Lord's grace I find in it, to my pitiable confusion, nothing
but cause to praise His mercy, and to increase the love and
respect which in numerous ways I owe to you. I beseech
you whenever it may be necessary (would it might not be)
without regard to my being ill of a fever or what not, to
correct me. For, by the grace of Our Lord, although I am
grieved that there should be occasion and that I do not
amend, since there is occasion, I accept lovingly all that
you say lovingly; . . . In answer to what you say, after
consideration and asking God's favor, as you bid me, I
answer to your first point: I recognize many notable faults,
not merely because you find them (though that, I think,
would be enough to persuade me, for it is easy to believe
that he of sharper sight sees best) but because, even with
my poor illumination and poor sense of humility, I see that
such things have set a bad example to my neighbor, and
may have hindered the better service of our Lord, and
certainly have pained and disturbed you, my Superior,
turning your policy (which you were guiding with loftier
purpose) towards a less fitting direction, although it was
my duty, especially in view of the task assigned to me, not
to swerve, but to take the direction ordered by the captain
of the ship.

As to my choice of penitence, Father—seeing that it is
now about twenty years since I set my mind on serving
God by spreading the gospel, and that though I have had
much to help me I have borne scanty fruit, and that the
end of life is not far off—during these last days I have come

to entertain a special desire to die to myself and to all that belongs to me, and to live solely for God, desiring to fulfil His holy will and please Him. Wherefore I have thought to myself, that if I were treated outwardly as I deserve, as foul refuse, I should find that that would help me to live within my soul in the company of God, devoting myself wholly to His praise, dead to the world, and the world dead to me.

And so, when your letter came, asking God to bless me, I made my choice with many tears (a rare matter with me), and now, shedding a few more, I choose, for my errors and for the root from which they spring, that you (and in so doing I unburden my conscience, obeying quietly whatever you lay upon me), for the love of God, will take from me the charge over others that I now have, and preaching and study, leaving me only the breviary, and bid me go begging my way to Rome, and there work in the kitchen, or in waiting on table, or in the garden, or anywhere; or, if I were of no use in that way, then to teach the lowest classes at school. And to do this until I die, heedless of myself, as to all except my soul, as if I were an old broom. Such penitence is my first choice.

As to the second head, I make the same proposal, limiting the time to one, two, or three years, or more, as you shall determine.

As to the third head my proposal is, to go without supper during Advent, and in winter undergo a discipline in my room, to be deprived of my charge, and hereafter, whenever I have occasion to write to you, first to commit myself to God, and think what I am to write about, and after writing to read the letter over, looking carefully to see that I have made no mistakes, nor written in a way to vex you, either in matter or manner, but rather to comfort and aid you. For I recognize that that is my duty, if for no other reason than that you act in that way towards me; and besides I know a thousand other reasons. And I mean to take this same care not to offend you by my actions or by my words, whether absent or present, and also I shall try to do the same down in my heart, although (thanks to

God) I have had little difficulty in doing that all my life, except perhaps in those temptations that befell me in Rome and of which I told you. And since you say some persons have suffered in edification by what I have done, I suggest that you show them this letter, in which I acknowledge truthfully that I recognize my faults and that I am very sorry, and mean to do better; and I beg them for love of God to forgive me and to help me with their prayers.

One of these three courses is the penitence I ask for; but what will please me better than any of these is whatever you may think well to lay upon me, since, as I have said, I do not wish to do my will, but God's and yours, and all I beg is that in your soul before God you shall not reject or cast out my soul, but help and comfort it, as you have done for so many years; and as to outward behaviour I care not if you pay no attention to me, but make me go straight ahead carrying our Lord's cross in all humility, desiring only His glory. May He keep you, and increase His gifts and mercies to you, as we all wish and need.

Your unworthy son and servant in Jesus Christ,

LAINEZ.

And to give another touch to this sketch of this remarkable man, I will add a letter that he wrote to his mother, who wished to see him when his father died.

To, ELISABETH GOMEZ DE LEÓN.

TRENT, August 10, 1546.

May the grace and peace of Christ, our Lord, and the comfort of the Holy Ghost and the strength of the Father be always in our hearts, Amen.

. . . As to my going to Spain, you have already learned from my letters that I was all ready to do so several months ago, thinking that God was directing me there, as I was to be sent there by virtue of my vow of obedience. Since then, you have seen that my going was prevented by my coming to Trent, where the Council is being held, and I accepted this as right, in a belief that God was also directing this, and from not knowing in these matters anything more fitting. And now, since I have taken the vow of obedience to God (and by His grace I desire to keep it during the few years I have to live), I can do nothing more than to write to Rome what you wish, and what my father wished (God keep him). So I shall leave it for my Superior to decide, and I shall deem whatever he orders best. If I shall be free to go, the task will be a pleasure; if my going is barred, I shall never cease to be with you so long as I live, in my prayers and letters. And besides I am of so little account, that I am sure that whoever knows me, would care little to see me in bodily presence; and so, for love of our God, I beseech you, too, to deem that good which God shall ordain, and despise the help that I would give were I to violate my calling and my vow of obedience. And be sure that I shall truly be doing my duty towards you, if I do it towards God, who desires that all persons shall put their hope in Him only, especially widows, of whom St. Paul says, I Tim. V. 5: Let the widow that is desolate hope in God and persevere in prayer night and day. . . .

He that desires your greatest good,

LAINEZ.

CHAPTER XII

THE fourth disciple was Alfonso Salmerón, of Toledo. He was born in September, 1515, and in due course went up to the University of Alcalá. He studied Latin, Greek and philosophy, and then went with Lainez on to Paris in order to take a course in theology. As with the other early Fathers, little or nothing is told of his youth or of his personal traits. In after life his most noted service was the part he played at the Council of Trent. His learning was unquestionable, and he seems to have been somewhat of an orator; it is said that his wits were keen, his voice agreeable, his gestures dignified, and his command of language copious. With reference to the Council of Trent, Polanco says:

When Fathers Lainez and Salmerón, at the request of the papal Legates, delivered their opinions before the assembled theologians [the subject under discussion was Justification] they did so well (by God's help) that they found extraordinary favor with the Legates and all the prelates and theologians. The Spanish bishops, in particular, who had previously looked askance at them, changed their minds and could not see enough of them.

For the benefit of any reader more interested in poetry than theology, I had better add that when Vittoria Colonna besought Ignatius to send one of the fathers to Ferrara, where she could hear him preach, Salmerón was chosen to go, and preached to her great satisfaction. These were peaceful undertakings, but Salmerón's life did not lack its

117

share of adventure. He and Father Broët were sent on a mad expedition to Ireland, where they ran the risk of summary execution, in the days when Henry VIII was raging against the Pope and his emissaries. I shall return to this later.

Salmerón's letters, like those of the others, confine themselves strictly to business, but the language of the ballot he cast in favor of Ignatius, April 4, 1541, when voting for the first general, reveals the tenderer side of these austere Christians. In every one of the first Fathers, I believe, may be found touches of early Franciscan love and simplicity, but they must be sought diligently, turning over many leaves, as one searches for the first May flowers in March.

I, Alfonso Salmerón, a most unworthy member of the Society, after praying to God and reflecting maturely over the matter to the best of my judgment, choose and proclaim as General and Superior for myself and for the whole Society, Don Ignatius Loyola, who according to the wisdom given to him of God begot us in Christ and fed his little ones on milk, but now that we are grown up in Christ he feeds us with the strong meat of obedience, and guides us through the rich pastures of Paradise to the fountain of eternal life, so that when he shall deliver his little flock to Jesus Christ, that great Shepherd of the sheep, we may truthfully say, "We are the people of his pasture and the sheep of his hand," and he, verily, may say, "Lord, of them which thou gavest me, have I lost none." May Jesus himself, the good Shepherd, deign to grant this unto us. Amen. This is my vote.

I also quote a minute of thanksgiving entered in a letter to Loyola after recovery from an illness while at the Council of Trent:

May the Lord be always blessed and praised for the great mercies He has deigned to confer upon me in this illness, in that, besides having favored me with the Sacraments of the

Church and such goodly company [Lainez?], He has comforted me in the extremity to which I was come, bringing
my will, to my great content and joy, into conformity with
His holy will, and giving me a keen realization of my sins
and shortcomings, and a lively hope in the greatness of His
compassion and mercy, by which He has been pleased, contrary to the expectations of the physicians and all—to restore me to life, if I may rightly use this expression.   May
it please His Divine Majesty that my life may be to His
greater service, glory and praise.

The next disciple in order was Simon Rodriguez, a Portuguese. At that time, I believe, the University of Coimbra
either did not teach theology or taught it but indifferently
well, and the King of Portugal, as I have said, maintained a
number of deserving students at the University of Paris,
paying their expenses out of his royal purse.   Dr. Govea,
the principal of Sainte Barbe, had seen to it that his young
fellow countrymen should go to his college; and so, Rodriguez, who had won this *Prix de Paris,* went there, made the
acquaintance of Loyola, and touched to the heart by the
"immenso hominum salutis desiderio" with which Loyola
was on fire, he joined the little band that cared above all
things else to serve their God. Of all the first Fathers
Rodriguez, perhaps, was the least successful in attaining to
the high ideal that Ignatius set before his disciples.   Vigorous qualities he must have possessed for when the King of
Portugal asked that some Fathers should be sent to India,
he was selected to go with Francis Xavier; but on his way
through Portugal, waiting for the final preparations of his
voyage, he made himself so acceptable to everybody that
Ignatius, at the King's request, decided to leave him there
at the head of the Jesuit mission.   So he stayed; but the
decision proved unfortunate, for he brought the affairs of
the Society into much confusion.   He was of a volatile disposition, and when he wanted to do a thing, he was for
doing it at once without waiting for orders.   He was impulsive and imprudent, at least it appeared so to fellow
members of the Order. He took too lively an interest in the

royal court and its concerns; he lowered the standard of
austerity in the matter of physical comfort, he failed sometimes in brotherly love, he neglected discipline, permitting
superior and subaltern to be on even footing; he was lax in
observing, both for himself and those in authority under
him, the vow of obedience, the prime duty of all Jesuits;
and he suffered discussions and denials of his prudence right
under his nose. But at other times he carried his self-
conceit to such a point that he spoke disparagingly of
Ignatius, and when the latter disapproved of what he had
done or proposed to do, murmured that the general had
been governed by motives of ambition. To his more obedient comrades he appeared to be under the dominion of
some spirit not of God, whether his own or of the devil, they
could not tell. But these defects which seem to have proceeded from instability of purpose, rather than from any
deeper fault, belong to a time twenty-five years later than
these undergraduate days and did not reveal themselves
then; on the contrary, when the little band of disciples left
Paris to join Ignatius in Italy, Rodriguez mocked the efforts
of his worldly friends, who did all they could to persuade
him to turn back, and stuck to his purpose. In his old age
he wrote a treatise *On the Origin and Progress of the Company*. This and his letters show him to have possessed a
faithful and loving heart, but no very great intelligence.
At any rate, he was not in the least intellectual.

The next among these fishers of men's souls is Nicholas
Alfonso, usually called Bobadilla from the name of the little
town in Old Castile where he was born, about the year 1507.
He says that his parents were very devout Christians, who
went regularly to mass and brought him up in the fear of
the Lord. He prepared for college at Valladolid, and went
to the University of Alcalá, where he took a degree in the
arts and philosophy. He then returned to Valladolid to attend lectures at the University there upon Thomas Aquinas,
and supported himself by teaching logic. His ambition was
to study Greek, Latin and Hebrew and take more advanced
courses in literature; in order to do this he went to Paris,
where he matriculated in the College of Calviac, near the

Sorbonne.   His purse was light, empty probably, and having got wind of Loyola's reputation for helping poor students to a means of livelihood, he sought him out, received aid, and like other serious young men who came within Loyola's magnetic attraction, felt himself drawn to a life of self-consecration.   Under Loyola's exhortations he abandoned the learned languages in favor of a course in dogmatic theology; this he was the more ready to do because he found Paris infected by the Lutheran heresy, and report said that the humanists who cultivated Greek literature were chief among those who inclined to the new ideas.   In the jargon of undergraduate Latin he says *qui graecizabant lutheranizabant*.

Bobadilla in after life did much that called forth great praise.   The famous English Cardinal, Reginald Pole, lauded him for the goodly fruits of his labors in Viterbo, "for his preaching, his teaching and the praiseworthy example of his life."   Others speak of his *vita innocentissima*, of his *scientia, bonitas, sinceritas et erga Deum fervor,* and call him *dottissimo e simplicissimo*.   But in addition to diligence, perseverance and many other virtues, Bobadilla had his faults; he lacked tact, talked over-freely, gave loose rein to his impatience when he should have curbed it, and was too ready to exhibit complacency at his successes and his elevation in the world.   Some of these faults showed themselves in Germany.   The Emperor had issued a decree known as the *Augsburg Interim* which from an orthodox point of view was far too favorable to the Protestants; for instance, it granted the priests permission to marry, and to the laity communion in both kinds.   Bobadilla lost his temper, and in high indignation, drew up and circulated memorials against it.   Partisans of the decree, in their turn, were angry with Bobadilla, and induced the Emperor to issue an order directing him to leave Germany.   This was a great vexation to Loyola, always fully alive to the importance of securing the good will of persons in high place.   A letter from Father Salmerón, then at the Council of Trent, who was much troubled in spirit by Bobadilla's conduct even before this, also complains of him:

What I am now going to say is not for the sake of causing you [Loyola] anxiety nor for complaining of my neighbor, but to satisfy our consciences, and in order that you may, by prayer or any other way that you see fit, apply the remedy in Bobadilla's case. It is perfectly true, as Magister Claude Jay and others say, that he serves the Lord in some ways and causes some souls to bear fruit, nevertheless there are so many things in the other balance that they should be looked to. These are, first: he puts his fingers into decisions as to where he shall be sent, as for instance not long ago he tried to be recalled from Germany, and now he does the same in order to come to Trent, according to what Cardinal Pole said to Magister Jay. And also in Germany he interfered in order to be sent from one place to another, as for example to stay at Cologne, and then to go to Passau. So, unless you take steps, it may well be that he will come here. Second: it is said that he talks a great deal too much, interrupts other people, and discourses at great length on the policies of princes and kingdoms, and gets into great disputes, and both gives offence and excites ridicule. At times, too, he quarrels; as he did once with the Papal Nuncios, and provoked them to speak sharply to him, and to say not very nice things of him behind his back. Third: in writing he oversteps all bounds, as in writing letters to royalties and cardinals without taking any advice,—please God that he doesn't write foolishness. Among other letters he wrote one to Dr. Scott full of bad manners and insults. Luckily it fell into Magister Jay's hands and he did not deliver it. Again he oversteps bounds, in writing pamphlets and presenting them to princes, and one he had translated into German in order to give it to the Queen of Austria. He also made Canisio put another into proper style, wasting his time, and we are afraid that he will print it. And he proposes to expound one of his books in Ratisbon, and to invite princes, bishops, and ambassadors to hear him, and he speaks in his letters as if they came regularly to his lectures, whereas they could not have gone but once, for somebody wrote to Magister Jay, "Magister Bobadilla has begun to lecture on some book or other, but I do not think he will have any audience." Fourth: his behaviour is so free that he often plays chess with laymen, for instance with the Venetian ambassador. Besides some one here said to Magister Jay, that he once got heated in arguing and drank so much with some other men that he could hardly walk home; however, Magister Jay says he has never seen any such fault in him, but thinks that his gestures and gesticulations in argument make people think that he has drunk too much, although he has not.

When we read that his freedom of behaviour carried him to a game of chess, we may rest assured that his lively southern temperament and lack of tact and self-control,—grievous faults according to the stern discipline of the Society—were the worst that can be said of him. After Loyola's death, Bobadilla now and again became contentious, he criticised the constitution of the Society, and denied the validity of Lainez's election as Vicar. But, on the other-hand, the generosity of his nature showed itself later, when, after Lainez had been elected general, the question arose whether it would be better to limit his term of office to a period of three years, as Pope Paul IV had wished, or to continue it for life as the Constitution provided. He wrote to Lainez as follows:

Very Reverend Father in Christ. *Gratia et pax Christi Domini sit semper vobiscum.* Amen. As to the office of General, my vote is that it shall always be for life, as the Constitution says; and may it be yours solidly enough to last for a hundred years, and if you should die but were immediately to rise again from the dead, I vote that you be confirmed in it until Judgment day, and I beseech you to accept it for the love of Jesus Christ.

That neither Bobadilla nor Rodriguez was a weakling is sufficiently proved by the fact that they were the first two brethren chosen to go upon the mission to India. Bobadilla was ill and could not go, and Rodriguez was detained in Portugal.

Ignatius also tried to attach to himself a young Spaniard, Jerome Nadal, who had been at the university at Alcalá while he was there. The attempt was unsuccessful and Nadal did not join till years later, but as the brief record in Nadal's autobiography sheds a little light on Loyola's method, I quote it:

He took me to the little old church that is near the gate of St. Jacques, and by the baptismal font read me a long letter that he had written to some nephew of his in Spain, of which the purport was to win him from the world to a life of perfection. The Devil perceived very well the efficacy of the letter and of its writer, and dragged me forcibly from the spiritual power that sought me. So, as we went out and were standing within the space in front of the church door, I said to Ignatius (I had the New Testament in my hands), "I propose to follow this book; I don't know in what direction you are headed; please do not do any more in this matter and don't concern yourself about me."

CHAPTER XIII

THE "SPIRITUAL EXERCISES"

It is now time to speak of Loyola's set of rules and counsels for religious practices, the *Spiritual Exercises,* for they were the chief means by which he imposed his vision and his will upon the young disciples. This book is the fruit of his own needs and experiences; he entertained an unshakeable assurance that what had proved of great succour and consolation to him, a tonic and source of strength, would do as much for other sincere souls, and further, that there could be no better test of a man's fitness for a religious life than the manner in which he was affected by these exercises. He wrote the main part of the treatise at Manresa, in the first flood of religious emotion, but undoubtedly made additions and alterations at later times. The concluding chapter, which contains rules for rejecting private judgments and accepting the guidance of the Church, was evidently added later, probably at Alcalá, after his evangelical mission had attracted the notice of the Inquisition, or perhaps in Paris; and one particular clause—"to attain the truth in all things, we ought always to hold that we believe what seems to us white to be black, if the Hierarchical Church so defines it" —belongs, I think, to the period of his residence in Rome, after the Society had been stationed in the van of the phalanx that upheld the doctrine of blind obedience to the Sovereign Pontiff. I do not for a moment suggest that Ignatius expressed in this last chapter more than he fully believed; I merely mean that he gave clear expression to his belief, when it became prudent perhaps advantageous, to do so.

It seems likely that at the monastery of Montserrat he had become acquainted with a book of spiritual guidance called

the *Ejercitatorio Espiritual,* written by a former abbot of
the place, Francisco Garcia de Cisneros; and various unfriendly controversalists have seized upon this likelihood to
deny originality to Loyola's book. It may well be that
Ignatius got the idea of his book from this precedent, but
if so, the starting point counted for little or nothing with
him; he was completely absorbed by his own emotions, and
swept along by a passionate desire to render the lessons of
his experience valuable to others. As both books treat of
the same general subject there is of necessity some slight
resemblance between them, but the plans and the purposes
are different, and the triumphant vindication of Loyola's
originality lies in the fact that whereas only a few scholars
know of Cisneros' book, the whole Roman Catholic world
is as familiar with Loyola's *Spiritual Exercises* as Protestant England, for instance, is with *Pilgrim's Progress.*
Loyola, also, no doubt derived some of his ideas from other
sources, for he was neither so foolish nor so arrogant as to
reject approved ideas that fitted in his schemes, merely because in some form or another they had been used before.
In this case, as in others to which I shall refer hereafter,
he took his raw materials as chance or Providence put them
within reach, transformed them in the fiery furnace of his
passionate purpose to serve God, perfectly oblivious of what
he had taken. He would have been bewildered by any
question of originality; how could that matter? He was
not thinking of himself, or of his own reputation, but of the
salvation of souls and the greater glory of God.

It is necessary, at the outset, to say, that the book is not
meant to be put in the hands of a novice. It is a book of
instruction for a spiritual director, and contains many suggestions as to the method of imparting the contents and
imposing the discipline. An experienced director would sup-
plement the text by oral explanations and amplifications.
For this reason, in part at least, the book is stark and bare
from beginning to end. All superfluity, emotional and intellectual, is stripped off, very much as nurses prepare the
operating room of a hospital. The counsels are free from
sentimental weakness; they may move the novice to re-

pentance, to a passionate aspiration for an ideal, to tears
and contortions, but not by tenderness.   It is ·essentially a
masculine book, and needs the kindly exposition of a
Fénelon, or a François de Sales, to soften its severity.   And,
we must remember that for Loyola, as well as for his contemporaries, Catholic or Protestant, and for many since his
time, the mediæval dogmas of Christian faith existed in
their naked simplicity.   By Adam's sin all his descendants
were doomed to eternal damnation; but "the Three Divine
Persons . . . seeing all men descending into Hell, determined, in Their eternity, that the Second Person should become man to save the human race."   Christ's sacrifice
redeemed Adam's fall.   Nevertheless, the Atonement is not
sufficient for human salvation: it is still necessary for man
to be baptized, to believe a series of dogmas, and to abstain,
or at least to be absolved, from mortal sin.   The brief span
of a few years determines his everlasting weal or woe: *qui
bona egerunt, ibunt in vitam æternam, qui vero mala, in
ignem æternum.*   Life is a sort of grim game in which the
players run from bourne to bourne across the field of time,
while two orders of superhuman beings interfere; one to
help the players safely across, the other, furnished with all
sorts of tricks and devices,—wine, women, offices, honors—
strive to intercept and catch them.   Under such an aspect
life is far more dramatic and serious than it can be under any
naturalistic theory that humanity is merely a chance manifestation of the chaotic forces that create the universe; and
much of Loyola's power was due to the intense vividness
with which he believed this creed.   The horror of lost souls
scourged him on to action and passionate prayer.   It mattered nothing to him in what national clay the soul was
housed, or what the color of the skin; if it was in mortal
danger, he felt a personal fear and a personal responsibility.

The full title of the book is *Spiritual Exercises to conquer
self and regulate one's life and to avoid coming to a determination through any inordinate affection.*   He says:

By this name of *Spiritual Exercises* is meant any method
of examining one's conscience, of meditating, contemplat-

ing, praying aloud or to oneself, or performing any other spiritual operations. For, just as sauntering, walking briskly, or running, are corporal exercises, so spiritual exercises are any method at all that prepares and disposes the soul to cast away all inordinate affections, and after it shall cast them off, to seek and find the Will of God as to the ordering of one's life and the salvation of one's soul.

And the foundation on which the whole teaching rests is a dogma of the purpose of human life. "Man was created for this end, that he might praise and reverence the Lord his God, and by serving Him to attain to salvation."

The *Exercises* are intended for a period lasting about four weeks. Time is of no great importance, except in the matter of sequence, in that a novice should not proceed to a new exercise before he shall have mastered the exercise preceding it. To these four weeks are assigned respectively four several topics. In the first week the novice follows the purgative way, and is bidden to fix his mind on the foulness of sin; during the three other weeks he is to contemplate the beauty of righteousness, under varying conditions, in the person of Christ. There are two objects in view: first, the immediate, to inspire the heart with a desire for holiness, and to discipline it by means of the practices enjoined; second, the permanent, to improve the novice for all his life by teaching him to understand the true values of things.

The duties of the novice in the course of a day during the first week, are roughly as follows: He is to rise from his bed at midnight and pray to God that "all his intentions, actions and operations may be ordained purely to the service and praise of His Divine Majesty." Then he is to frame before his mind's eye some scriptural picture, say of Christ at Bethany, with all the physical surroundings just as they were in life, bringing himself as it were into the actual presence of the living Christ. With his imagination fixed upon this picture, he is to pray for shame and confusion at the thought of his wrongdoings, and of the eternal damnation that he deserves. After these preliminaries he is to think of sin: first the sin by which the angels fell, then Adam's sin, and, third, any definite mortal sin. These sins are, as it were, to be handled, touched and weighed, as if gross and palpable to the senses, by means of will and imagination. After an hour spent in such contemplation, there follows an imaginary dialogue. The novice, bowed beneath an overpowering sense of treason against Infinite Goodness, must imagine Christ before him nailed to the cross, must talk to Him, and ask Him, how it could be that He, God the Creator, had taken upon Himself death for man's sake; and then he is to turn and ask himself, what he has done for Christ, what he is doing, and what he ought to do. This colloquy is to be conducted as if a servant were talking to his master, or a friend to a friend, and ends with a *pater noster*.

It is impossible to deny the power that such a visual imagining would exert upon a sensitive soul; and remember that this is at midnight, and after a fast of twenty-four hours; none of the First Fathers (except one, owing to sickmen, if I remember aright) when they took the Exercise fasted for less than three days. The second Exercise is to be performed on getting up. Again the prayer for grace and the imagined corporal presence of Christ at Bethany, and a passionate prayer for grief over sin. Thus quickened, the novice must hold an inquest upon his own guiltiness, must fetch before his conscience all the sins of all his life, recalling the house where he lived, conversations with his family or friends, his occupations, and so forth, in order that these remembered sins shall appear in all the inexcusable shamelessness of their native setting. His thoughts must dwell on the foulness of those sins, and on his own infinite littleness, and that littleness so loathsome. "Let me look"—Loyola is thinking of his own case, and often speaks in the first person—"at the corruption of my whole self, the wickedness of my soul, the pollution of my body, and account myself a kind of ulcer or abscess, from which so great and noisome a flood of sins, so vast a pestilence of vices, has flowed forth." These thoughts are to be succeeded by an awful sense of the omnipotence, the justice, and the goodness of God, in contrast with the weakness, iniquity and malice of the sinner. At this point comes the one poetical fancy in the stark discipline: the sinner bursts into "an exclamation of wonderment and of intense gratitude, as I run through the list of all creatures in my mind,— that they have suffered me to live, have even preserved me in life; how the angels . . . have borne with me, and have guarded me, and prayed for me; how the saints have been interceding and praying for me; how the heavens, the sun, the moon, the stars and the elements, the fruits of the earth, the birds, the fishes and the beasts, have endured me; how the ground has not opened to swallow me up, nor created new hells that I might suffer in them forever." And then the Exercise, having lasted about an hour, closes with a colloquy between the sinner and Christ, and with promises by help of His grace to amend, and finally, as before, with a *pater noster*.

The third Exercise is to be made before dinner, the fourth at the hour of Vespers, and the fifth an hour before supper. The former two are in the main repetitions of the first and second, while the fifth is a meditation on hell, in order that, if love of God shall be of no avail, fear may save the sinner. Here the five senses,—sight, hearing, smell, taste and touch —are in dreadful coöperation to conjure up hell in all its horrors before the fearful imagination, to summon up in palpable presence infernal fires and souls in pits of flame, to render audible howlings and blasphemies, to offend the nostrils by stenches of filth and putrefaction, to taste with the tongue and palate of imagination the worm of conscience and the bitterness of tears, and feel the fire scorching the sinner's soul. Loyola is as grim as Dante; he always employs the definite, concrete, image, as the poet does, never touching the abstract, the pure idea. After this contemplation, which according to the usual schedule is to last about an hour, there is, as always at the close of an exercise, a colloquy with Christ, this time upon the topic of souls in hell.

For the other three weeks the exercises are concerned respectively with events in the life of Christ; in the first week, with the main incidents up to Palm Sunday, in the second, with episodes of the Passion, and, in the third, with those of the Resurrection and Ascension. The whole course follows the three-fold way, familiar to mystical literature: the Purgative Way, on which the soul is cleansed and purified by repentance and fear; the Illuminative Way, whereby, as I take it, the soul comes to see with spiritual eyes the light of mystical truth to which worldly eyes are blind, and learns to cast aside the false values of the world for the true values of eternal life; and the Unitive Way, in which it feels the ineffable joy of the enveloping presence of God.

Among these Exercises are one or two memorable passages that for convenience' sake I did not refer to in their places, for instance this, known as the meditation upon the *Two Standards*: The novice is to think of Christ and Satan as the leaders of two opposing hosts; Satan, on the one side, sending forth innumerable devils to ensnare souls by means of riches, honors and pleasant vices, while Christ, on the other, commends to His disciples humility and poverty. And elsewhere, keeping the same allegory, the book bids the novice bring before the eyes of his imagination a human king who shall say to his people:

My purpose is to bring all the countries of the infidels under my sway. Whosoever chooses to follow me, let him be ready to take no food, clothing or similar things, other than such as he sees me serve myself with; he must stand fast by me in trials, vigils and hardships, so that, as he was a companion of my toil and pain, he shall also be a partaker in my victory and felicity.

Then follows the interpretation of the parable. Christ says:

It is my righteous will to claim for myself the dominion of the whole world, to conquer all my enemies, and thereby to enter into the glory of my Father. Whosoever desires to come thither with Me, he must needs labor with Me, for the reward shall be according to the labor.

At this (the book says) surely every man of sound mind will be ready to trample down the rebellions of the flesh, all love of self and of the world, and he will say: "Behold, O Thou Supreme King and Lord of all things, I, though most unworthy, yet relying on Thy grace and help, offer myself altogether to Thee, and submit all that is mine to Thee; testifying before Thy infinite goodness, as also in the sight of Thy glorious Virgin Mother and of the whole Court of Heaven, that it is my will, my desire, and my fixed determination, to follow Thee as close as possible, and to imitate Thee in bearing all injuries and adversities with true poverty, in things material as well as in things spiritual, if it shall please Thy Holy Majesty to choose me, and to receive me, for such ordination of my life." This is Christian doctrine in its widest aspect, Protestant quite as much as Catholic:

> The Son of God goes forth to war,
>   A kingly crown to gain;
> His blood-red banner streams afar;
>   Who follows in his train?

Other counsels concern particular questions that beset scrupulous souls. Suppose that a rich man be perplexed as to the right attitude toward his money; his duty is neither to wish to keep the money, nor to give it up, but solely to do with it whatever may be for the better service of God. Or, suppose a man is to make election as to important matters of conduct; let him consider that there are some times better than others for coming to an impartial decision: God may give plain indication of His will; or, some interior joy of spiritual increase, or perhaps, a feeling of desolation, may throw light; and, always that time is best, when the soul is in a state of tranquillity. And having waited for this state of tranquillity, the chooser must remember that the end for which he was created is to praise God and to save his own soul. Let him put away all inordinate affections, bring himself into a state of indifference, and pray God to direct his will in the right way; and finally, considering all that may tend to the praise of God and salvation of his own soul from either choice, let him set the reasons on one side and on the other in a balance, and see which way the balance inclines. Besides this method there is another: Let the chooser be sure that the love which determines him to choose one way rather than the other descends from on high, from the love of God; let him imagine somebody else, whose eternal welfare he desires, as making the choice; let him reflect what his choice would be were he on the point of death; and, finally, let him bear in mind what decision he will wish that he had made when his soul shall be before the judgment seat. And the chooser must remember that he will make progress in all spiritual matters in proportion as he shall have divested himself of his own self-love, his own will and his own self-interest.

Then there are rules for the discernment of spirits, by which Ignatius means the way to tell whether feelings of elation and happiness on the one hand, and feelings of depression on the other, are to be interpreted as coming from a good or evil source, whether they indicate spiritual health or spiritual sickness. There is also an exposition of the three degrees of humility; the first, in which I so humble myself before God that I would not commit a mortal sin for all the world; the second, in which I am indifferent whether I have riches or poverty, honor or dishonor, a long or a short life, so long as the alternatives are irrelevant to the service of God; and the third, where "in order the better to imitate Christ our Lord, and to become more like Him, I desire and choose rather poverty with Christ poor, than riches; to be scorned with Christ scorned, than to possess honors; and to be esteemed useless and foolish for Christ's sake, since He was held to be such, rather than to be accounted wise and prudent in the things of this world." There are also provisions for confession and daily self-examinations, suggestions for keeping a chart to see if one has made progress in bridling and diminishing some particular sin, and rules for penance and abstinence, for giving alms, rules as to scruples, and rules for thinking as the Church thinks, and so forth.

For those who go to the book not to practise its teachings

but to become better acquainted with Loyola, it possesses a biographical interest, for it is really the story, cast into the form of a manual for directors, of his own spiritual experiences, what he felt and what he did for the salvation of his soul and the greater glory of God; and, here and there, though rarely, a passage reveals his passionate temperament:

Take, O Lord, and keep all my liberty, my memory, my understanding, and all my will, whatsoever I have and possess. Thou hast given all these things to me; to Thee, O Lord, I restore them: All are Thine, dispose of them all according to Thy will. Give me Thy love and Thy grace; that is enough for me.

To my mind the order and arrangement of the Exercises does not appear to be determined by a very close logical connection, but the commentators are all agreed that the discipline proceeds from thought to thought, from meditation to meditation, from prayer to prayer, according to the very best system for bringing the novice to the wished for state of mind. Whether they are right or not, the underlying purpose is plain enough. Man's work is to do God's will, and he cannot do this, unless he becomes a tool for divine grace to work with, and to make himself a tool he must renounce self, and strive to follow the example of Christ on earth. In one of his letters, Ignatius says: "There are very few persons, perhaps none, who understand to the full how much a man hinders what God wishes to accomplish through him, and would accomplish through him, but for such hindering." His hope was to enable men to break down these hindrances within them, by persuading them to lift up their eyes to eternal values. Thomas-à-Kempis says: *Beati qui interna penetrant, et ad capienda arcana cœlestia magis ac magis per quotidiana exercitia se student præparare.* (Blessed are they that enter into the things of the spirit, and by daily exercises strive to fit themselves more and more to understand the mysteries of heaven.)

CHAPTER XIV

IGNATIUS stayed seven years in Paris. During these years he made his first real acquaintance with an educational force of far greater influence upon him than any academic studies. In an earlier chapter I laid stress upon the importance of his visit to Italy. The effect of the spirit of the Renaissance upon him had been that of the wind upon the traveller. In Paris, Loyola felt the fresh breezes of the Reformation, and again he wrapped the cloak of mediæval tradition the closer about him. The result was of such magnitude in his later life that I must digress a little to describe how it came about; much as a biographer of Voltaire would feel obliged to dwell upon the state of the Roman Catholic hierarchy in France during his youth, or a biographer of Burke upon the French Revolution.

The new religious movement was still in its infancy. For generations there had been great discontent with the conduct of monks and of the priesthood, and ecclesiastical reforms of one kind or another had long been mooted, but the present agitation was of a wider scope and more dangerous temper. The strong wine of the Renaissance had begun to ferment in the old ecclesiastical bottles; and Luther's doings, like some disturbing chemical ingredients, had set it seething and foaming. The sixteenth century felt that it had reached its majority, and was free to ask such questions about life, about the meaning of things, about the truth of accepted opinions, as it might please. Speculation laid hands upon the traditions of the Church, the interpretation of the Bible, the doctrine of free will, of divine grace, and the relative merits of faith and good works, in short about the relations of God to man, and the ways in which

God's will is manifested. The storm was already violent in Germany, it had begun to rustle in the countries of the north, had touched Italy, and now, as I say, it was blowing westward over France.

I have space but for a hasty reference. In accordance with custom, I have spoken of Erasmus as the incarnation of the free spirit of inquiry and examination that marked those humanists, who were more interested in literature than in life; and of Luther as the embodiment of the ecclesiastical revolution in Germany. History is always easier to understand, or at least pleasanter to read, if we personify a movement in a man, and take a prominent actor as the symbol of very complex social phenomena. So, with regard to the manifestation of religious reform in France, I shall do the same, and speak of Lefèvre d'Étaples as comprehending in himself the first blossoming of the evangelical movement there. Lefèvre d'Étaples was a saintly scholar, full of sympathy for the mystical side of religious belief, full of desire to come closer and closer to the spirit of Christ, who, though bound by strong bonds of piety to the past, felt that the surer path was to be sought in the gospels rather than in scholastic philosophy. He was chief of the little group of righteous men who gathered about Briconnet, the good bishop of Meaux. His disposition was so gentle and loveable that one would like to conjecture that he belonged to the same blood as our friend Pierre Lefèvre, but I fear that there is no ground for doing so. As early as 1512 Lefèvre d'Étaples, then a professor of theology at the University of Paris, enunciated, in moderate form, the doctrine of justification by faith, and a few years later published a French translation of the New Testament. He was a noble spirit full of sweetness and light.

The outsider sometimes wonders if a way of reconciliation, some meeting place of charity, sympathy and mutual good will might not have been discovered. Lefèvre d'Étaples says:

You wear a hair shirt, you fast, you deny yourself; you punish your body, you pray, you shed tears; you roll in the dust so that God may have compassion on you—you do well, excellently, if, in doing all these things, you do not think of yourself and of what you do, but of God. . . . If you wear a hair shirt; wear it because Christ wore one for your sake. If you fast, fast for Christ's sake, since He fasted for yours. . . . If you deny yourself, do it because Christ denied Himself. . . . If you receive blows, receive them because Christ, our King, was beaten with rods for your sake. If you shed tears, do not weep over yourself, but weep because you have offended your Creator, the infinite Goodness, whom heaven and earth obey. . . . It is well to follow such an example; but you draw in still more of His spirit, if you will imitate His mercy, His goodness, His humility, in that spiritual delight and in that word of Christ which is the gospel of eternal peace.

Would it not have been easy to hold out a hand of sympathy and good will, and say, "God be with us both"?

One of Lefèvre's pupils, Maigret, a poet, lived in a spiritual cell where one might suppose Catholics would be at home and Protestants not loath to come. "First a pure serenity of soul. Then a second sacred good, penitence. . . . Add a third sacrifice that shall propitiate the God we have offended:—I will comfort those in tribulation, I will minister generously to the poor, I will aid the sick, I will pray often in thought, and after I shall have persevered in these things, I shall confess that I have done nothing, and I shall attribute thoughts and act more to Christ than to myself." Might not this sentiment be ascribed to humility and not to a Lutheran desire to reject good works?

But sweetness and light were not destined to play any very notable part in the ecclesiastical confusion of the sixteenth century. Reasonableness disappears when passion is afoot; and by the time Loyola had come to Paris, the tempest was already sweeping along. Lefèvre d'Étaples and his friends were like the moderate party of the Gironde in the French Revolution. Events brushed them aside, and the radicals began to show themselves. As early as 1519 Luther's writings were sold by thousands from the Alps to

the North Sea, and had made their way to Paris; more and
more followed.   One bookshop sold 1400 of these books or
pamphlets.   Violent words were spoken; one zealot called
the Roman Church *"fille de perdition, Antéchrist, courti-
sane, prostituée."*   Inevitably, the two great conservative
bodies, the University and the Parlement, became angry.
The Sorbonne condemned the Lutheran doctrines (1521).
Lefèvre himself was denounced as a precursor of Antichrist;
his words were distorted.   The Sorbonne said: "Lefèvre
mocks the discipline imposed by rule; he finds fault with
mortifications of the flesh. . . . He condemns, impiously, the
corporal exercises of the cloister, as if they were the ridicu-
lous institution of men."   The monastic orders cried aloud
for the suppression and extirpation of their critics.   Nevertheless, reformers began to show themselves all over France,
at Orléans, Toulouse, Rouen, Lyon, Grenoble and elsewhere,
as well as in Paris, Rabelais was beginning to formulate
their thoughts about doctors of the Sorbonne: *"maraulx,
sophistes, sorbillans, sorbonnagres, sorbonnigenes, sorboni-
coles, sorboniformes, sorbonisecques, boulgres, traistres,
. . . ennemies de Dieu et de Vertu."*   The humanists
scented freedom and a fresher air, and inclined, if only from
intellectual amiability, to give a hospitable reception to the
new ideas.   The King, always a friend to the humanists,
favored a measure of reform within the Church, and, at first,
welcomed what might prove a good card in playing his game
of politics with the Pope.   Marguerite, his distinguished
sister, openly befriended the reformers.   Even Louise of
Savoy, the Queen Mother, though not friendly to the new
ideas, had her moments of irritation against the friars; she
says, in her diary: "By the grace of the Holy Ghost, my
son and I begin to recognize hypocrites—white, black, gray,
dun, and all colors.   God save us from them!"

   But political considerations told heavily against the reformers.   The King went off to the wars, leaving his mother
regent, lost the battle of Pavia, was captured and carried
prisoner to Spain.   The monarchy felt itself a little insecure,
it could not afford to dispense with the support of the Sorbonne and the Parlement, it needed a united nation at its

back to defend France against her enemies.   Moreover, the insurrections of the Anabaptists in Germany had thoroughly alarmed the upper classes everywhere.   The Queen Regent was a shrewd politician.   In order to secure the release of the King, she did her best to propitiate the Papacy.   In 1525 she asked the Sorbonne for advice "how to eradicate Luther's damnable doctrine from their very Christian land," and the Sorbonne was very ready with suggestions for ferreting out and punishing.   Decrees were issued prohibiting printing or owning the Bible in France, and instructing the bishops to bid the clergy take precautions that their flocks should not catch the taint of Lutheran heresy.   Between the Regent, the Sorbonne and the Parlement, the reformers were roughly belabored.   Lefèvre d'Étaples fled to Strasburg, and the gentle reformers slunk into the background, while intemperate partisans began to perpetrate outrages upon the religious feelings of their fellow citizens.   Angry punishments followed.   A heretic was burned in the pig-market at Paris, in 1523.   In 1525 some fanatic fastened a placard to the door of the cathedral at Meaux, calling the Pope antichrist, and afterwards proceeded to Metz where he smashed sacred images, and, after suffering tortures too horrible to relate, was burned alive.   In Paris a young man blasphemed against God, Our Lady, and the Saints in Paradise; his tongue was pierced, he was strangled, and his body burned on the *Place Maubert*.   The next year (I am quoting from the diary of a *Bourgeois de Paris*) in April, a Lutheran, who had said that there was no advantage in praying for the dead, in sprinkling holy water, or in worshipping images, just escaped the stake; he was condemned to prison for seven years on a diet of bread and water.   In August, a deacon, because he denied the power of the Virgin Mary and the Saints, was burned alive in the *Place de Grève*.   On March 4, 1527, on the same square, another clerk was burned alive for blasphemy against Our Lord and His Glorious Mother.   The earlier sufferers belonged to the lower orders of society, but that same year a gentleman was burned alive in the pig-market for sowing the seeds of Lutheran heresy off in Scotland; and in December, a boatman who plied his boat on the Seine, was burned alive in the *Place de Grève* for saying that the Virgin Mary had no more power than the little image in his hand, which he broke as he uttered the blasphemy. Loyola arrived in Paris in February, 1528, and he must have heard of these doings. Three months later a statue of the Virgin was found wantonly broken, and the King, bareheaded, carrying a lighted taper, walked in the expiatory procession. That very year Noël Beda, dean of the Faculty of Theology in the University and Principal of the *Collège de Montaigu*, published his *"Apologie contre les Luthériens cachés."* The next year there was a very famous case. A gentleman of distinction, a humanist, a friend of Erasmus, whose *Enchiridion* he translated into French (1523), M. Louis de Berquin, who had escaped persecution for years owing to the King's favor, was arrested at a time when the King was absent from Paris, condemned, and strangled, and his body burned in the *Place de Grève* as a Lutheran heretic.

Further efforts at repression were made, both big and little; the Parlement of Paris issued its process against the poet, Clément Marot, because he was said to have eaten meat in Lent; in spite of all prohibition, however, the King declared, in 1533, that *"le crime d'hérésie pullule et croît en la bonne ville de Paris."* Moreover, the ribaldry and grossness of the scoffs and vituperations cast at the ancient ecclesiastical order must have alienated him. Rabelais was hot for the reformers at this time and continued to berate the monks: *"Jamais homme noble ne hayst le bon vin; c'est un apophthegme monachal."* In *Gargantua* he puts into the mouth of Brother Jean this comment on the disciples who abandoned their Lord at Gethsemane: *"Ensemble le diable me faille si j'eusse failly de coupper les jarretz à messieurs les Apostres qui fuyrent tant laschement après qu'ils eurent bien souppé, et laisserent leur bon maistre au besoing."* On he goes in his glorious scurrility: *"Brevis oratio penetrat celos, longa potatio evacuat scyphos."* Loyola somehow or other seems to have come within his range of vision, for in his famous list of books alleged to stand on the library shelves in the monastery of St. Victor, he includes *"Le*

Faguenat (bad odor) des Hespaignols supercoquelicanticqué par frai Inigo."

In 1534 followed the celebrated affair of the placards. During the night preceding Sunday, October 18th, placards entitled, "True articles concerning the atrocious and insupportable abuses of the papistical mass," etc., were posted in Paris, Orléans and elsewhere, and on the very door of the King's bed-chamber in the Château of Amboise. Popular excitement was intense; rewards were offered, spies hired, traitors bribed. In a few days some three hundred persons were arrested, and in November hangings and burnings followed one another. "You could see," one witness says, "men suspended over a fire, burning alive," and no doubt pious indignation was heightened by the news that England had broken loose from the Papacy (1534). In January, 1535, several weeks before Loyola left for Spain, there was a solemn procession of expiation in which the King walked bareheaded, carrying a wax taper, and by his side the Cardinal of Lorraine, followed by the great nobles of the Kingdom. After mass in Notre-Dame and a banquet in the archbishop's palace, the King addressed the assembled company, and turning towards the members of the Sorbonne, said:

Et vous, Messieurs de l'Université, je vous prie, prenez garde à vos colleges quelz regens il y a, affin que les jeunes enffans ne puissent estre gastez. Vous avez la foy en vos mains, vous estes appelez à cette vaccation [vocation?], faictes en votre debuoir à la descharge de voz consciences; et si vous en trouvez de mal versans, advertissez en la cour séculière. . . . Si ung des bras de mon corps estoit infecté de cette farine, je le voudrais coupper, et si mes enffans en estoient entachez, je les vouldrois moy mesme immoler.

The expiation finished with more hangings and burnings. Among the accused was Clément Marot, who, though protected by Marguerite, now Queen of Navarre, and by the King himself, fled post haste to Ferrara, where the Duchess Renée, a French princess, was kindly disposed to the new doctrines. In France the persecutions kept up until the King's desire for an understanding with the German Protestants compelled him to become lenient; and it is said that the Pope, Paul III, protested to the King against such cruelty.

Of all this turmoil, passion and punishment, there is no mention in the lives of these early Jesuits, nor any reference to the new doctrines, further than that Ignatius rescued Xavier from contamination, and persuaded Bobadilla to forsake the classics for theology. Nevertheless this contact with the world of religious revolt affected Ignatius profoundly. He probably recked little of hangings and burnings; punishment for treason is always cruel, and it is expedient that a few human bodies shall suffer torture for a few minutes in order to save multitudes of souls for all eternity. But he must have brooded over the awful thought that damnation might burst in from Germany and spread over the Latin world in the manner in which it was spreading far and wide among Teutonic peoples. Had the reforming movement remained within the Church, going no further than Lefèvre d'Étaples went, seeking the spirit of Christ as it appears in the New Testament and yet clinging to forms and dogmas hallowed by time and the passion of many generations, it is conceivable that Loyola might have looked upon Reform without repugnance, might have felt a greater confidence in the free search for God, and less in the strait and narrow way of tradition, that he was to help still further straiten and narrow. He might have avoided the difficulty of reconciling determinism and moral responsibility by ascribing to God the mobility, the variety, the unexpectedness that may be supposed to belong to an infinite being. He might have modified his teaching that men should do right for fear of hell and hope of heaven, since Lefèvre d'Étaples, who also accepted the mystic way of purgation, illumination and union with God, says: *"Les larmes, gectées par crainte d'enfer ou pour la perte de paradis simplement, sont . . . larmes demye-perdues."*

But such speculations are beside the mark, for the fanatical reformers outraged public opinion and took a position that could only, as it turned out, be maintained by force of arms. Ignatius drew in his sympathies, and in so doing, as I have said, intensified them; he conceived his dogma of obedience—*sicut ac cadaver*—and went to work is if he were a smith hammering hot iron on an anvil, and disciplined his handful of Christian soldiers as Philip of Macedon drilled his phalanx. The nature of the Society of Jesus was (as I think) in great measure determined by Loyola's experience of the Lutheran heresy in Paris; and for this reason I have dwelt so long upon it.

CHAPTER XV

THE VOW AT MONTMARTRE AND NEW DISCIPLES (1534-1536)

THE little company consisted now, as I have said, of the master, and six devoted disciples, who were convinced that through him they had found the true way to serve their God. All were of one mind. They would take the vow of chastity, and the vow of poverty; after being invested with priesthood they would take no fees for performing any sacred office; they were not, however, while at the University, to deprive themselves of the means of study. They were to remain in Paris long enough to complete the theological course, and then go to Venice and take ship for the Holy Land, where they would spend their lives, devoting themselves to the service of souls; but, if it should happen that on account of war with the Turks no ship was sailing, they would wait at Venice for a year in hope, and on the expiration of the year betake themselves to Rome and put themselves at the Pope's disposal to do whatever he might bid them do for the good of human souls.

This was no sudden resolution, no flare up of religious zeal, no spurt of unstable emotion, but the matured purpose of a man who had now spent thirteen years preparing himself to prove his love of God, a purpose thought over, prayed over, and communicated solemnly to young men carefully chosen, and by them put to the test of examination and discussion, and confirmed by the peace which contemplation of the fulfillment of that purpose brought to their souls. The earlier companions, the three in Spain, and the first three in Paris, had started off at too great a pace, and had lost their wind; but these had received their training under Loyola's eye, and started off slow but sure, and like good athletes of the Lord, they would run the race to the end.

On August 15, 1534, the feast of the Assumption, at daybreak, Loyola and his companions, their minds made up and their hearts light, took their way from the *Quartier Latin* across the Pont St. Michel, through *la Cité,* across Pont du Change and through *la Ville,* and out of the city gates to the hill of Montmartre, on whose top the great church of the Sacré Cœur now stands. They mounted to the deserted little chapel of St. Denis, about halfway up the hill. Nobody else was there. Lefèvre, the only one of them already a priest, celebrated mass, and then taking the host in his hand, stood facing them; and each of the six, advancing in turn, fell on his knees, pronounced the vows agreed upon in a loud voice, and received the consecrated wafer. Lefèvre then did the same. The ceremony over, they left the chapel and walked round to the other side of the hill and down to the fountain, to which according to the story St. Denis had carried his own bleeding head in his hands and where he washed it. Here they spent the day *magna animorum lœtitia,* in great joy of soul, talking of nothing but the service of God, and at sundown went home, praising and blessing the Lord. Might this not have been St. Francis and his companions at the *Portiuncula* in Umbria? I will quote Balzac's feeling about it: "Who is there that would not admire the extraordinary spectacle of this union of seven men animated by a noble purpose, who turn toward Heaven, and under the roof of a chapel lay down their worldly wishes and hopes, and consecrate themselves to the happiness of their fellow men? They offer themselves as a sacrifice to the work of charity, that shall give them no property, nor power, nor pleasure; they renounce the present for the future, looking forward only to a hereafter in Heaven and content with no happiness on earth beyond what a pure conscience can bestow."

Long years afterwards, Father Rodriguez said: "These First Fathers gave themselves up to God, and held nothing back. They renounced their own wills so completely, they offered their oblation with so much joy, putting all their hope in the divine mercy, that when I think of it, I am all emotion, my piety swells and my wonderment grows and grows." And Ribadeneira, who used to listen respectfully while the First Fathers recalled these happy days, and is therefore perhaps a better witness, for he had already seen and tasted the fruits before he was told of the blossoms, says in his memorial:

They went about with a burning desire in their hearts to serve God. And they were comforted and quickened in their good purpose by the vow of poverty, by familiar intercourse day by day with one another, by sweet peace, by concord, love, and the sharing of what they had and by the communion of their hearts. And they imitated the usage of the ancient Holy Fathers and invited one another to dinner, according to their means, and took advantage of the occasion to talk of the spirit, and urge one another to a contempt of this world and a desire for things divine. These means were so efficacious, that all the while they stayed in Paris to finish their theological studies there was no faintness nor lukewarmness in their zeal for perfection, rather it went on growing with marked increase day by day.

Ignatius himself fell into very poor health. His lack of proper food disarranged all the processes of digestion. He suffered very much, and the physicians said his one chance was to go back to Spain and try the effect of his native air. He was the more willing to accede, as it was necessary to transact some business there on behalf of his Spanish disciples and to see their families, before they should put the plan of renouncing ordinary life into operation. But before following Ignatius to Spain, it will be as well to introduce the three new-comers who joined the little group in Paris after his departure, and rounded out the full number of the ten *primeros padres,* as they were afterwards called in all reverence.

The first of the three is Claude Jay, who was born at Mieussy, a little town in Haute Savoie. He was a year or two older than his compatriot Father Lefèvre, and must have been born about 1504. Little is known of his boyhood, but it is said that he came *"de bien bonne maison."*

He, too, went to school at *La Roche,* under the saintly schoolmaster, Peter Villiardus, and though the school was very large, he may have known Lefèvre. He stayed there for many years and studied theology with the head master, perhaps he became one of the staff; at any rate he did not go to Paris and matriculate at the Collège de Sainte Barbe until the autumn of 1534. The next year he took his degree as licentiate, and, after that, probably, was ordained priest, and the year after, perhaps at the same time with Lefèvre, was made master of arts. It does not appear that he had any personal acquaintance with Ignatius at this time, and we may assume that he joined the saintly fellowship under the influence of Lefèvre. His after life must have crowned the expectations of his schoolmaster, but I know of neither special traits nor strange adventures that distinguished his laborious apostolic life from the lives of the other First Fathers. One anecdote I will repeat, of the year 1537, while the comrades were engaged upon their evangelical missions in Venetia, before the Society received its charter from the Pope. He and Rodriguez went together to Ferrara. I quote from the latter's narrative:

There was fog, a frosty air, and bitter cold, immoderate rains, and cloudy sky. We lodged in the most poverty-stricken hospice in the city, a great big habitation of clay, damp as could be, with the winds blowing through wherever they listed. This hospitable lodging was entrusted to the care of a shrewish little old woman, who would not let anybody get into bed with any garment on. Before she retired, she compelled every poor man to take off his outer clothes and his undergarments right under her eyes, so that in case they had sores or any infectious disease, they might be sent elsewhere. If they passed inspection, they had to lay their clothes on a remote bench, before they got into bed, in order that sheets and blankets should not be fouled with lice. The brothers behaved with as great modesty as was possible in this very delicate situation. As soon as they woke from their first sleep they got up, struck a spark and lit a little lamp, and putting on their miserable garments, began to recite their morning prayers; and so spent their nights in pious orisons. The little old woman, however, used to keep a sharp eye on what these brothers did so quietly and secretly. Besides, she observed that they ate very little, and taught Christian principles to the other poor people, and coming to the conclusion that they were overlaid with sanctity, proclaimed her opinion in a most laudatory fashion. Now it happened that the very noble and virtuous Marchesa di Pescara [Vittoria Colonna] was living in the city at the time, and had long in mind to make a pilgrimage to Jerusalem to see the holy places, and she wished to learn about the character and religious life of the Fathers, not by gossip, but by authentic information. She had often seen them in one of the city churches, so she went up to one of them and asked him, if he did not belong to that group of theologians from Paris, who were said to be waiting for an opportunity of sailing to Jerusalem. When she learned that they did, she asked where they lodged; and as she knew the hospice, she went there privily while we were out, and asked the woman in charge of the hospital ward, who and what sort of men we were. The woman answered most garrulously and most satisfactorily. She said: "They are saints, anybody can see, and they deserve great praise for their spotless behaviour and their blameless habits, and their teaching is wonderfully true. They neither eat nor drink; they are on their knees all night long and pour out their prayers. I have seen them often with my own eyes and spied on them sharply." So the brothers finally accepted food from the Marchesa, and by her kindness they were transferred to a more commodious poorhouse, where they had a room, and bed and food every night, and lived a little less pinched, although still slenderly.

In later years Father Jay labored in various places in Germany, and for a time occupied the chair of theology in the University of Ingolstadt, left vacant by the death of Johann Eck, Luther's famous opponent. I notice that in one letter to Loyola he writes; *"Non ci manca la croce per*

multi rispetti; non di meno il Signore ci consola. We are
not without our crosses, but the Lord comforts us"; and
in another, "As to the fruits of my teaching and preaching
I can't say; but if what a good many people have said to
me is true, they have been more satisfactory to others than
to me." In one German town threats were made to throw
him into the river. "It is as easy," he said, "to go to heaven
by water as by land." He also was a good deal of the time
in Italy, including two years in Ferrara, where he won the
favor and affection, it would seem, of the duke, Ercole II,
son of Lucrezia Borgia. Jay died a few years before
Ignatius.

The next to join was Paschase Broët, a Frenchman, who
came from a little town in Picardy. He was a few years
older than the other disciples, and had already been made
a priest. His personality was of no very marked character,
but he was so good and innocent that Loyola used to call
him the angel of the Society. He did his duty as he saw
it, *"nullis parcens laboribus, nullis fractus adversitatibus,*
he passed his life striving to lead his fellow-men away from
the company of the vicious into the perfectness of Christian
life." His most remarkable experience was the mission to
Ireland, which I shall relate in another chapter. After this
we find him in Italy, at Faenza or Bologna, but the chief
work of his manhood lay in Paris. He was put at the head
of the French province, and there he labored with great
prudence for ten years, when he died of the plague. His
last written communication is an index of his unselfish life.

I Paschase Broët declare that since I caught the plague,
I have not been to the garret, and I have touched nothing,
I have not even gone to the old refectory, I have not
touched the books in the library. In my room I have
touched some little books of devotion in manuscript, and
three or four others in print, such as the breviary, the book
on medicines, and a little book of advice about the plague.
I have touched some coins, some of which are in the wooden
box beside the window by the stalls in the library, the rest
I gave to John the cook. I commend my soul to the

Reverend Lord God, and to all the court of Heaven, and to our Reverend Father General and to all the Society, and to all of you scattered on account of the plague, and I beg you all to pray the Lord God to forgive all my sins. I also ask forgiveness of all whom I have offended. I hope that through the prayers of the Society the Lord God of His mercy will forgive me.

September 11, 1562.

PASCHASE BROËT.

Of the third of these three new disciples, Father Coduri, there is little to say, for he lived but a scant year after the founding of the Society, and the few references merely speak of him as sharing in the general experiences of the fellowship. One incident, however, casts a little light upon his character. While the ten comrades were still tarrying, during the year of waiting for a ship to Jaffa, Coduri and a young man, Hoces, who had come under Loyola's influence in Venice, went to Padua, and there the "Bachelor," as Hoces was called in distinction to the others who were all masters of arts, died. In life he was an ugly youth of swarthy complexion, but as he lay dead, to the loving eyes of Jean Coduri, his countenance looked beautiful, like the face of an angel, so that Coduri wept for joy, and could not gaze upon the dead face enough. After the foundation of the Society, because of his poor health, he stayed in Rome, working in the garden. There he died, and if—so his comrades thought—integrity of life, love of his neighbor, and sanctity at death availed, he went from earth to Heaven; and it became the fashion among them to speak of him as *"el buen Magistro Juan, che está en gloria."*

These three new brothers took the same vows as the others, and on the first and second anniversaries of the day of self-consecration at Montmartre, repaired thither with them, and all shared in a repetition of the sacred ceremony.

CHAPTER XVI

BACK IN SPAIN (1535)

LOYOLA did not complete his course in theology at the University. His health gave out. At this time, and all his life long, improper and insufficient nourishment played havoc with his stomach. It was imperative to change his mode of life, and apart from the physician's advice, there were various reasons for going to Spain. It had been said that he was a fugitive and durst not go back; naturally he wished to prove this accusation false; and it was proper to acquaint the families of his Spanish disciples with their purposes, and important to make some arrangements whereby the families should continue to support them, as well as to obtain assurance from his own friends in Barcelona, or elsewhere, that they would continue to make provision for him. He left early in the year 1535. Having appointed Pierre Lefèvre to act as father, in his stead, of the little flock, and having enjoined upon them frequent communion, penitence, prayer, and daily meditation over holy thoughts, he mounted a little horse, which his friends had provided for his sickly body, and rode off, probably by way of Orléans, Tours and Bayonne, and over the border, direct to Azpeitia, where his elder brother lived. Here Loyola insisted upon a behaviour that bears to our eyes a look of ostentation, or at least of exaggerated humility. But we must beware of our modern judgments; for we are all inclined to regard ways and customs that clash with our own as outlandish, as barbarian or Gentile. Ignatius lays it down, in the *Spiritual Exercises* as a principle, that if a choice of conduct is in itself a matter of indifference in that it does not affect the glory of God, nevertheless, if one way means a closer walk in the footsteps of Christ, a way of poverty, of reproach and contumely, then that is the path to be followed. With this principle in mind he refused his brother's proffered hospitality, betook himself to the pilgrims' hospice and even rejected a bed that his brother sent him. He also insisted upon begging his food. Such stiffness of principle after an absence of eight years runs counter to our notions of brotherly kindness. But Ignatius had taken a vow of poverty, and it would hardly have been consistent with this vow to accept his brother's comforts and luxuries. And, we must remember, that Ignatius was a lover; he had a passionate longing, a passionate ambition perhaps I ought to say, to do what the great saints had done; and that being so, to part company with Lady Poverty even for a day, would have been for him an act of spiritual privation. His conduct seems in the end to have commended itself to his brother.

Ignatius stayed at Azpeitia for about three months. He spent his time teaching little children and discoursing to older people "concerning the things of God." When he proposed to teach, his brother said: "No one will come"; to which Ignatius answered, "One will be enough." But in fact many came and among them his brother. He also preached on Sundays, and people rode in from miles away in order to hear him. In addition to these evangelical practices, he busied himself with the concerns of the town; and I shall quote at length from one of the town ordinances, adopted at his instigation, in the hope to disarm, even at the cost of tediousness, any reader, bred upon the principles of a Charity Organization Society, who may feel a prejudice against Loyola's seeming encouragement of mendicancy by begging himself and teaching his disciples to live by begging. His biographers, as I have said, lay stress upon the mediæval aspects of his conduct, as if such mediæval conduct were the prime interest in the biography of a saint; whereas the immense and dazzling success of Loyola's work was due to the very quality that it was not mediæval, but thoroughly modern, adapted to the needs of his generation and of the generations immediately to follow. The distinction that he drew between begging for the sake of

saintliness and begging from idleness, appears clearly from
this document. He himself, in his *Memoirs,* refers to the
episode very briefly: *"Il Pelegrino"* (the Pilgrim as he calls
himself) "brought about an ordinance that alms for the
poor should be given by public agency and according to
fixed regulations." The details are these: On May 23,
1535, a meeting was held in the town hall, at which Loyola's
brother, Martin García de Onaz, *Señor de la casa e scolar de
Loyola,* and other chief persons of the neighborhood were
present. The ordinance adopted reads as follows:

Ordinances for Relief of the Poor of Azpeitia

Experience shows that much inconvenience and waste are
caused by lack of due provision that in every town and
parish the poor shall be supported and fed in accordance
with rules laid down by the magistrates. Many persons
who could work and maintain themselves by their labor
and sweat, become vagabonds and tramps, making a jest
of Our Lord's name; and many other inconveniences ensue.

Therefore, We order, decree, and command that the
sheriffs and other officers of this city from now on, each
year, shall choose two honest, upright citizens, one in
orders, the other a layman, whose duty it shall be to ask,
collect, and store on ever Sunday and feast day alms for
all the poor of the town. And for this purpose, we exhort
all citizens of the town, and lay it on their conscience, to
give to these two bailiffs of the poor all the alms that they
have heretofore been accustomed to give to the poor,
whether natives or strangers, every one according to his
means and good will; and the said bailiffs shall divide and
distribute such alms among all the poor of the town, having
regard to the needs and qualities of each poor person. . . .

And We further order and command, that no alms-
gatherers or solicitors from any hospital, house or church,
whether in this province or out of it, shall dare to ask any
alms, whether from door to door, or in any other manner,
in this town, under a penalty for every offense of six days'
imprisonment, and also, for each repetition, fifty strokes

with the cat. And We command that no citizens shall give any alms to such solicitors under penalty of two reals for each offense proved, to be applied to the poor fund. . . .

And We further order and command that no mendicants, from outside the jurisdiction, shall ask alms from door to door within our jurisdiction, except that a mendicant, who cannot work and earn his food by labor and sweat, or a pilgrim upon his pilgrimage, may have recourse to the said bailiffs of the poor or either of them; and said bailiffs shall take into consideration their condition and need and give alms on which they can subsist, but without harboring them more than one night in the city.

And We command that nobody shall give alms to any such poor persons within this jurisdiction under penalty of two reals, to be applied as above, but that they must have recourse to the aforesaid bailiffs.

And We further order that, if strangers who are able to work, go a-begging within our jurisdiction, nobody shall give them alms, under penalty of two reals to be put in the poor box; but, on the contrary, every citizen shall denounce them and hand them over to the officers of the law, on the ground that they go begging although sturdy. And solicitors for churches or hospitals from outside the jurisdiction shall be punished for the first offense with six days in prison and for the second with a hundred lashes.

And We order and command that the poor of our jurisdiction shall not go begging, either within this jurisdiction or out of it, under penalty of three days in prison and for the second offense six days; it being understood, as provided hereinbefore, that the aforesaid bailiffs are charged with the duty of maintaining and feeding them according to their several necessities.

Further, in order to prevent persons who are able to support themselves by the labor of their hands from knavishly pretending that they are poor, so that they may receive the alms aforesaid, the officers of this town, now and hereafter, shall make a carefully prepared list of all the poor within this jurisdiction, and the bailiffs aforesaid shall employ the alms aforesaid to succour only those poor persons that have been investigated and are listed on the said roster by the town officers, and no others.

And We order and command that the directors of the hospitals of this town shall not admit into their hospitals any solicitors from outside the jurisdiction, nor any poor persons, who are capable of working and yet go about begging under penalty of three days in jail for the first offense, and payment of one hundred maravedis for the poor box, and for the second offense triple the penalty.

This document affords a good example of the consideration, care and precision with which Loyola drew up rules for conduct of any kind, as well as of his sagacity and good sense, but there was nothing original in what he did here. Mendicancy was a universal curse; sturdy beggars swarmed everywhere, and plans for reform were taken up by both Cortes and municipalities. Perhaps Ignatius got his ideas from Luis Vivés, whom he saw on his visit to Bruges; for that eminent thinker had recently drawn up an elaborate brief, *De Subventione Pauperum,* in which, among other things, he recommends that commissioners be appointed to visit the hospitals, and ascertain their incomes, the numbers and names of the inmates, and the reason why each one is there, to investigate homeless beggars, inquire why sturdy beggars are not at work and find or create employment for those that are able to work, to despatch physicians to look after the sick, and send wandering beggars back to their native towns. Besides this the Cortes, only the year before, had renewed its petition to the King to take some measures to diminish mendicancy. Here we find Loyola borrowing ideas and working them up into a plan that should best fit the needs of the situation before him. It was in this same general fashion that he had taken certain suggestions from Ludolf and others, and, expanding and amplifying, altering till the original nucleus was scarcely if at all recognizable, had wrought them into his *Spiritual Exercises.* And later on, when he drew up the constitution for the Society he availed himself of academic rules and regulations that he had learned in Paris. One of the faculties of his genius was this ability to take ideas that lay ready to hand and transmute them into instruments of social serviceableness, as Tubal Cain might take a lump of iron and out of it create a coulter, a shield or a trenchant blade. Other reforms, as well, were adopted at his instance, but with these we need not concern ourselves. On leaving Azpeitia, he gave the little horse which he had ridden from Paris, to the hospice where he had been staying. And out of this episode we get a glimpse of the impression he made upon people with whom he had merely casual dealings; for, when the horse grew old, the managers of the hospice turned it out at large in the fields, as a token of respect for its master.

When Ignatius set forth again on his journey, there was another contest between his humility and his brother's hospitality or family pride. The upshot was that Ignatius accepted a horse and the company of servants to the boundary of Guipuscoa, but no further, and from there continued his way on foot and alone. He went to Obaños, which lies a little to the south of Pamplona, to visit Xavier's family. No doubt he carried other letters of introduction from each of his three Spanish disciples to their families, but that from Francis Xavier is the only one that has been preserved. It is addressed to Xavier's brother Juan:

To my Lord, Captain Azpilcueta, Obaños

PARIS, March 25, 1535.

MY LORD:

I have written to you often of late, for many reasons. I owe you a great debt for the many acts of kindness I have received; and also because you are older than I. And, that you shall not think me careless or ungrateful, I will not fail to write every time that I find a messenger. And if all my letters shall not arrive—remember, the road is very long— please lay the blame on the numerous hindrances between Paris and Obaños. When I don't receive answers from you to all my letters, I always impute the blame to the long journey, on which many of our letters get lost.

I know that there is no lack of affection on your part; quite the contrary, you have a great deal for me. You don't know of the hardships and privations of my life at the University—I am without even the necessaries—or you, with your abundance of everything at home, would feel them as much as I do. I put up with my troubles, because I am sure that, when you learn about them, your generosity will provide an end to them.

I have met here lately Rev. Father Fray Vear who told me all about the grievances you held against me. From what he said I can see that you have been deeply pained. Nothing could prove more clearly the tenderness of your affection for me. My worst regret is that you have suffered so much from the stories of good-for-nothing rascals. I wish I knew just who they are, so that I could pay them back as richly as they deserve. But it is hard to discover them, for everybody here has behaved in a most friendly way. God knows how vexed I am by being obliged to defer the punishment they deserve. My one comfort is that *"quod differtur non aufertur."*

Now, in order that you may know beyond a doubt how great a benefit God has conferred on me by making me acquainted with Master Iñigo, I give you my word that never in all my life shall I be able to pay my debt to him. Over and over again, both with his purse and his friends, he has succoured my necessities; and, thanks to him, I have withdrawn from bad company which, owing to my lack of experience, I did not recognize. But now that these heresies have got about Paris, I would not have been of their fellowship for all the riches in the world. If this were the only service Master Iñigo had done for me, I don't know when I could repay him. I repeat, it was he that prevented me from consorting with people, who on the outside appeared good, but whose hearts were full of heresies, as the event proved. And, therefore, since his good deeds have laid me under so great an obligation, I beg you to give to him the same reception you would give to me. Remember that if he were what they reported him to be, he would not go to your house and deliver himself into your hands. No wrongdoer puts himself into the power of the man he has wronged. By this one fact you can see clearly the falsity of all that has been said to you about Master Iñigo.

And now, I entreat with all my heart, do not fail to get to know Master Iñigo, and to talk to him. Believe everything he says. He is so God-fearing and of such high character that you will derive great benefit from his conversation and counsels. Once more, I beg you for mercy's sake, do this. As for whatever Master Iñigo shall say to you from me, please believe him as you would me. You can learn of my needs and hardships from him better than from anybody else, for he knows them better than anybody else. And if you wish to relieve my poverty, you may hand over to Master Iñigo (the bearer of this letter) whatever you may choose to give me. He is obliged to go to Almazan [Old Castile] with letters from one of my friends [Diego Lainez] who comes from Almazan and is a student here. This friend of mine, who is well off, receives his remittances by a sure channel, and he is writing to his father, that if Señor Iñigo shall give him funds for students here in Paris, to send them on together with his, by the same method. And since there is so secure a way, I beg you to remember me.

I have no further news to tell you, since our dear nephew ran away from the University. I followed him as far as Notre-Dame de Cléry, thirty-four leagues from Paris. Please let me know whether he arrived in Navarre; I fear that he will never be good for much. As to what has happened here in the way of heresy, Master Iñigo will tell you all I could by writing. So I conclude, and kiss your hands and my Lady's a thousand times. And may God prosper your noble lives for all the years you may desire.

Your very faithful servant and younger brother,

FRANCIS XAVIER.

Without doubt Ignatius delivered the letter. From Obaños he went to Almazan to see the parents of Diego Lainez, thence to Siguenza, to Toledo, from there to Valencia, and up toward Segovia, near which was situated the Carthusian monastery where his old disciple, Juan de Castro, was living. He returned to Valencia and there took ship for Genoa. The voyage had a spice of danger, for Mohammedan pirates infested the sea. According to report, the Turkish admiral, Barbarossa, master of Algiers, had recently raided a town of Minorca, impaled a thousand Christians and taken prisoners four thousand more, while his right hand corsair, Cacciadiavolo, or a third, El Judeo, had laid waste the coasts of Sardinia and Minorca, and might well be lying off Valencia on the lookout for prizes. However, as it turned out, the Emperor's expedition against Tunis at this time kept the pirates busy at home, and the worst misadventure was a terrible tempest, in which the rudder broke and many on board gave the ship up for lost. Loyola says that during the storm he prepared to meet death and examined his conscience, and found no fear of death, nor of damnation, but great trouble and sorrow because he had not put to good use the gifts and mercies that God had vouchsafed him.

CHAPTER XVII

VENICE (1536)

FROM Genoa Loyola went on foot to Bologna, across the Apennines. In his *Memoirs* he recalls one or two mishaps. At one point he lost the high-road and found himself on so difficult a path, between a rugged mountain side and a river far below, that he had to go on hands and feet for a long distance, and suffered great bodily exhaustion. This may have happened at Bismantova, a precipitous hill in Emilia, which stands almost on a line, as the crow flies, between Genoa and Bologna. Bismantova is an out of the way spot, but of immortal though pale renown, because Dante refers to it as an instance of a most difficult path, in order to help his reader imagine how hard his climb, as he goes crawling up the Mount of Purgatory on hands and feet,

e piedi e man voleva il suol di sotto.

Loyola, at this time, was a poor Italian scholar, and there is no record that he ever heard of Dante, but he may well have thought of Purgatory.

And when he was reaching Bologna the poor pilgrim tumbled off a bridge into water and mud, to the delight of the bystanders; and finally when he begged in the streets no one would give him a penny. Luckily he came upon the Spanish College and received its hospitality. At first he proposed to stay and study at the university until his comrades should come from Paris; but he fell ill and could do no work, so he changed his mind and went on to Venice about January 1st, where he lived for a whole year awaiting the tryst. A letter written not very long after his arrival speaks of his circumstances:

160

To Jaime Cazador, at Barcelona

VENICE, Feb. 12, 1536.

May the Grace and love of Christ, our Saviour, bless us and help us always.

[I omit the beginning.] You say that you will not fail in sending the usual remittance; I am merely to advise you as to when. Isabel Roser has written me that by next April she will provide me with what is necessary to finish my studies. That will be a very good arrangement for me, because I shall then be able to make provision for the whole year, both as to books and other necessaries. Meanwhile, though this city is very dear, and my health does not at present let me undergo privation or bodily labor (more than my studies lay on me), I am sufficiently supplied, because she has sent me twelve crowns, in addition to the alms that, out of love and service to Christ, you have sent me. I hope that I shall repay you in good coin, not only for what you do for me, but for the great solicitude you show for my needs; I don't believe that fathers show more for their own children.

About fifteen days before Christmas I was in Bologna, of those I spent seven in bed with chills and fever and pains of the stomach; so I decided to come to Venice (that is about six weeks ago), and my health is much better. It seems to me that I could not be better off in all these respects.

De bondad pobre (Poor in goodness),

IÑIGO.

Of Venice, then in her glory, Loyola never speaks. His eyes lacked speculation for corporeal things. There stood the Basilica of Saint Mark's, with its domes, its bronze horses, its gorgeous mosaics, and the nobly austere Campanile; there stood the Ducal Palace, the Clock Tower, the *Procuratie Vecchie,* then new and fresh, *San Giovanni e Paolo,* the *Frari, Santa Maria dei Miracoli.* The bronze

Colleoni, gilded and glorious, looking like Lucifer, bestrode his bronze steed as proud as himself. Palaces of potent magnificoes lined the Grand Canal. The Madonnas of Giovanni Bellini, the glorious women of Palma Vecchio, Bonifazio, Paris Bordone, Sebastiano del Piombo, of Titian in his prime, the sculptures of Alessandro Leopardi and the Lombardi were all there, in the triumphant splendor of recent creation. There were gondolas plying to and fro, zandolos pushing their way, barges of fruits from the mainland, fishing smacks of many colored sails, galleys and argosies; there were foreigners from everywhere, diplomats, merchants, traffickers, noblemen travelling for pleasure, refugees from persecutions at home, gaberdined Jews, turbaned Turks, Greek priests, Arabs, Moors, and all the gaiety and bustle of the most cosmopolitan city in the world.

Other travellers, even on their way to the Holy Land, had eyes for these things. Monsieur Le Saige, Monsieur Denis Possot, Monsieur Greffin Arfargart, all in Doge Grimani's or Doge Gritti's time, stared full of wonder and admiration at the Piazza, the Piazzetta, and their buildings, at the magnificent ceremonies in St. Mark's, at the merchandise of East and West heaped up along the Rialto, or, for instance, by the Fondaco dei Tedeschi, on docks, in court yards, in shops and ware-rooms,—this street devoted to silks, that to cottons, a third to weapons, a fourth to copper utensils, a fifth to iron work,—at the multitude of ships (more boats, Arfargart wrote, pass through the canals than mules and horses through the streets of Paris), at the churches, at holy relics, at the multitude of mingling nationalities. Englishmen felt in the same way. When James Howell went there he rejoiced in Venice, "gay, flourishing, fresh, and flowing with all kinds of Bravery and Delight; . . . I admired her magnificent buildings, her marvellous situation, her dainty, smooth, neat streets, whereon you may walk most days in the year in a silk stocking and satin slippers, without soiling them." Clément Marot was there, a fugitive from Ferrara, afraid to go back to France and face the charge of heresy. He writes in a letter to the Duchess of Ferrara, *Sa très illustre Dame:*

That it would be impossible to do more than the Venetians do to gratify the body and delight the eye; would that they were as solicitous for their souls, for to judge from their actions they do not care whether they have a soul or not, or if they have, they regard it but as a member of the body; they never lift their eyes above the earth, or pay heed to the glorious banquet of eternal life. Their Signors are very wise in worldly matters, prudent to plan and quick to execute; pomp and pleasure abound, but it is hard to discern marks of Christianity; they call themselves by the name of Christ but follow the precepts of Epicurus. Every sense is pampered, and the body ministered to as though it harbored man's highest good; and more than elsewhere, among lesser delights Venus sits enthroned triumphant.

But if Venus was enthroned too high in the hearts of the Venetians, art—the ennoblement of material things by giving them forms of beauty—was enthroned beside her. While Loyola was tending the sick and praying by the bedside of wretches in the Hospital for Incurables, not far from there, where the *Fondamenta Nuove* now are, stood a house, half palatial, in a garden. The land sloped down from terraces to the lagoon. Tall trees cast a grateful shade against the summer heat, and rustled their leaves in welcome breezes from the north. Flowers and statues showed their colors, or their marble hues, against the dark blue of the Adriatic. Toward sundown gondolas passed, like flocks of black swans, filled with handsome women, singers and musicians. And at a table under the trees, laden with viands, fruits and wines, Titian welcomed the clever men of Venice, Pietro Aretino, "that notorious ribald of Arezzo, dreaded, and yet dear to the Italian Courtiers," Sansovino, the great architect and sculptor, some fellow painters, or distinguished foreigners from other cities, Jacopo Nardi, the Florentine historian, or Benvenuto Cellini, or some learned grammarian or humanist. There they sat, perhaps quietly, musing over the fresh canvases that their host had just shown them, and looking at the lovely outline of

Murano as the sun went down, or at the hills and far off peaks on the mainland; or, in boisterous discussion, if for instance Aretino heard someone praise Latin above the Tuscan tongue, for then he would jump to his feet and pour out passionate invectives.

Nothing, perhaps, shows better Loyola's fixed purpose to live for the greater glory of God, than his utter oblivious-ness to the pleasures of sense, gross or delicate. Saints do not, as a rule, record their admiration of the things of this world; but St. Augustine praised Cicero, St. Benedict chose for his first hermitage a spot on the river Anio that Words-worth might have celebrated in a sequence of sonnets, and St. Francis loved the sun and stars, fire and water; and, although Loyola, too, loved the stars, it was merely, I think, as symbols of heaven. The chief criticism, perhaps, to which he lies exposed, is that he was not sensitive to the poetry in nature or art. The beauty of the world, the charm of human communion, the drama of the emotions, the love-liness of women, the enchantment of youth, meant, it would seem, nothing at all to him. This was no doubt in the main due to the tremendous experience of his conversion and to his stern self-suppression, but not altogether. There was a certain bleak and stark barrenness on that side of him, like the southern slopes of the Californian Sierras, as if the rock within rejected fruitfulness out of disdain for it as a sort of effeminate weakness. He was as stern as Calvin, as inflexible as John Knox; and if he had not had the saints and angels of the Catholic creed to fill his mind with gracious images, he might well have been as hard as Calvin, as dour as Knox. He did not even notice the richness of the Venetian churches and the splendor of their ritual, the singing of the choristers, the gilded images, the painted walls, which Clément Marot notices and com-ments upon, though he piously says to his Protestant protectress,

C'est ung abbus d'ydollatres sorty.

Loyola went about his business in his own fashion, as in-different to the ripe beauty of Venice as the most bigoted

crusader might be to the delicate beauty of Moorish or
Arabian art. And, it is but fair to add, that another
attribute of Venice, for which we honor her, must have
horrified him,—liberty. *"Venise* (as one of the French pilgrims I have quoted says) *est une cité de liberté; car ilz
permettent toutes manières de gens vivre avecques eulx
comme juifs, turcs, maures, et Chrétiens grecs scismatiques.
Ilz permettent un chacun vivre selon son rite et façon en
leur payant tribut."* Think of it! To permit disrespect,
insult, treason to God, and for money! No wonder that
Loyola never speaks of Venice.

As to his studies, I find nothing but the most vague reference, such as that contained in his letter to Cazador. But,
as usual, he spent much of his time trying to bring home
to those about him a realization of the spiritual life. Never
did he forget the great injunction, "Lovest thou me? Feed
my sheep." In particular he became intimate with two
gentlemen from Navarre, brothers, it is said, of the printer
who befriended him at Alcalá, Don Diego and Don Estevan
de Eguia, who were on their way back from a pilgrimage
to the Holy Land. Both finally became members of the
Society. Diego lived to be a *"venerandus et sanctus senex,"*
and for a time acted as Loyola's confessor. He often used
to say, "Oh, if I might but tell what I know of Master
Ignatius! Oh, if my mouth were not closed, how many
great things I could tell you!" He had also received an
express command, in virtue of holy obedience, never to
speak of Loyola's private personal matters. Besides these,
there was a young Spaniard from Malaga, Diego Hoces,
to whom I have already alluded, a student of theology.
Loyola wished to give him the *Spiritual Exercises,* but
Hoces, although *divini servitii cupidus* was fearful lest there
might be something heretical in them, and fetched a quantity of theological books to test them by; after deliberation
the test proved satisfactory, and he decided "to follow the
Pilgrim's way of life." He is reckoned the tenth among the
first companions, allthought he died before the Society received the papal sanction. He left to his comrades the
memory of a youth "most fervent in spirit and by no means

slothful both in divine worship and in seeking to serve the souls of his neighbors."

Two others, of greater note in the world, also became his friends, Pietro Contarini, a relation of the good Cardinal Contarini, to whom he taught the *Spiritual Exercises,* and Gaspar de Doctis, a doctor of law, canon of the cathedral at Vercelli, and vicar to the papal legate. Loyola was also made acquainted with a gentleman of importance, who had formerly been an archbishop, and was destined to become a personage of the very highest ecclesiastical rank, Giovanni Pietro Caraffa, the future cardinal and Pope, Paul IV. Caraffa was a remarkable man; haughty, impetuous, ardent, hard and inflexible, yet of stainless life, high character and great piety. Erasmus praises his eloquence, his dignified bearing and his knowledge of theology, of Latin, Greek and Hebrew. Caraffa was zealous for a reform of the clergy, and had recently given proof of his single-mindedness by renouncing two bishoprics and joining in the foundation of the new Order of the Teatini. This was an association of priests, bound by the three vows, and directly subject to the Pope, who hoped by their example, their preaching and good works to effect a general reform in the habits of the Italian priests. The vow of poverty was very strict; they were not even to beg, but to await the gifts of the charitable. They practised prayer and meditation, studied the Bible, looked after the sick and pilgrims, and took care of souls. The Superior was elected for three years. At the time of the sack of Rome, the little band—there were but twelve—managed to escape to Venice, thanks to the Venetian ambassador. By the time Loyola arrived in Venice, there were about twenty, and the Order had become a sort of seminary for priests. Just where, how, or under what circumstances these two men met, we do not know, but something passed between them that gave offense to Caraffa. It seems that Loyola criticized certain matters connected with the new Order more freely than was acceptable to the distinguished prelate. As that criticism is probably contained in the following letter, although the address is not certain, I quote it:

To Giovanni Pietro Caraffa

VENICE, 1536.

Considering how our eternal happiness has its being in a true love of God, and that it obliges us all to a true affection . . . I have thought to write this letter, not with those customary compliments (which are not out of place, if there is no forgetting of God's ordinances); for he that forsakes the world, its dignities and offices, does not care to be addressed with ceremonious speech, since he knows whosoever makes himself least in this world, will be the greatest hereafter. So . . . for the love of Christ our Saviour, I beg you to read this with the same good will that it is written with; my love is so genuine, that with all the vigor God has given me, I beg Him to grant me in this life and in the next the same good that I beg and beseech Him to bestow upon you, in body and soul.

In this state of mind, therefore, I will speak of three matters with as much directness as if I were talking to my own self, not for the sake of giving advice, for it is always more humble to receive advice than to give it, but to quicken us in asking counsel of the Lord, from whom all good counsels proceed.

First, I think that there are good and sufficient reasons enough why your Society should not separate and scatter. . . .

Second, As to this, that a person like yourself, of such high lineage, rank and place, and besides no longer young, should be a little luxurious in his dress, should have a large, well furnished apartment, not so much to receive members of your Society as for strangers and visitors—as to this I see neither scandal, nor lack of edification, because one may well adjust oneself to the needs and proprieties of the time being; but that which is not perfect, ought not to be considered perfect. So, it seems to belong to a ripe wisdom (as one recalls to mind those blessed saints, like St. Francis, St. Dominic, and many others, and how they did at the time they founded their orders, and

gave rules and set an example to their companions) to
have recourse to the true Wisdom, to ask for more light,
in order to arrange all to His greater service and praise;
for many things are lawful, that are not expedient, as St.
Paul says; and this is so that others shall not find occasion
for lax behaviour, but an example of going onward, especially persons of the household, who pay great heed to what
their master says and does.

Third, . . . [Under this head he discusses and indeed
seems to criticize the advisability of the principle adopted
by the Teatini that they should not beg for food but wait
for it to be given to them.]

INIGO.

Loyola was a man of much native courtesy, of rare tact,
and iron self-control, but none of these happy qualities
interfered with plain speech, if he deemed that plain speech
would tend to the service of God; and Caraffa, a man of
the highest rank, wide experience, and great piety, as well
as distinction, might think a shabbily dressed foreigner had
better be more reticent of his unfavorable opinions in a
matter blessed by the Pope and highly commended of clergy
and laity. It is quite possible, also, that the mere fact that
Ignatius was a Spaniard militated against him in Caraffa's
mind. Caraffa was no friend to Spain. When Gonsalvo
de Cordova conquered Naples for Ferdinand, Caraffa's
family, the principal nobles of the country, had been favorable to the ousted King; and Ferdinand in retaliation had
opposed Caraffa's confirmation as bishop. And, on the
other hand, Caraffa, as bishop, had felt called upon to
oppose various acts of the King's magistrates in Italy; and,
later, when Caraffa was sent as papal nuncio to Spain,
although he was appointed a member of the royal council
and for a time enjoyed the King's good graces, nevertheless he completely alienated the King by urging him to
renounce his claims upon Naples in favor of the former
dynasty. His appointment on the council, also, was not
popular in Spain, and he must have known it; "all that
the Neapolitans deserve," it was said, "is bread and

cudgellings"; and it was suspected that he reported back
to the Pope matters that came up for discussion. Caraffa
returned the ill will; and long after he had gone back to
Italy, and Charles V had appointed him to the arch-
bishopric of Brindisi, he still clung to the feeling. Whatever the trouble was, it caused Ignatius considerable anxiety
in later times when fortune had put into Caraffa's hands
the power to make or mar the Society of Jesus.

During his stay in Venice Ignatius took pains to maintain his relation of spiritual counsellor with his old friends
in Barcelona and Paris, and perhaps elsewhere. He wrote
direct to some, and communicated with others through his
disciples in Paris, or through one of the early disciples at
Alcalá, Lope de Caceres. Some of his early letters have
been preserved and tell much more than his biographers
do of his method in giving comfort and advice:

To Theresa Rezadella, my sister in Christ

VENICE, June 18, 1536.

May the grace and love of Christ bless and keep us
always.

A few days ago I received your letter. It caused me to
rejoice in the Lord, whom you serve and desire to serve
more and more, and to whom we must ascribe whatever
good appears in His creatures. You say that Caceres will
inform me fully of your affairs. He has done so, and not
only that, but he has told me what advice he gave you as
to each particular. After reading his letter, I found nothing
more for me to say. But the information you now give
requires some further counsel, for everybody can explain
their own feelings better than any one else can.

You ask me to take charge of you for love of Christ. In
truth, for many years His divine Majesty, without any
merit on my part, has made me want to do whatever I can
for all men and women who walk according to His will,
and to serve them that labor in His service. That you are
one of these, I do not doubt, and I trust that my advice
shall take substantial form in act and deed.

You also ask me to write you at length what the Lord may suggest to me, and to communicate my matured opinion. I am very glad to tell you what I feel in the Lord, and if it may appear harsh in any respect, its harshness will be directed against the Enemy who tries to disturb you, rather than against you. He disturbs you in two ways; and though he does not succeed in causing you to commit a sin that shall separate you from God, nevertheless he bars you from greater service of God, and discomposes your peace. His first way is to entice you into a state of false humility; the second is to inspire you with an extreme fear of God that takes possession of your thoughts beyond all reason.

Now, as to the first. The usual course that the Enemy adopts toward those who love the Lord and are beginning to serve Him, is to put obstacles in their way. That is his first weapon of offense. For instance, he instils the thought: How shall I be able to live all my life in such penitence, with no enjoyment of family, friends, or passions? How shall I live so solitary a life, without a little respite? He insinuates that you can save your soul without so many trials, and that just because of your hardships you should lead an easier life, but never a suggestion of the consolations which the Lord giveth to His new servant, if he will break down all obstacles and choose to suffer with his Creator. Next the Enemy comes out with his second weapon, that is, boastfulness and vanity, inducing one to believe that there is much goodness and sanctity in oneself, and to assume a higher place than he deserves. If the servant of the Lord, by means of humility and self-abasement, repels these shafts, and does not yield to evil suasions, then the Enemy draws his third weapon, which is false humility. I explain what I mean. When he sees the Lord's servant virtuous and humble, doing what the Lord commands and yet thinking that it avails him naught, and thinking about his own weakness, quite free from vanity, then he slips in this thought: "If I shall speak of any grace of God granted to me—good works, good purposes or aspirations—I shall sin from a species of vainglory, for I shall be

speaking in my own praise." So the Enemy induces him
to hold his tongue concerning graces granted to him by the
Lord; and so they bear no fruit, neither in others, nor in
him. And the Enemy is aware that if the Lord's servant
keeps thinking of grace received, it helps him climb to
higher things. However, one should only speak of graces
received with great circumspection, and only for the sake
of spiritual advantage for himself or for others; that is,
supposing that he finds those others prepared, and believes
that they will profit by it.

And, there is a further point with regard to humility.
The Enemy tries to entice us into another kind of false
humility, that is, into an extreme and wholly wrong
humility. Your case affords a good illustration of this.
You ascribe some weaknesses and apprehensions, and then
you say: "I am a good-for-little nun," and "I *seem* to desire
to serve Christ." You don't venture to say, "I desire to
serve Christ," or "the Lord inspires me with a desire to
serve Him." If you will consider, you will understand that
those desires to serve Christ are not of your doing, but the
gift of the Lord. So, you ought to say: "the Lord hath
increased my desire to serve the Lord." You praise Him
in order to publish His good gift and glorify Him, not
yourself; for you are not attributing this grace to yourself.

If the Enemy puffs us up, we must be on the watch to
abase ourselves and run over the inventory of our sins and
wickedness; but, if he abases us and thrusts us down, then
we must rise up in faith and hope in the Lord, and go over
the blessings we have received, and remember how much
hope we have of salvation. The Enemy recks not whether
he speaks truth or falsehood, his object is to win us. Remember how the martyrs, when they were brought before
pagan judges, declared that they were servants of Christ;
but you, before the Enemy of mankind, when he tempts
you and tries to make you weak and fearful with his tricks
and artifices, you do not even dare to say, "I desire to serve
our Lord." But you should confess without fear that you
are His servant and that rather than leave His service you
would die first. If the Enemy harps on justice, you hold

to mercy; if he insinuates mercy, you allege justice. In this way we must proceed in order not to be confounded, and leave that mocker mocked, following the authority of Holy Writ which says: "Be ye careful that ye be not so humble that out of humility ye cast yourselves into foolishness. . . ."

De bondad pobre,

IGNACIO.

To the same:

VENICE, Sept. 11th, 1536.

May the Grace and love of Christ bless us and keep us always.

I have received two letters from you at different times. I have answered the first at some length, . . . and now I will answer your other questions briefly. . . .

All meditations, during which the mind is at work, tire the body; but meditations that follow one another in quick succession without making the mind work or calling on the deeper parts of the intelligence, do not demand any effort, interior or exterior. Such meditations do not fatigue the body, rather they rest it, except under two conditions. First, when the body lacks the nourishment and recreation which nature requires it to have. As to lack of nourishment, I mean for instance, in the case where a man is absorbed in meditation and does not remember to give his body natural sustenance, letting the usual hours for food go by unnoticed. As to recreation, I mean pious relaxation, letting our thoughts wander off whither they will, on good or indifferent matters, provided they do not busy themselves with wrong matters.

Another thing often happens to persons who are given to prayer or contemplation just before it is time to go to sleep; their minds are stimulated by the effort, they think over what they have contemplated or imagined, and then they cannot sleep. From this condition of things the Enemy tries to derive advantage; because without sleep the body is an easy prey. This must be wholly avoided. With your body well, you can do much; but if your body is sick, I don't know what you can do. A healthy body is a great help both for doing good and doing evil; much evil to those whose will is depraved and morals bad, much good to those who set their whole will on God, and whose way of life is virtuous. . . .

Above all, remember that our Lord loves you (for I do not doubt that), and repay Him with the same love; and do not vex yourself about thoughts, though they are evil, sexual or shameful, or about trifles, or lukewarmness, provided that they are against your will, for neither St. Peter nor St. Paul was able to prevent such thoughts from coming. And if you do not succeed in expelling them, you can do much by paying no heed to them. Just as my salvation does not depend on the good works of good angels, so I shall not be damned for the weaknesses and evil thoughts which wicked angels—the world and the flesh—spread before me. God wishes my soul to conform to His will, and then the soul, by such conformity, makes the body also, willy-nilly, conform to the divine will. That is our fighting ground. Such is the pleasure of Eternal Goodness. May He, of His infinite grace and mercy, keep us always in His hands.

De bondad pobre,

IÑIGO.

To Father Manuel Miona, in Paris

VENICE, November 16, 1536.

May the Grace and love of Christ bless us and keep us always.

I want very much to know how things have gone with you, and no wonder, for I owe you so much in spiritual matters, as a son to his father. And since it is my duty to repay so much loving affection as you have always had for me and shown in your actions, I do not know what better I can do for you in this life than to get you to practise the *Spiritual Exercises* for a month with the person I named; besides you said you were ready to do so. And please, for God's sake, if you have tried and enjoyed them, write me about it; and if not, I beg you by His love and by the bitter death He suffered for us, to practise them. And if you regret doing so, besides the pain you will give me, which I will submit to, put me down as a mocker of the spiritual persons to whom I owe everything.

I have not written to you personally up to now, because when I write to one of you I write to all; and besides Lefèvre can tell you all you want to know about me; you can get it from my letters to him.

Twice, thrice, and as many more times as I can, I beg you for God's sake to do what I ask, so that hereafter His divine Majesty shall not ask me why I did not beg you with all my might. For these exercises are the best thing I can imagine, or feel, or understand, in this life, first to help a man win advantage for himself, and second to be able to help and benefit many others and render them fruitful. For if, as to the first, you shall not feel a need of them, nevertheless as to the second you will see beyond all measure how much it shall be of service to you.

So, I conclude, supplicating the infinite mercy of God to give us grace to learn His holy will, and to perform it fully, according to the talents committed to each of us, so that He shall not say to us "Thou wicked and slothful servant, thou knewest that I reap where I sowed not," etc.

Wholly yours in the Lord,

IÑIGO.

In Venice, Ignatius was again the object of suspicion and slander. It was said that he had been condemned several times, that he had been burned in effigy both in Spain and in Paris, and that he had fled to Venice in order to escape death, and what not. He took the same stand that he had done under similar circumstances in Paris, at Salamanca and Alcalá—he went to the ecclesiastical judge, Dr. Gaspar de Doctis, deputy of the Apostolic Legate, asked for an investigation and offered to appear at any time; a proceeding was held, a time was set for all to appear that might wish to testify against him, depositions were taken and witnesses examined in behalf of the accusations and also for the defense; and after the matter had been duly considered, judgment was finally given on October 13th, 1537. The charges were dismissed as frivolous, empty and false, and Loyola declared "to have been and to be a priest of good and religious life and orthodox belief, as well as of very high reputation, and to have taught religion and morality in Venice up to this day."

CHAPTER XVIII

FROM VENICE TO ROME (1537-1538)

IGNATIUS passed a whole year in Venice, waiting for the time agreed upon when his companions were to come. The agreement had been that they should set forth from Paris on January 25, 1537, but in the preceding summer war broke out anew between the King of France and the Emperor, and the Fathers in Paris, apprehensive lest the Spaniards among them should be arrested, or the area of battle extend to the north and bar the roads into Italy, decided to forestall such contingencies, and left Paris abruptly on November 15, 1536. A letter from Ignatius to the confessor of the French Queen, sister of Charles V, a Spanish priest who had accompanied her Majesty to Paris, reveals his perturbation over their journey:

May the grace and love of Jesus Christ always bless us and help us.

I remember well the kind and obliging good will which, from your love and service toward God, you have always shown to me, in spite of my unworthiness, and so I have come . . . to ask for still more kindness to the end of serving and praising Almighty God. . . . Master Pierre Lefèvre and some companions are about to start on a very hard journey, of which you can get full information from them. I am fearful because of the wars and troubles that, on account of our sins, have grown so great in Christendom, lest they find themselves in great distress. So for God's sake, please help them as God may prompt you and as may be feasible. All will be for the love and glory of God, and I shall regard whatever you do as if done for me personally.

The little band might turn their backs on the world and rise superior to national ambitions and enmity, nevertheless the war "kindled by our wickedness" as they humbly

176

said, affected them, not only directly by obliging them to
make a premature start and interfering with the progress
of their journey, but also, in a less obvious but more permanent manner, by its indirect effect upon the policy of the
Pope and of the various princes and states of Italy. And,
therefore, before taking up the narrative of their journey
and further doings, I shall make a short digression in order
to refresh the reader's memory of the political situation.

For several years Charles V and Francis I had held to
the treaty of peace that had followed rather lamely upon
the battle of Pavia, but circumstances had altered, and
fortune looked with a more smiling face upon France. Great
factors in European politics veered towards her side. Henry
VIII, who in earlier years had usually inclined to his
nephew the Emperor, now that he had divorced Catherine
of Aragon and broken with the Papacy, leaned toward
France; the Protestant princes of Germany had organized
a league and looked to Francis as a protector; Prince Henry
of Orléans, Francis's second son, had married the Pope's
niece, Catherine de' Medici; and the Turks were threatening
Austria. These favoring circumstances confirmed the
French King in his purpose to recover Milan when he
should get a good chance, and he pressed his advantages.
He grew more and more cordial to the Protestant princes,
and even invited Melanchthon to come to Paris to discuss
ways and means of mutual understanding and reconciliation between the new opinions and the old; and he made
a secret alliance with the Sultan of Turkey against their
"common enemy." To his disappointment, Clement VII
died, and the Medici marriage lost its political value, but
he believed that he could win the good will of the new Pope,
Alessandro Farnese, Paul III, and despatched a very clever
man as special ambassador, Jean du Bellay, archbishop
of Paris. At this juncture Francesco Sforza, who had been
reseated upon the ducal throne of Milan by the Emperor
after having been ousted by the French, died without children. This afforded Francis his opportunity to revive the
French claim. Making a pretext of civil war in Savoy,
he overran that duchy and entered Piedmont. The

Emperor struck back by invading Provence. In this campaign an incident occurred which connects at one small point the history of the Society of Jesus with that of Spanish arms and Spanish literature. The Imperial army advanced beyond Cannes as far as Fréjus. Near here, in the village of Muey, a detachment under the command of a Spanish officer attempted to storm an outlying tower. This officer, Don Garcilaso de la Vega, although but thirty-three years old, had seen considerable service. In 1520 he had fought for the King against the *Comuneros,* and had been wounded about the same time as Loyola; he had served in the vain attempt to relieve the island of Rhodes, when besieged by the Turks; he had taken part in the capture of Fuentarabia, when Xavier's brothers were officers of the French garrison; in 1530 he had assisted at the siege of republican Florence, memorable because Michelangelo had fortified the city along the heights of San Miniato; and in 1535 he had accompanied the Emperor in the successful attack upon Tunis. Nevertheless, his fame is due, not to his sword, but to his pen; for he is still the most brilliant lyrical poet in the Castilian tongue. He led the scaling party against the tower in a mad, dare-devil fashion, was desperately wounded, and died three weeks later in the arms of another gallant soldier, the marquis of Lombay, subsequently duke of Gandia, who is known to history as St. Francis Borgia, third general of the Society of Jesus. Shortly after this, the Imperial army was repulsed before Marseilles and retreated ignominiously to Italy; but we may take leave of the war, which was destined to last for two more years, and return to the pilgrims.

Fearful of difficulties, as I have said, they took the shortest road out of France into Lorraine, via Meaux to Metz. They journeyed on foot, poorly clad, with their skirts tucked up in their belts, each with a wallet on his back, containing Bible, breviary, papers, and little else. They made a singular group, but in spite of their dress they presented the appearance of gentlemen. Francis Xavier came of a noble family; Lainez perhaps had the delicacy of features that sometimes indicates an admixture of the blood of Spanish

Jews; Broët is said to have been a tall man of good carriage and handsome face, with delicate profile and reddish beard; while Salmerón, a Spaniard, was big, black-bearded, with an olive skin, and both had an aristocratic look.   Pierre Lefèvre, the leader, possessed without doubt a saintly presence, and all must have been of a refined and ascetic countenance. They overheard some people who were staring at them ask a peasant who they were, and his answer: "Some reformers who are going to reform some country or other."   It was their custom every morning when they started forth, to say a prayer, and again in the evening when they reached their night's lodging.   The three that were already priests, Lefèvre, Jay and Broët, celebrated mass every morning in order to give them all courage for the hardships of the day, and as they trudged along, they meditated or conversed on religious things.   They ate what the poor eat; and whenever a decision was to be made, they took a vote and followed the opinion of the majority.   From Metz they travelled south to Basel and Constance.   In France it rained every day, while in Germany and Switzerland the roads were deep in snow.   Crossing the Alps was especially laborious.   Besides the physical difficulties, they were in constant danger of arrest from French soldiers.   When challenged by French sentries, the French fathers answered for all, "We are students from Paris," and the Spaniards contrived to escape notice.   After leaving Lorraine, they passed through Protestant lands, and were treated with scant courtesy by both clergymen and laity.   But at the end of about seven weeks they reached Venice and joined Ignatius, on January 6th, 1537; as Bobadilla says, *"Gavisi sunt valde omnes."*

Their wish was to go immediately to Rome for two objects: to obtain from the Pope permission to make the pilgrimage to Jerusalem, and also license to such as were not already ordained for ordination as priests, because not being residents of any particular diocese and having no means of support they were canonically disqualified.   But it was necessary for them to wait until spring for the roads to open.   In the meantime they devoted themselves to works of charity.   The little band, divided in two; half lodged at the hospital of San Giovanni e Paolo, which lies close beside the church, and the others at the hospital of Incurables, which was situated, I believe, about where the barracks now stand, while Ignatius stayed where he was.   All passed their days in religious devotions and care of the sick.   By the middle of Lent the roads were passable.   Ignatius, however, deemed it prudent to let the others go without him, fearing lest he might hinder the success of their mission, for the reason that he was *persona non grata* to two personages of great influence.   One was Caraffa, the other Dr. Pedro Ortiz, a famous theologian and canon lawyer of the Sorbonne, who while in Paris had had some official relation to the charges laid against Ignatius and had been inclined to treat them seriously.   Dr. Ortiz had been retained by the Emperor as counsel for Queen Catherine in the divorce case, and was now in Rome defending her rights before the Pope; as counsel in a case of the very greatest political importance, he was a person of high consequence and to be dealt with gingerly.   For these reasons Loyola, who combined, to a degree rarely if ever seen, worldly shrewdness and spiritual passion,—the prudence of the serpent and the guilelessness of the dove—stayed behind and let his disciples go alone on their mission.

The nine journeyed three by three, mingling nationalities, with a priest in each group.   They went on foot, as before, and begged their way, often getting no more than bread and water.   The season was rainy, and the water courses, often little more than a succession of stagnant pools in the dry months, were become torrents.   Sometimes the Fathers were obliged to wade up to their waists.   But they took it all in good part, rejoicing that they were privileged to suffer privations and endure hardships for the sake of the Lord, and sang psalms as they trudged along.   The exercise and outdoor life—they were able to cover twenty-eight miles on one Sunday—did them much good; and one of them, Jean Coduri, who had what Ribadeneira calls a sort of leprosy of the legs, was quite cured.

It would however be neither a truthful tale of these heroic

Companions, nor a faithful picture of their religious ideas, if I were to give only what seems to me the nobler and more rational side of their doings. The grotesque, at this period of the Renaissance, is not confined to such as Rabelais. Father Rodriguez, who had not received from nature a delicately tempered mind, nor acquired a large notion of religion, tells this anecdote that occurred while they were in Ravenna:

It happened that three of the Companions went to the same hospital. The beds offered them had been much used and were very dirty, the sheets were foul and badly spotted with blood. Nevertheless, two of them, one with his clothes on, the other stripped, were not afraid to get in. The third [it is supposed that this was Rodriguez himself], kept back by horror of the filth, sought another spot. But as he went he reflected on what he had done, and grieved greatly that he had shirked in the battle. He laid it to weakness, self-indulgence and delicacy of body, and mightily desired that a new occasion would offer itself in which he might retrieve the flabby act. God did not fail him. For when he and another brother arrived at the hospital of some village, the matron informed them that there was no bed except one which a patient had occupied who had died that day of the lousy disease; the sheets, she said, were clean, for the patient had not used them while alive, but they had been laid under his dead body, out of respect for the cross and for the priests who had come to the infirmary to say the last rites and bury the body. The matron did not exaggerate; the sheets had been sprinkled with holy water, and were thick with great big lice which accompany that disease. The Father, who had once been vanquished, now saw his way to win a victory over himself, and seized the opportunity. He took off all his clothes and jumped quickly between the sheets. The lice rushed incontinently upon him, pricked and stung him all night long, and made his body smart till it sweated. Of a truth the Father conquered himself, he conquered and won the field gloriously. His companion also lay down in the same place but kept his clothes on.

In Rome, to their surprise, Dr. Ortiz showed them very particular kindness. He procured them an interview with the Pope, eulogized their goodness, their learning and their great desire to glorify God. The introduction served them well. Paul III was both a reforming Pope and a clever man of the world; he wished to serve his religion and his country, but he shared with many a predecessor the passion of nepotism, as it is called, lavished honors on his worthless son, Pier Luigi Farnese, and made his two young grandsons cardinals. He employed Michelangelo to crown the Palazzo Farnese with its magnificent cornice, enjoyed the arts of the jeweler and goldsmith, and also took pleasure in the company of good and learned men. His worldly traits are those usually remembered, but he deserves to be known as the first of the Popes of the reformation within the Church. He received the nine Companions very graciously, and put them to the proof then and there, by requesting a discussion on a point of theology. They stood the test so well, that he granted them permission to make the pilgrimage to Jerusalem, and headed a subscription with sixty crowns to pay for their journey. Others of the curia, principally Spaniards, also contributed, and in all two hundred and ten gold crowns were raised. It must be said at once that the Companions regarded this sum as destined solely to pay their way to Jerusalem, and when it became apparent that they could not go, they returned the money to the givers. License was also granted them, in virtue of their learning and their vow of poverty, to take priest's orders, without obligation of accepting a benefice, that is, leaving them free of parochial duties. Their objects thus attained, they went back to Venice.

The Seigniory was at war with the Turks and little prospect showed itself of a passenger ship sailing for Jaffa; nevertheless the brethren held fast to their plan of waiting for a year. Those not already priests, except Salmerón who was still a year or so too young, were ordained, and then, in their humility, determined before saying their first mass, to undergo special spiritual preparation by means of a retreat for forty days with prayer and meditation, and all proposed to spend the rest of the time conducting evangelical missions. For this purpose they left Venice, going in twos or threes to different towns roundabout. Loyola, Lefèvre and Lainez went to Vicenza, Xavier and Salmerón to Monte Celso, Hoces and Coduri to Treviso, Jay and Rodriguez to Bassano, Broët and Bobadilla to Verona. Loyola's party established themselves in a deserted monastery wrecked by soldiers in the open country about a mile outside the walls of Vicenza; it had neither door nor windows, and the wind blew through the openings at will. Straw strewn on the floor was their only bed. Twice a day two of them went their rounds begging in Vicenza, and were hardly given enough to support life; no wine, no meat, only a little bread, hardly ever any butter or oil, while the third stayed at home and boiled the bread in order to make it soft enough to eat. The rest of the day was spent in prayer and contemplation. After the prescribed period of forty days had elapsed, Jean Coduri joined these three, and they set about their evangelical work. Going into town, they separated, and repaired to four several squares. Then each shouted aloud and waved his hat in order to catch the attention of passers-by and draw a crowd; then each began to preach, but in an Italian rendered difficult of understanding by bad grammar, foreign words and idioms, and by their respective Spanish, French and Savoyard accents. Nevertheless people listened; possibly in the crowd that clustered about one or another of these outlandish preachers was a lad of twenty, a native of the town, Andrea Palladio. The preachers preached on the ugliness of vice, the beauty of virtue, on the love of God, on contempt of the world, how dreadful sin is, and upon whatever topic they hoped would rouse the hearts of their hearers to strive for the attainment of that blessed end for which mankind was created. The people of Vicenza were touched, the seed fell on good soil and brought forth abundantly; and thereafter alms were given in plenty.

What the Companions considered and spoke of as plenty would probably square but poorly with our modern ideas of diet and hygiene. Loyola was ill, Lainez also, when word came that Simon Rodriguez lay at death's door in a poor

hermitage near Bassano. The place was a day's journey
from Vicenza, but Loyola, fever-stricken as he was, immediately got up, left Lainez in a hospital, and started on the
road to Bassano at so smart a pace that Lefèvre had great
difficulty to keep up with him. At one point Ignatius out-
stripped him and stopped to pray for Rodriguez, and, when
his companion rejoined him, said with joyful confidence,
"We need not be distressed, Brother Lefèvre, for Simon will
not die of this illness." And when they reached Bassano
and found Rodriguez emaciated in pitiable plight, Loyola
spoke comfort to him: "Don't be afraid, Brother Simon,
this time you shall get well." So he did, and both he and
Lefèvre ascribed his recovery to Loyola's prayers. Lefèvre
on their return, recounted this episode to Lainez, and he
himself told Ribadeneira, who publishes it in his biography.
Other signs of divine visitation were bestowed upon Loyola
at this time. He had many spiritual visions, and other experiences of spiritual comfort, especially at Venice while he
was preparing his mind to receive sacred orders, and whenever he went on a journey he was favored with supernatural
manifestations, such as he used to meet with at Manresa.

Meanwhile the others likewise had preached, prayed, and
lived on scraps at their respective places, and now all met
together at Vicenza. They were very happy over the first
fruits of the harvest. Rodriguez says: "And the Companions, when they beheld the rich crop which the most
merciful Lord of the Vineyard was gathering in, esteemed
hunger, cold and other hardships as sweetest dainties for
their souls, and singular proofs of divine beneficence.
Thanks and praise without end be unto Him for such great
mercies." But, however abundant the crop, preaching in
Vicenza was not the object of their association, and the
little Company of Jesus, as they had begun to call themselves, seeing that winter was drawing on and that there was
no hope of taking ship for Jerusalem, agreed that the primary purpose of their covenant must be renounced, and
that they must adopt the alternate purpose, and offer themselves and their services to the Holy See. It was decided to
separate. Loyola, Lainez and Lefèvre set out for Rome,

but the others went, two and two, to Padua, Ferrara, Bologna, Siena, all seats of universities, in the hope of persuading some young scholars to join them. Their experiences were varied. Coduri and Hoces, who went to Padua, by mischance spent their first night in prison, whereas Claude Jay and Simon Rodriguez, who went to Ferrara, were well treated by Duke Ercole. For this they seem to have been indebted to Vittoria Colonna. He listened to their sermons, confessed to them, received the eucharist at their hands, and promised to pay the cost of their journey to Jerusalem. One cannot but fear that the duke, who was at the time allied to the Emperor and Pope against Francis I, was willing to lay an emphasis upon the difference between his orthodoxy and the wayward opinions of his French wife, the Duchess Renée, who had harbored Calvin and Clément Marot, and been most friendly to the French ambassador, Jean du Bellay, and his secretary, François Rabelais, and other members of the embassy.

For the most part, these wandering preachers, reformed priests or Parisian priests as they were called, conducted their missions very much as Loyola and his two companions had done at Vicenza; they preached in the public squares, they taught children and the uneducated, they frequented hospitals, they tended the sick, they comforted the downhearted, "in a word, they neglected nothing which they thought might conduce to the glory of God and the spiritual welfare of their neighbor." But to return to Loyola. It was his habit, on the way to Rome, to partake of the eucharist daily, in preparation for the office of priest, and to pray in particular to the Madonna. I am coming to what he regarded, I think, as the most important episode in his life, and I had better introduce it with his own words.

In his *Memoirs* he always speaks of himself in the third person, usually as the Pilgrim, *Il Pelegrino,* for he dictated in Italian: "After he had been made priest, he had decided to pass a whole year before saying mass, giving himself up to preparation and to prayers to the Madonna that she would set him with her Son." As the episode to which this preparation is leading up is important, and Loyola has expressed himself so simply, I will quote also Father Riba-deneira, his secretary and biographer, who expands his brief sentences, and I do so the more readily as this quotation will indicate the way in which the biographical style of the Jesuits was tending:

After the Blessed Father had been raised to the sacerdotal dignity, as he knew full well what sanctity it requires, he took a whole year, virtually in solitude, to prepare himself to take in his hands the sacred body of Christ Our Lord, and to offer it as a living sacrifice for the sins of men. He thought he should spend at least that length of time in preparing himself for his first mass. In fact the accomplishment was still later than he anticipated, for he did not have that happiness until Christmas Eve in the year 1538, at Rome, in the chapel of Santa Maria Maggiore, where the Saviour's manger is kept. That was a year and a half after his ordination. During this time he gave himself up day and night with extreme ardor to the contemplation of things divine, humbly praying the Glorious Virgin, Mother of God, to place him near her Son, and give him means of approach to Him, for she is both the door of heaven and the mediatrix between Jesus and mankind. By favor of her protection he hoped to be brought to the notice of the divine Child, and also to know Him, speak to Him, and worship Him with tender respect. Wonderful were the divine favors that he had received at Venice, Vicenza, and other cities, and on the highroad, so that he thought himself to have gone back to the time of abundant consolations that had blessed him at Manresa.

After such preparation, and with such thoughts ever present to his mind, and heavenly habitants hovering, as it were, near his head, Ignatius and his two companions, stopped at a village, Storta, a few miles before reaching Rome, on the road from Siena. There they went into a little chapel to pray. And as he prayed he felt a sort of transfiguration of his soul, and he beheld God the Father, and God the Son with His heavy cross. The Father, turning to the Son, tenderly commended Ignatius and his companions, to His care, and Jesus welcomed them, and said to Ignatius with a loving look: *Ego vobis Romœ propitius ero* (I will be a friend to you in Rome). And having finished his prayers, Loyola, all joy, said to Lefèvre and Lainez: "My brothers, I do not know what God wishes of us, whether we shall die on the cross or under torture; but of this I am sure, come what may, Jesus will stand our friend." And he recounted to them what he had seen and heard. This vision contributed not a little to confirm them in the choice of name, Company of Jesus, which they finally adopted when the Company was formally founded. This name also avoided the offense to his humility caused by people here and there who fell into the way of calling his companions *Ignatians,* or *The Company of Ignatius,* or by some such phrase. He used to declare afterwards, that, even if the brethren had opposed the name instead of joyfully acclaiming it, he would have insisted, he was so sure that it was God's wish, and he informed all who joined them that they were entering the Company and service of Jesus Christ, enlisting under the banner of that great Captain, and must carry His cross, and fix their eyes on Him.

CHAPTER XIX

But in spite of the promise of divine support, the way was not smooth, and Loyola foresaw that it would not be. When they got to Rome he said: "I see that the windows have their shutters up." The great affair that lay before them was the foundation of the Order; but first I will give some account of how Loyola and his brethren employed their time, and then of the accusations cast up at them and of their deliverance and triumph, and after that I shall return to the story of the foundation.

It seems that Loyola must have been preceded or accompanied by a reputation highly to his credit, for very soon he was sufficiently familiar with several men of consequence to lay before them the *Spiritual Exercises*. Chief of these was Cardinal Contarini, a man of saintly life, one of the leaders of the reformation within the Church, and a relation of the Contarini who had already become Loyola's friend; he used to go about saying that he found Father Ignatius a most sympathetic teacher, and wrote out a copy of the *Spiritual Exercises* with his own hand. Dr. Ortiz went further. In order to be able to practise the exercises apart from the interruptions of business and friendship, he took Loyola to Monte Cassino, stayed there forty days, and followed the whole course of spiritual instruction. So keenly did he feel, as he says, "What a difference there is between the study that prepares us to instruct others and that which teaches us to guide ourselves!" All his life he remained a firm friend of the Society, and even, it is said, felt a strong inclination to join it, but corpulency rendered him unable to perform the physical duties imposed by the rules, and probably the world had too many just claims upon him to permit him to abandon it. While at Monte Cassino a

vision appeared to Loyola, which, had it not been explicitly
referred to in his own *Memoirs,* one would be inclined to
look upon as a sort of pious repetition, or echo, created out
of the imagination by credulous disciples, of a very similar
vision that had been vouchsafed to St. Benedict, when he
was at Monte Cassino, a thousand years before. "I saw,"
Loyola says, "the Bachelor Hoces enter into Heaven; I wept
but felt great comfort of spirit; and I beheld this so vividly
that to deny it, would be a downright lie." Ignatius had
known that Hoces was ill at Padua, and had expected him
to die, but the vision is said to have taken place at the very
hour of his death.

Already before Loyola went to Monte Cassino, Paul III,
who was trying to set on its feet the college of *La Sapienza,*
which had been wrecked in the sack of Rome, had appointed
Lefèvre to teach sacred scripture there, and Lainez to teach
scholastic theology; and after the other brothers joined them
in the spring of 1538, all laid out their work with greater
regard to a common purpose. They all lived together in a
house, which had been lent them, near *Santa Trinità dei
Monti,* begged food and what else they needed, and preached
in various churches throughout the city. Ignatius preached
in the Spanish language at Santa Maria of Montserrat, the
national Spanish church, near the Palazzo Farnese; Jay, in
French I surmise, at San Lodovico, the French church next
to Palazzo Madama, where the Emperor's daughter, Margaret of Parma, was living; Lefèvre in San Lorenzo in
Damaso, a church appurtenant to the palace now known as
the Cancelleria, while Lainez, Rodriguez, Salmerón and
Bobadilla, preached elsewhere, all five in Italian. Part of
the good that preaching in Italian accomplished, as they
themselves perceived, was their own mortification, *por
mortificacion del predicador;* afterwards, when they had
better mastered the language, they did good to the congregation, and even in the earlier days, as they thought, they
planted seeds of spiritual fruit, and at any rate made themselves known and talked about. Schoolmasters took their
pupils to hear them, and many persons came to confession
and communion. Ignatius must have been a remarkable

preacher. Sincerity and passionate love of souls are the parents of true eloquence. Dr. Ortiz considered himself fortunate not to have missed any of his sermons; and another theologian, Dr. Arce, used to say that he had never heard so virile a preacher, for he spoke as one that had authority and not as the scribes.

Besides preaching, the practical labors of charity were the especial care of the brethren. It was just ten years since the terrible sack of Rome, and in consequence the rich still suffered discomforts, and the poor privations. The biographers speak in particular of Loyola's tireless activity in matters of charity; to this I shall return in a later chapter. By his influence a certain rich man contributed generously to the Jesuit charities, and also to the needs of the little band of Fathers, so that they were released from the burden of begging alms for themselves and left free to attend to higher things; and, later on, this same generous friend by his labors more than by his purse enabled them to procure a church of their own, and to build a house on the site where the church of the Gesù now stands. In the meantime the Fathers had moved from the neighborhood of Santa Trinità dei Monti, and lodged in an ampler house near a tower, *Torre de la Melangola,* bordering upon the ground once covered by the Circus Flaminius. The need of charity was doubled by a great famine in the land, and many poor people, according to report, were found dead of hunger and cold in the streets. The Fathers converted their new building into a sort of charitable lodging-house, and took in the destitute. Soon the number cared for reached a hundred, then two, three, and even four hundred. These poor people were housed and kept warm, the feebler had what beds there were, while the more robust slept on straw. As many as could be were fed, and all were preached to and prayed over. This work was noised abroad, and well to do citizens came to see how they could help, and some if they had nothing else to spare, gave their coats and cloaks. Even alms intended for the Fathers were spent in charity. This state of affairs lasted till the next year's harvest. In all more than 3000 persons were taken in and looked after. Besides their

care of this household, the Fathers, and also some new
comers who joined them, went about the hospitals and private houses, ministering both to body and soul. I shall
return to the matter of Loyola's practical philanthropy
hereafter; but it is impossible to touch upon these two years
prior to the granting of the charter without saying a word
as to the faithful, laborious, and self-sacrificing devotion
shown by Ignatius and his Companions to the sick and
destitute. At the same time one must remember that to
Loyola, men's bodies were mere temporary houses of clay,
but their souls the everlasting temples of God's holy spirit.
Loyola himself was always mindful of the benefits received
by those who serve others; the more his zeal to serve souls,
the closer he came to God, as he says, *sempre crescendo in
devotione, id est, in facilità di trovare Iddio*. With this, I
leave the aspect of his work as a practical philanthropist,
and go back to the ill wind of misunderstanding, dislike and
jealousy, that blew about his head. Father Polanco begins
his account of it, *"Cum Satanas, . . ."* but I shall start a
little differently.

The storm arose in this fashion. An Augustinian monk,
from Piedmont, a great preacher, who was at that time
preaching in Rome, seemed to the Jesuits to be larding his
sermons with Lutheran doctrines; thereupon, they did what
they believed to be their duty, by unmasking him from their
pulpits and refuting his teachings. For some reason or
other, that we can but guess at, certain Spaniards, connected with the papal curia, espoused the monk's side, and
spread evil reports about the Jesuits; and they also got hold
of a rascally Spaniard, Michael by name, who had known
Ignatius and the others in Paris. This Michael had wished
to join their Society, but as he did not seem a suitable person, he was refused. Encouraged, apparently, by the
friends of the monk, he went about saying publicly that
Ignatius had been condemned as a heretic in Spain, in
Paris and in Venice, and implied, if he did not say, that
they were all runaways and had been obliged to take refuge
in Italy, and he also did what he could to bring the *Spiritual
Exercises* into bad odor. People began to look askance at

the Jesuits, and reports of these alleged exposures were carried back to various cities and places where Ignatius had preached.

Ignatius acted as he always did under false accusations: he insisted upon publicity, a full investigation of the facts, and an official adjudication of his innocence.   In this case the charges were laid before the Governor of the city as judge.   The fellow Michael appeared as complainant, and repeated under oath the slanders he had been spreading abroad.   The cross-examination, if I may call it so, was decisive.   Ignatius produced the following letter written to him by Michael within the year.   I quote it at length because this accusation is the first of a long series brought against the Jesuits by those out of sympathy with them, and the ready refutation thereof when investigated, though it had begun to spread infection, points a moral; and also because it throws light upon the volatile character of many of the people with whom Loyola had to deal, people who were afraid of hell, but with no courage to bear the hardships on the path of virtue.

To Father Ignatius de Loyola

VENICE, Sept. 12, 1537.

May God of His infinite mercy keep you and hold you in His hand.   Amen.

I left your habitation with the intention of returning within a few days, or at least to write you fully of how things went with me, and I think I gave you my promise. My promises have been, not only now but all my life, poorly truthful; to this I bear truthful witness, for every day I do sorry things, starting out with high purposes and coming back with failure.   May it please God to give me grace and strength to do battle for His glory and my salvation against those fierce beasts that hold me in their clutches, I mean the world, the flesh and the devil.

The day I left you I dined with Master Arias, who greeted me with joyful looks, as I thought.   Before dinner, and while we were at table, and afterwards, he inquired of me with solicitude and particularity, about each one of you, and how you are, and what was said of him.

As to the first question I told him all I knew. As to the second, I answered that I was very much surprised that a man of his discretion and experience, who got at the marrow of things, hidden or not, should suspect that the companions would speak ill, or say anything they should not, of anybody, or give any information that was not true; for it was well known that their way of life was very pious and very close to the apostolic life,—without any false touch of the illumined, those pretended servants of God, but really servants of Satan—and that he well knew the companions worked hard to bring back to the right road those who had strayed, and in return for the good they did received evil.

To which he answered: "I do not think that they speak ill of me or of anybody else; I want to know what they say of my leaving them." I answered: "When I asked them about you, they answered my questions, and told me what had happened. I was bewildered by it, and I am bewildered still. Suppose a student at the Sorbonne, who had passed his examinations, should invite all the doctors of the University of Paris, and the Rector, to go to Notre-Dame in order for him to take his degree; and then when they were all there, should say 'I have decided not to take it' and that they might go home; they would all think him under-witted. Such a matter should be more carefully considered in the beginning." I told him, I felt badly, just as if he were my brother, over what would be said of him, whether he was in Italy, or Spain, or any other part of the world; both his friends and those who were not his friends would know all about it. "What you should do (I said), is to go back to them; or, let us both go to a hermitage." He answered: "What do I care what they say about me? How do they know whether or not I have given my money to the poor, or have got absolution from Rome?"

We talked about this and other things until it was time for me to get aboard ship; he went with me to the dock, and said we should see one another within three days in Venice. Three days have gone by and I have not seen him. The report that he has gone to Rome may be true. I do not know whether it is or not.

One day, walking through the piazza of San Marco, I met a woman from Padua, who had been his landlady; she recognized me and asked me about Master Arias, her saint. I asked her what reason she had for asking me. She said: I left my house in his hands, just as if he had been my husband. [I need not continue this episode, the object of which seems to be to show that Master Arias was one of the vicious *illuminati,* and to throw on him the blame of Michael's backsliding.] . . .

I mean to make an effort to find out where he is, and if I do, I will have him up before the Pope. . . . I mean to get even with him for what he did to me on the way to Rome and add something more, for he is responsible for taking me away from you, *and in taking me from you he took me away from the service of God.*

As for me I have no peace unless I study; and as I see I shall get no aid from men, I trust myself to God, and I am going to leave Venice this week to seek whatever may come. I am always fixed in my determination to return and serve God; but, unless I study, I shall not be able to serve God as I wish to serve Him. Always, whatever He may wish me to do, I offer myself to you; and some day, by means of your prayers and those of my brethren, I hope that He will have mercy and enlighten my understanding, if in coming to this decision it is blind.

If you will write me, it will comfort me very much and I shall be deeply obliged. Be it as God may prompt you. Please remember me to my brethren in Christ.

He that wishes to be remembered in your prayers, the least of all,

Yours,
Michael.

The prosecution threw up the case; Michael was condemned as a slanderer, fined, and banished. So far, so good; but Ignatius demanded that the Spaniards of consequence who had backed Michael should come into court and proffer their charges. They, however, were cautious and endeavored to avoid the issue; they had been mistaken (they said), they entertained a high opinion of Ignatius and his associates, they admired their mode of life, their teaching and their charitable actions. In this way they hoped to slink out and leave the cause with an impotent conclusion; and to this end they used what influence they had. They went to the papal legate, Gian Vincenzo Caraffa and acknowledged their mistake; and he supported their attempt to suppress the matter quietly. The Governor took the same position, and various prelates also; even Loyola's companions thought it would be wiser not to press the suit in court. But they had the wrong sow by the ear. Ignatius insisted. The case had been brought into court, and the court must render judgment. The judge refused to act. Ignatius went to the Pope, laid before him a full account of his whole life, his doings and his purposes, the opposition he had received, his imprisonments and so forth, and besought him, for the sake of his companions and himself, to command the judge to give judgment. The Pope did so. And by a very singular coincidence, all the men who had been judges in the divers accusations and complaints brought against Loyola, were all present in Rome at that very time, and all appeared and deposed their evidence before the Judge had concluded. There was Dr. Figueroa, the Vicar General at Alcalá, on his way back from Naples where he had been upon an important mission on behalf of the Emperor; there was Dr. Matthew Ori, the French inquisitor, before whom Loyola had twice been hauled in Paris; there was Dr. Gaspar de Doctis, vicar of the Apostolic Nuncio, who had had cognizance of the charges laid against Ignatius in Venice. Other testimonies from various places where the companions had been,—Venice, Vicenza, Bologna, Ferrara and Siena—were introduced in evidence. Very respectable gentlemen of Rome also testified in their favor. The Governor, therefore, in his decision, November 18, 1538, condemned the detractors of the Company, and not only acquitted Loyola but also praised his life, his teaching, and good works, and, by express mention, the *Spiritual Exercises*.

In spite of some repetition I will quote from a letter of Loyola's, in which he tells the whole story:

To Isabel Roser

ROME, December 19, 1538.

May the grace and the love of Christ always bless and keep you.

I can well understand that you are anxious, and not less amazed, because I have not written to you as often as I wanted to; indeed, if I were to forget the great deal that I owe to God, for what your hands have given me with such loving good will, I think that His divine Majesty would not remember me, since you, out of love and reverence for Him, have always done so much for me. The excuse for my delay in writing has been because we have been constantly hoping to despatch a certain affair here from day to day, or rather from month to month, and to be able to tell you definitely about our situation. The affair is so serious, that in all our lives we have never passed through such rough maltreatment as during these last eight months. I don't mean that they have laid hands on us, or arrested us, or anything like that; but a report has gone round among the people, suggesting things they had never heard of, and roused suspicion and offensive gossip; so we felt obliged on account of the scandal to go before the Legate, Cardinal Vincenzo Caraffa, and the Governor of the City, the Vice-Chamberlain, Benedict Conversinus (for the Pope had gone to Nice), and we summoned the persons who had spoken insolently against us to lay before our superiors whatever evil they had found in our lives and in our teaching. I will tell the whole story from the beginning so that you shall understand it.

More than a year ago, three of us (Lefèvre, Lainez and I,) came to Rome, as I remember I wrote you. The other two began to teach gratis in the academy of the *Sapienza* one positive theology, the other scholastic theology, by the Pope's orders; while I devoted myself to imparting my *Spiritual Exercises* both in the city and out. This we ar-

ranged in order to have some educated people, men of
consequence on our side (or rather, on the side of the honor
of God, for all our concern is to serve and praise His divine
Majesty,) so that we should not meet so much opposition
among people in general, and that we might afterwards
preach His holy word freely,—for the earth here, so dry of
good fruit, reeks from its abundance of evil fruits.   By
this method of procedure (God helping), we won over some
persons to our side, persons of education and good repute,
and four months after our arrival, we decided to have all
our band together in Rome.   As soon as the members came,
we applied for license to preach, to exhort, and to hear confession; the Legate granted this very fully, although people
told many false things about us to the Legate's Vicar, and
delayed the issuance of the license.   After we had got it,
four or five of us began to preach in various churches on
Sundays and feast days, and we also expounded to boys the
Ten Commandments, the mortal sins, etc.; the courses at
the *Sapienza* and hearing confessions going on all the while.
I preached in Spanish, all the others in Italian.   There was
always a good congregation at the sermons, ever so many
more than we expected.   We thought there would be few
for three reasons: First, it was an unusual time for preaching, because we began after Easter, after the other
preachers, who preached in lent and on the great feast days,
had stopped.   In this country it is the custom to preach
only in lent and advent.   Second, after the sermons and
privations of lent, many people, for our sins, incline more to
diversions and pleasures than to a new set of devotional
exercises.   Third, because we do not make any account of
elegance and an accomplished manner in what we do, but
in spite of that we do make account of this,—relying on our
experience,—that God, in His infinite goodness, shall not
forget us, but through us, who are of no account, shall help
many other people.

After we had come before the court, and two men had
been summoned, and one of them had got from the judges
very much the opposite of what he had expected to get, the
others against whom we had made application for a sum-

mons, became so fearful that they neither wanted nor
dared to appear, but kept putting hindrances in our way to
prevent our going on with the case. And as some of them
were men of large incomes, six hundred ducats or a thousand, and some with influence, all men of affairs connected
with the curia, they twisted the cardinals about, and other
personages of position in the papal court, and made us
spend much time in carrying on the fight.

At last, however, the chief men among them, were summoned and appeared before the Legate and the Governor,
and said that they had heard our sermons and teachings and
so forth, and found nothing at all to take exception to either
in our doctrines or our conduct. At that the Legate and
the Governor, expressing a high opinion of us, advised that
the matter be hushed up, both as to these defendants and
others. But we asked repeatedly, as we thought it but
justice, that there should be a written decision concerning
our doctrine, whether it was evil or good, so that the people
should have no cause for scandal; but this we could not obtain from them, either as a matter of justice or law. From
this time on, however, from fear of legal proceedings, nothing was said against us, at least not in public. Then, as we
could not succeed in getting a judgment or a declaration as
to our matters, a friend of ours spoke to the Pope, when
he came back from Nice, asking him to issue a pronounce-
ment in the matter. The Pope agreed, but as nothing was
done, two of our Company also spoke to him. And as His
Holiness went right off again to Frascati, I followed him
there and talked to him all alone in his room for about an
hour. I spoke at length about our purposes, and gave a
clear account of all the suits that had been brought against
me in Spain and in Paris, as well as of how I had been
locked up at Alcalá and Salamanca. I did this so that nobody should be able to tell him anything which I had not
told him, and also to persuade him to make an investigation
of us, so that some judgment or definite declaration concerning our teaching should be made. Finally, as it was
particularly necessary for our preaching and exhortations, to
enjoy good repute, before the world as well as before God,

and to be free from suspicion both as to doctrine and to conduct, I begged His Holiness, in the name of all of us, to use
his power and apply the remedy, and have our doctrines
and our mode of life investigated by any judge of ordinary
jurisdiction that he might order; so that if any wrong were
found we might be corrected and punished, and if none, that
His Holiness would show us his favor. The Pope, though
he had ground from what I had told him for some suspicion,
took it in very good part, praised us for putting our minds
to good things, and, after he had talked and encouraged me
for a time (and indeed his language was that of a good
shepherd, no hireling), gave an express command to the
Governor, who is a bishop and chief judge of the city both
in ecclesiastical and civil matters, to proceed at once with
our case. In consequence, the Governor began afresh with
much expedition; and the Pope came back to Rome and
several times spoke a good word for us before everybody,
when our Company was present, for every other week they
go to debate some question while the Pope is at dinner.
And the consequence was that most of the storm blew over,
and some piece of luck has happened every day, so that it
appears to me that things are going very much as we wish
for the service and glory of God, and we are much impor-
tuned by some prelates and others (by God's help) to sow
the seed of good fruits in this part of the world; but we are
waiting for a more appropriate opportunity.

Now it has pleased God that our case has been adjudged.
And at this juncture a very surprising episode occurred. It
had been said of us that we had run away from various
countries, and in particular from Paris, from Spain, from
Venice; and now just when the court was about to give
judgment, there turned up, here in Rome, just arrived, the
regent Figueroa, who had arrested me in Alcalá, and instituted two proceedings against me, and the Vicar General of
the papal legate at Venice who had also started proceedings
against me at the time when we began to preach in Venice,
and Dr. Ori, who likewise had taken proceedings against me
in Paris, and the bishop of Vicenza, where four of us
preached for a time; and so all these testified in our favor.

Besides, in like manner, the cities of Siena, Bologna and Ferrara sent certified evidence, and the duke of Ferrara, in addition to sending evidence (taking to heart the disrespect shown to God in this treatment of us) wrote at various times to his ambassador and to our Society making our cause his own, because he had seen what had been accomplished in Ferrara and also in the other cities where we had been.

For this we render thanks to God, because, from the time we began to the present, we have never failed to give two or three sermons on every feast day, and two lessons every day, and some have been always busy with hearing confession and some in giving the *Spiritual Exercises*. Now that judgment has been pronounced we hope to deliver more sermons and to do more teaching among boys. · And, seeing that the soil is dry and sterile, and that we have met great opposition, we cannot say truthfully that we have lacked something to do, and that God has not wrought more than our knowledge and intelligence of themselves could accomplish.

In order not to exceed all bounds, I will not specify more details; on the whole God has made us very well satisfied. I will only say that there are four or five who have made up their minds to enter our Society, and have persevered in their purpose for many months; but we do not dare admit them, because one of the points they made against us is that we took in members and were making a congregation, or religious order, without apostolic authority. As it is now, although we are not all agreed as to what course to pursue, we are all of one mind that we should come to some definite plan for the future; and we hope that God will so dispose this to His best service and praise.

Now that you have heard how our affairs stand, for the love and worship of God I beseech you, that we may all have great patience, desiring that He may work in us whatever may be most to His praise and glory; for matters are just now in a critical state. I shall keep you informed very often of what happens; for I say, if I forget you, I feel that I shall be forgotten by my Lord and Master. However,

I care little to express my thanks in words, but of this be sure that,—apart from the fact that all you have done for me out of a love and worship of God lives in His presence— in whatever His divine Majesty shall do through me, making it meritorious by His divine grace, you shall be a sharer so long as I live, since you have always given me great help in serving and praising Him. Please commend me to all our friends and acquaintances, who are of a religious life and at one in Christ.

I end my letter, with a prayer to God that of His infinite goodness He will give us grace to perceive His holy will and to perform it.

De bondad pobre,

INIGO.

P. S. As I write this, the Pope has directed the Governor to see that orders are issued for the city that the boys' schools shall be united, and that we shall give them instructions in Christian doctrine, as we had begun to do before all this trouble. May it please God, since it is His affair, to give us strength for greater service and praise.

CHAPTER XX

WE now approach the culmination of nineteen years of preparation; but the final act was not achieved without difficulty. Already in the spring of 1538 Ignatius had called his companions to Rome with a view of taking some decisive step. It was first necessary, however, to clear away all the dust and smoke kicked up by the false accusers before the little group could discuss calmly and properly the wisdom of forming a permanent organization, and decide upon its character and constitution. In mid-Lent, 1539, their deliberations began. At the outset the Fathers were of various minds; so they betook themselves to prayer and offered masses, in order to learn the will of God, feeling great hope that He would inspire them with what would best please Him and most redound to His honor. They met every evening; and each man was to declare his opinion in turn, giving his reasons point by point, and the voices of the majority were to control. The first question was, should this little band of men, brought together as if by Providence from different countries, break up and scatter, each to go his several way, or should they bind themselves by some permanent bond of union? To this there was a prompt answer in the affirmative. The vows of chastity and poverty were accepted as of course; but should they add a third vow, that of obedience to a superior to be elected from among them, as a means to enable them more fully to do the will of God and of His Vicar on earth? This was more difficult to decide; and considerable uncertainty was felt. Some appear to have been fearful lest they might be commanded to enter some order already existing and to abide by its rule, and so be diverted from what they re-

202

garded as the true way for them to work for the salvation both of themselves and others. In this perplexity they adhered very closely to Loyola's rules as to an election, contained in the *Spiritual Exercises*. They prayed God to incline their hearts to go counter to self-love rather than with it; they refrained from discussing with one another, leaving each to reflect upon the question by himself, alone with God; and each endeavored to put himself in the position of an outsider, and as such consider what advice he would give under these circumstances to other men for the greater glory of God. After this, there was further debate and deliberation in company; at last the vote was put and unanimously carried. Other articles, concerning the novitiate and time of probation, the establishment of colleges, the ownership of houses and of churches, the nature of their duty of obedience to the Pope, obedience to superiors, the teaching of children, the election of a general, and so forth, seem to have been readily agreed upon. Loyola himself, when considering and discussing important matters, was accustomed to receive what he deemed a divine revelation. Christ would appear to him in a vision, shining like the sun, and thereafter he had no doubt. He told Gonzalez that this often happened to him when deliberating over the constitution of the Society; and he showed him daily records in his diary, in which he had noted down how visions came to him in confirmation of one or another article in the constitution, sometimes a vision of God the Father, sometimes of the Three Persons of the Trinity, or of the Madonna, either interceding or approving. During his deliberations, his practice was to say mass every day, to pray, and lay the particular matter under consideration before God; and when he celebrated mass, or prayed, his eyes were wet with tears. His was the plan of the Company; his was the will and the passion that brought it to birth. And yet, at this time, however he may have behaved later, he was far from being an autocrat; on the contrary, the remarkable fact concerning these deliberations and conclusions, is that they are really the work of ten minds acting together, all in the end concordant and at one, not because of the tyrannical

mastery of Loyola's genius, but because during long years
of intimacy his comrades had been persuaded, trained, illumined and inspired by his ideas, and therefore, in spite of
their diverse capacities and dispositions, they arrived at
one harmonious agreement. Lainez ascribes Loyola's
powers of leadership to these qualities:

Great knowledge of the things of God, and great devotion
to them, and the more metaphysical these matters were, and
over our heads, the better he knew them; great good sense
and prudence in matters of business; the divine gift of discretion; great fortitude and magnanimity in tribulation;
great guilelessness in not judging others, and in putting a
favorable interpretation on all things; and great skill in
knowing how to set himself and others to work for the service of God.

By St. John the Baptist's day, June 24, 1539, all
matters had been settled, and Ignatius drew up under five
heads a compendious statement of their decision, a sort of
brief constitution. Paul III, who had been through stormy
months, putting down riots caused by his salt taxes, and
subduing disobedient members of the Colonna family, was
then resting at Tivoli, and Cardinal Contarini, the Venetian
cardinal, kinsman to Loyola's friend, and, as I have said,
one of the principal reformers in the papal curia, undertook
to lay the document before him. He did so on September
3rd. The Pope expressed his approval and the cardinal
wrote the good news at once to Ignatius:

TIVOLI, September 3, 1539.

REVERENDO DON IGNAZIO,

I received yesterday from M. Antonio, your Spanish
friend, the copy of your constitution together with a little
note from the Master of the Sacred Palace. I waited upon
the Pope today, and, besides making your petition by word
of mouth, I read to His Holiness your five heads. They
were highly satisfactory to him, and with right good will he
approved and confirmed them. We shall return with his

Holiness to Rome on Friday and an order will be given to
the Very Reverend Ghinucci to make out the brief or bull.
Remember me in your prayers. My kind regards to our
friend Lactancius. *Bene vale in Domino.*

Vestri amantissimus,

G. Card. Contarini.

However, on his return to Rome, the Pope thought it
proper, following no doubt the usual course in such matters, to submit the petition to a committee for examination.
This procedure does not seem to have caused the Company
any apprehensions; for on September 25th Father
Salmerón, in writing to Señor Juan Lainez, the father of
Diego, says incidentally: "You will be able to get full
particulars from the carrier of this letter, how the Pope, in
spite of accusations, slanders and law suits, has approved
and confirmed our mode of living together after a definite
system, and has given us full permission to have such constitution and laws for ourselves as we shall think best."

This news, however, was premature. The charter was
held up, not so much because of any specific objections to
its provisions, or to the Jesuits themselves, as because of a
general objection to new orders. There had been such an
outcry against monks and friars, that many of the reforming
cardinals were not only opposed to new orders, but wished
to do away with many of those already existing. And it
happened that an important member of the committee (as
it may be informally called), to which the charter had been
referred, Cardinal Guidiccioni, "the glory and honor of
Lucca," a man of piety and learning, had expressed such an
opinion most emphatically. It is said that he had written
a book in support of his views. He was so much irritated
by the mere notion of a new order that for months he would
not even look at the papers in the matter. There was
nothing for the Fathers to do but pray God to touch his
heart, and Loyola promised two thousand masses or more,
which were afterwards punctually celebrated. In consequence of these prayers, as they believed, or, of the interposition of the Duke of Ferrara, to whom Loyola himself

ascribes the success of the application, or, as I believe, on a hint from the sagacious Pope himself, Cardinal Guidiccioni turned from an opponent into a strong supporter of the new order. He said to the Pope (according to Father Ribadeneira): "I do not approve of new orders; but I do not dare to oppose the foundation of this order, for I feel my heart drawn toward it. I have such an extraordinary feeling for it, that reason yields to this manifestation of the divine will, and [he adds, anticipating Pascal] the heart triumphs over all the arguments of the mind." The Pope caught his enthusiasm—*"Digitus Dei est hic"* (Here is the finger of God)—and the bull of confirmation was issued on September 27, 1540.

Pierre Lefèvre says:

In this year occurred the memorable blessing, the foundation of the Company, when we presented ourselves as an offering before the Supreme Pontiff Paul III, for him to determine how we could serve Christ to the edification of all those who are under the jurisdiction of the Apostolic See in perpetual poverty, and ready to go, in obedience to his command, to the ends of India. It was God's good pleasure that he should accept us and rejoice in our purposes. Wherefore I shall always be obliged, and all of us, to render thanks to the Lord of the harvest of the Universal Catholic Church, i.e., to Jesus Christ our Lord, who deigned to declare by the voice of His Vicar on earth His good pleasure, and to indicate His will that we should serve Him, and that He would use us forever.

The bull itself incorporated Loyola's petition, with the exception of two paragraphs that did not meet with favor. I quote the document at some length, on account of its importance. The style is bad, but the very length and elaboration of the sentences show how anxious Loyola was not to make any definite statement without its proper qualifications. Indeed, the document reads as if suggestions from one or another of the Company had been inserted, as they were offered, without regard to form or phraseology:

Whosoever desires to be a soldier of God under the banner of the Cross in this Company (which it is our wish shall be known by the name of Jesus), and serve his Lord and the Roman Pontiff, His Vicar on earth,—having first vowed the vow of perpetual chastity—must take note that he is a member of a Company instituted: (first of all) to advance souls on the way of Christian life and doctrine, to propagate the faith by public preaching and expounding holy scripture, to give the *Spiritual Exercises,* to do works of charity, and, in especial, to instruct children and the uneducated in Christian truth, and finally, to try to bring spiritual consolation to the faithful by hearing confession. Then, all shall endeavor, first, always to keep God before their eyes, and next the welfare of this Institution, which is our road that leads to Him, and to make every effort to attain that end, according as God disposes; nevertheless, each shall try to employ himself according to the grace which the Holy Spirit may impart, and according to his grade in the Society, so that no one shall be dragged aside, here or there, by well meant but inconsiderate zeal. It shall belong to the General, or Superior, whom we shall elect, to assign to each his grade and his duties, in order to secure the harmony necessary to every well ordered community. The General shall possess authority to draw up a Constitution that shall give effect to the purposes we set before us, taking counsel with his companions, and deciding each matter by a majority of the votes. It is to be understood that, as to the more important and permanent matters, the majority of the whole Company (that the General can conveniently get together) are to give advice, whereas in unimportant and transitory matters, only those Fathers who may be present in the place where the General resides. The executive power shall lie in the hands of the General.

Members of the Company must understand that not only at the time of making profession, but always as long as they live, the whole Company and every one of its sons are soldiers of God, and that they fight under the orders of our very holy lord the Roman Pontiff, and of future Popes, his successors. And, although the Gospel teaches us (as we also know by reason of our orthodox faith and firmly believe) that all faithful Christians are subjects of the Roman Pontiff, since he is their head and the Vicar of Jesus Christ, nevertheless, for the greater humility of our Company, and for the more perfect mortification of each one, and the abnegation of our own wills, we think it highly fit and becoming to bind ourselves to this by a separate vow, in addition to the common obligation of all Christians. So that, without equivocation or excuse, with all possible promptitude, we must fulfil all that the present Roman Pontiff and his successors shall command us to do for the good of souls, and the propagation of the faith, in whatever countries he may wish to send us, whether to the Turks, or other infidels, or to the regions called India, or to the lands of heretics, schismatics, or of faithful Christians. Wherefore, those that mean to join us, before laying this burden on their backs, should consider long and carefully whether they possess sufficient gifts of the spirit to enable them to complete the building of this fortress according to the plan of the Lord; that is to say, whether the Holy Spirit, which impels them, promises them so much grace that they are hopeful by its help to carry the weight of this calling; and, afterwards when, under God's impelling, they have enrolled themselves in this soldiery of Jesus Christ, they must be girded and ready, day and night, to fulfil so weighty a promise.

And in order that no one among us shall make any effort either to obtain, or to refuse, any mission or any country, each one promises that he will never have any negotiations, direct or indirect, with the Roman Pontiff, in order to be sent to this region or that, but will leave all such matters to God and to the Pontiff, His Vicar, and to the General of the Company, who also promises, like the others, that he will not have any negotiations with the Pontiff to be sent to any particular place, except with the advice of the Company. All shall make a vow to obey the General of the Company in all things that appertain to keeping this rule; and the General shall command what he may deem proper to attain the end that God and the Company have

prescribed for him. In governing he shall always remember
Christ's kindness, gentleness and love, and the precepts laid
down by St. Peter and St. Paul, to which he, and his counsellors, must always give heed. Specially enjoined upon
them is the instruction of children, and the uneducated, in
Christian doctrine, teaching the Ten Commandments, and
the principles of faith, which, according to the circumstances
of person, place and time, shall seem to them appropriate.
Very necessary is it that the General and his counsellors
attend with especial vigilance to this ministry, for the edifice of the faith cannot be built up among those who are
our neighbors without this foundation, and there is danger
lest our brethren, the more learned they become, may likewise become the more disinclined to this work, for it appears
less brilliant at first sight, although there is none so useful,
both for the edification of our neighbors, and to exercise our
brethren in the virtues of charity and humility. On their
part, the members, both for the general good of the Order,
as well as on purpose to secure the continual exercise (which
can never be sufficiently praised) of humility, shall always
be obliged to obey the General in all that pertains to the
Institution of the Company, and they shall acknowledge
and reverence him, as is befitting, as they would Christ,
if He were present in person.

As we know by experience that the religious life is the
more agreeable, pure and edifying, according to the measure
by which it is separated from all contagion of avarice and
conforms to evangelical poverty,—and as we also know
that our Lord, Jesus Christ, will provide for His servants,
who seek nothing but the heavenly kingdom, what food and
clothing may be necessary for them—therefore we all take,
every one of us, the vow of perpetual poverty; and by that
we mean that not only each man as an individual but also
all together, shall receive no permanent property, or rents,
or income, or legal rights, for the support or use of the
Company. All shall content themselves with receiving only
things to be consumed, and whatever necessaries may be
given them. Nevertheless, in the universities, college or
colleges, that they may have, they shall be at liberty to

receive income or own possessions, applicable to the needs and use of the students. The General of the Society shall possess absolute government and superintendence over said colleges and their students, in all that concerns the election of superiors and as to the admission, dismissal, reception or exclusion of students, and the making of rules concerning instruction, higher studies, edification and correction of said students, the manner of distributing among them food and clothing, and concerning all that appertains to the care, direction and government of the same; and he shall do so in such a way, that the said students shall not misuse such belongings, nor the Company apply them to its own use, but keep them for supplying the needs of students.

Students after proving that they have advanced in spirit and in their studies, and after passing sufficient tests, may be admitted to our Company. All the members in sacred orders, although they do not possess benefices or ecclesiastical revenues, shall be obliged to say the Church office, according to the ritual, each by himself and not all together.

The foregoing are the things that, with the approval of our lord the Pope, Paul, and of the Apostolic See, we are able to set forth with regard to our profession and way of life. We do this in order to inform, in summary fashion, both those who inquire as to our manner of life, and also those who may come after us, if God shall grant that there shall be hereafter imitators of our mode of life. As we have learned by experience that many grave difficulties beset such a way of life, we have thought it fitting to decide that no one shall be received into the Company without a long and thorough probation. When a novice shall have shown himself wise in Christ and well advanced in the doctrine and the purity of the Christian life, then he shall be admitted into this soldiery of Christ; may He deign to favor our poor beginnings for the glory of God the Father, to whom alone is due honor and glory for ever and ever, Amen.

A few years later the charter was amended and enlarged in some particulars—a limitation upon the number of members to sixty was removed—but it is not necessary to expatiate upon that. At this period of his life, as it seems to me, Ignatius had attained his full growth. His years of education and preparation were over; his years of administration begun. His general conceptions of the ills that afflicted the world, and of the work that lay before him, were cast in their final mould. Those opinions had passed through three phases: In the first, he entertained elementary mediæval notions of religion, picked up during childhood and youth in Guipuscoa and Navarre, which denounced somewhat vaguely the World, the Flesh and the Devil, and very definitely Moors and Turks, as enemies of Christ; in the second, the period of his travels in Italy, he became acquainted with the evil spirit of the Renaissance, the Spirit that Questions; and in the third, that of his sojourn in Paris, he learned to believe that the demon of Disobedience and Private Judgment was as hurtful to the old ecclesiastical order as Infidelity or Doubt.

Now, with the forces of Satan, all visible, all drawn up before his eyes in battle array, he girded himself to the task of recruiting and drilling a battalion of light horse that should, at the command of the general in chief, Christ's Vicar on Earth, be ready for service at all times, in any place, reckless of everything except the greater glory of God.

CHAPTER XXI

Now that the charter had been granted, the next step was the election of a general. Some new members had already joined, but the original band, the First Fathers, were regarded as the source of authority, and they alone took part in the election. Xavier and Rodriguez were already in Portugal, but knowing of the proposed action, they had left their ballots; Lefèvre, who was in Germany, sent his. Bobadilla was unexpectedly delayed in southern Italy, and lost his vote. Altogether there were but six actually present in Rome, in April, 1541, when the election was held. The voting was conducted as if it had been a religious ceremony. Each wrote the name of his choice upon a ballot, and then all the ballots, including the three from absentees, were put in a box, where they were left for three days, during which the Fathers prayed for God's favor, and then taken out and read. The ballots, in addition to the names, contained some explanation or sentiment. Salmerón's I have already quoted. Broët's had the brevity of a foregone conclusion: "In the name of Our Lord Jesus Christ, Amen. I, Paschase Broët, choose Don Ignatius Loyola for Superior. Paschase." Coduri, ill and somewhat disquieted in spirit at the prospect of going to Ireland—for he had been selected, and would have gone but for his illness—wrote:

With no thought but for the greater glory of God and the greater good of the whole Society, I vote for the man who in my judgment, ought to be head and minister of the Society. That man,—and I bear witness that I have always known him zealous for the honor of God and most ardent

212

for the salvation of souls, and he ought to be set over others for the reason that he has ministered to them and made himself the least among them,—is our honored Father, Don Ignatius Loyola; and after him I choose a man not less endowed with virtues, our honored Father Peter Favre. This is the truth before God the Father and our Lord Jesus Christ; nor should I say otherwise even if I knew for sure that this was the last hour of my life.   Johannes Coduri.

Rodriguez's ballot is also characteristic.   He thought that he was on his way to India.

To the praise of God and His Virgin Mother.   It seems to me, according to the light which I unworthy unworthily possess, that Ignatius is the man whom we ought to choose from among us for president and rector, and if death or some mischance prevent, then Peter Favre should take his place.   And as I feel in this way in my conscience, I wish to confirm it, dear Brethren, by writing my name with my own hand.   And I assert that I have not been persuaded by anybody directly or indirectly, but act of my own free will, and I believe that you will do the same.   And as up to now there has been no question of ambition among us, so I hope it will continue to be, and when, dear Brethren, God shall have blessed your wishes remember your brothers. Lift up your hearts for their sakes.   I say good-bye to you all, Brothers.   Rome, March 5th, on which day I leave Rome, in the year of our Lord, one thousand five hundred and forty.   SYMAON RODRIGUEZ.

Of course, all the votes were for Ignatius, except his own, which was cast for whoever, other than himself, should receive the most.   Then followed one of those scenes of humility that are a tax on the reader who is not familiar with the great tradition of Catholic self-abnegation. Humility is not a fashionable quality in the modern world; we have not been taught that it is like truthfulness or

loyalty, one of the virtues most acceptable to God; and
when we read of the refusal of honors or office, knowing
that in the end the refusal will be withdrawn, we find it
very difficult not to think of the classical scene on the feast
of the Lupercal, and to fancy that we are witnessing a
little high-flown ecclesiastical politeness. But if we suspect
Ignatius, we must also suspect many popes and princes as
well as illustrious persons in our own country, who have
expressed an unwillingness, were it not for the overpowering
duty of patriotism, to accept high office. At any rate,
Ignatius acted as the virtue of humility required. He
said that he had a greater inclination to be ruled than to
rule, that he was inadequate to govern himself and still less
adequate to govern others, and therefore, remembering his
evil ways, both those past and those still continuing, his
many sins, wrongdoings, faults and wretchedness, refused
to accept the position, said he never would unless he should
receive more light than he then had; and he besought them,
in the Lord's name, to commend themselves to God and
consider further for three or four days, who would be the
fittest for the position. Accordingly, after four days the
Fathers met again; and again voted for Loyola. After
reflecting upon the matter from this side and from that,
to see what should be for the greater service of God, he
answered that he would leave it in the hands of his confessor. So he did. He passed three days at San Pietro in
Montorio, making a full confession of all his sins from the
day that he first was morally able to commit sin up to
the present, told all his bodily infirmities, and then bade the
confessor, as if in Christ's place, say what he ought to do.
The priest replied that the refusal seemed to be contrary
to the will of the Holy Ghost; nevertheless, Loyola's scruples of humility still persisted. Finally the priest wrote
his affirmative decision on a sheet of paper, sealed it up,
and sent it to the Society; and at this Ignatius yielded and
accepted the charge.

On Friday, April 22nd, the Fathers visited the seven
pilgrimage churches, ending at St. Paul's outside the walls.
Here Ignatius said mass, and when the time came for giving

the eucharist, he took in one hand the paten with the host upon it, and in the other a paper on which his vow was written, and, turning towards his brethren, knelt, and repeated aloud, in Latin, the words of the vow:

I, Ignatius Loyola, vow to God Almighty, and to the Supreme Pontiff, His vicar on earth, in the presence of the Virgin His Mother and of the whole Court of Heaven, and in the presence of the Company, perpetual poverty, chastity and obedience, in accordance with the provisions of the Bull confirming the Company of Our Lord Jesus, and contained in the constitution as drawn or to be drawn. Moreover, I vow obedience in particular to the Supreme Pontiff concerning missions as set forth in the Bull. And I further vow that I will teach boys in the principles of the faith according to the Bull and the constitution.

He then partook of the sacrament; and after him, each of his companions in turn took a similar vow, only instead of addressing it to God and to the Pope they addressed it to God *"et tibi, Reverende Pater, locum Dei tenenti,"* and they also partook of the sacrament, and after mass was finished Ignatius embraced each of them and gave each the kiss of peace.

One final act remained to be done, the Society must have a constitution. It was obvious that Fathers who were off on missions could not possibly attend to framing a constitution, so it was decided by those who had come up for the election, to leave the whole matter in the hands of the two Fathers who were to remain in Rome, Ignatius and Coduri. The latter, however, died soon after, and the task devolved on Ignatius alone. But his health was not good, and he was heavily laden with the affairs of the Company, and little was accomplished until 1547, when he was given a secretary to help him, Juan de Polanco, a young Spaniard who had recently finished his studies at Padua.

Loyola's task, in his own eyes at least, was far more

religious than legal. He told Father Gonzalez de Camara that "while he was at work on the constitution, he used to say mass every day and to lay each several article before the Lord and pray over it." The first complete draft was not finished until 1550; this draft was read to various Fathers who happened to come to Rome, and received some alterations and amendments, and then, in its amended form, proclaimed as the Constitution (1552), in spite of the fact that it had not been ratified by a vote of the Society, as the charter required; so great was Loyola's authority and the religious sanction that in the eyes of his companions consecrated what he did.

The Constitution I shall touch upon but lightly, doing little more than mention even its most important provisions. It is preceded by a long *Primum ac generale Examen,* which is an exposition of what is required by members of the Society. At the threshold it states: *"Finis hujus Societatis est, non solum saluti et perfectioni propriarum animarum cum Divina gratia vacane, sed cum eadem impense in salutem, et perfectionem proximorum incumbere"* ("The object of this Society is to labor not only for the salvation and perfection of our own souls, by the help of God's grace, but also, by the same help, to devote ourselves zealously to the salvation and perfection of our neighbors.") All the members, at the end of the noviciate, take the three regular vows, and the professed members also vow to go in the interest of religion wherever the Pope shall command. The mode of life—so it says—does not outwardly differ from that of ordinary men *(majus Dei obsequium semper intuendo);* penances or bodily chastisements are not obligatory, but each one may, with permission of his Superior, inflict upon himself whatever discipline he may judge will be for the good of his soul. The members are divided into classes. (1) The Professed, all priests, who have passed the necessary tests and have taken the four vows; (2) Coadjutors, who serve either in a spiritual or secular capacity, and take but the three vows; (3) Scholars, who, according to their talents and proficiency may pass on into the first or second class, *ad majorem Dei gloriam;* (4) Persons awaiting a determination as to their grade. A noviciate of two years is required before taking the vows, and scholars must wait an additional year, or longer, after completion of their studies before they are admitted to a higher class.

Chapter II enumerates the five impediments which bar a man from the Society: heresy, homicide, membership in another order, marriage or servitude, and mental deficiency. On all these points the applicant is to be very carefully examined, and also as to his habits, inclinations, and his readiness to forsake all in order to follow the precepts of Christ, *an omnino decreverit sœculum relinquere et consilia Domini Nostri Jesu Christi sequi.* Is he firmly resolved to live and die in the Society of Jesus? The candidate is then told that he must follow the counsel of perfection, "Go and sell all thou hast," and other rules of great self-abnegation. "Since every communication, verbal or written, with family or friends, usually does more to disturb the peace of those who give themselves up to the things of the Spirit, than to do them good, let the candidates be asked if they are willing to forego all communication, neither to write nor to receive letters, except as the Superior may permit, and that, all the time they are in a house of the Society, their letters, from them or to them, be read, and that the Father in charge of this matter, may pass such letters on or hold them back according as he shall judge most expedient." Let the applicant remember the words of Christ: "If any man come to me, and hate not his father and mother, and wife, and children, and brethren, and sisters, yea, and his own life also, he cannot be my disciple." And will he consent that all his faults be reported by any one to his Superiors, and do as full members do, revealing all they do to one another, in due charity, *ad majorem Dei gloriam?*

During the noviciate the candidates are subjected to six preliminary tests: They shall take the *Spiritual Exercises* for a month; serve in a hospital for a month; travel for a month without money, begging their food from door to door; they shall perform the most menial services in a house of the Society; teach the catechism to children; and hold themselves ready to preach and hear confession. And the novice must remember that in the performance of services, of whatever sort, at the command of a Superior, that it is not to him or for his sake that obedience is rendered, *sed soli Deo et propter solum Deum Creatorem ac Dominum nostrum.* And, in order that the Superior may know those under him, both to enable him to counsel and direct them, and also to know what service will best suit their capacities, let the novice at the beginning render to him a full account of all that he has ever done, and again, at the end of every six months, of what he shall have done in the interval, and once more before taking the vows. Finally, after two years of preparation, the novice, having shown himself always obedient, having been a pattern of edification during all his probation, having humbly submitted to all penances imposed on him for error, negligence or wrongdoing,—and both he and the Superior being in accord that it is for the best—he may then be admitted into the body of the Society, consecrate himself to God, and take the vows according to the grade he is to enter. Let him think well how much it avails for progress in spiritual life *omnino et non ex parte abhorrere ab omnibus quæ mundus amat et amplectitur;* and be sure that he is ready to suffer insult, injury and mockery, whether from a member of the household, or of the Society, or from a stranger, not returning evil for evil but good for evil, and bearing it patiently for God's grace. And he must make it his study to renounce self absolutely and to submit to continual mortification in every possible thing. For, as Thomas-à-Kempis says: *"Homo qui necdum perfecte in se mortuus est, cito tentatur, et vincitur in parvis et vilibus rebus."*

The Examen shows the care employed to make the novice and the Society known to one another before the great vows "that shall incorporate and make them one" are taken. I have given larger space to it than I had meant; but greater conciseness might have prevented the reader from appreciating how solemnly the novice is warned before dedicating himself for life to a task beyond his strength.

The Constitution

Part I.

On admission to the novitiate.

Chap. I.   On who has the right to grant admission.
       II. On who may be admitted.
       III. On impediments that prevent admission.
       IV. The procedure of admission.

Part II

On the matter of dismissing those who, having been
admitted to probation, are found unsuited to the
Society.

Chap. I.   Who may be dismissed, and at whose command.
       II. On the causes for which it is proper to dismiss.
       III. On the procedure of dismissal.
       IV. How the Society shall behave to those who leave
            voluntarily, and to those that are dismissed.

Part III

Concerning what shall be done in the care, keeping,
and advancement of the novices.

Chap. I.   On taking care of novices in matters that concern
            the soul, and progress in virtue.
            For this, it is very necessary for the novices to
            avoid all communication which might chill their
            purpose; they must not go out of the house except
            at the time prescribed, and with an appointed com-
            panion, and while in the house converse only with
            those whom the Superior shall designate; they
            must keep watch and ward over eyes, ears and
            tongues; they should speak in words apt for edifi-
            cation *(in circonspectione et œdificatione ver-
            borum)*, wear modest looks, walk with unhurried
            gait, and never a gesture showing pride or im-
            patience; they should in all matters leave the
            better things to others, look upon themselves as
            inferior, and treat every one with the respect due
            to his station; indeed, each should see in every
            other an image of God. And it is of the first im-

portance for spiritual progress that all shall give
themselves over to a perfect obedience, looking
upon the Superior, whoever he may be, as in the
place of Christ, and performing not only in outward act but with inward reverence and love,
what he shall command, however hard, *integre,
prompte, fortiter,* with due humility, without a
murmur, without an excuse. Novices shall love
Poverty like a mother; they shall strive after
righteousness *(rectam intentionem),* and learn to
divest themselves, as much as may be possible, of
love of all creatures in order to turn all their
affection toward the Creator.

Chap. II. On the care of the body.

Part IV

On the manner of instructing those who remain in
the Society, in liberal studies (litteræ) and other
things that serve to help our neighbors.

Chap. I. On the gratitude to be shown towards Founders and
Benefactors of Colleges.

II. On the property of Colleges.

III. On the students to be matriculated therein.

IV. On dealing with students who have been admitted.

V. On studies.

These shall consist of grammar, rhetoric, languages,
logic, natural and moral philosophy, metaphysics,
theology, both scholastic and positive, and the Holy
Scriptures. As a rule Latin is to be spoken. And
so on; with provisions for schools to be opened
in connection with the colleges, for the government
of the colleges, and for studies in any possible
Jesuit university. Some text books are prescribed:
in theology, the Old and New Testaments; in
scholastic doctrine, St. Thomas Aquinas; in positive theology, part of the Canon Law and decisions
of Councils; in logic, metaphysics, natural and
moral philosophy, the treatises of Aristotle. In
Greek and Latin literature care is to be taken in
the choice of books, unless they have been expurgated. This Fourth Part does not go into great
detail, but it contains the germ of what afterwards
became, some thirty or forty years later, the
famous *Ratio Studiorum* which occupied the youth
of the upper classes in Europe for generations.

Part V

Deals with admission to the Society, and designates various grades. The lowest is the novitiate; next there is an intermediate class of *Scholastici approbati,* who devote themselves to their studies, or to spiritual discipline; from this intermediate stage members pass into that either of the *Coadjutores formati,* or of the Professi. The coadjutors are divided into the spiritual and the temporal; the former are priests, or to become priests, and occupy themselves with religious matters, while the latter have strictly secular employment. Of the Professed, the greater number add to the three regular vows, the additional fourth vow; a few, who have too little talent for preaching or are not sufficiently learned, do not.

Part VI

On those who are admitted and received into the body of the Society.

Chap.   I.   On what appertains to obedience.
Sancta Obedientia: All must observe obedience and strive to excel in it; not only in routine, but in everything, not waiting for express command, but on the mere indication of the Superior's will. All must keep God before their eyes, obey from love and not from fear, and strain every nerve of their strength in the virtue. "Dropping every occupation,—leaving unfinished the letter we have begun—and banding all our strength and purpose in the Lord to that end, so that holy obedience be perfect in us in every respect, in execution, in will, and in understanding; obedience in execution consists in doing what is ordered; obedience in will, in having no other will than his from whom we receive the order; obedience in understanding, in thinking as the Superior thinks, and in believing what he ordains is rightly ordained. Otherwise obedience is imperfect. We are to do whatever shall be commanded us, with great promptitude, and spiritual joy and steadfastness; persuading ourselves that all commands are righteous; and laying aside in blind obedience our own opinion to

the contrary; yea, in everything prescribed by the Superior—where it cannot definitely be shown that some kind of sin is involved. Let every one convince himself that those who live under Obedience, should be led and governed by Divine Providence through their Superiors, *perinde ac si cadaver essent,* as a corpse would be, that allows itself to be carried here or there, and handled after any fashion; or like an old man's staff, which suffers itself to be used everywhere, and in any way, that he who holds it wishes."

Chap. II. Concerning Poverty.
III. On what members of the Society may do, and what not.
IV. On the aid given to those that are in the Society.
V. That the Constitution does not impose obligations under the penalty of sin.

Part VII

On missions.

Part VIII

On the means of maintaining union between the members scattered abroad, with one another and with the General.

Part IX

On the General and his mode of government. This chapter deals with the qualities desirable in a General, with his authority and functions, with the limitations and checks upon his power, which are extremely elaborate, and cut down his autocratic prerogatives very greatly.

Part X

How to preserve and increase the Society.

I have also quoted these articles more fully than I had intended, for they bear in every chapter the individual stamp of their author. They are obviously not the work of a trained codifier, such as were the men who drew up the *Constitution of the United States,* or *The Code Napoleon;* they are the labor of a man who wrestles with the difficulty of putting into concise and logical form rules and counsels that he has learned in life through manifold experience, who is accustomed to govern by force of character and emotional intensity, rather than by cold reason. Friends of the Society have greatly extolled this Constitution. One Pope declared that it was more the result of Divine inspiration than of human prudence. Such is the orthodox opinion. Father Astrain, who is notable for moderation and good sense, says: *"El Espiritu Sancto fué el principal maestro de Ignacio."* Nevertheless, an outsider cannot but remember that Sir William Blackstone praised the Common Law of England as a perfect work of human reason, and Henri de Boulainvilliers, calls the French feudal government *le chef-d'œuvre de l'esprit humain.* However, the proof of the pudding lies in the eating; not in the judgment of those who merely read the receipt. The Constitution of the Order of Jesus can only be judged by those who are familiar with it in operation. It is less common, however, to find fault with the form and style of the Constitution than with its substance. Protestants have declaimed against what they call the iron constraint put upon the human soul. But if one stops to think, how does the Jesuit training differ, unless perhaps in conscientious intensity, from that at West Point or Saint-Cyr? In a military academy the whole weight of authority comes down on the individual soul. Substitute the flag for the cross, country for church, famous generals and marshals for saints and martyrs, honor for grace, and you will find that the constraint in either case is very much the same. Obedience is of equal obligation, the word of the superior as indisputable, the period of preparation about as long. As for liberty of thought, there is no more room for patriotic agnosticism in West Point than for religious agnosticism in a Jesuit College. In New York state men have been sent to prison for insult to the symbol of our patriotic faith. The difference is that we have lost our belief in supernatural religion, but not as yet our faith in nationality.

But whatever the plausibility of this comparison, there is, in truth, something humanly sacrilegious in coldly criticising a document, every clause of which was prayed over with tears, and offered to the Lord.

CHAPTER XXII

THE charter of the Company of Jesus is a declaration of purposes, and the Constitution prescribes the methods by which the Company shall fit itself to carry out those purposes; but documents at best furnish no more than a diagram, or mechanical plan, and tell little or nothing of the organism's vital processes. It will therefore be necessary to describe, or rather to indicate by a few details and episodes, what the Company did; for as we can best estimate the character and talents of a commander-in-chief by following the course of the campaign and the movements of his troops, so by following the doings of the early Jesuits, at first but a dozen, and then gradually increasing in numbers, we shall get a clearer idea of Loyola's genius. I shall therefore take a brief survey of the labors of these new apostles as they trudged from city to city, going about their business of saving souls, and doing whatever they believed to be for the greater glory of God.

As a general rule the Fathers conducted missions. They preached, sometimes in a church, in the cathedral perhaps, sometimes in the streets, either expounding the Bible, or discoursing on ethics or religious topics; they visited the sick in hospitals; they heard confessions, and administered the eucharist; they attended the dying; they gave the *Spiritual Exercises;* they taught children the catechism, and older boys the doctrines of the Church; they combatted heresy; occasionally they converted a Jew or a Turk; they did their best to persuade persons living in concubinage to marry or to separate. They slept in a hospital or some charity lodging house, and lived upon alms. What they received beyond their immediate needs they gave to the poor. Sometimes they were sent to reform a monastery or nunnery, sometimes to found a Jesuit college, or to perform some special task imposed by the Pope—*ad zizaniam extirpandam quam aliqui Satanœ operarii superseminaverunt—;* but the usual employment was upon evangelical missions. They travelled over a great part of Europe,—Italy, Spain, Portugal, France, Southern Germany, the Low Countries, even going to Ireland,—across the seas to Ethiopia, and India, and beyond. It seems plain that the clever Pope, Paul III, and the more clear-sighted prelates, recognized at once the great service that this Company of spiritual knights errant could render to the Papacy; and, indeed, they must have been dull of mind if they did not, for the Papacy had not had such defenders since Francis and Dominic had come to its rescue three hundred years before.

Their missions began even before the Company had been approved by the Pope. In the summer of 1539 the Cardinal of Santangelo, governor of Parma (at that time under papal jurisdiction) took Lainez and Lefèvre with him. A letter from Lainez gives some account of their life there:

To Father Ignatius Loyola

PARMA, June 2nd, 1540.

May the grace and peace of our Lord Jesus Christ be with us, Amen. . . . Spiritual matters here by the grace of our Lord advance every day from good to better. I continue my preaching, with considerable fruit and comfort for the listeners, and as a consequence, not without some opposition,—but *vincit veritas,* and all things work together for good. So it comes about that some do not want me to preach in the cathedral, because they say it interferes with the services, and that the season is over. Nevertheless they are calming down. I don't know how long it will last.

Confessions multiply to a glorious extent; a large number of the parish priests have begun to hear confession once a month, and five churches, beside ours, celebrate the communion every feast day. The *Exercises* grow day by day, for many of those who have taken them instruct others; one gives them to ten, another to fourteen. As soon as one brood is hatched, another begins, so that we see the children of children unto the third and fourth generation; and everybody has changed their way of living so that it is something to praise God for. And some persons whom God has called have died with so much courage and joy, calling on Jesus, that anybody would be edified; and the sick are a great deal more patient than they used to be.

And, besides this, our Lord has opened up a new field in the nunneries. A Benedictine convent, the richest in this neighborhood, asked me to come and preach once to the nuns, and I went and preached six times, with no one else there but the chaplain. During the course of my sermons, an outsider, a cousin of the abbess and dressmaker for the nunnery, to whom Brother Don Pablo had given the *Exercises*, went and told them about the *Exercises* and aroused their interest; and our Lord moved them so that at my last sermon one of the nuns said that she wanted to speak to me, and up to fourteen more followed her, and all said they wished the *Exercises*. And I, without more ado, gave one *Exercise*, and left instructions that Don Pablo should go on giving them. And that was done . . . I can't recount all the fruits that have sprung up—knowledge of God, tears, reform of habits. All are eager to do something, and they give up various little luxuries; one gives her clothes-press to the infirmary, another her coffer to the sacristy. They no longer want to work on dainty articles; they don't wish rich litters, as they used to. They are most content in their vocation, very obedient, no contentions, all bent on conquering their wills and overcoming temptation, and upon perseverance in prayer, in fastings, and in all the discipline of the rule; and, withal, they think they are in paradise, and, as it seems to me, they deserve to. There was a good deal of opposition from the confessor, who was once a friar, as well as from the older nuns; but we have held our own, because the abbess has always been on our side, and the vicar was not against us. Now the confessor dissembles; and the nuns say nothing;

even the most hostile are almost ready to join our side.
So we hope for a great harvest in this nunnery. . . .

And besides the attitude in the city, all the villages
roundabout are well disposed to us—if there were only
laborers for the harvest! On my way to Piacenza, before
Pentecost, I passed through a large village, and somebody
who had heard me in Parma recognized me, and told the
canons, who despatched one of their number to invite
me to preach. So I made a halt, went to the chief church,
and got into the pulpit; and I did the same on my way
back. The congregation was so excited, that many times
messengers came to tell me to hurry along as all the town
was waiting for me, etc. . . . I don't think of anything else
to write about of matters here, except that Don Pablo is
well by the grace of our Lord, although I am somewhat
tired. I am afraid of some such sickness as I usually get;
but I hope that it will not be so discourteous as not to wait
till Master Pedro [Lefèvre] is well. . . . This is all we
have to say. We should like to know from you what you
have heard about those who have gone to India, and to
Ireland, and about Caceres [in Paris] and Araoz [in
Spain]. . . .

Yours in Christ,

Lainez.

From there Lainez went to Piacenza, where his experiences
were sufficiently similar to those in Parma to make it unnecessary for me to narrate them. Then he was in Rome
for a time, assisting Ignatius. In 1542 he took up his abode
in Venice, where he stayed for three years, going on frequent missions to towns in the neighborhood, Verona,
Vicenza, Brescia, Bassano and elsewhere. In Padua he
started a college, and admitted among the first students
André Desfreux, commonly called Frusio, a Frenchman, a
person of note in the early history of the Order, and Juan
de Polanco, who subsequently became Loyola's private
secretary and finally his biographer. A few years later,
after attendance upon the Council of Trent, Lainez accepted a warm invitation from Duke Cosimo, and went to

Florence, about the time that Benvenuto Cellini was there, busy with modelling and casting his *Medusa* and *Perseus*, and hammering and chiselling gold and silver vessels to the great contentment (as he says) of his patrons.

Lainez was an excellent preacher. André Desfreux, after hearing him preach in Florence, wrote:

It seemed to me that everybody, if not with his lips then in his heart, said: "No man has ever spoken like that in our time"; and I can say on my conscience that I have never heard, and never hope to hear in my life, sermons of greater perfection, in spirit, doctrine, or delivery. His restraint in gesture is admirable, and such clarity, and such readiness of expression; and he has a way of explaining by familiar illustrations, when his thought is too deep or too subtle for the ordinary intelligence, so that even the most uneducated women can follow him.

From Florence, Lainez returned to Venice, stopping on the way at Gubbio, Monte Pulciano and Siena. A few months later he went down to Naples, and across to Palermo, and from there sailed with the Spanish fleet on a three months' campaign against the Turks in Tripoli (1550), and after that he made a visit to Pisa. Two years later he was named Provincial of Upper Italy, and among other labors, opened a Jesuit college in Genoa. I go into these details in order to show how much ground these early Jesuit missionaries covered, how far and wide they sowed their seed. Other Fathers toiled in other Italian cities; they all did very much the same sort of things that Lainez did. Bobadilla went to Naples where he wrestled with heresy and helped break up a meeting at which Juan Valdés "was vomiting forth blasphemies." Nadal, too, should be mentioned, for he seems to have been the first to start in practice the *Ratio Studiorum,* the course of studies that afterwards became world-famous; he displayed his liberality and good sense by making use of text books by Erasmus, Lefèvre d'Étaples, Lorenzo Valla, and Luis Vivés, all highly obnoxious for one reason and another to bigoted conservatives. I shall leave them, to describe adventures of another kind, in a different part of the world. The expedition of Fathers Broët and Salmerón to Ireland was far from successful. It was utterly ill judged, and reveals how ignorant the Papal Curia was of the conditions there; but it also shows the extreme confidence that already at this time, 1541, the Pope placed in the courage and devotion of the new Order. I will merely remind the reader that Henry VIII some years before had established the Anglican Church in England, and was doing his best to stamp out Catholicism in Ireland; and with that I will let the Fathers tell their own story:

To Marcellus Cervinus, Cardinal of Santa Croce.

EDINBURGH, 9 April, 1542.

MOST REVEREND AND ILLUSTRIOUS LORD:

As we think that you already know about our journey up to the time we reached Scotland by various letters which we have written to our Superior, Father Ignatius, in order to avoid tedious repetition we shall not say much of that here. This letter will confine itself to a brief account of the mission itself with which we were charged.

First, after we left Dieppe, we embarked at a port in Flanders, and sailed for Scotland, where we arrived on the last day of 1541. We experienced—our voyage being in the month of December—various sorts of bad weather. We ran other dangers, too, for twice the winds obliged us to put into English ports and stay ten or twelve days. Our clothes and our ignorance of the language exposed us to suspicion, but by Christ's intervention we escaped. At Lyons we met Cardinal Beaton of Scotland, and delivered the document we had brought for him from the Pope. He advised us by no means to proceed with our undertaking, because, as he said, every town, village, castle and stronghold was in the possession of the King of England, and his soldiers guarded every port, and because the Irish were the wildest people in the world, barbarians, and incapable of any civilization. In Scotland, too, we received the same advice from many men of high position, among others, the Archbishop of Glasgow, and the bishop of the Isles,—as the Isles are very near Ireland, this prelate would be likely to know the condition of Ireland and the manners of its princes—and also from many others, even Irishmen, that on no account should we go to Ireland, if we valued our lives.

We were somewhat disturbed by this testimony, but could not rest content with it, nor did we deem such a course consistent with our commission. We thought it best to see the island and the difficulties there for ourselves. Nobody else took that view, but as the event turned out, perhaps a good spirit urged us on. . . . Our plan was that if it proved not to be safe to stay, then to shake the dust from our feet and return as quickly as possible; at least, we should be able to testify concerning the state of Ireland from what we had seen with our own eyes and not from hearsay.

We landed in Ireland on the second day of Lent and stayed there about 34 days. In that time we questioned, inquired and examined; and, in short, found that what we had been told about Ireland was true, or rather that conditions were even worse. Not one stone had been left on another; for to begin at the most deplorable end, the princes have been forced into subjection to the King of England. This has been done within the last few months. There are three princes, much more powerful than the rest, who rule over all the wild parts of Ireland, Oynell [O'Neil], Odonel [O'Donnell] and Onell [O'Neil]. First, O'Donel, as we learn on good authority, was summoned by the Royal Deputy to Dublin, and there made terms, pledging his allegiance to the King, and subscribing in particular to two articles, first to recognize the King of England as supreme head of Ireland, in spiritual as well as in temporal matters, and, second, to deliver up to the Royal Deputy every Apostolic legate or anyone else bringing Apostolic letters from the Papal Curia. The Abbot of Derry and the Bishop of Derry were present when he signed, and they swore that all this was true. And the fact was corroborated, because when that same prince knew that we had come to his dominions, he wrote to the Abbot of Derry to fetch us, but with the utmost secrecy, lest word of it reach the ears of the Royal Deputy and he get into trouble for breaking the treaty. These letters and his signature we saw with our own eyes. But as we had been sent openly and had entered Ireland openly, we did not think it consistent with the dignity of the Apostolic See that we should be received in a secret interview, so we first postponed our visit to the Prince, and then, a few days later, left. He knew of our departure but did not ask for us.

Prince Oynell, after a manful resistance for several years to the King's fury, with the loss of thousands of men on each side, and after his lands had been devastated so that he hardly had a safe place to go to, submitted to the King and plighted his allegiance; and he was obliged to deliver up his son as hostage for observance of the treaty. This was about four or five months ago. . . . Prince Onell, like-wise, the third of the three, who is a little farther away from the Royal Deputy, has also been summoned to Dublin to do as the other two have done. If he refuses to go, he knows that the English will attack him. So, finally, almost all that part of Ireland to which we have been sent,—the wild region—the only part that remained faithful, has been, partly voluntarily, partly by force and fear, sub-jected to the King. If any corner remains free, it will probably soon be subjugated. As a token of this subju-gation, the King, who formerly called himself Lord of Ire-land, has now usurped the grander title of King of Ireland.

Besides, our particular purpose—as the very reverend Cardinals, who planned and directed our mission, told us—was to establish peace among the princes and lords of Ireland, to the end that by their union they should be better able to defend themselves from the King, and even make war on him, if necessary, for the sake of our religion, and of extending the Apostolic sway, which the King is wild to destroy. But we met some of the princes, Maculin [Mac-Quillan], Ochan [O'Cahen] and several others, and could see how desperate and incurable this disease of intestine feuds is. Their hatred of one another is rooted in the long past; and their ways are fierce and barbarous, brutal rather, to a degree unbelievable to any one who has not seen them. And if they do make peace, they violate it before the end of the month and things are worse than before; for then they have but one object—to steal cattle and horses, and set fire to one another's villages and churches. The most successful freebooter is the most respected. Of this we were witnesses, for while we were staying in the territory of lord Maculin, and not over two miles away from his house, he set out on a foray against his enemies, harried the countryside for sixty miles around, and drove back two thousand horses and cows, as we hear, burnt villages and killed many men. We think the only remedy for this evil, and for a general reformation of the island, is to have a Catholic monarch, whom they will be afraid of and obey, and who will punish criminals and establish justice. But that can't be done, for every prince would want to be king. . . .

Moreover, to come down to matters of less importance, almost all the monasteries of this island have been suppressed and the monks driven away, even in the comparatively safe region where we are. A few had been left as a favor to the princes, which was granted in an interlude of friendly relations. But now Odonel is daily beset to destroy the monasteries in his lands. The few monks still there are making ready to go into exile this summer, or to hide,—as they have repeatedly told us,—because they expect the English to come, erect forts and build houses, as the land would be very fertile, if it were cultivated. And the Irish bishops, who have been appointed in Rome, as soon as they land, are forced to surrender their Apostolic letters to the Deputy to be burned (together with their bearers); although sometimes—as we have been told in the case of one bishop—they obtain a new grant of the bishopric from the Deputy. Those who are conscientious and fear God, are compelled to fly from their bishoprics and hide in the woods, to wait till the King dies, like the Archbishop of Tuain, the Bishop of Kildare, and many others. . . .

However, we have come upon a few simple honest god-fearing folk in the island, who are devoted to the Apostolic See and have not bent the knee to Baal, and who have received us with kindness and respect, after the fashion of the country. They confessed and partook of the eucharist for the sake of the indulgences that are granted them, in accordance with the powers conferred upon us; but they are very poor and can hardly support themselves, how much less support us, especially as the princes, on whom we relied as the base of everything, are bound over to the King.

We granted pardons for bastardy and incest, of which there is an immense amount. Many of these pardons we gave gratis for the love of God. From a few we collected some money, but not much, because the country is incredibly poor and we did not wish to get their money but to lift them out of sin; for pardon, or no pardon, they would go on doing in the same way till the day of their deaths, as ample experience testifies. But all the money collected we gave away publicly to the poor or to some pious charities, to the great astonishment and edification of the bishops who saw it, and of others who heard of it.

So, we considered all the circumstances:—there was no safe place to stay; the English were ready to bribe the Irish to deliver us up; there was no city nor town; there was no hope of making peace between the princes, and they had sworn allegiance to the King, honestly or not; it was not consistent with the dignity of the Apostolic See to conceal ourselves in the woods and other hiding places; and we had been commanded by the Cardinals, deputed to arrange our mission, that if we found Ireland in the state in which we did, to shake the dust off our feet and return; and besides, many honorable Irishmen advised us to leave for the sake of our lives and the dignity of the Apostolic See; and our consciences told us not to run the risk of probable death without hope of doing any good. So for all these reasons we decided to go back to Scotland, etc., etc. . . .

Your unworthy servants,
PASCHASIUS BROËT
ALPHONSUS SALMERÓN.

CHAPTER XXIII

THE Society of Jesus, as the last chapter shows, started upon its world-wide career almost at once, even before the proposed charter had been granted. Chance, or Providence, seemed to have a trick of holding out its hand to Ignatius, and each time he grasped it. King John of Portugal, a very pious and somewhat superstitious prince, felt troubled in conscience at the thought of all the heathen in his far-flung empire, and asked Dr. Govea, principal of the College of Sainte-Barbe, how he should get missionaries; or, perhaps the first suggestion came from Govea. At any rate Dr. Govea bade him apply to Loyola. As a consequence, Xavier and Rodriguez were assigned to this duty; but upon their arrival in Lisbon, they started so lively a religious revival, that King, nobles and clergy wished them to stay in Portugal. It was finally decided to keep Rodriguez and send Xavier to India. This was done. Xavier sailed in April, 1541, while Rodriguez remained as head of the Jesuit mission in Portugal.

It is not my purpose to say more of this Portuguese mission than may be necessary to give an idea of Loyola's generalship. The Jesuit Fathers became very much the fashion, they were known as the "apostles," and all the world went to hear them preach; no one but a Turk, it was said, would stay away. Many new recruits of high social position joined them, among others a young nobleman, Louis Gonzalez de Camara, to whom Ignatius dictated the *Memoirs* that I have quoted so often. In spite of this success, however, there were trials and vexations. Satan, as the Fathers often noticed, went about scattering tares among the good seed. Rodriguez proved to be the wrong man for head of a mission. Ignatius, however, is

not to be blamed for the appointment, as Rodriguez had
been selected to go to India, quite a different task; but having been detained by the King and become a court favorite,
it would have been highly impolitic, very likely impossible,
to have put in any one else to fill what was virtually the
office of Provincial for Portugal.

It is difficult for our generation to pass judgment upon
what was regarded as saintliness four hundred years ago;
for very much of what in those days to passionate pilgrims, trudging through the valley of preparation, seemed
a sort of solemn ritual, to us looks fanatical, or even, supposing that we lack imaginative sympathy, childish and
silly. What was once a language of palpitating emotion is
now no more than a series of fantastic hieroglyphs. In
this case, strange doings went on among the students of the
newly founded, and highly successful, Jesuit College at
Coimbra. I will set forth the facts as they appeared to
the principal of the college, Father Martin Santa Cruz.
The following letter was written by his secretary:

To Father Peter Favre

COIMBRA, August, 1545.

May Jesus Christ keep you.

Father Santa Cruz being too busy to write as fully to you
as he wished, has bidden me write on his behalf, to give you
an account of some things that have taken place among us
here concerning mortifications and exercises in humility
that some brothers of this college have performed, in part
with permission of Father Rodriguez, who was with us at
that time, and also in part by his express command.

The beginning of these things was in this wise. Antonio
Figueredo [one of the students] got the idea of carrying
into the lecture room a dead man's skull, which Cardoso
[another student] had in his room. Figueredo felt some
repugnance to do this because of the shame involved, but
out of a wish to overcome that feeling, after consulting
Christopher Leyton [also a student], he took the skull into
class, put it in front of him on a bench, and remained gazing

at it for the two hours while the lesson lasted, in presence of everybody. When Father Rodriguez got home, as this had been done without his permission, he ordered both him and Christopher Leyton, who had assented to the plan, to take the death's head and go to Figueredo's mother's house, in the city, and tell her on their knees the whole story, asking forgiveness for the shame her son had brought upon her. When they came back, after doing as they had been told, they found that they were not allowed to enter, so both sat down in the street near the door, where they stayed till near dark, when the Rector of the University, on his way home, espied them sitting on the ground. Guessing what the trouble was, he sent his chaplain to Father Rodriguez, to say that he had no doubt that the men deserved to stay there for some fault they had committed, but, as this was the first favor he had asked, perhaps he might consent to pardon them, and that he himself was much edified to have seen them in this plight. Father Rodriguez forgave them, and sent the Rector word by the same chaplain of his reason for forbidding them to come in.

An order was given to all the brothers not to speak to them until they received permission to do so, and so the two were for several days without a word from anybody. One day Figueredo entered the refectory while the brothers were at dinner, barefoot, bare-headed, with his hands tied and a cord round his neck, and his tongue tied by the same cord between two sticks. Father Rodriguez bade him leave the room because he had come in such a fashion without permission. That same day, at supper, Christopher Leyton (who had approved of taking the skull into the lecture room) started to come into the refectory, stripped to the waist, scourge in hand, barefoot, and a rope round his neck. As soon as he saw him, Father Rodriguez sent him back, because he acted without permission. They invented these acts of penitence in order that Father Rodriguez should permit conversation again with the brothers.

The letter goes on to tell of a young musician, who had been rejected by Father Rodriguez because of his feeble con-

stitution. Many religious organizations were eager to receive him for his musical talents, but he had a pious desire
to go where such talents were not valued; and, therefore,
in the hope to overcome Father Rodriguez's unwillingness,
he walked all through the town, carrying a death's head,
and asking the crowd of boys who followed him please to
kick him or throw stones at him. This conduct effected his
purpose; he was admitted to the Jesuit college, where, instead of touching musical keys, he handled heavy logs, and
burned his fingers cooking. Other students went upon
menial errands, bare-headed, in ragged clothes, or with
neither cloak nor shoes, and did other unconventional
things. For instance, one student lost a shoe in the street,
and went back crying out, "Who has found a shoe?" Others
went round the streets, ringing a bell and shouting: "Hell
for all those who are in mortal sin!" Others carried bas-
kets, begging for victuals, till the town officers hurried up
to relieve such destitution. One Sunday ten or twelve students went through the town, ringing a bell, and yelling:
"Sinners, depart from sin; for ye must die!" And once
while the brothers sat at dinner Father Rodriguez sent one
of them to the church for holy water; the brother fetched
it and then walked round the table, saying *Miserere mei*,
and sprinkled all the brothers one by one. And again, one
brother, in the middle of dinner, having been told to do so
by Father Rodriguez, gave a great slap on the table saying,
Conclusum est contra manicheos, and started an argument.
And, to give a final instance, a lad from the college went to
the square, and there, half naked, tied himself to a pillar,
and stood for some time, crying out, "O Lord Jesus, who for
our sins wast tied to a pillar in Pilate's house, forgive the
sins of this city!"

The writer adds that some people murmured at some
of these proceedings, but refrains from all comment himself. Rodriguez was the superior of Father Santa Cruz, and
any criticism would have been improper. However, as the
letter was written at about the time when Ignatius, troubled
by reports from Portugal, had arranged matters so that
Rodriguez—ostensibly for other reasons—should go to

Rome, it seems plain that Santa Cruz was quite out of sympathy with these novel methods of self-mortification. He was not alone in this opinion. A Flemish Father at the College, also wrote Lefèvre a long letter to tell him the same story.

That these extravagances were, in part at least, the causes of the complaints against Rodriguez, is plain from a letter that he wrote some time afterwards to Ignatius, explaining the disagreement between himself and Santa Cruz, Strada, and Lefèvre, who all disapproved of the extreme mortifications that the students at Coimbra put upon themselves. Rodriguez maintained that the Society was founded on contempt for the world, that it was necessary to be fools for Christ's sake, and to wish for the world's derision, for "God hath chosen the foolish things of the world to confound the wise, and the weak things of the world to confound the things which are mighty; and base things of the world, and things which are despised hath God chosen"(1 Cor. I, 27, 28). For this reason he had bidden the students despise the world, and to undergo hardships and mortifications, that would increase their strength. As a consequence there was intense fervor among the students,—they were like lions— such as there had been among the disciples of Christ at Pentecost. Certainly, he says, it is far more in accordance with the flesh to give up such self-mortification than to submit to it, and yet, nevertheless, the superiors of the College (his critics) have greater trouble to stop the students than to incite them to it. Santa Cruz and Strada are fearful lest the college be misjudged and disapproved of. "I cite St. Francis (he says); Strada answers that 'St. Francis acted under a special inspiration from God, and that these practices will do when another St. Francis comes, or God grants a fresh inspiration.' The influence of Strada and Lefèvre has cooled the fine fervor, and so *factum est prælium magnum* in the college. Strada says that there are more mortifications in Portugal than the first Fathers ever suffered, and Santa Cruz quotes Lefèvre that our mortifications mortify him in Castile. *'El inimigo sembró esta mala simiente'* (It is the Devil that sows this seed.)" He adds that he has made Luis Gonzalez de Camara rector, and concludes by asking Ignatius to write his opinion. This Ignatius did, and the letter is an admirable exposition of his method of procedure.

The case was difficult. Rodriguez was one of the *primeros padres,* he had the favor of the King and Queen, he was virtually the creator of the college in question, he was a man of peculiar qualities, full of zeal and self-confidence. On the other hand, the men of better judgment were opposed to him, and it was to be feared, and justly as events proved, that if Rodriguez were given a free hand for his extravagant zeal, he would look upon freedom of action as his right. Here is Loyola's letter:

To the Fathers and Brothers at Coimbra

ROME, May 7, 1547.

May the grace and everlasting love of Christ our Lord be with us and bless us. Amen.

[Ignatius begins with an elaborate prologue. He sets forth his deep satisfaction with the news of their zeal and desire to serve the Lord, says what great expectations they have raised, and yet how difficult it will be to live up to them, and dwells on their special obligation to be faithful and diligent.] And above all I should wish that you have no motives other than the pure love of Christ and desire for His honor and for the salvation of the souls that He redeemed, because you are His soldiers, in His Company, by a special title and with special pay. I say *special,* because there are many general reasons that oblige you to render Him honor and do Him service. All that you have and are, is your pay; He gave you life and being, and all the qualities and faculties of your minds and bodies, and all external things, and He preserves them. Your pay is the spiritual gift of His grace, which out of His bounty and goodness He has conferred on you and continues to confer, even when you are disobedient and rebellious. Your pay is the inestimable worth of His glory, which, with no advantage to Himself, He has promised you and has prepared for you.

. . . Your pay is all the universe and all that in it is, corporeal and spiritual, because He has caused to minister
unto us not only all that is underneath the sky, but also His
most glorious court, not excepting any of the celestial
hierarchy—'Are they not all ministering spirits, sent forth
to minister for them who shall be heirs of salvation?' (Heb.
I, 14). And as if that sum of wages was not enough, He
made Himself your pay, becoming our brother in the flesh,
paying for our salvation on the cross, and by the eucharist,
upholding and accompanying our pilgrimage. What a
caitiff soldier must he be, whom such wages will not stir to
work for the honor of such a Prince?

[And Loyola continues to lay solemn emphasis upon the
personal debt and the grave responsibility of a soldier of
Christ, how every one must give devoted, unstinted, un-
measured, service]:

But what I have said up to now to wake up them that
slumbered, or hurry up those that might tarry on the way,
must not be interpreted as an approval of the extreme contrary of indiscreet fervor. St. Paul says (Rom. XII, 1),
'Your *reasonable* service' for he knew that the psalmist's
words were true (Psalm CXVIII, 4) 'The King's strength
loveth *judgment*' i. e. discretion, and also that which is said
allegorically in Leviticus, 'Every oblation of thy meat offering shalt thou season with salt' (II, 13). And, as St.
Bernard says, 'The enemy has no contrivance so apt to take
the charity from the heart, as pricking it on to proceed
rashly and not according to spiritual reasonableness.' The
philosopher's counsel, *Ne quid nimis,* should be observed in
all things, even in matters of righteousness, and we read in
Ecclesiastes, *Noli esse justus nimium*—Be not righteous
overmuch (VII, 16). If moderation be not observed, then
good is turned into evil, and virtue into vice, and many
unseemly things follow, contrary to the purpose of him
that oversteps.

First. One cannot serve God without some restraint; a
horse exhausted by his first stages cannot finish his journey,
and others have to take care of him.

Second. That which is gained with immoderate eagerness is not kept, as the Bible says: "Wealth gotten by vanity shall be diminished" (Prov. XIII, 11). And not only is it diminished, but it is a stumbling matter: "He that hasteneth with his feet, sinneth" (Prov. XIX, 2), and if he falls, the greater the height the greater the danger, for he will not stop till he reach the bottom of the stairs.

Third. Avoid the risk of overloading your boat; for though it be dangerous to take it empty, for it will flounder about amid temptations, do not load it so that it shall sink.

Fourth. It may come about, that in crucifying the old man, you crucify the new, so that from sheer weakness he cannot practise the virtues. . . .

Besides, there are other inconveniences, such as carrying weapons so heavy that you cannot use them, as David with Saul's armor; or putting on spurs, but no bridle, to ride a fiery horse. So you see that discretion is necessary, in order to keep virtuous practices between the two extremes.

And after quoting various proverbial sayings, such as Spaniards delighted in, Ignatius continues: "I would not have you think from the things I have just written, that I do not approve of what has been told me of your mortifications; for I know that the saints made use of such, and of other holy follies *(locuras sanctas)*, to their advantage, and that they are useful in order to overcome self and acquire grace, especially in the beginning; but for those who have most control over self-love, what I have written concerning the middle way of discretion, I hold to be the better course, not forgetting obedience, which I commend to you most earnestly, and that summary of all virtue, which Jesus Christ enjoins 'This is my Commandment, that ye love one another' " (St. John, XV, 12). And he concludes with the general rule that the way to help one's fellows is to practise virtue and set an example of a truly Christian life.

I do not think that rebuke could be expressed more tactfully or more kindly, than in this letter. Rodriguez, however, did not profit by it as he should have done. His behaviour caused much dissatisfaction, and he was finally recalled and sent into a sort of exile near Venice. This is a lamentable episode, which I need not expatiate upon; and, after all, it was but an episode in a long life, dedicated to the service of what he believed to be the cause of righteousness.

CHAPTER XXIV

SPAIN AND FRANCE

Before the charter was granted Ignatius had established the headquarters of the Society in Rome, and he himself always lived there, never going away, except for exceedingly brief absences, such as a visit to the Pope at Tivoli, all his life. From the very first he had an unbounded faith in the future of the Society—*Romæ Ego vobis propitius ero* always rang in his ears—and, as a consequence, he never entertained the thought of establishing its seat of government in any place but Rome, the capital of Christendom, the abode of the Supreme Pontiff. In Rome he had many local duties, but I shall defer an account of them, until I shall have completed my little sketch of the beginnings of the Society in Europe and across the seas.

To my mind the most brilliant achievement of these First Fathers was in Spain; Xavier's mission in India and Japan impresses the imagination more, but his heroic labors secured much less solid and permanent results. It is characteristic of Ignatius that he did not launch the Spanish campaign until chance circumstances had given the Society a foothold there; this was partly because the Fathers had their hands full with what they had to do in Italy, Germany, and elsewhere, and it was not Loyola's way to undertake more than he was likely to accomplish; and partly, because he waited for some sign that he could interpret as the finger of God pointing to what he should do. Perhaps his mind lacked inventiveness, did not prowl about to find new matter for thought and action, but lay couchant waiting for opportunity to come in its way. It was so with the missions to Portugal and India. However, as soon as first one, and then a second, Jesuit happened to go to Spain,

244

and reported that the harvest was ripe for the reapers, Ignatius directed the campaign with the foresight and thoroughness that were the two wings of his genius. He understood better than anybody else that the surest way to beat back heretics to the north and infidels to the east, was not to send theologians, preachers, or missionaries to the confines of Catholic Christendom where the enemy were, though that was well, but rather to rouse the enthusiasm and resolution of the faithful to the fighting pitch throughout the length and breadth of Catholic lands. Then, as now, international issues were to be determined by the faith and pertinacity of the populations at home. If the Roman Church was to maintain itself against the Teutonic rebels, it needs must draw upon stores of religious energy in the Latin lands and chiefly in Spain, which, flushed with adventure and self-confidence, was ready to answer the call of any leader that should touch her imagination. As Menendez y Pelayo says, Spain put herself at the head of the Catholic party, and kept back the northern flood within the dykes that it has never passed; and it would be rash to deny that the Jesuits are entitled to the lion's share of the credit for her doing so.

The chance circumstances to which I alluded are these: A young relation of Loyola's, Antonio de Araoz, who had recently joined the Society, went to Spain in the year 1539, to attend to some family matters. Loyola undoubtedly gave him instructions, bade him reconnoitre the ground and report his observations. Two years later Dr. Ortiz had occasion to go from Germany back to Spain on some ecclesiastical matters, and took Pierre Lefèvre with him. These were the haphazard causes that laid the first foundation for the Jesuit missions in Spain. Both Fathers were highly accomplished missionaries; they knew their business, and faithfully followed Loyola's tactics. They preached, they heard confession, they visited the sick, they gave the *Spiritual Exercises,* and, where it was possible, they made friends with people of importance. Ignatius never lost sight of the fact that power, position, and wealth are potent factors for good as well as for evil, and always took the greatest pains, and charged his disciples to do the same, to win the favor and assistance of princes and noblemen. I shall not recount the doings of Father Araoz and Father Lefèvre in Spain, or of their comrades and followers. The directing mind of Loyola was always there; his will was their North Star. One fact deserves to be recorded, because it shows how soon Loyola's reputation had reached his native province. When Araoz went to Azpeitia to preach, the people flocked in multitudes from all the villages roundabout to hear him, the church could not hold a tithe of the congregation. A pulpit was set up in the open, and listeners climbed into trees and on the roofs of houses.

Araoz and Lefèvre led the way, but new members, Nadal Villanueva, Miron, Oviedo, and others, ably seconded them. Suffice it to say that within fifteen years, in Loyola's own lifetime, colleges had been founded, most of them no doubt in a small way, at Alcalá, Valladolid, Valencia, Gandia, Barcelona, Salamanca, Medina del Campo, Onato, Cordoba, Avila, Burgos, Zaragoza, and elsewhere. This extraordinary success was due to several co-operating causes: the directing genius of Ignatius; the zeal, devotion, tact and ability of the missionaries; the favor of princes; the accession of Francis Borgia, duke of Gandia; and the temperamental ardor of the Spanish people that to so great an extent found its outlet in religion.

Francis Borgia was one of the principal nobles of Aragon, great-grandson to Rodrigo Borgia (Pope Alexander VI, the father of Cæsar and Lucretia,) and also to King Ferdinand, the husband of Queen Isabella. No Spanish lineage could be more illustrious. He was a serious, pious, hard-working, painstaking, conscientious man. On the death of his wife, he laid aside his dukedom, and asking Lefèvre's advice, decided to become a Jesuit. It was a great day for the young Order when the descendant of a line of kings dismounted at its house in Rome and took up his lodgings there. He stayed three months, "in deep humility and self-abnegation, and in complete obedience and reverence to Padre Ignacio"; and when Ignatius dined in his apartment, he waited on the table, serving the meats and pouring the wine, and he

proposed to wash the dishes, but Ignatius interfered. His
conversion is evidence of the religious ardor of the Spanish
people at this time, which, as I have said, favored the
Jesuits so greatly. But before dropping the subject of
Spain and passing on to France, I shall cite another instance
of this religious ardor, more celebrated even than Borgia's.

I quote from St. Theresa's autobiography, for her Jesuit
confessors serve to connect her with the Society. She was a
genius and of an emotional sensibility far beyond ordinary
people; nevertheless, the intensity of her feelings will serve
as an index to show how deeply religious a society must
have been in order to provide a soil in which such feelings
could germinate and find superabundant nutriment.   At
this time she was a woman of thirty.   I take the following
passage from her own account of what she felt when she
entered the Carmelite order some ten years before:

The day I put on the nun's dress, God enlightened me
with a refulgent light; I understood how much He favors
those who conquer themselves in order to serve Him. . . .
A happiness so pure flowed over my soul that nothing has
ever been able to dry it up. . . . All the practices of religious life became a source of delight to me. . . . Even in
this life the Divine Master is pleased to repay a great courage in His service by intimate joys, known only to the souls
that taste their ineffable sweetness. . . . At the end of nine
months, Our Lord, not content with the delights He had
accorded me, deigned to lift me up to the orison of contemplation, and sometimes even to the orison of union. . . .
I was not twenty years old, and yet I trampled down under
my feet, methought, a conquered world. . . . Here is my
way of praying.   I tried, all I could, to consider with atten-
tive sight, our Master Jesus Christ, as present in the background of my soul.   Whenever I meditated upon a mystery
in His life, I pictured it in this inner shrine. . . . However
defective and imperfect were my works, my adorable Master
deigned to better them, and give them worth.   As to my
faults and sins, He hastened to throw a veil over them. . . .
At that time my soul habitually enjoyed an intoxicating

delight in God, and my sweetest pleasure—the only subject of my conversation—was to talk of Him.

The success of the Jesuits, however, was not obtained without great opposition. Melchior Cano, the Dominican professor at Salamanca, with whom Lainez afterwards, at the Council of Trent, lost his temper, was the most violent. The Archbishop of Toledo, Primate of Spain, was also very down on them. The real reason for this opposition was jealousy and Spanish conservatism; but there may also have been some truth in the ostensible reasons put forward. Adversaries said that the Jesuits introduced innovations; that they condemned other Orders, at least by implication, in that they did not adopt a distinctive dress, as other Orders did, and did not deign to receive monks from other Orders; that they did not celebrate the musical service as all other Orders did; that they arrogantly assumed the name of Jesus, as if it were personal to themselves; that they omitted or skimped corporal penance—this sounds like an odd accusation, and is probably one of the reasons why Jesuit biographies are so full of flagellations, vigils, fasts, etc.—that they refused ecclesiastical dignities, that they taught suspicious spiritual exercises, and so forth.

The Society had powerful friends and proved too strong for professor and Primate. I shall say no more of these troubles except to quote from a letter that Ignatius wrote to the Archbishop, after the latter had given way, for it shows how courteous, almost subservient, his manners were in dealing with persons in high place who had power to help or hinder the work of the Society. It was a definite part of his policy—based perhaps on a sense of Christian duty, but as to that I do not feel clear—to do all he could, after a quarrel, to prevent leaving wounded feelings behind, and, more than that, to turn his old adversary into a new friend. Let me caution the reader against imagining that there is any irony or sarcasm in these mellifluous sentences:

ROME, June 1, 1552.

My very illustrious and reverend Lord:

. . . Although it is a new thing for me to write to your

Lordship, it should not be a new thing for any one to feel and to show gratitude for favors received, and as I have learned of those that your Lordship bestowed upon our humble Society a little while ago, I not only hold myself deeply obliged to ask the Divine Goodness to reward them with a very generous and everlasting reward; but it also seems to me my duty while writing, I do not say to give thanks, for I leave that to God's love, but rather to show to your Lordship that you have not done those favors to ungrateful men. And though there is little that our poor Order can do for one whom God has raised to so high an estate in His Church, nevertheless I beseech your Lordship to consider us all as wholly devoted to you in the Lord, and to make use of us as such for the greater glory of His divine majesty. And in token that we consider your Lordship our lord and father, and always shall, I am writing to our brothers there, not to admit, either in Alcalá or anywhere else in Spain, anybody to our Society who is not satisfactory to your Lordship, and although the Apostolic See has granted us many privileges in order to aid souls, I am also writing not to make use of those privileges except so far as your Lordship shall think we had better do so for the purpose of helping you carry some little portion of the heavy load that God has laid upon your Lordship. For as I attribute the dealings that passed between us before you were informed of our ways and proceedings, to your Lordship's great zeal for God's service, so, now that you are informed, I am persuaded that your Lordship will be our protector and father, etc., etc.

Your Lordship's humble servant in the Lord,

IGNATIUS.

In France the Society was slow, at least in comparison with its success in Spain, to gain a foothold. The antagonism between the two countries was largely responsible for this; but also, as I have said, Loyola's policy was to refrain from the initiative. He preferred to wait for Providence to lead the way. At first his disciples went to Paris solely for the sake of study. Don Diego Eguia conducted a small company of young men there in the spring of 1540; others soon joined them. Some of them became conspicuous in the early history of the Order, Diego Miron, Francisco de Rojas, Francisco and Antonio Estrada, and Pedro de Ribadeneira, a lad of fifteen, who afterwards wrote Loyola's life. These students were very poor, and had to eke out what funds could be spared for their use, with scholarships and odds and ends of charity. They entered the College of the Lombards, where poor Italians were received gratis, and "the Italian charity pensioners [I quote this in fulfillment of my promise to repeat whatever instances of dissimulation I may come across] took the others into their rooms as fellow lodgers, without letting the outside students know that they belonged to a religious order." They had not been settled in this college a year when war again broke out between Francis I and the Emperor, and the Spanish students either were obliged, or found it prudent, to make haste across the border into Belgium, where they founded a Jesuit community at Louvain.

The real beginning of the establishment in France took place at Trent, where Guillaume Duprat, bishop of Clermont, made the acquaintance of Father Jay, as well as of Lainez and Salmerón. Everybody who met Claude Jay, perceived that he was a saint. He told Duprat about the Society, and of its students who desired to get a theological education, and Duprat put a house in Paris at their disposition, and thus started the College of Clermont. Later, the bishop founded another college at the University of Billon in Auvergne. Another, and perhaps no less significant, consequence of the bishop's good graces was the advice that Loyola should make the acquaintance of Charles de Guise, Cardinal of Lorraine, who went to Rome to attend the conclave on the death of Paul III. Ignatius, as I have said, always grasped the opportunity which a favoring Providence, or kindly chance, extended. He went to pay his respects; the call was returned, and the Cardinal promised to be the protector of the Order in France. There was great need of powerful protection. The bishop of Paris, Eustache du Bellay, cousin of Cardinal Jean du Bellay, the Sorbonne,

and the Parlement, were united in opposition.   The Society
tried in vain for years to obtain legal sanction.   The Sorbonne said:

This new Society, which has assumed the name of Jesus,
and takes in without discrimination all sorts of people, no
matter whether they are criminals, bastards, or infamous,
. . . seems to wrong the honor of the monastic profession;
it takes all the strength out of the laborious, pious and most
necessary, practice of the virtues, out of abstinence, out of
ritual, and of austerity; it deprives lords ecclesiastical and
lords temporal of their rights, and causes vexation to both;
it breeds law-suits, disputes, quarrels, jealousies, separa-
tions, and schisms. . . . It appears to be a source of danger
in the matter of Faith, disturbs the peace of the Church,
hurts the monastic profession, and is more apt to destroy
than to edify.

This decree was a hard blow.   Several younger members
of the Society in Rome,—Nadal, Olave and Frusio,—were
outraged and indignant; they were hot to publish an angry
denial of these charges, and fell to discussing who should
write it.   They reckoned without their host.   Ignatius
would not hear of any such thing.   One always finds him
with the double aspect of Christian charity and worldly
prudence, always obedient to both clauses of Christ's injunction: "Be ye wise as serpents, harmless as doves."   He
used to say: "It is better not to write words that bite."
When the hot heads crowded about him, he quoted the
gospel: "My peace I give you, my peace I leave you," and
said how much he disapproved of the passions and hard
feelings that were sown by books and pamphlets, and did
not think that the Society should defend itself in any such
fashion, nor was it prudent to get into permanent disfavor
with the University.   Even when somebody suggested that
it would be well to write a friendly letter, and that some
graduate of the University should be the writer, Ignatius
thought it better not.   He told Ribadeneira afterwards,
that with God's grace the Society would live long, and that

the University of Paris was eternal and of great authority, and it would not be well to build up a perpetual enmity between the Society and the University. The vindication he had in mind, was to write to all the members of the Society, stationed all over, wherever they were, without telling the reason, and bid them request kings, princes, dignitaries, spiritual and temporal, and the universities, to collect information concerning the lives and conduct of the members of the Society in their respective domains, and to certify under seal whatever reports they received, whether to the credit of the Society or not, and to send such reports to the General of the Order, and that when those documents came, he would submit them to the Pope (for the Pope was concerned in the matter since he had confirmed the Society and granted it privileges), and then it would appear which was of greater weight, the decree of the University of Paris or the concordant testimony of all the world.

So it was done. Kings, dukes, archbishops, bishops, inquisitors, magistrates and universities, sent in most flattering reports, as may be seen in the mighty volume, Acta Sanctorum, VII Julii. And in due time, but not till years after Loyola's death, the Society triumphed over its enemies and obtained whatever legal authority was necessary for it in France.

CHAPTER XXV

AN important episode in the early history of the Society was its participation in the Council of Trent. This famous assembly, after many vain discussions and proposals, finally met together in 1545, and formally opened its proceedings in the month of December. The first demand for it had come from Luther when he was condemned at the Diet of Augsburg, and since then requests, appeals, supplications had been addressed to Pope and Emperor from all over Christendom. At first the gravity of the Lutheran movement was not understood, and pious people had no doubt that if an ecumenical council would reform the monastic orders, check the sale of indulgences, suppress the extortions of the Roman courts, and in general correct the most crying abuses, then the German malcontents would return of themselves. But the Lutherans attacked dogmas as well as ecclesiastical practices, and it became evident that a council, if it was to effect a reconciliation, must deal with matters of creed as well as of practices, must discover some way to grant a certain latitude of belief, to broaden this doctrine, modify that, and leave some discretion to the individual mind and conscience; nevertheless, hopeful Catholics continued to believe that, if passion and prejudice were laid aside, the traditional order might be restored, and one flock still herd together under one shepherd. But for any such hopes matters had gone wrong from the beginning. Passion and prejudice were not laid aside; on the contrary they grew greater and more violent. And yet if it had been possible to isolate ecclesiastical and religious questions from politics, compromise and reunion might perhaps have been accomplished; but politics intermeddled from the first. Charles V, good Catholic though he was, thought that it belonged to him as Emperor to decide where a council should be held, and how; nor was he blind to the political advantages to be got from the Lutheran revolt in his dealings with the Pope, and therefore wished to effect the reconciliation in his own way. The King of France, for his part, had interests at stake; the preponderance of the imperial power was a cause of constant solicitude, and he opposed any action that would confer upon that power greater unity and strength. His policy was to face both ways; to aid and abet the Lutheran princes and also to keep friends with the Holy See, for it was essential to have the papal support in his struggle with the Emperor for possession of Milan. This double dealing was a delicate matter, and, for the most part, led him to put obstacles in the way of a council, openly or in secret. The Protestant princes, when they were weak, appealed to an ecumenical council; but they approached the matter cautiously, they would not accept a council that was to be under the Pope's thumb, and, as an essential preliminary, since the schism was a German affair, they demanded that it be held in Germany. Finally, when they found themselves strong enough, they jeered at all the Catholic overtures. Paul III also was on his guard. Although a *grand seigneur,* with tastes acquired under Alexander VI and Leo X, and hampered by a passion to promote the worldly interests of his grandchildren, he was a genuine reformer, and sought to promote the best interests of religion, as he saw it. He understood the situation in Germany far better than Clement VII had done, and recognized that sweeping reforms must constitute an essential part in any scheme of reconciliation. He was ready to go great lengths in order to stop the mouth of criticism and deprive secession of plausibility. A Council was not merely the best plan, but the only possible plan; otherwise Germany might follow the example of England, hold a national synod and establish a national church. The project, however, was hedged about by difficulties. The Pope wished to suppress the Lutheran rebellion and re-establish papal jurisdiction throughout Germany, yet he did not wish the Emperor to have any more power than he had, and it was as plain as

the sun at noon that with a united and loyal Germany behind him, the Emperor would have the continent of
Europe, including the papacy, at his feet. Besides, there
might be trouble lest a convocation of bishops, supported
by the Emperor and the King of France, should wish to
increase their power at the expense of the papacy. Altogether a great deal of circumspection was necessary. His
wish was for the Council to busy itself mainly with a definition of the doctrines of the Church and a refutation of
Protestant errors, and to deal with ecclesiastical reforms as
discreetly as possible; for, though he honestly wished to
purify the Church, nevertheless, as a practical politician, he
feared a too sudden eradication of long established abuses.
Besides, he wished to keep all these matters in his own
hands. To this end, he made an adroit use of his influence
and authority. He hoped, in the first place, to set up a
bulwark against Protestantism and win over those who
might be wavering between the new order and the old, and
in the second, to defend the papacy from all attempts to
clip and trim its power, and even to bring it forth from the
ordeal in greater strength and vigor than before, and by
accomplishing all this, outgeneral both the Emperor and
the King of France. With reference to that part of his
plan that concerned the theological duties of the Council, he
had recourse to the young Order, whose members had
pledged themselves to a devout obedience to the Holy See,
and asked Ignatius to select three of them to act as his representative theologians at the Council. Ignatius appointed
Lefèvre, Lainez and Salmerón; Lefèvre died soon afterwards
and the other two went alone.

When they set forth, Ignatius gave them, in his method-
ical way, a list of instructions for their conduct. It seems
certain from these instructions that neither he nor they
foresaw just the nature or the importance of the rôle they
were to play; evidently, all anticipated little more than that
the representatives were to attend an assembly of the
ecclesiastical notables of Latin Christendom, where they
would be seen and heard, and that the Society would be
judged by their behaviour. The instructions were ele-

mentary. Ignatius knew that the two men were humble-minded, and would not feel hurt by elementary counsels; and if, contrary to his belief, they were not properly humble, as became members of the Order, it was his duty to administer such discipline to their vanity as would be for their good. Since Loyola's method here of dealing with his subordinates is characteristic, and the matter of the Council important, I shall give an outline of these instructions:

He begins by saying that as a general rule, when people discuss spiritual things for spiritual advantage, they benefit by such discussion; nevertheless, members of the Society stand on a peculiar footing, and must be on their guard, otherwise more harm than good will befall, and therefore it will be prudent to think beforehand over the best methods to be pursued. The rules he shall lay down are not to be taken too literally, rather as a set of suggestions that may be modified to suit shifting circumstances. As was his custom, Ignatius, in giving advice looked upon the matter before him as if he were to be the actor, and often says, instead of "you should do this or that," "I would do so and so."

    I. I should be slow to speak, and then only after reflection, and in a friendly spirit; especially on any matters that may come up for discussion before the Council.

    II. And, just as it is profitable to be slow to speak, so it is profitable to listen quietly, in order to understand the kind of mind the speakers have, their feelings, their wills, and be the better able to speak in answer—or to remain silent.

    III. Whenever you speak upon the general subject under discussion,—or whether you branch off from it—it is a good thing to enumerate the reasons on both sides, in order not to appear set in your own opinion; and, at the same time try not to annoy any one.

    IV. I should not adduce any persons, especially if they are persons of consequence, as my authorities, except in matters thoroughly considered, making myself friendly with all, but not too much of a partisan of anybody's.

V. When the matters under discussion are so plainly right that one neither could nor should hold one's tongue, one should give one's opinion with the utmost possible calmness and modesty, and end with *salvo meliori judicio*—subject to a wiser opinion.

VI. Finally, if I wished to speak in a discussion upon qualities acquired or divinely imparted, I should not consider my own leisure, nor hurry for lack of time, nor regard my personal convenience, but suit the convenience of the other person, in order to arouse him to the greater glory of God.

After these preliminary counsels, Ignatius goes on to say that the best they can do for the greater glory of God is to preach, to hear confession, to read the Bible, teach boys, give the *Exercises,* visit the poor in hospitals, exhort, and so forth, each according to his talents and aptitudes, and to pray God—and urge others to do so, too,—to pour His divine spirit upon all members of the Council. When preaching, they are not to touch on matters upon which Protestants and Catholics differ, but to confine themselves to morals and attendance at Church, exhorting the congregation to a sense of spiritual realities and to a love of God, but they are to speak frequently of the Council, and always at the end of a sermon, and to say a prayer for it. And he concludes with rules for their own spiritual welfare: They are to set apart an hour in the evening to tell one another what has been done during the day and what had better be undertaken on the following day; and to come to an agreement, whether as to things past or future, whether by voting, or in any other way. And, each in turn is to ask the others to correct him as they think best, and he is not to answer back, unless they ask him to justify what he has been corrected for. In the morning, resolutions are to be made, and twice a day self-examination as to the performance of those resolutions. These last few rules, I conjecture, made a part of the instructions given whenever several Fathers went on any mission together. Ignatius foresaw that the delegated Fathers would require a little time to look about and adjust themselves, so the instructions were not to go into effect until five days after their arrival.

Lainez and Salmerón reached Trent in May, 1546,—why they did not go sooner, I don't know—; Claude Jay was also present, as procurator for the Cardinal of Augsburg, and Father Covillon, a new member of the Society, as theologian for the Duke of Bavaria. The Council, even at its best, hardly deserves the term *ecumenical*, for there were no Protestants there, and no delegates, so far as I remember, from Oriental Christendom, and even after several months there were but about three score voting members, some forty Italian prelates, twenty Spaniards, and a few scattering from here and there, such as Reginald Pole, a refugee from England, and Robert Wauchope, the titular Archbishop of Armagh. Under the system of organization adopted, only cardinals, bishops, heads of religious orders, and some abbots, possessed the right to vote. Theologians, such as Lainez and Salmerón, were there to give their opinions on matters laid before them, but with no further privilege.

Lainez and Salmerón conducted themselves with extreme prudence, keeping modestly in the background; they studied the matters that were to come up before the Council, made the best of what opportunities they got to express their views to one prelate or another in private conversation or by brief letters, and spent their time going about to hear confessions, or tending the sick and the poor. It was some little time before they received license to preach. They attended certain subdivisions of the Council that considered the definition of dogma, and when they were asked to give their opinions, succeeded in doing so "to the satisfaction of their hearers, both prelates and theologians," and soon found themselves looked upon with interest and kindness. By July they were able to feel that they were of service to the Council, and had brought distinction and good repute *(lustre y odor)* to the Company; French, Spanish and Italian bishops showed them favors, and expressed a wish to have members established in their dioceses; and various dignitaries, before voting, would come to them for advice.

At a session of the Congregation of Theologians, held in October, Lainez greatly distinguished himself. The Council had defined certain fundamental dogmas, such as original sin, and had taken up the burning question of Justification. There was no one present to defend Justification by faith only, but one member, illustrious for his piety and learning, had propounded a doctrine dangerously close to heresy. He suggested, that, in order to be absolved before the judgment seat of God, in addition to our righteousness, it might be necessary to impute the righteousness of Christ to us, that is the merits of His passion and death, for the purpose of supplying the defect in our righteousness, which is always deficient. It seems (I quote Dr. Ludwig Pastor) that the true doctrine is that "inherent righteousness through God's mercy contains already everything necessary to salvation, and that the acceptance of an imputed justice is quite unnecessary in order to venerate, in the justifying and redeeming grace of Christ the basis and root of man's justification." Lainez made a very long, clear and convincing argument to show the erroneousness of the heterodox opinion. His "erudition and brilliant powers of exposition" made a deep impression upon his audience, and from that time the Jesuit Fathers were persons of considerable importance at the Council. Lainez himself acquired such a reputation that, whereas one hour was the usual period allotted to speakers, the President permitted him to speak for three hours at a time, or longer. His success, apparently, was not at once reported to Ignatius, and, at the very time when the Council was defining the dogma of Justification, in sixteen chapters, containing thirty-three canons, "formulating with clearness and precision the standard of Catholic Truth as distinguished from Pelagian error on the one hand and Protestant on the other," Ignatius was planning to send him elsewhere. In great alarm, Salmerón at once wrote to protest:

TRENT, Jan. 20, 1547.

To FATHER IGNATIUS:

I think it will redound greatly to God's service, that Master Lainez shall stay on here; his presence is so necessary now that I really believe that if your Reverence were here, you would feel it to be against your conscience to deprive the whole Council—this is no hyperbole—of an eye. There are many delicate matters to be discussed and very few persons have the distinction, the grace, and the good will of the Cardinals and prelates of all nations to such an extent, as to be able to get their views accepted. I say this, although up to now I have obeyed your Reverence in trying to facilitate his going, nevertheless I see that his presence is imperative and of the utmost use to the Council.

SALMERÓN.

Ignatius gave way, and Lainez and Salmerón stayed at Trent throughout the sessions of the Council, and when it adjourned to Bologna, in March, 1547, they went, too. They also attended subsequent sessions at Trent, when the Council met together again, from May, 1551, to April, 1552. But, as will appear from the following letter, neither their reputation for learning nor their position as representatives of the Pope, availed to secure them any great attention, so far as their physical wants were concerned. It is but fair to suppose that in the little city of Trent, perched high among the Alps, and suddenly crowded to overflowing, commodious lodgings were hard to get:

TRENT, August 11, 1551.

To FATHER IGNATIUS LOYOLA:

We will inform your Reverence about what has happened to us since we came here, and about our lodgings, not to find fault with anybody, unless it be ourselves, but to let you know the facts, lest they may be reported in Rome after another fashion.

When we arrived here, the Very Reverend Legate (Cardinal Marcello Crescenzi) received us, as far as we could judge, with great cordiality, for even before we had got here he had spoken of our coming to many prelates, saying he was glad to have us; and they said nice things about us, as we know both from him and from them. He said he would lodge us both in a room in his house, and that an inn should be at once looked up, which he hoped would be near by in order the better to enjoy our society, and he also hoped that we would regularly dine with him, but if we preferred to dine in our own room, dinner should be served there. We kissed his hands, and took our leave.

Our expectation was that he would speak to the Secretary of the Council, and tell him to take charge of us until an inn was found. The Secretary took us to his own house and said that, as we were not lodged at an inn, we should come there for just that one night; and he gave us all three, for our joint apartment, a little, tiny, smoky oven of a room, with a bed in it and a trucklebed (which when pulled out did not leave space to take two steps in the room). There was no table for us to study at, or write a letter, and as for chairs only one foot-stool, but there were lots of boots, belonging to him and his valet, and a big wallet, an old harp, and the valet's sword, which were kept in our *oven*. I said to Master Salmerón: "See here, this is a little more than we bargained for; let's stay at the inn, and to-morrow on my way to the palace, I will tell the Secretary that, in order not to go changing inns, and as long as he said we were to be here for only one night, we had decided to stay at the inn." But Salmerón thought it was better to come to the *oven* in spite of the heat, in order not to show any signs of discontent with the room, or any dissatisfaction. So Salmerón slept that night upon a chest, and John [a companion] and I upon the beds; but the next day Salmerón betook himself to the house of the Bishop of Verona, which was near by, to sleep, but though I was offered the same, in order that we should not all leave the apartment, John and I continued to sleep in the *oven*. One day the Legate's Secretary came and asked if we lacked anything; and I answered with my usual freedom, or foolishness: "You can see; we lack everything." And he said: "That's so; but at the present moment, what do you need?"

So I answered: "At least we need a candle to go to bed by." Then he asked: "What more?" And I said, laughing all the time, "A candle-stick to put it in." However, the keeper of the store closet was out, so we couldn't have a candle that night: nevertheless we were the gainers, for we got a torch to go to bed by.

After about a week, having paid visits upon almost everybody, we went to the Cardinal to beg him to give us a room; for everybody was asking us where we lodged, and a good many people wanted to come to see us, but we did not think that we could receive visitors where we were. He told us that they would surely give us a room; however, the owner of the house, where he wished to lodge us, was away, but that as soon as he came back, he would take us in. The owner did return in three or four days, and offered us rooms; but as the house was new and still unfinished, and as there were neither doors nor windows, he asked for an advance of ten ducats on the rent in order to complete the rooms. When he went to ask the Secretary of the Council for the ducats—I was present—the Secretary answered sharply, that he was a dreadful man, etc. After the landlord had gone, I said to the Secretary: "It would have been a good thing, if you had given him those ducats, for in the end they come out of the rent, and it makes little difference." To which he said: "What rent do you think we have to pay for those rooms per month, anyhow, that you increase the cost that we shall have to bear in hiring them?" I answered, a little indignantly: "Well, there is some expense for every one that comes to the Council; do you think you spend much for us? Don't you know that we don't eat our bread for nothing, but that we work as hard as the others? The Pope knows that, and that is why he sent us; and you have done a thing, that has neither head nor tail, in putting two priests, sent by the Pope, into your servant's room, and such a room, that I am astonished at you. And since you are not spending your own money, you ought to spend according to the orders you receive from the Pope, and not keep us all this time where you do; Salmerón had to sleep on a chest the first night, and hasn't been willing to

sleep there again; and I should have liked to do the
same, if it had not been that I didn't want to show
your shortcomings. But I promise you I shall tell the
Cardinal how we are situated, and that I shall write it to
Rome."

That's the whole story, and the full extent of my bad
temper. The good man was scandalized, and (so I have
heard) told the Cardinal; and I, quite without anger, rather
to please Master Angelo, Secretary of the Council, and the
Cardinal, told the Cardinal, after supper, laughing, in the
presence of Master Angelo, all that had passed. I didn't
blame Master Angelo, but rather my own bad temper and
freedom, although at the time it seemed to me right, and
seems to me so now, and that's why I told the Cardinal.
His Reverence, forewarned by Master Angelo, said that our
having no rooms was from no lack of good will on his part,
but because of the chance absence of the house-owner; and
he excused Master Angelo, saying that as we were in the
habit of preaching patience, we must also practise it. And
I told him truthfully, that I had not done this in order to
escape discomfort, for the year before I had passed three
months in Africa under a sheet, suffering from heat by day
and from cold by night, and that in the *oven* I could laugh
and be content, but that I had spoken out because it was
not fit and proper for us to have no conveniences for study,
whether to prepare to preach, or to read, or anything else,
nor towards those that sent us, nor towards his Eminence,
nor for any members of the Council who might wish to
come to see us. And I told him truthfully, that I had not
expressed any discontent to anybody except to his Eminence and to Master Angelo, and that he should take this
freedom on my part as in the line of my duty; and that if I
had done wrong in any way, he should impose penance upon
me, and I would perform it very gladly, provided that he
would harbor no ill feelings against the Society or against
us and that in time, if the Council continued, he would see
our fidelity and our wish to serve him in every good thing
that we could. In this way we remain good friends; and I
at least had the satisfaction of telling him what was on my

mind. And next day, seeing that the matter of the house dragged, for the owner had gone away again, and the greater part of it was full of the Cardinal's retinue and there was no place for religious services, and it was expensive for Master Angelo, we went to see our old host of last time, and got from him the same rooms we had had before, for so much a month, and he did it most willingly, offering them to us at once, and, as he needs the money, and gives us three rooms, washing and cooking, and what else we need, we have agreed to give him three crowns a month. And so, as the Cardinal is satisfied, we have come here with his permission, and on the understanding that we shall dine with him once a week. And his Eminence supplies us from his own house with a generous portion of bread and wine, and ten crowns a month, at the Pope's charges, which we asked for, three for our lodgings and seven for other expenses, as Trent is dearer than last time. The Cardinal is to give us also all we need for clothes, etc.; for he does not wish us to take anything from anybody else. We made the same arrangement last time with the Cardinal of Santa Cruz [Marcello Cervini] that we do now.

We have been four days at this inn, after having spent eleven or twelve in the *oven*. . . . We have wanted to write this to your Reverence, not to make a complaint of any one, for we certainly have none; but in order that, in case complaints may have been written from here (but we don't think so) you may know the facts, and be able to make use of them. And also because, in accordance with my character, I should not be at peace, if I had not advised you of this fault, so that you might correct me. . . .

LAINEZ.

In the final session of the Council of Trent, in 1561, which Lainez attended as General of the Society of Jesus, he represented the extreme ultramontane view, and did all he could to strengthen the Pope's autocratic powers; but that period lies beyond the limits of my subject. There is, however, one more episode to which I shall refer, as it shows that, notwithstanding the severe discipline which the Jesuit

Fathers had undergone, notwithstanding their humility and their habitual self-control, the old Adam had not been wholly expelled, but that they were sensitive to provocation and irritation, like ourselves. At the second reunion of the Council, Lainez and Salmerón went about paying their respects to all the prelates and theologians, in the hope of making the Society favorably known to them. In this they were successful except in the case of the learned Dominican monk, Melchior Cano, who for some reason or other, not very clear,—as I have told in an earlier chapter,—had already fallen foul of the Jesuit Fathers who had been conducting missions in Spain. It seems likely that he had met Ignatius at Salamanca in early days, but nothing is known about their meeting; and in the meantime he had become a distinguished professor of theology at Salamanca, and was now at the Council as one of the Emperor's theologians. Cano's quarrel with the Society in Spain had been notorious and perhaps it was partly in the hope to effect a reconciliation that Lainez and Salmerón went to see him at Trent. They explained the nature and purposes of the Society; Cano raised objections and attacked the arguments put forward by his visitors in its favor. For two hours the dispute waxed hotter and hotter. Finally Lainez said: "For charity's sake, Father, answer me one question: Are you anything more than a simple Dominican friar in the Church of God?" Cano: "No." Lainez: "Why, then, do you take upon yourself the office of the bishops and the Pope, God's Vicar, and what's more, condemn those very persons whom the bishops and the Pope have approved and do approve?" Cano, smiling ironically: "O Lord! Is your Worship not pleased to have the dogs bark when the shepherds snooze?" Lainez: "Let them bark, but at the wolves and not at other watchdogs." By this time both had lost their tempers, and Cano shouted out: "Oh, throw away your new ideas," insinuating that the Jesuits had introduced unorthodox usages and doctrines. This was more than Lainez could bear. Dropping Latin for Spanish, in his excitement, he shouted back a very improper word, and dashed out of the room; but he had hardly got to the street door, than in a fit of repentance he ran back, up into Cano's room, flung himself down before him on his knees, and begged his pardon for the gross word he had uttered in a fit of anger.

CHAPTER XXVI

It is now time to say something of those achievements of the Society that have won the greatest celebrity and admiration, and are most colored with high romance. Among all the adventurers of those early days, Magellan, Albuquerque, de Soto, Cortez, Pizarro, Cabot, Raleigh, Champlain, not one was more heroic than Francis Xavier; all unwittingly, and in the innocence of complete indifference to human praise, he set up to himself in the temple of Fame as enduring a memorial as the best of them. Albuquerque presented an empire to the Kingdom of Portugal, Cortez and Pizarro annexed great Provinces to Spain, Champlain added Canada to France, but Xavier, during his ten years of missionary labors, converted (it is said) hundreds of thousands of heathens to Christianity; and the religion that he taught, whatever one may think of certain aspects of it, was a religion of decency, devotion and love.

It was in 1538, I believe, that King John of Portugal, through the mediation of Dr. Diego de Govea, applied to Ignatius for some of the Fathers to go as missionaries to India. The Portuguese ambassador asked for six. Ignatius replied: "Gracious Heavens, Mr. Ambassador, if out of the ten that we number, six go to India, who will be left for the rest of the world?" He consented to send two, and at the ambassador's suggestion chose Rodriguez, the Portuguese by birth, and Bobadilla; but as the latter was ill in health, he summoned Xavier: "You have heard, Brother Francis, that by command of the Pope two of us are to go to India, and that Bobadilla, who was selected for the enterprise, is prevented by sickness. The Ambassador is in such a hurry that he cannot wait. So it is you that God will employ upon this mission." To which Xavier answered:

"Father, I am ready."   Ignatius furnished him with the following letter, and he started off the next day, never to come back:

To Beltrano de Loyola

ROME, March 20, 1540.

May God bless us and keep us always:

I haven't time to write at length, as I should like to do, on account of the rush and hurry, which they put upon us, in order to send some of us to the Indies, others to Ireland and to other parts of Italy.

Master Francis Xavier, of Navarre, son of Señor de Xavier, a member of the Society, will bring this letter; he is going under the Pope's orders, on the requisition of the King of Portugal, beside two others who go by sea to the same King.   Master Francis knows all about these matters and will tell you all from me, as if I were there myself.

You must know that the Ambassador of the King of Portugal, with whom Master Francis is going, is on the most friendly terms with us; we are much indebted to him; and in matters that concern the service of God, he will recommend us to the King and do all he can.   Please therefore, for the service of God, show him all the courtesy you can. Treat Araoz as a member of the family; and accept all that Master Francis says as you would do with me.   Please remember me most kindly to your wife and the family.

May the Lord bless us and keep us always.

De bondad pobre,

IÑIGO.

Xavier's readiness to go provides us with a measure of his love of God, for he dearly loved his friends.   In a letter written from Bologna, on his journey to Portugal, he says to Ignatius:

On Easter day I received some letters from you in the post-bag that came for the Ambassador; the Lord knows what pleasure and comfort they brought me.   And since I think that by letters only we shall behold one another in

this life—but in the other face to face with many embraces
—in the little space of life left to us, we must see one another by frequent letters.

And, again, he wrote from Lisbon, a year later, on the
eve of sailing:

There is nothing more to tell except that we are soon to go
aboard. So I end, with a petition to Our Lord Jesus Christ
to grant that we may meet and see one another in another
life in bodily shape, since I doubt if in this life we shall see
one another again, for Rome is a long way from India, and
there is so great a harvest there that there will be no need to
go looking elsewhere. And let whoever enters first into the
other life, and does not find a brother whom he loves in the
Lord, pray to Christ, to unite all of us there in His glory.

On April 7, 1541, he sailed away, in his shabby clothes,
with no superfluity other than a few books. Some Portuguese gentlemen wished to fit him out in the manner suitable for a messenger honored by the King and the Pope,
with servants and so forth, but "he answered with much
grace and wiseness, that God gave what repute and credit
were needful through the contempt of worldly honors and
of oneself; and that this very desire to acquire repute by
decking oneself out with worldly ceremony, had brought religion in many places to the pass in which we saw it." Two
missionaries went with him, Paolo da Camerino, an Italian
priest, and Francisco Mansilhas, a Portuguese student.

Xavier must have known what to expect. The voyage to
India lasted six months. The usual course was to make a
continuous voyage round the Cape of Good Hope to Mozambique, to put in there for repairs, supplies, and rest, and
then on, along the coast of Arabia, across the Indian Ocean,
to the port of Goa. Twice they crossed the equator, and
rounding the Cape of Good Hope went far south, so that at
times they were perspiring and at other times almost frozen.
The ships were considered *"grandes y poderosas"* (large and
powerful), but the cabins were so small that a passenger
could scarce lie down, and the poorer folks were huddled

together in the hold.   The rations consisted of biscuit, salt
fish and salt beef; but the mode of cooking failed to render
them palatable.   The fresh water did not keep well, and the
quantity doled out to each man was very scanty, especially
during the hot stretches of the voyage.   The ship's doctor
had more than he could do, and his supplies usually gave
out.   In short, quite apart from perils of winds and waves,
of reefs, of fire, of French corsairs believed to be manned by
heretics, not only the steerage but also the cabin passengers
were badly off.   Contagious diseases often broke out, and
on some voyages, two, three, or four hundred people died.
One can see how crowded the ships must have been.   Part
of the difficulty was that ignorant emigrants had no idea
of what they needed, or else no means to buy it, and went on
board with one shirt, two loaves of bread, a cheese, a pot of
marmalade, and nothing else.

On Xavier's ship, the Santiago, the number of sick and
ailing was very large, "but the charity and patience of
Father Francis was still greater than all the difficulties."
He tended the sick, he taught the catechism to children and
slaves, he preached; he seemed more like one of the ship's
hands than a person of so much importance; he performed
the most menial offices, washing not only his own clothes
but those of the sick.   Altogether, his life on board was such
that for the greater part of the voyage (as he said) his bed
consisted of a coil of rope.   His tact and gentle ways made
him master of all hearts.   He was so ready and gay in conversation, and the serenity of his soul showed so plainly in
his countenance, that he got on well with everybody.   The
hardest sinners, such as generally avoid good men and
priests, were very glad to talk to him, and in a little while
found themselves changed from what they had been.   In
short, he was so beloved that he could do pretty much what
he wished with everybody.

The voyage was not prosperous; they were obliged to
stop for months at Mozambique, and Xavier did not arrive
at Goa until May 6, 1542.   There his missionary work
began among the Portuguese; for absence from home, the
love of customs of the country, the demoralization of living

among an inferior people, had smoothed the way for much
laxity of life. But after a few months he went southward
to the natives along the coast of Malabar. I will quote
from a long letter he wrote after he had been gone from
Rome nearly four years:

To the Comrades in Rome

COCHIN, INDIA, Jan. 15, 1544.

May the grace and love of Christ, our Lord, always be
with us and bless us.

It is two years and nine months since I left Portugal,
and since then I have written three times, but I have only
received one letter since I arrived in India, written on
January 18, 1542. The Lord knows what comfort it gave
me. It reached me two months ago; the delay was because
the ship spent the winter in Mozambique.

Master Paul, Francisco de Mansilhas, and I are very well.
Master Paul is at Goa, in the college of Santa Fe; he has
charge of the students in the house. Francisco and I are
here among the Christians at Cape Cormorin; we have been
here more than a year. There are many Christians here,
and many are converted every day. As soon as I came to
this coast, where they live, I tried to find out what they
knew about Christ, and asked them about the particulars
of their faith, and what more they believed now that they
were Christians than they had when they were heathen;
I got no other answer except, "We are Christians." They
do not know our language, and so they don't know what
they ought to believe. And as I can't understand them,
nor they me, because their native tongue is Malabar and
mine Basque, I got together the most intelligent of them,
and sought out some persons who knew both languages.
After many meetings, and with much difficulty, we translated the prayers from Latin into Malabar, beginning with
directions as to the manner of blessing oneself, and con-
fessing that the Three Persons are one God, then the creed,
the commandments, the Lord's prayer, Ave Maria, Salve
Regina, and the general confession. After these had been

translated into their language and I had learned them by heart, I went through the village ringing a bell, collecting all the men and boys that I could, and after I had got them together, I gave them a lesson twice every day. In the space of a month I taught the prayers, and bade the boys teach their fathers and mothers, and the whole household, what they had learned at school.

Every Sunday I assembled the whole village, men and women, old and young, to say their prayers in their language. They enjoyed it and came with great glee. They begin with the acknowledgment of one God, Three in One, then they say the creed aloud in their language; I lead and they follow. After the creed has been said, then I speak alone. I repeat each of the twelve articles by itself, pausing over each, and explain to them that to be a Christian means to believe these articles without a doubt. Then I ask if they firmly believe in each article; and then, all together, men and women, old and young, with their arms crossed on their breasts, shout out loud, "Yes" to every article. I make them repeat the creed oftener than anything else, because a man is a Christian in consequence of his belief in the twelve articles. After the creed I proceed to the Commandments, explaining that these contain the Christian law, and that if a Christian keep them he is good, but if he breaks them he is a bad Christian. All were amazed, Christians and heathen, to learn how righteous the law of Christ is, and how it conforms to natural reason. From the creed we proceed to the Lord's prayer, and the Ave Maria. [He goes on to recount how carefully he drills his pupils. They repeat twelve *pater nosters* and twelve *Ave Marias* in honor of the twelve articles of the creed, then ten of each in honor of the Ten Commandments, and pray for grace firmly to believe each article, and to keep the several commandments. After they were able to say that they firmly believed, then he baptized them.]

I hope and believe that the boys will be better men than their fathers, for they show much love for our law, and eagerness to learn and to teach our prayers, and they abhor the idolatry of the heathen. They often are con-

tentious with the heathen, and rebuke their fathers and
mothers, if they see them worship idols, and find fault with
them in my presence. When they report to me that idolatry
is practised anywhere in the countryside, I collect all the
boys and repair with them to the spot; and the dishonor
that the Devil gets from the boys outweighs the honor
he gets from their parents and relations, for the children
take the idols and break them into bits, and spit on them,
and trample on them, and do other things, that are just
as well not named, but it is quite proper for the boys to
do them to that Power which was bold enough to persuade
their fathers to worship him.

[He continues the account of how he teaches the boys
to go and pray with the old and the sick, and so forth; and
deplores the lack of laborers for the harvest.] Often and
often I am moved to go to the universities of Europe, and
cry aloud, like a man who has lost his wits, most of all
to the University of Paris, and say in the Sorbonne to
those that have more learning than good will to set about
putting it to use, 'How many souls will ye lose from glory
and let go to hell because of your neglect?' If they paid
as much heed to the reckoning that God will exact of them,
and to the talents that He has given them, as they do to
their studies, many would bestir themselves, and take
measures and spiritual exercises so that they should feel
God's will within their souls, and obey it rather than their
own inclinations, and say, 'Lord, here I am, what wouldst
Thou have me do? Send me whither Thou wilt, even to
India, if that be the thing to do.' [He fears that the students
pursue learning more for worldly advancement than for
God's glory.] I have wanted [he says] to write to the
University of Paris, at least to our friend Master de Corni-
bus and to Doctor Picard, how thousands upon thousands
of heathen would become Christian, if there were laborers
minded to go to them. . . . The multitude of people in
this land who are ready to become Christians is so great,
that it often happens that my arms are wearied out with
baptizing, and that I cannot continue to repeat in their
language the creed and commandments and prayers, and

the explanation of what Christianity means, and what Paradise is, and what Hell is, and who go to the one and who to the other.

[He describes, in no very flattering terms, the brahmins who look after the pagodas and the worship of idols, and exact gifts from the people.] As I was going about to visit Christians in those villages I passed many pagodas, in one of which there were 200 brahmins who came out to see me. And in our conversation I asked the question, 'Please tell me what your gods and idols command you to do in order to go to heaven?' There was great dispute among them as to who should answer me; finally they told one of the oldest to answer, and an aged man, over eighty, said: 'You tell me first what the God of the Christians tells you to do.' But I saw through his trickery, and refused to answer until he had. So he was obliged to reveal his ignorance. He answered that their gods commanded men to do two things in order to go where the gods were: first, not to kill cows which they worship; second, to give alms to the brahmins who tend the pagodas. When I heard this answer, I was grieved that devils should rule our neighbors after that fashion, and get themselves worshipped instead of God, and I stood up, and I cried aloud to the brahmins seated there, and repeated the creed and the commandments in their language, and dwelt a little while on each commandment; and after I had finished the commandments, I repeated my admonition in their language, telling what heaven is and what hell, and who go to the one and who to the other. And when I had finished talking, the brahmins got up and embraced me, and said, 'Verily the God of the Christians is the true God, since his commandments are so completely in accord with natural reason.' They asked me if our soul dies with the body, like the soul of a brute; and God gave me arguments suitable to their understanding, so that I explained clearly the immortality of the soul, and they expressed great pleasure and contentment. The arguments to be given to this idiot people need not be so subtle as those in the books of our scholastic doctors. [And so on, at much length.]

There is nothing more to write you concerning matters here, except that the consolation that God confers upon those who go among the heathen, converting them to Christianity, is such, that if there is content in this life, it is here. . . . So I make an end, with a prayer to God that since of His mercy He united us, and for His service has separated us so far from one another, that He will reunite us in His holy heaven. And in order to attain that reward, let us take for intercessors and advocates all those holy souls of this land, where I am, which God has taken to His holy heaven after I had baptized them and before they lost the state of innocency,—of which there are more than a thousand, I think. I pray all those holy souls, to obtain this grace from God for us, that for all the time that we may be in this state of exile we shall realize in our souls His holy will and fulfill it perfectly.

Your dear brother in Christ,

FRANCISCO.

Of his letters that have been preserved those written to Europe are more or less narratives of this character, while those to his subordinates in Goa, Malacca, or elsewhere,— for as years went by other Jesuits were sent to help him— contain advice, instructions or plans, and generally stick very closely to the matters in hand. Occasionally, a passage or a sentence reveals his homesickness and his deep affection for his friends:

So I end, though I never could end if I were to write the great love that I bear to you all and to each one. If the hearts of those who love one another in Christ could be looked into in this present life, be sure, *Hermanos mios charissimos,* that you would see yourselves clearly in mine; and if while gazing at yourselves in it, you should not recognize yourselves, it would be because I rate you so high, and you in your humility rate yourselves so low; and for that reason you would fail to know your pictures, and not because they are not imprinted on my heart and soul. And I beg that there shall be a true love between you, suffering no bitterness of spirit to spring up, . . . for you remember that Christ says that by this He knows His disciples, if they have love one to another.

And in another letter he says:

I beg you for the love of our Lord God, Dearest Brothers, to write me at length about all the members of the Society; for since I no longer hope to see you face to face in this life, at least let it be as through a glass darkly, that is, by letters. And to Ignatius: So I close, beseeching Christ, since of His infinite mercy, He has joined us together in this life, that after death He will bring us to His glory.

Your son in Christ

Francis Xavier.

The most interesting parts of his letters, at least to me, are a few expressions, here and there—where his emotion strips off that sentiment of shyness akin to shame with which the Jesuits accustomed themselves to cloak human affections—expressions of the deep love he felt for Ignatius, for they bear eloquent testimony to what must have been an almost feminine tenderness and loveableness in that stern ascetic, which, like planetary forces known only by their visible control of subject bodies, were revealed to very few: *"Verdadero Padre mio," "Vuestra santa Charidad," "Padre mio de mi anima observantissimo," "Padre mio in Christi visceribus unico," "Padre mio de mi alma."* And one letter ends: "I conclude, kneeling upon the ground as I write, as if you were here before me, beseeching that you will commend me to God in your holy prayers, that He will let me know His holy will in this life, and give me grace to perform it. Amen."

I insist upon this point of Xavier's love for Ignatius, because, I repeat, it is an index to Ignatius's character; and in order to establish it beyond a peradventure, I will quote from a letter, written from Cochin, on January 29, 1552:

Verdadero Padre mio, I received a letter from your *Santa Charydad,* at Malacca when I got back from Japan. God knows how much my soul was comforted to get news so longed for of your health. Among the many other comforting and holy words in your letter, I read those at the end, "All thine, without the possibility of ever forgetting, Ignatius." I read them with tears, and I write them down with tears, remembering the past and how much love you always have had for me and still have, and thinking, too, how Our Lord delivered me out of many toils and dangers in Japan through the intercession of your holy prayers. . . . Your *santa Charydad* says how great is the desire you have to see me before you die. The Lord knows what an impression these words of great love made upon my soul, and how many tears I shed each time I think of them; and in my opinion, I may take comfort from them, for with holy obedience nothing is impossible. . . . And so I conclude with a prayer to God—taking you for my intercessor on earth and all the Society, together with all the Church Militant, and for my intercessors in heaven, all the saints who in this life were of the Company of Jesus, and all the Church Triumphant, so that by their prayers and merits Our Lord in this life will grant me to know His holy will, and grace to accomplish it to the uttermost.

The least of your sons, but the first in exile,

FRANCISCO.

I shall not dwell upon the dangers that he underwent on his missionary expeditions, dangers of travel by land and sea, dangers from marauders and pirates, dangers of fevers and pestilence. His friends would try to deter him. "My best friends are dismayed by my purpose to take so long and dangerous a voyage, and picture the perils of storm, reefs and robbers; but I am more dismayed to see what little faith they possess. All things are in God's power, and my only fear is punishment for negligence in His service and failure to spread Christ's name among the heathen." Physical dangers were real enough; but apart from them, other difficulties crowded in front of him. The

natives were of many different tribes and languages; and
their system of caste, their idolatry, their cruel religious
customs, their mendacity, their gross vices, their instability
of purpose, caused him perplexity and uneasiness. Once,
while he was on board a Chinese junk, the crew, in fear of a
storm, sacrificed to idols and cast lots as to what course to lay
the ship; he tried, in vain, to interfere.   "It is very hard,"
he said, "to be in the hands of the Devil and his ministers."

And, besides, the Portuguese merchants, who were
Christians, finding themselves free from the restraining influences of home, had, as I have intimated, yielded to
licentious Oriental ways, and had got into a mire of *di-
soluciones, abominaciones y pecados.* Venturesome men
had come thousands of miles and braved many dangers in
order to exchange the manufactures of Europe for the
products of the East, and they sought to soothe their
absence from civilization with the charms of the native
women. Xavier was often sadly disheartened; he writes
to one of his fellow missionaries: "Sometimes, I admit, I
am weary of life; and it seems to me that I should accomplish more for our holy faith by dying than by living, since
I see so many wrongs and insults to God that we are
powerless to help."

But such moments of depression were rare. He is usually
full of abounding courage, and no one is more overflowing
with gratitude than he. To our way of thinking his consolations are very unsubstantial. In sleep he sometimes
dreams that he is with his brethren, *"estar con vosostros,
charissimos,"* and waking he often thinks of them, *"re-
cordarme muchas vezes de vosostros, charisimos hermanos
mios";* and, he says:

In order that I may never forget you, I want to tell you,
Charisimos Hermanos, that for my consolation, as an ever
present means of recollection, I have cut out from the
letters you have written me your names written by your
own hands, and putting them together with my own vow
of profession, I carry them about with me all the time for
the sake of the great consolation that they give me.

And, once, after a tribe of natives had been baptized, and some heathen King had come down in wrath and in the cruelest ways massacred great numbers of them, he wrote: "For this we must give many thanks to the Lord, that in our days there is no failure of martyrs."

Indeed, tribulations of all kinds were to him occasions for great religious consolation, and what with illness, idolatry, the immorality and murderous habits of the people, he found plenty of them. "The islands (he says) are well fitted to blind a man in a few years by an abundance of tears of consolation." All these ills he underwent out of a love and desire to serve his God. He was more than ready to lay down his life for his neighbor's soul,

Hoping [as he writes home to the brethren] with my feeble strength to obey the precept of the Gospel, *Qui voluerit animam suam salvam facere perdet eam, qui autem perdiderit eam propter me inveniet eam.* (Whosoever will save his life shall lose it: and whosoever will lose his life for my sake shall find it.) And, my dear Brothers, be sure that though the Latin of this sentence is easy to understand in the abstract, when a man comes in actual fact to make up his mind to lay down his life for the Lord, confronting dangers in which he expects to lose it, then that Latin, that seems so plain, becomes obscure, and he only understands it to whom God in His infinite mercy gives the power of understanding.

But whatever his habitual mood may have been, Xavier went about with a high spirit and no outward show of dejection or hesitancy. Men find every countenance fair to look upon from which courage, faith, and innocence shine forth; and, in addition to such radiance, Xavier had a genial charm, a social gift, and a native tact, that long intimacy with Ignatius must have quickened and increased. He would watch the soldiers at their games, and if out of deference toward him they wished to stop, he bade them go on, saying that they were soldiers not monks; and he would go to their houses and chat with them; and, if he stayed to a meal, he would praise the food and the cooking, ask who could prepare such dishes, and when the pleased host called in the cook, he would compliment and thank her. One particular instance of his behaviour will, perhaps, make clearer the nature of his influence. On a certain voyage the pilot of the ship acknowledged that he had not been to confession for a long time,—I quote from Xavier's earliest biographer—:

But finally he disclosed his wound to Father Francisco, who encouraged him and did all he could to facilitate the cure, and so the pilot promised to confess to him when they got ashore; nevertheless, embarrassed and dismayed by shame and timidity, he avoided the Father, tried to escape, and even hid himself. But in vain he tried to escape from him that was in pursuit; for the Father met him on the beach. The pilot was in great confusion from shamefacedness, but the Father greeted him most cordially, began chatting familiarly, and gave him time to collect himself, and then in order to make confession easy, said, "Why not confess as we walk up and down the beach?" And he walked along, side by side with him, in order to relieve his embarrassment. So the pilot plucked up courage, and little by little began to tell one thing and then another, until finally Father Francis with his ready ways, his graciousness, and his charity, won him over, and he felt his heart so pricked by compunction that, sobbing and crying, he made up his mind to unbosom himself completely. They went into a church; the pilot made a full confession, and resolved to live a new life. And so he did until he died, making much account of his conscience, and going to confession.

Xavier's success in saving multitudes of souls, as he believed, and the love that he inspired among people everywhere, both the Portuguese and natives, must have been of great comfort to him, especially after more Jesuits came out, as they did from time to time, and he felt that the Society he loved so much was accomplishing a great work. Nevertheless the yearning for his old friends never left

him. Mails came at best but twice a year, and often less
frequently because of the uncertainties of navigation. On
January 27, 1545, he writes:

It is four years since I left Portugal and in all this time
I have only received one letter from you in Rome, and two
from Master Simon in Portugal. I want to hear every year
news of you and of all the members of the Society, all the
particulars. I am sure that you must have written every
year, just as I write regularly every year. But I am afraid
that, as I have not received your letters, you have not received mine.

The story of these years contains much poetry; but it is
seldom, if ever, that the tale of a missionary's labors does
not require some chapters to be told in prose. There seems
to be an inevitable connection between missionaries,
merchants and punitive expeditions. I quote again from
the Jesuit Father, Alessandro Valignani, Xavier's earliest
biographer:

He used to tell the natives that if they became Christians,
they would have the good will of the Portuguese, and live
in security, for under the protection of their fleets they
could trade and fish freely. The Commandant at Quilom,
with the Father's approval, often interfered with their fishing, in order both to quicken their interest and to punish
their misbehaviour. . . . Xavier sometimes promised fa-
vours; sometimes he added menaces that the Commandant
would stop their fishing and trading, and so he induced
a great many to become Christians, as the Lord says,
"*compellendo eos intrare ad nuptias.*"

But if we can save men from eternal damnation by driving them into the Christian fold, should we be discriminating and fastidious and cavil over the manner of getting
them in? Nobody who believed in eternal damnation ever
hesitated to approve such action. Criticism of these means
of conversion only begins when men come to believe that
there are other doors to eternal life than a particular church,
or that there is no damnation hereafter.

Xavier's labors in the East lasted about ten years. Death crowned his life in a most fitting fashion. He was on his way to China. The Chinese authorities would not permit Europeans to enter, and Xavier bided his time on a barren coast, waiting to be smuggled in. An old hulk, with some Portuguese aboard, was anchored off shore, but Xavier, being ill, and distressed by the rolling of the vessel, was taken to a little hut of mud and branches on the beach. He grew worse, could not eat the poor food that the ship sent him, and with no doctor or priest, in the company of two Chinese boys only, he breathed his last. So virtuous and blameless was his life, that all the people in that part of the world repeated to one another stories of the miracles he had wrought.

The fruits of his labors and sacrifice were not confined to Asia. His letters were copied—circularized is the word we use now—and copies sent to all the Jesuit missions in Europe, and served as most potent propaganda to win the good will and support of persons in authority.

CHAPTER XXVII

I HAVE now given in rude outline a sketch, or rather a suggestion, of what the Jesuit Fathers accomplished in Italy, Portugal, Spain, France, Germany, Austria and India, during Loyola's lifetime. My purpose has been to tell no more than was necessary in order to understand Loyola's purposes and ambitions, and the devotion with which he inspired his disciples. To understand the head or heart, it is necessary to know what the hands and feet are doing. I think, however, that, bearing in mind the reader's gratitude for brevity and the limits of my subject, I have said enough; I shall pass over without further mention the missions to Brazil and Ethiopia.

The impression, I think, that these last chapters would be likely to convey, is an impression of dash and energy, of a blind obedience, like that of the Light Brigade at Balaklava. And, perhaps, a criticism similar to that made upon the famous charge, may spring to the reader's mind: *C'est magnifique mais ce n'est pas la religion.* I will not attempt to define religion. It seems to me a very personal matter, consisting mainly perhaps in the emotions that color man's consciousness of his relations with whatever he conceives reality to be. I wish, however, not to slur over the fact,— as one might be in danger of doing in an exposition of such achievements of constructive organization—that the early disciples of Ignatius were men of loving, innocent hearts, some of them holy men. Obedience and energy were not their only qualities; nor was it in the main to those qualities, or to their knowledge of theology and power of exposition, that their success was due. They possessed, in varying degrees, the apostolic virtues. That of loveableness appears more clearly in Pierre Lefèvre, perhaps, than in any of the others, not even excepting Xavier or Claude Jay, because of his innocent simplicity of soul; and therefore, before going into the details of Loyola's life in Rome, I shall devote a few pages to him, merely reminding the reader again that one must judge a man by his friends, that Lefèvre was Loyola's first disciple, that the two were drawn together at once and remained devoted comrades all their lives.

The editors of Lefèvre's letters call him *Catholicorum columen, Haeresum impugnator, Societatis amplificator.* Those are not the epithets I should have chosen, but no doubt they are deserved. He conducted missions in the same general fashion as Lainez and the others, first in Northern Italy and afterwards in Germany. Ignatius used to say that he taught the *Spiritual Exercises* better than any of them. And a younger companion says: "He was able to comfort such as were in affliction or tormented with doubt, he gave strength to those in temptation, and, taught by what he himself had suffered, he had learned compassion." At the Diet of Worms, held in 1540, he came into contact with the Lutheran Reformers, and perceived how badly things were going for the conservatives. Melanchthon was also in attendance; and some Catholics were desirous that Lefèvre should hold conference with him, but it was judged more prudent that religious discussions should be left in the hands of the accredited representatives of the Church. This decision was probably wrong. The ancient ecclesiastical order of Latin Christendom was doomed. The old conception of unity, originally handed down by the Roman Empire to the Roman Church, of one head, one administrative whole, one common interpretation of things unseen embodied in a common formula, had cracked under the pulls and tugs of centrifugal forces, under the egotisms of race, of nationality, of personal and dynastic ambitions. But the degrees of loosening and separation, or local self-control, were still to be determined, and it was still to be proved whether these changes should be carried out in kindliness of spirit or in passion and anger. Lefèvre no doubt was ignorant of the intellectual currents that had

unscrewed the bolts and undone the knots that had held
Christendom together, and his simple piety would have
been no match for the fierce dogmatism of the Lutheran
extremists, but his sweetness of character could hardly have
failed to beget a strong personal regard in Melanchthon. At
any rate their meeting could have done the Catholic cause
no harm. Eck and Pflug argued and disputed, and only
widened the rift.

Lefèvre felt a great tenderness for the Germans. He
says:

*Grandes ramos de amor y charidad me penetran muy á
menudo desta nación, y grandes speranças de poder hazer
mucho fruto con tiempo por nuestro modo de proceder:*
(Great shoots of love and charity for this nation go through
and through me, and great hopes that our way of procedure
will with time bring forth much fruit.)

Altogether it was a period of emotional exaltation, and
Lefèvre in his *Memoriale* records both his trials and his
spiritual blessings:

Forget not, O my soul, the memorable consolations which
God bestowed upon thee in answer to thy prayers at Worms,
a knowledge of new ways to pray, new ways to render
thanks to God, to ask for favors for thyself, and both for
the living and for the dead,—prayers suggested to thee by
the Holy Ghost.

At the Diet Lefèvre did not play a public part of any
great consequence. He was not a great preacher, his
health was poor, and his body frail; and he usually confined himself to personal persuasion and exhortation, with
but one or two hearers at a time. He brings to one's mind
the first disciples of St. Francis of Assisi, Brother Bernard,
or Giles, or Sylvester. When he went through the country
from one town to another, he used to pray to the archangel that watched over the whole region, and to all the
several guardian angels of the townsfolk and peasants, and

to the Christ *"qui est in ecclesia eiusdem loci,"* beseeching
them to bless him, his companions, and all the people of
the place who might be in want, or ill health or need of
any kind, and also for the remission of their sins. In Germany he commended himself in especial to the Three Kings,
to the Eleven Thousand Virgins of Cologne, to St. Ursula,
and to St. Pinosa "whose head I saw with my own eyes
in a monastery of St. Benedict." One of his disciples,
Canisius, says of him:

Lefèvre had a wonderful sedulousness in prayer, especially
while he was sojourning in Germany, where he besought
God for the salvation of the Germans, all of them together
and each individually. He used to return thanks, in the
name of the country and of the town where he was living,
for the divine benefits that had been received. Sometimes
he would beg for God's mercy upon the children of the inhabitants; sometimes he besought spiritual and temporal
blessings on the clergy and people present, and he always
bore the threats and insults of rowdy adversaries with an
undaunted heart, for he had learned to rejoice in persecution
for Jesus' sake.

Of his stay in Cologne the following anecdote is recorded.
The Reformed opinions were prevalent, and sundry persons
animated by ill will toward the Catholics cast about for
some excuse for backbiting; so his friends cautioned him to
satisfy everybody.

Ah, my friends, he answered, if there were none others
to satisfy except the citizens of Cologne, we should have
an easy job; but there are other spectators who look and
criticize us; God, angels, archangels, powers, dominions, and
all the goodly fellowship of saints—to please them and do
nothing to offend them is a greater labor and needs greater
vigilance; but I thank you for your kind caution.

And I may add that in Cologne by his means Canisius,
who played a great part in his day and has left a great

tradition in Vienna, was brought into the Society; and it is interesting to find here a third link to connect the Society with the main tradition of mediæval German mysticism, for Canisius edited the writings of Johann Tauler, and Tauler was one of the Friends of God and, if not a pupil of Ludolf of Saxony, was at least acquainted with him.

From Germany, as we have seen, Lefèvre set out in company with Dr. Ortiz for Spain. On their way through France they were cast into prison for a week.

And for this [Lefèvre says] I shall never forget God's great goodness, for He freed us of His grace from those who imprisoned us, and granted us the favor of conversing with them, and of sowing good seed in their souls, as the captain of the soldiers admitted to me. For it came to pass that the bowels of compassion that God had given us were not made captive, nor troubled, nor vexed with our captors.

A little later he says:

On the day of Saint Elizabeth, Queen of Hungary, I worshipped long, and held in my thoughts eight persons, without regard to their errors, while I prayed for them;— the Pope, the Emperor, the King of France, the King of England, the Grand Turk, Bucer and Philip Melanchthon. The reason was that I knew that they were condemned by many, and so a holy compassion sent by the Holy Ghost sprang up within me.

On entering Spain he commended himself and his labors to the principalities, powers, archangels, guardian angels, and saints, of the various places to which he should go, and to the special saints of cities and towns by name. It was the old pagan belief in the genius loci, picked up perhaps in his boyhood among the country people of Savoy, and ennobled by neo-Platonic and Christian notions, that through local spiritual agents the Universal Spirit of God manifested itself. In Savoy he had worshipped (*habeo devotionem* are his words) St. Bruno, the founder of the

Carthusian Order, and, among others, "Peter Villiardus, my old teacher, whom, though he has not been canonized, I regard as a saint."

At Alcalá de Henares he saw Beatriz Ramirez and Mencía de Benavente, two women who, the reader will remember, had been among Ignatius's first listeners, and had testified concerning his missions, when he was under investigation by the Inquisition. Both women were old and infirm. Beatriz Ramirez had gone to a hospital to be taken care of.

But [to quote Lefèvre's letter] she remembers the good works she did when she could go about freely, and her spirit is still vigorous. She says that if Padre Iñigo should say to her that it was better for her to carry her cross about the streets, working for her neighbors, than to stay in the hospital, she would do whatever he told her; or if something else seemed best, in the same way she would abide by what he said. So it would be well for Father Iñigo to write her a line.

At Barcelona he saw more old disciples of Ignatius, among others Isabella Roser. In a letter to Ignatius he says:

When I was talking to Isabella Roser, she said that by Easter, between her and another person, they would furnish some money for Peter Codacius's church [which he was building in Rome for the Society]; that she would scrape together a little at a time and provide all she could; and she was only waiting to hear what Master Iñigo thought, to know what course to pursue for the rest of her life; and that she was prepared, if Padre Iñigo should give her that advice, to go to Rome, in order to serve God better and more freely, and to take with her 3800 ducats, to dispose of as they should counsel. Doña Isabel de Josa also is making a great to-do about leaving Barcelona and going to Rome. I don't know what will come of it.

From Spain he was ordered back to Germany. The journey from Madrid to Spire was beset with difficulties and dangers, robbers in Catalonia, soldiers in France, heretics in Savoy, pestilence in Germany; but such trials and troubles could do nothing against a man armed strong in desire to serve his God. He says:

On this journey God bestowed upon me great feelings of love and hope for the heretics and for the whole world, just as He had done before, and also a special devotion, in faith, hope and charity, that shall last till I die, for the good of seven cities, to wit: Wittemberg in Saxony; a particular city in Sarmatia, the name of which I don't know; Geneva in the duchy of Savoy; Constantinople in Greece; Antioch, also in Greece; Jerusalem; and Alexandria in Africa. I mean to keep all these cities in mind, in the hope that I or somebody of the Society of Jesus Christ will at last celebrate divine worship in all of them.

While in Germany he composed a religious tract, or rather a series of prayers, hopes, praises, pious purposes and ejaculations—a sort of religious diary—following the headings of the different days in the Church calendar. Among them is this passage concerning the Society of Jesus:

With regard to my ever-present solicitude for our Society, I feel, under God's disposing, and in devout reverence of mind, a strong desire, and not for the first time. It is this: I have been wishing that somehow it might come about that our Society should grow in size and in virtue,—in the number of its members and in their quality—to such an extent that it would at last be able to build up the ruins of all our religious doctrines and usages, for some are in ruins now, and others will be in a short time, unless God prevent. For this I have been wishing that a great number of secular and ecclesiastical persons could be found, who would forsake all they have, and offer to do whatever should be commanded them, according to the Roman Church. Some of them could be chosen for our Society,

and undergo the novitiate; and others for other Orders.
God grant that this be brought to pass. May He bring
forward persons who are able to judge spirits, whether or
no they are of God; and further to judge concerning persons
that are of God, who should live together under one rule
and constitution, and who in other ways. May Jesus grant
us men and women so universally Catholic in faith, hope
and charity, and so impelled hither and thither, far and
near by this universal desire for the restoration of all old
conditions in the Church, that all monasteries, all seats of
monks and nuns, may be filled again; and last (but which
is first in importance), that the minds, memories, wills,
hearts and bodies of all men may become sanctified and
perfect in Christ Jesus. Amen.

His piety breathes forth from whatever he writes. I
quote from a letter to a French relation:

MAYENCE, 28 May, 1543.

Très cher et très aymé cosin et frère.
*La grace de nostre Seigneur Jesus-Christ et sa doulce
paix soyt havec vous, vous gardant et saulvant, à présent et
à tous jamais. Amen. . . .*
I begin to perceive that these heresies of the present time
are nothing else than a lack of devotion, lack of humility,
of patience, chastity, and charity. For that reason, we must
practise those virtues, seeking earnestly for the grace of
God that is always ready at hand for those that ask it, and
are willing to die in the asking.
Let us up and wage war against *our* mortal enemies; and,
when of our own free will we can take vengeance upon our
servants, let us do so, I mean on the flesh and our desires
for outward things.
Even if in time of prayer we are led astray by the dis-
tractions of vice, or vanity or business, let us take extra
heed when we are exhorting others, not to fix our attention
on temporal things. Whenever we perceive idle imaginings
among our thoughts, let us straightway search for the roots
from which these weeds sprung up. We shall find repose

in church, if all the time we are *out of church* we will struggle continually with ourselves. If we will battle vigorously and resist sins that we know to be venial, we shall soon conquer sins that are mortal; *il n'est pas possible trouver paix en nostre âme, si nous volons reposer hors de nous mesmes. . . . Les curiosités et inutilités, par le moyent des livres, sans profit d'esprit, évités-les, et pareillement les confabulations qui n'induysent point à la paix éternelle. . . . Il se faut vaincre; il se faut renoncer à soy-mesmes et se faire guerre. . . . Laissant nous-mesmes, nous gagnons Dieu tout-puissant, le Père, le Fils et le benoyt Saint-Esprit; laissant le monde, nous gangnons le reaulme des cieulx, qui est une terre ferme et à tout jamais incommutable; finalment, vainquant les mauvais esprits, lesquielx cherchent nostre éternelle ruine, nous acquérons la faveur et la bonne grâce de tous les amis de Dieu, qui sont les bons anges, et tous saincts et sainctes de paradis. . . .*

C'est de Magonce (Mayence), par le tout vostre, en chair cosin, et en Jesus Christ frère.

PIERRE FAVRE,
de la Compagnie de Jésus Christ.

From Germany he was sent back again to Spain. The heir apparent, afterwards Philip II, who subsequently married Bloody Mary, had married the daughter of the King of Portugal, and it seemed an excellent opportunity, as the royal house of Portugal was most friendly, to give the Society of Jesus a real foundation in Spain. After some delay from illness Lefèvre went (1544), carrying with him the head of one of the Eleven Thousand Virgins of Cologne and other sacred bones, which he presented to the Jesuit College at Coimbra. He did more than that, he wrote (it would seem for the students there) a little tract on obedience, a virtue of which, as we have seen, they stood in need. The voice is the voice of Lefèvre, but the words are the words of Ignatius:

Obedience must be blind; that is to say, he that is truly obedient must not look for love, nor reasonableness, nor any understanding of what fruit there may be in the work upon which he is sent.

When it shall happen by God's grace (and from the very fact that we go blindfold) that a perception of what fruit there is in the labors to which we are sent opens before us, nevertheless, we must try not to lose the spirit with which we bow in blind obedience, even though a new and different task be commanded, and we be called off from what we were doing. It is necessary for those subject to command never to settle down to rest anywhere, no, not to a labor commanded, not even if they feel a clear and saintly desire in it; I mean to rest in any such fashion as to slacken the promptitude that belongs to obedience. . . .

To sum up, obedience, as I have said, must be blind, both in contemplation of the work and in execution, dispassionate and free from any fleshly or worldly affection, taking as its pattern those words of perfection that Christ our Lord spoke to us in the Gospel: "If any man will come after me, let him deny himself, and take up his cross, and follow me," that is to say denying to ourselves every personal inclination, capacity, feeling, will and opinion, and submitting ourselves in every respect to the inclination, capacity, feeling, will and opinion of our superiors, taking up our own cross and not another's, although his may seem to us an easier cross to bear; and, with all humility and patience, being ready to suffer whatever may befall us at the hand of our Lord, following Christ with the cross of such labors, at whose hand we hope to receive our reward, as is said: "The husbandman that laboreth must be first partaker of the fruits."

From Coimbra Lefèvre set out on his mission to establish the Society in Spain. He was still at Valladolid when the Princess Mary, wife of Philip, died, leaving the unfortunate infant Don Carlos to grow up to mystery and tragedy; and he was still there when the Emperor's daughter Margaret, Duchess of Parma—destined to become famous in history as Regent of the Netherlands in the time of William the Silent and the beginning of the Dutch struggle for independence

from Spain—gave birth to twins in Rome, one of whom,
at the parents' request, was baptized by Ignatius. I mention these dealings with royalty, for they are straws to
show how the wind blows; the Jesuits are already in close
intimacy with the King and Queen of Portugal, and on
friendly terms with the royal house of Spain, and the royal
house of Spain is the dominant power in European politics.

While at Valladolid, Lefèvre wrote this entry in his
Memoriale:

Another day, when I was very low in my mind and de-
pressed by troubles and bitterness due to a lack of true
brotherly love and humility towards those who had found
fault with me, I lifted up my soul toward God, and I perceived that all other things are as nothing; and that the
very best remedy in such moments is for me to lift my soul.
For then, when my soul is lifted up on high, no darts that
can be thrown have power to hurt it; I do not feel them.
Neither word, nor sting, can follow there; nor mount up
to the spirit that stands erect before God. No scourge
comes near His tabernacle. So lift up your mind right
speedily when aught of earth, in word or deed, touches your
spirit; and that, whether it tend to human joy or to vain
sorrow. And a longing comes over me of advancing towards
the mystery of the ascension of our Lord, for in His ascension we are lifted above earthly things, now only in the
spirit, but at last also in the body, even according to physical sense.

And in another entry:

An inclination always comes over me when I am at an
inn, to edify by teaching and exhortation. It is always of
profit in the sight of Christ and His court, to leave in inns
or houses, where we happen to stop, some signs of holy
living; for everywhere we can build up, everywhere we can
either plant or reap, and we are debtors to all men in every
condition, in every place. Let us humbly imitate the Most
High God who takes heed of us and comforts us; we also
are His fellow-laborers.

A little later we find him writing to Lainez, rules or counsels for winning back heretics. I think that they all went to Lefèvre when they had need of sweetness; for light they went to Ignatius. Lefèvre's first rule is: whoever wishes to do good to heretics at the present day, must see that he has much charity towards them, and loves them truly, casting out from his spirit all antagonisms.

When he left Spain, the colleges at Coimbra, Alcalá, Valencia, Gandia and Barcelona had been, at least informally, founded. He got back to Rome in July, and died on the 1st of August, 1546. According to the records of the Company his spirit joined that of Jean Coduri: "Their souls found one another in heaven (as their bodies met together in Santa Maria della Strada), and both, in one another's company, likewise abide with us here in Rome."

CHAPTER XXVIII

ROME, in the years round and about 1540 and 1550, lay shrunken within the Aurelian walls, as if enveloped in a giant's robe. On the Pincian Hill there was scarce a building to be seen, the charming new villa erected for Cardinal Ricci, now the Villa Medici, stood on what might have been the edge of an English common; and as one went from the Villa Medici to Santa Trinità dei Monti, and then on along the Via Felix, now the Via Sistina, to Santa Maria Maggiore, all the space within the walls to the north and east, as far as the Porta Salaria, Porta Pia and the Campo Militare, was occupied by gardens, vineyards, olive groves, and vegetable patches, shaded by rows or clumps of trees, with a few churches and villas scattered in among them. And the streets that ran from Santa Maria Maggiore south-westerly towards the Forum virtually separated town from country, for all the region east and south of the Esquiline and Palatine hills, was a sort of wild park for horticulture or nature to take its ease in. So was the Aventine Hill. The Forum Romanum "overwrought with forest branches and the trodden weed" was half a cow pasture, half a waste haunted by Silence and slow Time; at the foot of the Palatine Hill, in the cool of the ruined arches that once supported the imperial palace, goat-herds lay on the grass in summer days and watched their goats, while shepherd lads drove their sheep along the Sacra Via or drovers shouted at cattle that ran loose up the Clivus Victoriæ. The site of the Circus Maximus was cut up into vegetable beds and irrigated by the little brook Marrana. Remains of ancient edifices lay all about, much more than now. Within the inhabited district, pavements, fragments of wall and scattered blocks testified to the magnificence of the colonnades and arched walks that once connected the Roman Forum with Trajan's; and, out in the southerly parts, in the fields within the walls, where hunters went fowling, masons quarried and lovers of ancient art went digging for treasures, the mighty ruins of the imperial thermæ, covered with weeds, wild herbs, bushes and grasses, showed like fantastical creations of nature. Across the river, in Trastevere, over the flat land and up the hill to San Pietro in Montorio, and on all the slopes of the Janiculum, the story was much the same, vineyards, vegetable patches, or pleasure gardens with flowers and orange trees, encompassed a villa here and a church there.

The built-up parts of the city began to the north of the Capitoline Hill. Houses, sometimes detached, sometimes close to one another with walls in common, were grouped in blocks, called islands, which were separated and surrounded by little crooked, unpaved streets; excepting those of the rich, they were of a simple somewhat distrustful appearance, usually of two stories; the roofs were ridged and tiled, the windows few and round topped, the doors protected by a penthouse. The *Corso* was almost the only straight road in the city; kept so, it might seem, for the gay days of the carnival, when horses, donkeys, buffaloes, and aged Jews ran involuntary races. The dwelling first occupied by Ignatius was at the foot of the hill that leads up to Santa Trinità dei Monti, near the present Piazza di Spagna, and looked out on the open hillside with vineyards and fields; whereas the house by the Torre de la Melangola was in a built-up neighborhood, to the west of the Palazzo Venezia, near the little church of Santa Maria della Strada, which was afterwards pulled down to make room for the Gesù. The first house built for the Jesuits (1543) was also put there.

At this time most of the famous buildings of the Renaissance had been already built, the palace of the Cancelleria, the Villa Farnesina, the Palazzo Madama, where the Emperor's daughter, Margaret, the friend and patron of the early Jesuits, dwelt, the Palazzo Farnese though still lacking the glorious cornice that Michelangelo was to add, and some forty other palaces and mansions, belonging mostly to great prelates or to their near relations. The Basilica of St. Peter's was in the course of construction under plans that kept changing as one architect succeeded to another, the new choir was not finished, and the great dome not yet begun; the old nave still stood and the façade of the old church still looked upon the time-honored piazza. Michelangelo had been put in charge in the early years of Paul III, and his autocratic, contemptuous ways were driving the board of works crazy with apprehensions and vexation. The long covered way between the Vatican and the Castle of St. Angelo, which had enabled Clement VII to escape when Bourbon's soldiers scaled the walls of the Borgo, showed how little the Papal Curia dared trust to law and order. The Sistine Chapel, Raphael's Stanze, the Appartamenti Borgia, statues and frescoes in a score of churches, are proof enough of the genius that had been lavished to make Rome beautiful. Nevertheless, the Eternal City was not what she had been in the pontificate of Leo X; she had been maimed and disfigured in the terrible sack of 1527, and, like a mutilated statue of Hera, was destined never to recover the radiance of her former beauty.

There were many who thought that Rome deserved what she got. Juan Valdés makes St. Peter say, "Behold the judgment of God." However that may be, the corrupt régime paid the penalty, and came to an end in horror and suffering. From that date—I speak approximately—the Catholic Reform began. I am not concerned with the old régime. The peculiar rottenness of morals and manners under the Borgias passed with them, but the generation now dominant in papal affairs had been bred in that atmosphere. Paul III owed his cardinal's hat, which he received at the age of twenty-five, to the beauty of his sister, *"belle à merveilles"* according to the reputation that lingered on, and confirmed by a picture of the Madonna painted in her likeness; and Paul III, though he became a great reformer, made no bones as to his relation to his *nipoti*. Such abominations as the Borgias perpetrated were not continued, but the military fervor of Julius II and the luxurious tastes of Leo X smacked equally little of Christianity. Pietro Aretino writes to a friend (1537): *"L'innocentia è una bestiuola parlante e inquieta; e l'honore un' bestionaccio sensitivo, e ritroso."* ("Innocence is a restless chattering little beast, and honor an irritable, obstinate big brute.") I recall this indifference of the Renaissance to religion solely in order to give the proper background to the reforming spirit; and I shall confine myself to two references, one to politics, the other to the interest in pagan art.

On the death of Leo X, both Charles V and Henry VIII, that "most beloved, most excellent, and most puissant Prince, our most dear brother, cousin and fair Uncle," were deeply interested in the choice of his successor. But intermeddling was risky for it might act like a boomerang. Henry despatched two letters to his ambassador in Rome, couched in identical language, advocating the choice of Wolsey in one, and of Cardinal Giulio dei Medici in the other, and advised his dear nephew Charles to do the same. Wolsey was craftily ambitious for the tiara; he told these two sovereigns that the chief advantage from his election would be that "they might direct and dispose of his power and authority as if the Holy See were in their possession." Charles inquired what he could do to help so desirable an issue. Wolsey was clear enough: "Nothing would contribute more towards determining the election in my favor than the march of the Imperial troops now in Italy towards Rome; and in case neither presents nor good words have their effect on the College of Cardinals, they should be compelled by main force to the choice which his Majesty approves." He, himself, was ready to pay out 100,000 ducats. Charles, who had inherited much of the political hypocrisy that had done so much for his grandfather, Ferdinand of Aragon,—Macchiavelli's hero—answered that he would leave nothing undone, he was ready with letters and harangues, *"mais aussy quand il serait besoing avec la main, y en emploiant toute l'armée que j'ay en Italie, que n'est pas petite."* It is not surprising that Baldassare Castiglione during a papal conclave exclaimed, *"Nostro Signor Dio mandi al Spirito Santo, che ve n'è grandissimo bisogno."*

("Please God send the Holy Ghost for there is great need of
Him.") Charles V was no whit worse than other monarchs.
Pietro Aretino ran no risk of shocking Francis I's sensibilities by writing to him (1538): "Political interest pays no
regard to right, it knows nothing sacred, does not swerve
aside for the blandishments of honesty, and when it is in
pursuit of something, wrong is right, and the blameworthy
becomes laudable." The policy and practice of the Papal
Curia was of a piece with this. Cardinal Jean du Bellay
from his experience as ambassador in Rome, concluded that
cardinals were not to be talked over but to be bought, that
the one motive power was *"auriflue énergie."* Ribadeneira, who lived for a time as page in the palace of Cardinal
Alessandro Farnese, calls that household "a bog, a quagmire,
an abyss of hell." All this is only too familiar. I shall,
however, make one further reference to what Loyola must
have thought the very unchristian interest in pagan
antiquities.

Jean du Bellay, bishop of Paris, and later Cardinal, had
come to Rome, as French ambassador, for the purpose,
among others, of arranging the marriage of Prince Henry
of France with Catherine dei Medici, and had conducted
negotiations dexterously enough with Clement VII, *"ce bon-
homme,"* as he called him when matters went smoothly, or
"le vieux renard" when they did not. Du Bellay had in his
suite, a vivacious man of many talents and variegated experience, François Rabelais, already known in France as the
author of a book called *Pantagruel.* Matters did not go
quite so well after Clement's death; the ambassador was
obliged to spend much of his time in making honeyed promises to Paul III, and in bestowing pensions and gifts on
cardinals, condottieri, and other gentlemen of indigence and
appetite who might be of use in persuading the straddling
Pope to incline the balance towards King Francis and away
from Charles, such as the Orsini, the Colonnesi, and others.
But there were periods of relaxation, unless the good bishop
of Mâcon belied the words of his kind letter that invited du
Bellay to lodge with him. *"D'une chose vous suplye-je: à
vostre arrivée ne prendre aultre maison que la myenne. . . .*

Si trouverez la cave assez bien garnye et espère vous faire boyre froict." But the chief diversion was the study of antique art. Du Bellay and Rabelais purchased a vineyard and began excavations, and Rabelais worked over a plan of the monuments of ancient Rome. Du Bellay enriched his own collection of *"anticailles"* and hunted about to provide *objets d'art* for his friend Anne de Montmorency, afterwards High Constable of France, who was at that time furnishing his château of Chantilly. Crafty Italians were at hand to supply what rich foreigners might want. One Signor Valerio, secretary to an Italian cardinal, graciously filled the office of art dealer, and found half a dozen antique heads, among them one of Cæsar, and, apparently, a very unusual head of a woman:

Una testa di donna. . . . V. S. può esser certa che è bellissima et antica. È il vero che l'ho fatta un poco ritoccar nel naso e ne la bocca da maestro Alfonso. V. S. vedra la piu bella acconciatura de capegli et cosi finita che Ella vedessi gran pezzo fa. Secondo che mi verrano de le cose alle mani che sian degne di Lei, me ne ricorderò. . . . Io fo un poco rassettar una testa che ho per S. Ex [Montmorency] et non Le dispiacera et, subito rassettata, la daro medesimamente a M. di Mâcon. ("Your Excellency may rest assured that the head is antique and very beautiful. I have had maestro Alfonso touch it up as to the nose and mouth. Your Excellency will see the loveliest coiffure and so carefully finished!—such as you have not seen in a long time. I shall keep you in mind whenever any things worthy of you come in my way. . . . I have had a head that is to go to Sieur de Montmorency a little touched up. You will be pleased with it, and as soon as the touching up is finished, I will give it at once to the Bishop of Mâcon.")

In this way Signor Valerio and Maestro Alfonso provided French amateurs with antique art *"ben rassettato"* serving together, all at once, politics, art and Mammon. And, of course, interest in antique art did not stand by itself. Paul III merely swam with the stream when he sat to Titian for his portrait, to Giacomo della Porta for his bust, bade Michelangelo paint the *Last Judgment* in the Sistine Chapel, fresco the walls of the Cappella Paolina, complete the Palazzo Farnese, and take charge of the works of St. Peter's basilica, or when he directed that comedies of Terence or Macchiavelli be played in the Vatican.

All this was very harmless, but it is evidence how complete the reign of pagan interests at Rome had been during the golden days of the High Renaissance. Luther's blows, straight out from the shoulder, changed the whole face of things. The idle, evil, foolish, lovers of pleasure hid their heads, and innocent-minded, high-souled reformers came to the fore. Paul III himself led the way. Cardinals Contarini, Sadoleto, Caraffa, Pole, Aleander, Fregoso, Badia, Morone and Cortese; bishops Giberti of Verona, Pio of Carpi, and many others, came in with new brooms, and, under the Pope's direction or encouragement, set vigorously to work. I cannot attempt even a sketch of the Counter Reformation. The task of reforming the Church was a labor for Hercules, and would hardly have been possible, had it not been for the attack from without. The Papal Curia was worldly, selfish, corrupt; the cardinals as a rule were men of pleasure; bishops often did not reside in their dioceses, nor parish priests always in their parishes; many prelates held a plurality of benefices; the secular clergy was in large measure ignorant and lazy; the monastic orders careless of their rules or worse. To all these evils the reformers within the Church addressed themselves with a will. I shall not recount their doings, neither their successes nor failures. I merely wish to lay stress on the fact that when Ignatius came to Rome, the flood of reform was setting it. He is not entitled to the credit of a pioneer reformer. He was, however, the one genius in the Catholic party, and he laid the foundations of religious reform—where for true building it must lie—in the soul and conscience of the individual layman. Nor was the Society of Jesus by any means, as one might be led to think from Jesuit books, the first organization dedicated to reform; it was the ablest, the most energetic, the most thorough, the most devoted.

Other new orders had preceded it. The earliest was the Oratory of Divine Love. This Society was an outgrowth of a reaction against corruption, and was organized sometime before the Lutheran movement; the purpose of its members, both clergymen and laymen, was to ennoble their lives by religious exercises, by praying and preaching, by frequent recourse to the sacraments, by acts of charity, and so, by means of personal sanctification, to reform the Church. Sadoleto and Giberti were both members. In 1519 the *Confraternità della Carità* was organized for the purpose of looking after gentlefolks fallen upon evil days, of visiting prisons, and providing burial for the very poor. A few years later, the order of the *Teatini* was founded by Gaetano di Thiene and Gian Pietro Caraffa. This was the order that called out unsympathetic criticism from Loyola, and so brought about a lack of cordiality between him and Caraffa. The idea of it was to form a society of single-minded priests, bound by a rule, who should devote themselves to administering the sacraments, to preaching, and other religious and ecclesiastical matters, with the special purpose of setting an example to secular priests, and persuading them to return to an apostolic life. The members took the three vows. Poverty was of the first obligation; they were not even to beg, but to wait for alms to be given. Caraffa resigned his two sees and his benefices, and gave away his property; Gaetano was of a tender type, and used to burst into tears at the mystery of the mass. The new order aroused enmity and contempt. After the sack of Rome, the members, of whom there were but twelve, escaped to Venice, where they made close friends with the men in charge of the Hospital for Incurables as well as with Gasparo Contarini, who became Cardinal, Reginald Pole, and other reformers. It was very likely at this hospital that Loyola first heard of them.

In 1525 the Order of the Capuchins, a reformed branch of the Franciscan Order, was organized; its members lived like hermits, and preached repentance to peasants. Another reforming body was the Somaschi, who performed their charitable works in and about Bergamo and Brescia. This too

was about the year 1530.   The Order of the Barnabites was
founded, in 1533, at Milan; these priests held open-air
missions, rather after the fashion of the Salvation Army,
as I understand it.   I give these details concerning the nature and purposes of these reforming bodies, as evidence
that the Society of Jesus—as it was constituted by its
charter and constitution—did not start as an original idea
out of an inventive mind, but was created or compounded
out of ideas that were in the air, and partially in practice.
Altogether, there is evidence that there were many health-
giving forces lying about, some showing themselves, some
still latent, ready to be applied to the conservation of the
old ecclesiastical order, if a man of genius should come forward with the instrument by which they could be put to
use.   The purpose of this book has been to show how such
a man did come forward.

And I shall adduce one more indication of the spiritual
atmosphere in Rome which, however alien to any thoughts
or feelings that we find in Loyola and his companions, shows
how the nobler minds brooded, though not necessarily in an
ecclesiastical fashion, over spiritual welfare.   I refer to
Vittoria Colonna and to Michelangelo.   She—*"di spirto
generoso, di natura magnanima, d'ingegno pellegrino, di
virtù sola, di creanza nobile e di vita buona"* as a contemporary truly says, had come under the influence of Juan
Valdés, and was accused of heretical views, as were other
pious souls, such as Cardinal Contarini—who constitutes
one of the links between that intellectual group and Ignatius
Loyola—but in fact, she went no further than a region of
poetry and neo-Platonism, where aspiration and upward
yearning may have been a little careless of classified dogmas.

> Se per salir ad alta e vera luce
> Dai bassi, ombrosi e falsi sentier nostri,
> È ver che Amor la strada erta dimostri—

("Of a verity, Love shows the steep path up to the true
light, out from our low, o'ershadowed, wayward ways.")

> Se le dolcezze, che dal vivo fonte
> Divino stillan dentro un gentil core,

Apparissero al mondo ancor di fuore,
Con bella pace in puro amor congionte;
Forse sarebbon più palesi e conte
Le cagion da sdegnar ricchezza e onore:
Onde i più saggi, lieti, ebbri d'amore,
Andrebbon con la croce all' erto monte.

("If the sweetness that flows into the humble heart from the living fountain of God, should show itself visible to the world, attended by beauteous peace and pure love; perhaps the reasons for contempt of riches and honors would be more plain and clear, and those more wise would go in joy, and drunk with love, up the steep hill, carrying the cross.")

And Michelangelo cries out:

Mettimi in odio quanto 'l mondo vale,
E quante sue bellezze onoro e colo,
C'anzi morte caparri eterna vita—

Make me to hate all that the world holds dear,
All things of beauty that I love and cherish,
And gain eternal life instead of death.

Or, let me refer to his sonnet wherein he prays for faith:

De', porgi, Signor mio, quella catena
Che seco annoda ogni celeste dono:
La fede dico, a che mi stringo e sprono.

O God, reach down that chain,
To which is knotted every heavenly gift,
True faith, I mean, toward which I strive and strain.

And it was at this time, I think, that Palestrina was chapel master in Santa Maria Maggiore.

There are, I presume, all the time all sorts of forces, physical, chemical, vital, ethical, social and, perhaps, spiritual, lying idle, so far as mankind is concerned, about us; it is the task of genius to discover and put some, at least, of those forces to use. Ignatius was such a genius.

CHAPTER XXIX

Such as I have described in earlier chapters were, in a way, the occupations of the earliest Fathers. Before Ignatius died the Society had houses and colleges, either established or in the making, all over Catholic Europe; kings and princes were its friends and patrons; the Popes were its supporters and protectors, even the dreaded Caraffa, Paul IV, behaved towards the Society in so fatherly a fashion that Ignatius was able to say,—with a little exaggeration—that no Pope had done more for it than he; the orthodox bishops of Europe assembled at the Council of Trent, had learned to respect it. In fact, the reputation of the Society had suddenly grown so great that there was danger lest the Fathers should lose their heads. Ignatius had to caution one of them, pretty sharply, not to assume a tone of authority towards Duke Cosimo of Florence, because already an unfriendly report was going about Rome,— *"Que queremos governar todo el mundo"* ("That we want to govern the whole world"); and years before he died, he said, to one of his disciples: "If you live ten years more, you shall see great things." All this accomplishment, big with promise of greater achievements still, could not have been wrought without the talents, the zeal and the tireless energy of *los primeros padres;* and they were well seconded by their younger associates, Canisius, Araoz, Francisco de la Strada, Domenech, Miron, Miguel de Torres, Nadal, Polanco, Ribadeneira and others. Nevertheless, making full allowance for what these men did, the credit and the glory must be awarded to Ignatius. His was the imperial gift, as Cardinal Newman calls it, "to frame, to organize and to consolidate."

From the time he was elected General until his death, Ignatius, as I have said, virtually never left Rome at all.

His labors may be divided into two main categories: As director of the Jesuit house in Rome, and of various charitable institutions there, he had much to do in the city itself; and, as executive head of a rapidly spreading order, he was concerned with matters all over the world. At first he devoted the greater part of his attention to local duties, but as years went by he must have found it necessary to give more and more time to the superintendence of affairs away from home. I shall, however, leave chronology to one side, and say something of his various occupations in the sequence that shall seem most convenient.

First and foremost in importance comes his correspondence: letters from Jesuit Fathers, wherever they were, and his replies of instruction, suggestion and encouragement; letters from persons in high place outside the Society, both ecclesiastical and secular, and his written in answer; letters from persons of various sorts, with whom the Society, or he personally, had some connection; letters from relations, old friends, acquaintances and such. The table of contents for the volumes of his letters show how far and wide, even in these first years, the Society had stretched its branches, how deep it had pushed its roots. His letters to Popes, kings, princes and cardinals are always marked by extreme deference; they reveal his policy of working with established authority, never against it. In matters of principle, he was very firm; but, if principles were not involved, he always endeavored to win the good will and to conform to the wishes of the great. He knew that it lay with them to favor or obstruct the work of the Society. For instance, King John III wished to establish the Inquisition in Portugal, and at his request, Ignatius made every effort to induce the Apostolic See to grant the necessary charter; but when the King wished members of the Society to assume the office of inquisitors, he refused, for he had made it a principle for the Society not to accept any outside dignities. For this same reason, Jay, Bobadilla and Canisius refused bishoprics, and Lainez and Borgia asked to be excused from accepting a cardinal's hat. Ignatius was fearful lest the mere possibility of such prizes might tempt ambitious men to join the

Society, or hurt the humility of those within; besides, he wished the members all absolutely free to be sent at a moment's notice, near or far, to heretics or heathen: "We, (he said) are the light horse of the Church." The Popes hesitated before accepting this principle, and Marcellus II, while still a cardinal, argued the point with Dr. Olave, S. J. They could not agree, until the Jesuit said: "Well, it's enough for us that Father Ignatius thinks so," and the Cardinal answered: "I surrender; reason seems to be on my side, but the authority of Father Ignatius outweighs reason."

The great bulk of Loyola's correspondence was with the Jesuit Fathers scattered about Italy or in foreign parts. This correspondence was a matter of great solicitude; we find him frequently admonishing one or another of them, as to what he requires. The rules that he laid down are explicit. The superiors of colleges, houses or missions must write regularly. Those in India, once a year—the post would not permit more frequent letters—those in Italy, once a week, and those elsewhere in Europe once a month. These letters must contain full information on all matters that concern the Society; the doings of the Superior and those under him, as to preaching, teaching, giving the *Spiritual Exercises*, hearing confessions, etc., news as to health, as to the welcome given them, the attitude of princes and bishops, the character and talents of new recruits, the prosperity of the mission, the outlook for the future, and all such matters. Every letter must be carefully written, twice over if need be, in order to be clear and free from irrelevant details, and contain only such matters as could be shown with advantage to outsiders, *cosas de edificación.* If the writer wished to communicate matters that might not redound to the credit of the Society, or might be misinterpreted or misunderstood, or for one reason or another had better be reserved for Loyola's private ear, he was to write them privily on a separate sheet; and also, as the rules say:

When there is anything surpassingly praiseworthy, so that you would not like to say it of yourselves, if there should be a friend at hand who could write of it, well and good; and, if not, put it either in the supplementary letter, or in the principal letter in such fashion that it shall arouse no suspicion of vanity, even in the somewhat suspicious-minded.

Besides these letters, the Fathers Superior away from home were to write three times a year,—*Litteræ quadrimestres*—on the first days of January, May and September, giving a summary of the *cosas de edificación* that had taken place during the preceding four months.

Ignatius set great store by these rules, for it was his practice to send copies of the letters that contained good news to members of the Roman Curia and to the missionary Fathers at their various stations, who were charged to show them to people of importance, in order that all the world should learn of what the Society of Jesus was accomplishing. Xavier's letters were of the very greatest service to the Society.

There was frequent business with various cardinals, often with the Pope himself, with bishops, with the ambassadors from Spain and Portugal, with distinguished personages, such as the Lady Margaret, the Emperor's daughter, or other visitors in Rome, sometimes concerning the interests of the Society, sometimes concerning other things. All this I pass over and come at once to the ordinary routine. In the first place the usual religious means for stirring men to a sense of spiritual things were zealously employed. There was preaching, both in the Society's own churches, *Santa Maria de la Strada, Sant' Andrea de la Fracte,* and also in others, and there was hearing confession, giving *Spiritual Exercises,* and teaching. Ignatius himself used to teach. An anecdote told by his secretary, Ribadeneira, bears witness to his zeal:

A great many people came to listen to Father Ignatius, learned and ignorant, men and women, all sorts of people. In these lessons of his, two particular virtues displayed themselves, humility and holiness. He was far from eloquent, he had learning but no skill in speaking; and, worse than that, he did not know the Italian language very well. So, although I was a mere boy, I told this holy old man that there were many mistakes in what he said, much to be corrected, for he mixed Spanish in with his Italian. "Well," he said, "please note and tell me when it happens." So, the next day I set out to take careful notes of his foreign words, mispronunciations, and so forth. I found, however, that it was not this word or that which had to be altered, but the whole discourse; and out of sheer fatigue and despair I gave up trying to make the corrections, and told him how it was. Father Ignatius said: "Peter, for the Lord's sake, what am I to do?"

But in reality he had much of the orator's art, at least he had the gift of persuasion. His conviction and his extraordinary fervor stirred his hearers to the depths. Even when he mixed up Spanish and Italian, the divine love that radiated from his countenance touched their hearts. Ribadeneira says that his sermons were devoid of all the artifices of eloquence, but full of force and the spirit of God, that they were like St. Paul's who says, "And my speech and my preaching was not with enticing words of man's wisdom, but in demonstration of the Spirit and of power." And Gonzalez adds that Ignatius used to say, "Love God with all your might and all your soul," and say it with such energy and fervor of spirit that his face seemed on fire with flames of love, and that his hearers hurried away with groans and tears to confess their sins.

In addition to these evangelical labors he undertook certain specific charities. He founded a house for orphan boys and another for orphan girls, and also the nunnery of Saint Catherine for respectable girls, who lived in bad surroundings or had nobody to look after them. He also established a place of refuge for repentant prostitutes, known as *Saint Martha's Home*, and organized a society of charitable people under the name of *"Our Lady of Compassion"* to take care of them. Ribadeneira says:

I remember how, at the time when the Home of St.
Martha was founded, notorious harlots forsook their shameful quest and with tears betook themselves to the quest of
salvation, and how Father Ignatius used to accompany them
through the public streets, not in a group, but first one and
then another; it was a very beautiful sight to see this holy
man, like an attendant going on before, leading a sinful
handsome woman, in order that he might save her from
the jaws of cruelest tyranny, and place her in the hands of
Christ.

He also took advantage of a rich gift from Francis Borgia
to found the *Collegio Romano,* an institution of higher
education for teaching various branches of philosophy,
casuistry, and also theology; he took charge of the *German
College,* chartered by Paul III, a seminary where young
Germans should be trained for the priesthood, with the idea
of returning to Germany, as missionaries, to serve the orthodox faith; and he devised a system of instruction to be
used there.

The way that Ignatius set about these charitable foundations was this. He imparted his general idea to two or
three friends of character and sagacity; then, having obtained their approval, he laid the plan, in more elaborate
form, before men of opulent means, and after he had collected the necessary funds, and had set the project on its
feet and going, he would draw up rules for its government,
request some Cardinal to be its patron, and then induce
well-disposed persons to become a board of trustees and
take over the work. And then, that matter out of the way,
he would turn to something new.

He also busied himself with great zeal in the conversion
of Jews, of whom there were large numbers, living in the
Ghetto across the Tiber, and founded a house for catechumens. He was not only quite free from the popular prejudice against the Jewish race, but even asserted that it was a
great privilege to be of the same blood as Christ and the
Virgin Mary. Once a Spanish gentleman hearing him say
something of the sort, crossed himself in horror, and ex-

claimed scornfully, "A Jew!" and spat at the very thought. Ignatius said: "Señor Pedro de Çarate, let us reason together," and spoke so persuasively that before he finished, Pedro de Çarate wished that he too had been born a Jew. The Popes Julius III and Paul IV, with "great wisdom," obliged all the synagogues in Italy to contribute to the support of this house for catechumens. Ignatius also persuaded one or the other of them to repeal an old law which exacted that a converted Jew, in return for the treasure of heaven, should forfeit all his earthly possessions. And so, as Ribadeneira says: "the door to heaven was flung open wide to the Jews."

One would have supposed that such benevolent institutions might have been begun and set going without vexations; but quite the contrary came to pass. As to St. Martha's Home, an employee in the papal service, master of the posts, promulgated the grossest slanders, he called it the Jesuits' seraglio or some such name. Ignatius, as usual, brought the matter into the full light of day, and laid a complaint before the papal magistrate. Persons of no less consequence than the Spanish Viceroy of Sicily and his wife, whose good offices the master of the posts had sought, endeavored to persuade Ignatius to accept a retraction out of court and let the matter drop; but where the good name of the Society was in question, Ignatius was as obdurate as the rock of Gibraltar. The case was called, the slanderer made default. The Magistrate investigated the accusation, and declared that, so far from there being any wrong-doing, the Fathers deserved high praise. Other slanders were circulated by the priest who had been put at the head of the *Home for Catechumens*. Here again the Fathers were completely exonerated by a court of competent jurisdiction. Still another accusation was made. A Dr. Ferrer, a nephew of Doña Isabel Roser, denounced Ignatius as a hypocrite and a thief. The trouble arose in this way. This lady, who had been so kind and generous to Ignatius in early days when he was in Barcelona, had come to Rome, partly, I presume, to be near him and under his charge, and partly in order to marry off two young relations of hers. Ignatius received her gratefully, acted as her spiritual director, and admitted her to the vow of obedience. She stayed in Rome for two years, and, out of gratitude for her old kindness, one of the Fathers, Esteban de Eguia, now an old and venerable gentleman, was detailed to act as her steward, to provide her with food, apparel, shoes, to sweep her room, and so on. The nephew seems to have thought that Ignatius was using improper influence to get his aunt's money. The case was taken to court. Isabel Roser was in tears, and the nephew formally admitted that what he he said was wholly untrue. Warned by this occurrence, Ignatius insisted upon releasing Doña Isabel and two other ladies from their vows of obedience, and obtained a decree from the Pope that in the future the Fathers of the Society of Jesus should not be called upon to assume the spiritual direction of any women.

The Church of Santa Maria della Strada stood where the great church of the Gesù now stands, a little to the west of the Palazzo di Venezia, and the house of the Jesuit Fathers was close by. Here in 1545 there were over thirty inmates. To give an idea of the nature of the life there, and the nature of the discipline of humility to which all were subjected, I will quote from the brief autobiography of Father Benedetto Palmio, a young gentleman of breeding and education, at this time twenty-three years old. On his reception in the household he was put to work in the kitchen. He speaks of himself in the third person:

EXTRACTS

FROM FATHER BENEDETTO PALMIO'S AUTOBIOGRAPHY

Benedetto was used, following his natural inclination, to make a great ado over cleanliness and neatness, more than the ordinary, even to the point of daintiness; and therefore he felt great disgust at the dirt in the kitchen and dining hall. At this time there were two causes that contributed largely to make the house dirty: great scarcity, and the class of novices that attended to the household chores,—for they took little or no pains in the matter of personal cleanliness. The consequence was that Benedetto could not look at the horrid, dirty places, where he was at work, without being sick at his stomach, although he used to rebuke himself sharply for it. At last he hit upon a plan for getting over his disgust and squeamishness. A divine spirit urged him on, and he at once put the plan into practice. Under the kitchen was a cellar filled with filth; down into this cellar Benedetto went, rolled in the filth, and covered himself with it from head to foot, and in this guise went about the house in triumphant joy. By this means he overcame all his fastidious dislike.

When Ignatius saw him all covered with filth, he used these words: "Now at last you please me, Benedetto." For, although Ignatius greatly loved the niceties of cleanliness, nevertheless he would not put up with much of it in novices; he would say that where men were advanced in age, and wrong appetites had simmered down, the care of cleanliness was praiseworthy and added a grace to virtue; but in young men, only lately come forth out of the nastiness of worldly things, cleanliness was a matter of reproach and had a bad look, it offered a field for the tares of vain ostentation and tempted them from a whole-hearted study of philosophy. When he saw them shabbily dressed and neglectful of their persons, he would say that some good angel was on hand to destroy fastidiousness and pride in their hearts.

Full of joy at having overcome his disgust, as has just been told, Benedetto went back to the duties of the kitchen, and while busying himself over them, took to comforting himself with these thoughts. First, he kept pondering over the words that God addressed to the holy Apostle, whom he had always studied religiously, "Arise and go into the city, and there it shall be told thee what thou must do"; and since he felt sure that he had been brought to the Company by the special favor of God's providence, whenever he was bidden to do anything at all, he deemed that God was the giver of the order, and thought himself set to do the work by God's express admonition; and this thought filled his soul with a great joy.   Secondly, he went over in his mind the words of Christ, "Inasmuch as ye have done it unto one of the least of these my brethren," etc.; and therefore, whenever he undertook any work for any members of the Company, he thought to himself that it should all be done as if directly to Christ.   From his appreciation of this, so much joy flowed over his spirit, that he even shed tears.   Thirdly, he considered Martha's love and her devout piety to the Lord Christ, and thought within himself that he ought to minister to Christ, to the Blessed Virgin, and to the Holy Apostles, with equal devotion, solicitude and alacrity.   And these thoughts not a little inflamed Benedetto's heart to undertake and do everything for Christ's sake.

By this time Benedetto had declared war against his carnal nature, and was putting all his wits to complete the conquest.   Nevertheless he shrunk back violently from shame and disgrace, for they are hateful to a gentleman. He felt he must attack that shrinking with all the vigor of his soul, that he must not ask for respect from men of birth and position in the world, but, on the contrary, scorn and contumely.   He then assumed the dress and character of a beggar, and began to beg for things that were necessary for the brethren.   He even went for the portions of bread and wine supplied to our house in Rome by some cardinals and rich men, and carried them home.   For several months he performed this office with exquisite delight, for he knew that the daily insults and curses cast at him (as at this time our Society was the butt and scorn of all Rome) were, in truth, great embellishments and recompenses from the Holy Spirit.   Sometimes he was pushed out of palaces, as a crazy man, and hooted at.   And when he walked across a square, he was greeted with derision by the boys, and also (for they were set on by rude blacksmiths) with a banging of iron instruments.   All this seemed to him light and pleasant compared to the shameful insults and contumelies put upon Christ.   Nevertheless, he found the beginnings of this apostolic practice a little bitter; and when he met some gentlemen, with whom in his college days he had been on terms of familiar friendship, he was overcome by shamefacedness, and did not dare ask them for alms, although he made many an effort to do so. At last, very angry with himself, to think that respect in the sight of the world had had more power over him than respect in the sight of Christ, he cast aside all false sense of shame, and in his beggar's garb, went up to one of his old friends, with whom he had been on closest terms, and boldly made the request that he had not dared ask before. When this friend recognized Benedetto, he could not endure his unseemly dress and appearance, and upbraided him, and asked why he had let himself be brought to such a condition of idiocy. Benedetto smiled, and since he was on his way home, hurried along, after giving his friend an invitation to come to see him.

The friend accepted and went to the Jesuits' house. Benedetto took him into the garden, and a conversation of this sort passed between them: "Well, Galeazzo, what do you think of my foolishness?" Galeazzo answered: "Palmio, you seem to me to be a very grievous enemy both to yourself and to your reputation. Why, when we were at Bologna, who would have entertained the slightest suspicion that your future ways would turn out so silly? Weren't there other pious confraternities, respectable and gentlemanlike, in which you could have taken up your abode, far better than here? What is your opinion of this class of men, among whom you have enrolled yourself? They are the offscouring, the dung of the city. If you knew what is said of your Order in gentlemen's houses, you wouldn't stay in this Company one hour." Benedetto replied: "How deceived you are in your censure! Is it strange that men of the world should hate these brethren, when they have always been bitter against Christ, the Best and Greatest, and against His disciples and followers? . . . Did not Christ declare plainly to His disciples, "If ye were of the world, the world would love its own, but I have chosen you out of the world, therefore the world hates you"? . . . And so on. At last, when Galeazzo perceived how joyful and steadfast Benedetto was as he discoursed on the happy state of men in a religious order, and the dangerous life of attendance upon courts, he said: "Blessed art thou, Benedetto, for I see that God has been very good to thee." . . .

I will further illustrate the life in the house of the Society under Loyola's management, by another extract from this same diary:

It happened one day that a certain Spanish woman, named Catherine, pretty well on in years and aflame with piety, noticed that the door of the house was open, and, going into the kitchen and on into the dining-room, came upon Father Miona, who was eating his dinner; she sat down beside him and talked a long time very intimately. On that day Benedetto (now in an office of greater responsibility) had permitted the door-keeper to make the round of the seven churches; and the brother whom Benedetto had put in the door-keeper's place, had gone off for some reason and got back too late, as he acknowledged, so it was his fault that the door stood open to the woman. Benedetto at that moment was busy about some matters upstairs. Meanwhile, by chance, Ignatius had gone downstairs . . . to the little court which was opposite the door, and was walking about there. Benedetto also went downstairs, and going into the dining-room, perceived the woman, and was amazed, but said nothing because he saw that she was talking to Father Miona, who was in charge of the house. Going out of the room he walked toward Ignatius, who was pacing up and down; for Benedetto had the idea that the woman had been admitted into the house by Ignatius' permission. But Ignatius, quite put out, turned his back on him and went to his room; and Benedetto, who would not say a word to defend himself, stayed downstairs. In a short time Ignatius called Miona to him and gave orders that Benedetto and Giovanni Paolo, the door-keeper who had gone to the seven churches, and the brother who had been put in his place for the day, and Antonio Rion, who was cook, should flagellate themselves. Miona told Benedetto what orders he had received from Ignatius, and comforted him saying: "My son, be patient, you have done no wrong, but Father Ignatius lays these commands in order to prove you." Benedetto immediately called the others together, told them of the punishment Ignatius had appointed; and they went to the flagellating room. A flagellation was supposed to last while the psalm *Miserere* was being chanted, but because Giovanni Paolo, though a most religious brother, got the giggles, the time of flagellation was stretched out nearly to a full hour. The trouble was that Antonio Rion had set Giovanni Paolo off laughing because in flagellating himself he had used keys instead of thongs. Benedetto rebuked Giovanni Paolo because the penitence should be undergone with great humility of mind; however, while they were struggling to recite the psalm without laughter, almost an hour was consumed.

Ignatius was very fond of that kind of penitence, where there was no real wrongdoing, and imposed it freely, for he knew that it developed strength in the brethren to enable them to overcome the natural stubbornness of human nature. After Ignatius had been told of this flagellation, while walking in the garden, he saw Benedetto and called him, and asked him how an ailment with which he was afflicted was getting on, and in the sweetest paternal words expressed his sympathy, as he was wont to do when others were ill or in trouble.

While I am about it, I will give some further details of the life in the Roman community. Adjoining the house was a garden, and the Society also owned a vineyard on the Aventine, with a sort of lodge in it, for the benefit of the students in the *Collegio Romano;* and, as I understand it, the novices from the Jesuit house also had the privilege of resorting to this recreation ground. The young men played at quoits, and also at *piastrelle,* a game I should judge halfway between quoits and pitch-penny, which Ignatius had seen played at the Sorbonne; he designed a wax model for the *piastrella* himself. No other sport of any kind was allowed.

One day Dr. Olave, the rector of the College, then a man over forty and of distinguished reputation, young Ribadeneira, and some others, were tossing oranges about from one to another; part of the game being that whoever muffed was to say an *Ave Maria*. Ignatius caught them at it and imposed a good stiff penance. On another occasion he found out that some youngsters, recovering from sickness and therefore permitted to walk in the garden, were playing ball; he had all the balls brought to him and thrown into the fire. As Father Gonzalez says: "He stopped up the chinks by which distraction might sneak in." For this purpose he drew up a set of rules, that he intended should be a precedent for all Jesuit recreation grounds in the future:

RULES

No one shall go to the vineyard without permission of the Rector or of his deputy.

No one shall eat or touch grapes or other fruit without permission.

No one shall eat more grapes or fruit than he is allowed, in order to prevent sickness from any excess.

No one shall leave his clothes about the vineyard, but in the prescribed place.

No one shall go into the kitchen without permission from the cook, or some one in the cook's place.

No games shall be played in the vineyard except *piastrelle,* and singing.

Neither the players, nor any one else, shall lean against the espaliers, nor the trellises, nor get up on them.

No one shall break twigs from the trees or vines, or make marks on them.

No one shall play *piastrelle* on the little paths that run across the width of the vineyard.

The Rector shall appoint a monitor, who shall give out the *piastrelle* whenever the young men go to the vineyard; and when the game is over, he shall count them and put them back in the closet appropriated for that purpose.

Every player shall be careful to return the *piastrella* he has played with, at the gate of the house, and hand it to the monitor. No one shall make lines or other marks on the walls of the house or the rooms, either indoors or out.

No one shall throw anything into the well.

I quote these minute regulations because they indicate the extreme care with which Ignatius arranged details. He builded like the old Roman builders. His conception of the Jesuits' life was one of law. Liberty to him was a euphemism for license. His mind contemplated a definite idea of the perfect soldier of the Church, and he put his whole practical sagacity into the task of moulding every novice enlisted in the Company of Jesus, according to that pattern, so far as their several qualities and capacities would allow. Here, too, as perhaps with all great religious organizers, there was an element of personal ambition; Ignatius wished for good tools with which to do the work he hoped to accomplish. Few men, if any, can see the will of God as other than, in some particular at least, coincident with their own wills. Luther saw it so; Calvin, too; and Loyola as well.

The routine in the house was regulated with equal detail; the various officers had their respective duties, the superior, the minister, the subminister, the procurator, the gardener, the cook, the door-keeper, and so forth. Seven hours were allotted to sleep, then the "waker-up" knocked on the bedroom doors; a quarter of an hour later it was his duty to enter the bedroom, and if he found anyone still in bed, to pull the mattress half off the bed. Bells were rung for prayers and meals. At dinner three books were read aloud, the Bible, the life of a saint, and some treatise on contempt of this world. In the Refectory, a distinction in the food was made between Loyola's table, where *los primeros padres* and guests sat, and the other tables:

His table [Benedetto Palmio says] was always resplendent with parsimony and frugality, but it had nevertheless a savor of gentle usages. There were two or three brothers to wait upon it, more especially when outsiders were invited to dinner. The wine glasses were served with elegance; it could not have been better done, or more attractively, in a palace.

And Ignatius was very particular about manners at table; rustic or untrained actions were condemned as "inurbane." Beds must be made before sunrise, and rooms swept every day. But I have said enough on this subject; a full account of all the prescribed routine would be out of all proportion to its importance. Ignatius, himself, at least in his latter years, on getting up, would meditate for an hour; then he said mass. He then attended to whatever there was to do. In transacting business his way was to reflect before deciding, to pray for enlightenment, and never to reach a conclusion without consulting the Fathers best informed upon the matter in hand, and then he did the work himself or delegated it to another with general instructions. If he had business abroad he always took a companion with him; if he stayed at home he received members of the household or visitors. After dinner he used to talk on edifying topics, and then attended to details of his correspondence or signed letters. After supper he arranged matters for the following day, talked to his secretary, walked up and down the room with a stick, for with age his wounded leg limped a little, and closed the day by a complete surrender to holy thoughts. He allowed but four hours for sleep. He was very fond of music; when he felt ill or had no appetite, his best tonic was to listen to a hymn sung by one of the Fathers, or to hear Father André Desfreux play upon the harp. But these pleasures he regarded as self-indulgence, and hardly ever accepted.

CHAPTER XXX

Now that I have recounted the work of this remarkable man, I shall try to describe some of the mental and moral qualities that enabled him to accomplish it. Up to twenty-six he had been an ordinary young man. To be sure there is little that we know of his youth, but not a word of it suggests character or talents out of the ordinary; during that first stage of life, where men, not destined to accomplish a twentieth part of what he did, are wont to wear promises on their sleeves and fill their friends with hope, Ignatius leaves us in doubt if there be one talent wrapped in his napkin. His conversion was remarkable, but not like that of Saul of Tarsus, which came with a blinding light, nor that of St. Augustine who heard a voice, but more like those of unknown or little distinguished persons such as Harold Begbie tells of in his *Twice Born Men*. And, remarkable as his conversion was, it would not, of itself, lead us to expect a Roman strength of purpose, much less a rare genius for practical affairs of a kind that nature does not bestow once in a hundred years. There is no other record of such genius for statesmanship in the Roman Catholic Church since Hildebrand or Innocent III, and if they had a wider vision and a more intellectual outlook, I doubt if they had greater tenacity of purpose or a deeper insight into human nature.

In the first place this little man, with broad, bald, unwrinkled brow and deep set, deep seeing, eyes, grave aspect, and distinction of carriage, possessed great character; by which I mean steadfastness, patience, endurance, energy, courage, determination. He had, also, the quality of arousing confidence; something about him asserted that his side would win the victory. Ribadeneira says, "As soon as the Blessed Father had set his hand to anything, its success

321

seemed already assured." And more, much more than that, he was in their eyes a holy man. One of the household, André Desfreux, used to say that somehow the grace of God seemed to have been born in Father Ignatius at birth, as a part of him, for all inordinate and sinful affections had been so dominated and suppressed, and virtuous feelings so firmly rooted in righteousness, that all of them together, affections and feelings, had become ministers to holiness, and ascended up from him to God.

By nature Ignatius was of a choleric disposition, but he had learned to master it so absolutely, that physicians, who did not know this, set down his temperament in their diagnosis as phlegmatic. This does not mean that he never showed anger; on the contrary, though he did not feel it, he often affected the appearance of it, for the sake of discipline. Ribadeneira says:

Often and often we have seen him, in perfect calmness and with all the sweetness of manner that can be imagined, order some one brought before him for punishment; and when the offender came into his presence, it seemed as if he was transformed and all afire; and then, after he had finished speaking and the offender had gone, immediately, without the slightest interval of time, he returned to his former serenity and blitheness of countenance, as if nothing had happened. It was clear that there had been no irritation whatever within, and that he had made use of that sudden look as a mask, putting it on and laying it aside at will. . . .

And though his bodily condition had its ups and downs, for his health was inconstant, nevertheless his soul was invariably of an even temper. What I mean [I am quoting Ribadeneira] is that if you wished to ask for something from Father Ignatius, it made no difference whether he was on his way from mass or had had dinner, or whether he had just got out of bed, or had been at prayer, whether he had received good news or bad, whether things were quiet, or the world all upside down. With him there was no such thing as *feeling his pulse,* no *taking a reckoning by the North Star,* no *steering by a sea chart,* as is the usual way of dealing with men in authority, for he was always in a state of calm self-mastery.

And Father Gonzalez says: "His dominion over himself, is a thing to praise God for."

During the conclave on the death of Marcellus II, in 1555, it was known that Cardinal Caraffa would in all probability be elected Pope.

Loyola sat by his window waiting for news. When it arrived a visible change came over his countenance, and as I [Father Gonzalez] have heard since both from him and from old Fathers to whom he told it, all his bones shook in his body. Without a word he got up and went into the chapel to pray and shortly came back as cheerful and contented as if the election had been to his liking.

There can be no question but that his countenance was often a mask; Gonzalez confirms this:

In Father Ignatius [he says] consideration always seems to precede his smile, as well as all his other external manifestations of feeling; for instance, he often shows an angry face when he feels no anger, or appears gay and affectionate towards some one, when he does not feel any very great affection. In short, as far as those who live with him can judge, he is so complete a master of his inner feelings, that he only gives them play as reason dictates.

Ignatius himself remarked that "whoever measured his affection by what he showed, would be much deceived; and the same with regard to harshness or any lack of affection." Let me quote Lord Rosebery again, who is speaking of Cromwell:

A great general inured to tremendous hazards has to curb and disguise his emotions until he almost loses the sensations of nature. He has to appear calm when uneasy, imperturbable in the face of calamity, confident when least confident, so as to inspire his officers and his troops; he is, in fine, ground by fortune into temper harder than steel.   Little or nothing of nature survives or is possible.

Three years before his death Ignatius was able to say that he had not called anyone a fool or a blockhead (*fatuum vel stupidum*) for thirty years, or used any other insulting epithet.

Ignatius was stern to himself and stern to his followers. He regarded them as soldiers in the army of Christ, and enforced discipline.   Disobedience, as in an army, was the worst fault.   To novices he was gentle, but to those who had been in the Society long enough to understand the rules, he showed great rigor, and if the disobedience were serious, he expelled the offender without a moment's delay. He turned one backslider (who in a time of penitence had prayed leave to stay in the kitchen and be the scullion's scullion) out of the Society and out of the house into the street on a stormy night.   And when a brother of Lainez had left the Order in great destitution, Ignatius would give him nothing: "What! to a deserter, to a runaway soldier? If I were the owner of everything in the wide world, I would not give a penny to those who leave the Order, after they have once taken the vows."   And he was overheard to say to a Portuguese nobleman, a member of the Society: "Don Theutonio, I will not permit in my time any breach of our rules; and much less will I permit a man of rank, and learning, to step aside from the straight path than I would an unlettered man of low birth"; and when this nobleman did step aside, Ignatius expelled him from the Society, although almost all the Fathers, for fear of scandal, protested.

Once one of the Fathers was called suddenly to confess a woman; he could not find a companion on the instant and had gone alone, contrary to rule.   He was a man of well tried virtues; of the sort that no suspicion, no sinister rumor could come near.   Nevertheless, for the sake of example, lest in the course of time the necessary strictness of the rule be relaxed, Ignatius commanded him to scourge himself in the presence of eight priests, while they repeated psalms in turn. On another occasion, a venerable, elderly man, Father Diego

Eguia, spoke in terms of superlative praise about Ignatius, in the presence of some people who seem to have found fault with its extravagance, or put some misinterpretation upon it; when Ignatius heard of this, he bade Father Eguia scourge himself for the time it took to repeat three psalms, on three several days, in the presence of the persons who had taken his words in ill part, and between each psalm to say, "One must not say things liable to misinterpretation," etc. And, again, Ribadeneira says:

Father Ignatius and I were strolling about together after supper, and a good many others were walking about and talking of one thing or another at a little distance off. While we two were discussing spiritual matters, Father Ignatius paused, and stepping up to one of the brothers said: "Go, see who those are walking over yonder" (the spot was too far to be distinctly visible from where we stood).   The brother came back, and said it was one of our priests talking to a novice. Ignatius called the priest up, and asked, "What were you talking about to the novice?"   The priest replied: "Father, we got on the topic of humility and mortification, and I was telling him what I had seen myself, or had heard, in those respects, about Brother Texeda [this was a man of high repute but not a member of the Society of Jesus] in order to encourage the lad to follow his pattern." Father Ignatius said: "Are there no examples to be found in the Society, that you go seeking them from outsiders? Who gave you permission to talk to novices, when you have not sense enough?   Go to the minister, and bid him strike your name off that list, and don't speak again to a novice without leave from me."

Ribadeneira says, that Ignatius wished to teach both the priest, and the others who were standing by, that in conversations with a novice they must avoid all topics, however spiritual, that did not have to do with his novitiate, lest he be distracted, and rendered irresolute; meaning, I presume, that if Franciscans or Cistercians were held up as examples of virtue, the novice might think he would do better to join one of those orders. But to a reader today, not under the spell of Loyola's dominant character, it would appear that a slight touch, not more perhaps, of paternal jealousy entered into that abrupt rebuke. At another time he ordered an old Father, of marked piety, to scourge himself during the recitation of three psalms, because he had said to outsiders, that one of the Fathers in the house was out of his head with a fever and said things he would not have said if he had been in his right mind. These instances show, I think, that Ignatius was often very severe, but nobody ever questioned his justice; and he never asked for an act of obedience from another that he was not ready to exact of himself. Once he was in his own room alone, at prayers, when the porter came knocking at the door, and calling out importunately: "Father! Father!" Ignatius did not answer. The porter kept on knocking. Finally, Ignatius opened, and asked: "What do you want?" The porter said: "Here are letters for you which the messenger says have just come from Azpeitia, from your family," and handed him a bundle of letters. There was a fire in the room, because of the winter's cold. "Throw them into the fire," Ignatius said, and then shutting the door on the man, returned to his prayers.

I will now speak of the impression his tact made upon his companions. Ribadeneira says:

He possessed a very remarkable gift for bringing a perturbed conscience back to composure and peace; even when a sufferer found himself unable to explain his difficulty. Ignatius would set out before him everything that he felt in his soul as clearly as if he had been told; then he would recount some similar experience that he himself had passed through, and the remedy that he had discovered for a similar infirmity, and give serenity and peace, as if his hand had brushed aside a cloud.

And Lainez used to say, that "although Father Favre was greatly practised in spiritual matters, as we know and as can be seen from his letters and his book, nevertheless the difference between him and Ignatius as to knowledge how to direct a soul was the difference between a child and a sage." And Gonzalez records:

Father Ignatius has many skillful ways to learn a man's feelings and inclinations. One is to touch upon a world of topics, counting on the probability that the other will, apropos of some topic, reveal what there is in his mind. [And adds:] In conversation, Ignatius is so complete a master of himself and of the person with whom he is talking that even Polanco is as inferior to him as a little boy to a sensible man.

He was always just, and his knowledge of human nature told him when to be harsh and when to be tender. Gonzalez says:

It is remarkable how Father Ignatius uses contrary means in what seem to be similar cases. He treats one man with great severity, and another with great gentleness; and after the episode is over, it is always obvious that, though you could not tell beforehand, he employed the right remedy. But he is much more inclined to love, and so completely so, that his whole behaviour seems love. And he is so universally beloved by all, that there is not a man in the Society who does not feel deep affection for him, and does not believe that Father Ignatius is very fond of him.

And he explains their affection by Loyola's conduct toward them: first, his affability; second, the extreme care that he took of their health; and, third, his habit of giving disagreeable orders through his subordinates as if the orders emanated from them, but of bestowing all favors and privileges himself. This he did because he felt it of the utmost importance to the unity of the Society and to the spirit of loyalty within it, that all the members should be kindly disposed towards their General.

Of his care of the sick, of his concern with all the details of the infirmary, of their food, of the doctor's attendance, there can be no doubt.   And he wished all the officers of the Society to be equally solicitous.   His theory was that all reasonable care should be taken of the body, and if then sickness came it was to be accepted as a divine visitation and put to use as a means of spiritual regeneration.   Of this solicitude there is an anecdote.   The rector of the *Collegio Romano,* Dr. Olave, a stern man, not inclined to make allowances for ill health, was himself taken sick; Ignatius charged Ribadeneira with this message: "Tell Dr. Olave from me that we have a good Master, who teaches us that we should have compassion upon others."   It was the same with other matters that affected his household; Ignatius omitted nothing to make its inmates happy.   But his kindness went much further than this.   Though he was sparing of praise, he made it a point to say what good he could of everybody, and not to speak of faults, except so far as might be necessary to cure them.   Ribadeneira says that he does not remember hearing him say a single cross word in disparagement of anybody.   His refraining from all detraction, or evil speaking, was so perfect and wonderful, that his interpretations to excuse other people's failings, whether members of the Society or not, became a sort of proverb among them.   Besides that, when he heard that anybody was spoken ill of, he cast about for something commendable in him, and repeated it to those who spoke against him.   He liked to encourage those under him by praising their good qualities.   And what, perhaps, was more admirable still, he would listen with the greatest patience to the futile talk of outsiders, and also to long discourses from members of the household that might well have been cut short, and yet when he joined in he gave the conversation a turn to spiritual things, so that it was plain enough where his thoughts had been.   And he used to talk to his disciples about how wrong it was to write biting words.   People had often written very harsh things to him, and even though he had a good retort, he never answered back, for he did not wish to return evil for evil.   *Ita maternum sancti Patris cor omnem amovebat a se, non tantum actum, sed umbram ipsam novercalis animi* (as a Polish father said).

("In this manner our saintly Father's maternal heart rejected not only a stepmother's deeds, but even the shadow of a stepmother's disposition.")

A further reason for his hold upon his disciples is to be found in his devotion to the Society. The disciples were filled—I speak of the large majority—with a love of God and a desire to help their neighbors, but they also had a very strong *esprit de corps,* a pride in the Society. The General's loyalty to this corporate body, in which they all were members for the greater glory of God, inspired them with enthusiasm. I doubt if a day went by without some display of his love for the Society. He was wont to say to them that this thought often came to him: "Was it possible that some new, unheard-of thing, sad or bitter, could happen, that would trouble him and upset the composure of his mind? And after he had thought over everything he could only think of one thing: Suppose the Pope should dissolve the Society, and forbid its existence! But even if that should happen, after praying for a quarter of an hour, he would be able to lay aside his trouble and return to his former serenity." And a familiar remark of his was, that if anything could make him wish to live long, it would be to make it difficult for anyone to enter the Society. There is more than an abundance of evidence of his passionate interest in every matter that touched it. Over one chapter of the Constitution he had prayed and deliberated for forty days, over another for three, and he would not rest content with any provision in it until he felt that it had received God's sanction; even the least important he pondered over on seven separate occasions, with tears and prayers. And besides this, the brothers felt pride and confidence in his wisdom and in his holiness. When Nadal asked him how a man might attain to perfection, he answered: "Master Nadal, pray God to give you grace to suffer much for His sake, for in that good gift of His many others are enclosed." And all knew that he turned neither to right nor left for any human consideration when he beheld the gleam of God's glory leading him on.

CHAPTER XXXI

LOYOLA's especial distinction, that sets him far apart from other men—I can think of no parallel except St. Bernard—is that he not only possessed a genius for practical affairs, deep-seated piety, talents for meditation and contemplation, but also belonged to the little band called mystics. To begin with, he was profoundly religious minded; he believed, not as a theory only, but as a guide for living, that the controlling power in the universe is Spirit, that it is man's duty to serve that Spirit with all his might and main, and that the true way to serve is to do what the Holy Catholic Church, Roman and Apostolic, may direct. Spiritual powers, conceived under many forms and names, were as real to him as the phenomena of heat, light or falling bodies. He lived in this spiritual world, as a book-lover lives in a world of books; he ate, walked, slept, talked and did his daily duties in the world of sense, and then on his knees in his cubicle, or at the office of mass, or walking in the street, he would be rapt into the world of spiritual imaginings, to return to earth with the conviction that he had come down from peace everlasting to a temporary battlefield, where all good soldiers of God should *hazer de veras guerra al diablo,* make war in dead earnest against Satan.

He had trodden the purgative way and the illuminative way, and now, not with effort but by merely dropping the reins on the neck of his desire, he could transport himself into the immediate presence of God, *unirse con Dios.* Such almost involuntary sanctifications may have been more frequent in the early days of his conversion, but in his latter days he had more light on things divine, and a greater security of constancy and steadfastness. In a conversation

with Father Gonzalez, after he had finished dictating the
Memoirs, from which I have frequently quoted, Ignatius
said, that in his later years his power of communing with
God had increased, that whenever he wished he could find
God, and that he often had visions when he had important
matters to decide, especially of Jesus Christ, who appeared
to him like the sun.

After his death a note-book was found that contained
notes of his spiritual experiences during the time he was at
work on the constitution of the Society. He had noted
down his most intimate cogitations, and the heavenly light
and the visits that God vouchsafed him. For forty days he
gave his whole thought to the question whether the
churches joined to the professed houses should accept an
income for their maintenance; and he recorded all his
spiritual experiences throughout those forty days, at his
morning meditations, while celebrating or attending mass,
and while preparing for it. The notes reveal the scrupulous-
ness with which he examined his conscience, the fervor of
his prayers, his tears, the spiritual comfort descending
bountifully upon him that betrayed itself externally by a
paralysis of voice and breath, by violent pulsations in his
veins, and inwardly by the almost continuous revelations
that illumined his soul concerning the Trinity, the Divine
Essence, the procession of the Holy Ghost from the Father
and the Son, in short, many of the qualities and operations
of Godhead. These divine visitations were very frequent,
occurring in his cell, at table, indoors and out, day after
day, and ravished him from himself as if his soul were in
heaven and his body only left on earth. I will quote a
few lines, word for word, from the note-book:

Saturday, fifth mass of the Holy Trinity. At the usual
prayers, nothing very much at the beginning; then, towards
the middle of prayers, a sense of spiritual comfort, and the
sight of something very resplendent. When the altar was
being made ready, Jesus presented Himself to my soul, and
I felt moved to follow Him, in the conviction that He is the
chief and captain of the Company—(This conviction is the

strongest argument in favor of absolute poverty, although I have set forth other reasons in my chapter on Elections)— This thought stirred me to tears, and to steadfastness of purpose, so that if, either on that day or the days following, I had been deprived of tears at mass, this feeling would have been sufficient (I think) to make me strong in time of trial and temptation.

And Gonzalez says, that in the last years Ignatius would often stay at prayer in his private chapel, leaving him to attend to whatever business might come up, but that sometimes he needed to consult him. "And whenever I went in, and that was very often, his countenance shone so that I stood still in amazement."

The long practice of piety, vivified by his absolute domination of bodily appetites and impulses, and exalted by his passionate love of God, had carried him all along from the purgative way to this final stage of what the mystics call unity with God. There is superabundant testimony as to all these mystical experiences. Prayer in church, while there was music and singing, affected him especially; he told Gonzalez that if he went into church during the chants, at once he seemed wholly transported out of himself. On one occasion, when saying mass and holding Christ's body in his hands, he beheld Him also in heaven; and on another, while he was adoring the Most Blessed Sacrament, he saw up above a brightness so dazzling that he did not know whether to adore this or that, but then comprehended that the two were but one. At certain seasons, even as often as ten times a day, he was able to behold the presence of God, but these visitations were followed by great bodily exhaustion. The Lord, he said, had given him the spirit of *devoción,* and on account of his weakness and wretchedness visited him often; and that he did not think he could live without these spiritual comfortings, that is, could not live unless he could lay hold of something that neither was nor ever could be self,—unless his soul was resting upon God. He once told Lainez that he had read the lives of many saints; but that, though he dared not be so bold as to put himself ahead of the meanest saint, he would not exchange what he had felt and tasted of God for all their experiences; and, also, that if perfection consisted solely in holy desires, he would not yield to any man that ever lived. And again, he said, that at times it had been his wish, when he did wrong, to suffer some spiritual pain, like the diminution of grace or consolations, for then he felt that he would acquire greater mastery over himself, and yet it had never happened so, but on the contrary, it appeared that God had visited him all the more.

But his experiences at Manresa were the most striking of all. According to his own memoirs, while praying on the steps of a monastery, his understanding was lifted up, and he beheld (with overmastering tears and sobs) the Holy Trinity in its threefold form, like chords in unison, and again the act of creation mirrored itself in his understanding like a whiteness, shooting forth rays, from which God created light; and at mass, at the elevation of the Host, he saw with inward eye white radiations from on high, and with his own understanding, how Christ our Lord was present in the Holy Sacrament. These visions seem, if one may judge of such things, to have come to him more readily because of an extraordinary power of mental concentration. He seems to have been able to shut all windows of sense, to stop all crevices, through which the deceitful appearances of mortal things come in upon the mind, and to throw open wide some portal of the soul through which heavenly visitants descended at will. Not only when he said mass, but when he blessed the food, or rendered thanks, or was engaged in the most inconsiderable matters that bore a reference to God, he was so gathered within his innermost self, so rapt from things of sense, that it seemed to those about that he saw before him the Majesty of God.

Such visitations and visions, such bodying forth in seemingly solid form of ideas and symbols, are out of the course of our modern ways of thinking, and beyond the sympathies of most people, but they are no stranger than phenomena investigated every day by the *Society of Psychical Research;* human emotions and their power over the imagination remain constant, the imagery, the hieroglyphics, the pictured language, changes.   The apprehensive understanding catches the molten passion and pours it into the mould of what is most dearly beloved; and a vision of Christ, or of a son shot at the head of his company, stands glorious and triumphant, as visible as the most conspicuous object of sense in the light of high noon.   Sir Oliver Lodge says:

The idea of Angels is usually treated as fanciful.   Imaginative it is, but not altogether fanciful, and though the physical appearance and attributes of such imaginary beings may have been over-emphasized or misconceived, yet facts known to me indicate that we are not really lonely in our struggle, that our destiny is not left to haphazard, that there is no such thing as *laissez-faire* in a highly organized universe.   Help may be rejected, but help is available; a ministry of benevolence surrounds us—a cloud of witnesses —not witnesses only but helpers, agents like ourselves of the immanent God.

Ignatius would have smiled at such a milk-and-water statement; to him, if there were doubt as to either world, it was this palpable earth that needed a guarantee of reality.

Ignatius, of course, believed devoutly in the efficacy of prayer; whether to move the hearts of men, to check the course of illness, or stay the hand of death.   When Cardinal Guidiccioni opposed the grant of the charter, Ignatius commanded that several thousand masses be said; and, so again, a special mass when the Venetian Senate hesitated to confirm a grant of real property to the Society.   The Fathers believed that Ignatius's merits saved Claude Jay's life, and prevented Bobadilla from forsaking the Society.   And as his prayers brought aid from deity, from angels and saints, so, on the other hand, devils fought against the champion who balked them of their prey.   *In dæmones mirum exercuit imperium.*   "One night, while Ignatius was asleep in bed, the Devil (*ut creditur*) tried to suffocate him.   It seemed to him that he saw a man or a demon clutching him by the throat and squeezing his wind-pipe, and he cried out 'Jesus' with so violent an effort that for many days he was so hoarse that he could scarcely speak." And there were various other testimonies of the Devil's hostility. Usually, Ribadeneira says, one should not believe the Devil, even when he speaks the truth, for he only does so to deceive; nevertheless, the Lord often obliges evil spirits to testify against their wills. For instance, a young Biscayan was possessed of the Devil, and began talking Latin, a language which he did not know. The Devil flung the lad on the ground with great fury, but at the mention of Ignatius's name, howled and declared that he had no greater enemy than he. With such evidence, added to the visible holiness of his life, it is no wonder that his brethren recognized him to be a man apart. There is a pretty anecdote as to this, which Lainez himself told Ribadeneira:

Lainez had heard for certain from Father Araoz that the spiritual guardian who kept watch over Ignatius, was not a mere angel, as in the case of other men, but an archangel; so he asked Ignatius if it were true. Ignatius answered never a word, but such a flush came over his face, as when a most modest maiden is surprised by men.

The shame-faced look, the change of countenance, the blush, answered the question clearly enough with a yes.

I have said nothing of the quality that, perhaps, more than any other, impressed his companions with a sense of his rare spiritual nature,—his meekness. In the world, where, as La Rochefoucauld says, a man must impose his own good opinion of himself upon his fellows, the whole organization of secular society has developed the opposite qualities, self-confidence, self-assertion, and whatever other traits win for a man position, applause or riches, and has pushed this gentle virtue to the wall. The structure of society in Loyola's time was as unfavorable to meekness, as the feudal system had been, or as democracy is today. The spirit of arrogance was in the saddle. The nobles were taught that they were better than burghers, burghers that they were better than peasants; Christians were taught that

they were better than Mohammedans or Jews; Frenchmen
that they were better than Italians; Spaniards that they
were superior to all the world. There was little meekness
in Luther, none in Calvin. Only those men, Protestants
or Catholics, who honestly desired to follow the example of
Christ, really believed in meekness; it was the contrast between Christ's life and theirs that engendered the feeling.
When any man stands, let us suppose, on the prow of a ship
by night, and looks up at the bespangled sky, and sees
stars and stars stretching back into the abyss of space,
beyond the reach of human senses, beyond the very border-
land of thought, there comes over him a sense of the contrast between himself and the immeasurably great, and for
the moment meekness wells up in his heart. Loyola felt
such a feeling as he looked up to Christ. Today we do not
regard that attitude of mind as virtuous, but the believers
in Christ did. Like us, Ignatius in his youth, as a member
of a dominant people and a dominant religion, had been
taught arrogance; after his conversion he struggled to attain
meekness. But in spite of his efforts his underlying pagan
pride is often little more than varnished over by his
Christian principle, and for that reason anyone who reads
his letters and the pages of his biographers might, not un-
naturally, jump to the conclusion that his humility was
hypocritical. Nothing, I think, could be more unjust. At
bottom he was a very proud man; and after his death his
pride seems to have infected the whole Order. Voltaire
sums up in one word the causes, operating within the
Society, that finally united almost all Europe against it
and wrung from the Pope the bull of suppression,—*orgueil.*
Enough of this; I mention it in order to do full justice to
his valiant efforts to attain humility. Those efforts are
frequently very unattractive to our way of thinking. There
is an exaggeration about them, an utter disregard of the
happy mean which he himself praises. They look fantastic
and distorted. But, in order to do him justice, one must
regard him as a sort of Laocoön struggling in anguish to
save his children and himself from the strangulation of
pride.

Instead of picking out here and there bits of evidence to show where and how he succeeded in the pursuit of this virtue, I will quote the summing up of his biographer, Father Bartoli, S.J.:

To pass for an ill-bred, dull, unintelligent man; to acknowledge one's sins publicly and reproach oneself for them; to dress shabbily, expose oneself in public to the contempt of everybody, looking like a boor, barefoot, and hair unkempt; lodge at an alms-house, associate with beggars, and behave as they do in order to pass as such by birth instead of by choice; to beg from door to door, and choose houses where one would get more insults than crusts; to tarry there in order to rejoice in rough usage and in the jeers heaped upon one; to give thanks for brutality, and good for evil; to steer wide of places where he was known to be a gentleman and revered as a saint; to go back to his native land, among his own people, as a mendicant, and live like a mendicant, with no lodging but the alms-house, no food but bread begged from door to door; to rejoice when treated as a hypocrite, rascal, or sorcerer; when dragged into court, to refuse the assistance of counsel; when locked in jail to burst out into jubilation, when fettered to the prison wall to talk in so high a strain of the glory of suffering for Christ's sake, as to seem less a prisoner than a madman:—these, from the first days of his conversion, are some of the marks of Loyola's humility.

This is eloquent, this is a true picture of what Ignatius underwent; but is it humility or is it pride? I feel more clear as to other testimony, that may be grouped into three classes: (1) His companions are all agreed that he was meek of heart; *Pater humillimus fuit et suæ virtutis occultator.* (2) He was never dogmatic in his opinions, unless he felt that he had received illumination from God; he made it a practise to consult those who were better informed than himself, and "very readily" submitted to their judgment. (3) He was so secure in his consciousness of his own modesty, that on one of those rare occasions on which he unloosed his tongue as to his heavenly visitations, when Ribadeneira said to him, that a stranger might suspect him of vainglory, he answered that he had less fear of that sin than of any other, and added that he did not reveal the thousandth part of his gifts from God, for he did not think it suitable, as the listeners were not capable of understanding.

On the whole it may be that my partial disagreement with his eulogists as to his possession of this virtue, is not a question of substance but of words. What they call humility I call self-mortification; what I call humility, they would call the indwelling of heavenly grace. But whatever this quality was, heavenly grace, modesty or meekness, he strove to put it to use and live in accordance with its light. It showed itself in his continual endeavor to do better. When he had anything of consequence to do, his procedure was, first, to strip himself of all desire and self-love; second, to pray for help; third, to consider and think as best he could; and, fourth, to lay the matter before God. He told Father Gonzalez that he never ventured to do anything of importance, although all the reasons were in its favor, without having recourse to God. And Gonzalez adds:

I have heard him say that he would like to behave toward his neighbors as the angels behave toward us, and in two special respects: first, not to fail to give them all possible aid to deliver them from evil, spiritual and physical; second, not to lose his composure whatever should happen (as angels never cease to gaze upon God and enjoy Him) nor to be sorrowful in such a manner as to scant his worship. He also said that, even if God were to destroy the Society, he did not think his grief would diminish any of his devotion towards God.

Call it humility, or what you please, by his teaching and example, the things of this world became as dust in the eyes of his companions, and they held it to be their duty to proclaim their creed.

CHAPTER XXXII

I DO not know how some of these instances of Loyola's disposition will affect the reader. His character is subtle; its modelling is delicate, its color passes from shade to shade in almost imperceptible gradation, and what at the beginning of the scale seemed pure goodness of heart, further on looks like tact, and further on still seems to become prudence, and at the end almost an intense and fastidious pride. It is well nigh impossible to determine where one motive fades and another becomes dominant. He possessed prudence and tact to a rare degree, and pride as well; and each of these qualities affects his kindness, and his kindness also affects each one of them. I will quote an anecdote, in which I cannot tell whether Ignatius's controlling motive was Christian kindness or worldly prudence. The refectory in the house had no window, and was so dark that there was scarcely any light there at all. Its wall was a party wall, half owned by their neighbor, and a window might have been cut to look out on a court, without the slightest prejudice to him; but he would not consent. Ignatius was advised that the Society had a legal right to the window, but rather than quarrel and go to law, he preferred to have a dark refectory for eight years. Finally the Society bought the court and cut the window. Again; after the Society had bought of this same pleasant neighbor a house called the *Torre Rosso*, close by, the vendor without any right, carried away its doors, window shutters, iron-work, etc., but Ignatius would not hear of a law suit; he said that if a man dedicated to religion suffers for the love of our Lord, and loses things temporal for the sake of peace and charity, the Lord will reward him abundantly.

Another of his qualities was graciousness. For instance,

when going about the house, if he met one of the brothers
he looked at him with a most complaisant countenance as
if he would take him into his soul; and when a guest came
to dinner for the first time, or said good-bye on leaving the
city, his manners were affectionately cordial. And yet
dignity and gravity never forsook him. He was affable
towards every one, familiar with none. He always took into
account the humours and feelings of those under him, even
in trifling matters; for instance, when laying on a penance,
he would bid the offender say what he thought the penance
should be. His tact and consideration were those of an
accomplished man of the world. However frank in conversation, no one ever felt offended at his words or his
manner. But though nobody was more affectionate and
affable than he, yet if he did appear angry, nobody was
so feared. And his behaviour was always adjusted to those
with whom he was dealing. He was especially careful to
treat capable Fathers, on whom he needed to rely, with
great circumspection in order not to offend them, unless he
knew from experience that, whatever his manner, it was all
one to them. And it was his custom to get things done, if
possible, without giving a positive command. He liked it
best, if a brother should do what he wanted done as of his
own inclination, without any sign from him; and if it was
necessary to give directions, he preferred not to make them
peremptory. When something was asked of him, he immediately made up his mind whether he could grant it or
not, and if not, while the other was talking, he considered
how he could frame his refusal in such a way that the
petitioner should take no umbrage. Sometimes he would
say, this matter must be decided by some one else, sometimes he expatiated upon the difficulties hedging it about;
and he used such kind words, spoke so reasonably and
showed such real good will, that the other went away content, or, if he came, as sometimes happened, on a friend's
errand, with a conviction that his friend was wrong.

When two members of the Society were fond of one
another, he liked to praise each to the other; or, if two
happened to be at odds, he took pains to tell each separately

all the good that he knew or had heard of the other, or he would say complimentary things to a third person who he knew would repeat them, and so on.

In all such ways Ignatius showed tact, and also kindness. From that I pass on to what may more properly be called prudence, pure and simple. In his decisions, he never acted hastily; he never spoke at haphazard, but always upon consideration. When there was time, he would say: *"Dormiremos sobre ello."* ("We will sleep on this matter.") In consequence, the things he said, no matter when uttered or under what circumstances, were like the rules of a constitution, all dovetailed and fitted into one another. In his latter days he was able to tell his secretary that he had not made a rash promise for a dozen years. Whenever he wrote to persons in high place, or on business of importance, he was especially cautious and spent a long time considering what he should say, and would read the letter over and over, weighing each word, erasing here, amending there, and causing the draft to be copied out again and again. He said that such time and trouble were well spent. And he always made a point of telling the great personages he met of all the attacks and slanders that had been directed against him, so that they should know the truth and not take their first impressions from gossip or from unfriendly persons.

In one matter he was very wary. He would not suffer any criticism of the Pope, nor any suggestions, or insinuation, that the Pope might have done this, or commanded that, more to the advantage of his flock. This was particularly so after Caraffa, with whom, it will be remembered, he had once had a falling out, had mounted the pontifical throne. Lainez preached a sermon in one of the big Roman churches on simony; the sermon was most proper but because he feared that some one might misconstrue what Lainez had said into a reflection upon some measure that Caraffa had just sanctioned, he took him to task and punished him. And he warned Ribadeneira, who was setting off on a trip to Flanders, to beware how he spoke about matters that touched His Holiness, saying that, since some of the things the Pope had done were "hard to excuse" it would be as well to say nothing of him, but rather to expatiate upon all that his predecessor, Marcellus II, had done for the Society. And when he himself had an errand to this Pope, on some matter I think relating to the *Collegio Romano,* he waited till he had heard that the Pope was in good spirits over favorable news from England under Queen Mary. So, too, in the earlier days of the Society, he never allowed the purveyor of the house to ask alms of Paul III, for he thought that by refraining the Company was more likely to gain the Pope's good will, and thereby religious privileges; and he acted the same way towards gentlemen of means who were good friends to the Society.

Out of prudence, too, he was careful to avoid giving the Dominican friars cause for a quarrel. There had been trouble enough, he thought, with Melchior Cano in Spain. So when Dr. Olave was about to print a book that, among other things, asserted the Immaculate Conception of the Virgin, a doctrine which he firmly believed but the Dominicans did not, he bade him leave out the passage. And in delicate matters of business, where suspicion, malice or misinterpretation might induce those with whom he was dealing to pervert the truth, it was his wont, whether the persons concerned were members of the household or from outside, to call in witnesses; and in all serious cases within the Society, where accusations of wrong-doing were brought, he required the charges and countercharges put into writing. This virtue of prudence, it need hardly be said, belonged to him in his capacity of superior, not of subordinate. He said he should obey at once whatever mad act the Pope might command; some brother protested, and he answered, as Napoleon might have done,—"Prudence is a matter for those who command, not for those who are to obey."

His circumspection, his sternness, his self-mortification, and his passionate devotion to what he believed to be the service of God, might well make one think of him as wholly austere and serious, quite without any sense of humour;

but that would be wrong; from time to time he reveals touches of humour. I find but few instances, it is true, but that is because conventional hagiography, especially since the Counter Reformation, has affected to consider jests and laughter unspiritual qualities. It is one of the defects in Christianity, not to make much of mirth; and I dare say that the same reproach may be made against all religions, except Paganism, and certainly against almost all religious biography. It is not that great saints have lacked all sense of fun; but their biographers have been over-prudish and priggish. Loyola did not laugh often, he accepted Thomas-à-Kempis's teaching that life is a valley of tears; and even when he did relax, I suspect that Polanco, Gonzalez and Ribadeneira stopped their ears, or turned away. They were afraid of him, and took an unconscious revenge by making his dominant habit of austerity seem almost uninterrupted. They ventured, however, to preserve the following anecdotes:

Several of us were at dinner once with the Padre, including Bobadilla and Salmerón [most guileless of men, such as Phillips Brooks or Cardinal Gibbons] and somebody said that it was reported in Rome that we were all hypocrites. The Padre remarked that he wished that we had much more of that hypocrisy, and added, "I have been thinking over everybody in the Society, and I don't find a single hypocrite, unless it is Bobadilla and Salmerón."

And this:

The great pleasure he took in talking about and hearing about the affairs of the brothers is a sign of his great love for them. He made me read edifying letters about our new colleges two or three times over. . . . And he often talked of the brothers in Portugal and India, taking the greatest interest in hearing what they ate, how they slept, what they wore, and in all particulars and details. Once, while we were talking about the brothers in India, he said, "Oh, dear! how much I should like to know how many fleas bite them at night."

Here is a third:

A friend reported to Ignatius that a certain priest in Spain, Father Barbaran, was furious with the Society, and vowed that he would have every Jesuit from Perpignan to Seville burned at the stake. Ignatius wrote back:

DEAR FRIEND:

Please tell Father Barbaran—since he says that he will have all of us that he can find from Perpignan to Seville burned at the stake—that I say that it is my desire that he and all his friends, not only those to be found between Perpignan and Seville, but all that there are in all the world, shall be set on fire and burn with the Holy Spirit, that all may come into the glory of God. Tell him, also, that our affairs are in adjudication before the tribunal of the Governor and the Papal Vicar, and that they are about to pass judgment; and that if Father Barbaran has aught against us, I beg him to lay it before those judges. For if I am in debt, I wish to pay; and I prefer to suffer punishment alone rather than that all of our brethren between Perpignan and Seville should be burned at the stake.

INIGO.

There is another anecdote that I shall quote in this connection. I have been in doubt whether to take it *au pied de la lettre* or not; from the turn of phrase I incline to think that Ignatius's words, though serious, have a touch of humour, although Ribadeneira does not suspect it. One day Ignatius gave orders that everybody should assemble in the refectory after dinner, without a single exception, whether priest, or professed, or even the First Fathers, in order to hear Lainez explain some new rules, that Ignatius had drawn up. Such an assemblage was most unusual. All came in and while Lainez was in the midst of his talk, a great crash shook the refectory; everybody was frightened. After Lainez had finished, the brothers found that the roof which covered a corner of the garden, where the Fathers were in the habit of sitting after supper, had fallen down, and had it not been for the orders that no one should be excused from the meeting, undoubtedly somebody would have been killed or badly hurt. When this was told to Ignatius, he said: "God shows by this sign that the rules do not displease Him." Perhaps this speech may be wholly pious and serious. But remember Loyola's message to Dr. Olave, with respect to sickness, which contained a little kindly irony; and also that he had been a soldier until he was six and twenty, very far from pious, and that the one episode known of his youth is the carnival frolic, which seems to have been a practical joke of irritating dimensions. I do not think that Rodriguez would have made jokes as he does, or that Lainez would have written the letter he did about the little oven of a room at Trent, if he had not been able to count upon Loyola's sense of humour. And Nadal says: *Qui in ejus cubiculo lætissimi semper ac risibundi.* ("In Loyola's room everybody was laughing and jolly.")

There are some other details as to his character that should not be omitted. I quote Gonzalez:

It is remarkable to see what consideration he shows in his relations with everybody, whoever it may be, excepting with Nadal and Polanco, for he shows no regard at all for them, but treats them harshly and loads them with punishments.

Ribadeneira says the same thing:

He hardly ever said a good word to Master Juan de Polanco, his secretary, who had been his hands and feet for nine years, unless it was the day before he died, when he sent him to ask the Pope's blessing. And at times he gave Lainez such terrible scoldings (*dió tan terribles capellos*) that he made him cry. . . . What makes it more singular still is, that our blessed Father had said to me that there was no man in all the Society to whom it owed more than to Lainez, even including Francis Xavier. . . . The year before he died, he behaved to him with great harshness . . .

and Lainez felt so badly that he had recourse to the Lord, and said, "Lord, what have I done against our Society that this saint treats me in this fashion?"

The official interpretation of this asperity against these excellent, dutiful, able men is that it was specifically designed to develop their moral strength, their humility, or some such virtues; however, for my part, I cannot but think that Ignatius was suffering from an ill-used and ailing body, and being unable to control his physical irritability, vented it, as nervous invalids do, upon those nearest, and perhaps dearest, to them.

A second point is duplicity, which I have promised to point out whenever I come upon any traces. I do not know whether moralists will consider Loyola's practice of granting favors himself, and refusing them through others, who are not to reveal that they act on his orders, as double dealing or not. Here is an instance of a somewhat analogous method. Ignatius sent the following instructions to a Father far from Rome:

(1) Write me a letter, that can be shown to everybody, important people and unimportant people, to good and bad, without any words in it that reflect on any of them.

(2) In other letters that you write to me, you can put in all the particulars you wish, that you may think will be to the advantage of what we all believe is for the greater service of God.

This practice was always followed. There were some letters written to be passed around, and others that were not to be passed around. Such methods, I presume, have been followed by every corporation that ever existed, lay or religious, by all officials in the service of a state, or monarch, or house of business, as well as by many private persons. I doubt whether the apostles would have done so, or Marcus Aurelius, or Socrates. It does not seem consistent with perfect candor; and yet it is not a grave offense.

Here is another possible instance of duplicity; but as

the accusation comes from Simon Rodriguez in a moment
of irritation and peevishness, while smarting under punishment for his misbehaviour in Portugal, it is of no more substance than the others. In answer to Simon's complaints,
Ignatius wrote to him: "I declare before Heaven that I
yield to no creature of all there are on earth in my love
for you and in my wish for your spiritual and physical good,
to the divine honor and glory." To which Rodriguez
replied:

VENICE, Dec. 22, 1554.

To FATHER IGNATIUS LOYOLA:
  May the grace and love of Christ be in our souls. I have
received yours of the 15th of this month. As to what you
say, *that there is no one that loves me more in body and
soul*, etc.—the proof of love is to show it in actions, and
in this matter your actions should confirm what your letter
says.

  A committee of the Fathers had passed upon Rodriguez's
conduct, they had found fault, and Loyola had imposed
punishment, exiling the luckless Portuguese to a little place
near Venice. Rodriguez was very cross. That is all there
is to it. And his ill temper did not last long; in a letter,
dated *"Da la hermita de Basan* [Bassano] *lugar de peni-
tentia,"* he says that he is sorry to learn that Father
Ignatius is not pleased with his letters, and sends him a
blessing as big as the mountains of Bassano "where eighteen
years ago he came to see me when I was at the point of
death." And finally—for I have tried to let nothing concerning this charge of duplicity, whether touching Loyola
or any of his companions, escape me—I find in a letter of
condolence and warning written by Bobadilla to the Pope's
son, Cardinal Alessandro Farnese, on the murder of his
uncle, Pietro Aloisio Farnese, these words, *"la prudentia
ha de disimular algo, y proveer por via quieta á lo por-
venir."* ("Prudence must dissemble a little, and by some
quiet means make provision for what may happen.")
There! at any rate, I have disclosed the worst.

One more thing, and I shall leave this aspect of his character. I do not know whether Catholics, as a rule, approve of the institution of the Inquisition, or not; Protestants do not. I do not mean to suggest that Catholics approve of *autos-da-fé*, racks, dungeons, espionage, and whatever other deviltries can be held up against the Spanish Inquisition; I refer to the principle of an organized body of educated and conscientious men, charged with the duty of discovering those who think erroneously or wickedly, to their own ultimate harm, and perhaps to the grave danger of other people, on religious matters, and of persuading such persons, by some means to abandon error and accept truth, or else preventing them, in one way or another, from spreading corruption. It is very easy to see after the event that the system is wrong. It was based on the conviction that the truth was known, and that it was of everlasting importance to know that truth; believing this, it would have been brutal, non-human certainly, to see men drift away from truth down to hell without making frantic efforts to save them. The Bible spoke clearly: "It is profitable for thee that one of thy members should perish, and not that thy whole body should be cast into hell." The practice of toleration is partly due to a return from mediæval Christianity to the primitive Christianity of the gospels, but chiefly to doubts as to whether we possess religious truth, or what its nature may be. The Inquisition was an integral part of mediæval Christianity, and Ignatius accepted all mediæval Christianity and approved of the Inquisition; I shall not discuss whether he ought to have approved of it, but confine myself to his connection with it. I do not find that he had anything to do with the Spanish Inquisition, except on one occasion to ask for the pardon of certain Moriscos who had fallen back into error after baptism. The Spanish Inquisition was established, or rather revived and reinvigorated, by Ferdinand and Isabella years before Ignatius was born, to the great satisfaction of the Christian population, as an engine to deal with Jews and Moors; it persecuted Ignatius during his early missionary days, and did not get to ferreting out and punishing Protestants until after his death. His relations with the Inquisition concern its establishment in Portugal and in Italy.

John III, king of Portugal, was a bigot; he wished to persecute the Jews in his kingdom, and had done what he could, but without much success, to induce Pope Clement VII to give him a free hand in dealing with misbelievers and heretics. He began again with Paul III, and thanks to the support of the Emperor, obtained in part what he wanted; but as the Pope refused to accede to other demands, a quarrel ensued, and the King in his turn proposed to keep the papal nuncio out of his kingdom. I only allude to this, in order to show that other matters of contention were mixed up with the question of the Inquisition. Prince Henry, the King's brother, wrote to Ignatius asking him to use his influence with the Pope for the grant of full inquisitorial powers (May 29, 1542). This Ignatius did, with right good will, as appears from his letters to Simon Rodriguez; he says: *"De su alteza es mandar y de nosostros obedecir."* ("It is for his Highness to command, for us to obey.") The King's aid was of great consequence to the Society, and Loyola was most anxious to please him. But however much Loyola hated heresy and approved of the Inquisition, his support can hardly have counted for much. The desired bull was issued in 1547.

In Italy the Inquisition was established in 1542. Charles V had already issued a decree in Naples which forbade under pain of excommunication and death all dealings with persons suspected of heresy. The Church had its back to the wall. Heresy or questionings and speculations in the direction of heresy had become rife, not merely among little groups of intellectual persons, such as the friends of Juan Valdés, in Naples, but much more seriously in some northern cities, like Lucca, Modena, and Parma. Cardinal Guidiccioni wrote in alarm of *"quanto siano multiplicati quelli pestiferi errori di questa condannata setta lutherana in la nostra città"* [Lucca]. To have supporters of this German heresy appear in Italy was not only injury but insult. Cardinal Caraffa was "the chief originator" (according to Dr. Pastor), *die Seele* (according to Dr. Burchbell) of the plan for introducing the Inquisition. The Archbishop of Burgos, Juan de Toledo, son to the Duke of Alva, advised it; Caraffa and he were appointed inquisitors general. Ignatius also advocated the plan; and the Society, in its natural desire to magnify his influence, has spoken as if his advocacy had been of some consequence. I see no evidence to support such an idea; especially in view of the fact that the Archbishop of Burgos was a member of the Dominican Order, with which the Jesuits were on bad terms, and Caraffa had showed himself so unfriendly that, as I have said, when Loyola heard that he was elected Pope, "all his bones shook in his body." Besides, Paul III knew his own mind, and needed no counsel in this matter from Ignatius, who, I suspect, acted out of consideration for the people of importance who desired to see the Inquisition established in Italy.

One more word and I shall finish this chapter. Protestants have been long accustomed, out of charity, to impute to the Jesuits the doctrine *that the means justifies the end,* by which they imply that the Jesuits justify any act of wickedness that will further some end they have in view. I have read in Catholic sources that no evidence in support of this charge has ever been forthcoming against the Society. As to Ignatius and his companions, I have found nothing in word or deed, to suggest his or their approval or advocacy of any such doctrine, or any reference or allusion to it whatsoever. I will merely add a few words of exhortation from their early disciple Father Canisius to his congregation in Germany, as a sample of what the Jesuits really taught:

Let Truth and Simplicity be and remain our colors, and though we are persecuted and despitefully used, still we will always imitate Him, who prayed for His enemies, "Lord, forgive them, for they know not what they do."

CHAPTER XXXIII

His secretary, Ribadeneira, says that the character of what the General of the Society should be, as drawn by Ignatius in the Constitution, the Happy Warrior of religion, is his own.

Among the various qualities that a general should possess, the first is the closest possible union with God, familiar communion with Him, both in prayer and in every act, in order to obtain from the fount of all good, for the whole Society, a greater bestowal of gifts and grace, and to render all the means he may employ for the good of souls more effectual. And in the second place, that he be a pattern of all the virtues, and aid all the members of the Society to practise them; but, more than all, that the light of love shall shine in him towards his neighbor and particularly towards the Society; and that he shall show a true humility that makes a man dear to God and to his fellow men. He must be free from all inordinate affections, . . . his bearing and behaviour must be such, his speech so circumspect, that nothing about him, not a single word, but shall edify all men, and in especial the members of the Society, to which he must be mirror and model. He must unite rectitude and necessary severity to sweetness and benignity, and never turn aside from what he thinks will be acceptable to God; and he must be so full of compassion for his children, that those whom he rebukes or chastises, in spite of the smart, shall recognize that he fulfills his office with justice and charity in the Lord. He must have strength of soul and magnanimity, in order to bear the weakness of many and to undertake great things for the divine service and to

351

persevere without suffering discouragement from the most strenuous opposition, neither yielding to entreaty nor menaces in aught that touches the honor of God. . . . He must have judgment and good sense, . . . the gift of insight, . . . vigilance, . . . energy. He should be adorned with all the virtues . . . or, if some must of necessity be lacking, let it not be a shining honesty, nor love of the Society, nor good judgment, nor a suitable education.

This is great praise, but Ribadeneira knew him well. And he adds:

We have often see him make the most trifling thing a means to lift himself towards God, who is so great even in the least of His creatures. At the mere sight of a plant, a blade of grass, a leaf, a flower, a fruit, a worm, his spirit flew away up to heaven, and with a wonderful wisdom he drew a moral for the spiritual life.

It was complete conformity to the will of God, that gave him perfect tranquillity of soul. Once he turned in the course of some conversation to Lainez, and said:

Tell me, Master Lainez, what would you do, were God to say to you, "If you wish to die this minute, I will free you from your corporal prison and give you everlasting glory. But if you wish to live on, I will not answer for what may happen. I leave you to your own resources. If you persevere, I will reward you; if not, I shall pass judgment according as I shall find you." If God put that alternative to you, but you knew that if you stayed on in this world you might render Him greater service, what would you do?" Lainez answered: "For my part, Padre, I admit that I should choose to depart at once to enter into the joy of my Lord, and make sure of my salvation, a matter of great importance." "By heaven, not I," Ignatius said. "If I could do the meanest service to God, I should beseech Him to leave me here until that task were done; I should look to His interest more than to mine."

If these men were justified in their conception of God, then Lainez was surely right: *"Complacuit sibi Dominus in anima servi sui Ignatii."*

During the last years Ignatius's health failed. He had been frail and ailing ever since his self-mortifications at Manresa, but it was a proverb among the brethren that "as soon as there was any hard work to be done the Padre was well again." He said, that by God's Providence he had been subject to all physical ills, and therefore had understanding and sympathy with pain and suffering: "If I were robust and strong, and could lead a life of great austerity without relaxation,—for I always want to be urging my companions on—nobody could follow me, but by the lesson of my broken body God teaches me to be sick with the sick and to make allowances for human frailty."

His constitution was naturally good, but no constitution could stand the rack and strain to which he subjected his. Privations, trials, fasts and labors, such as he said he would not undergo again for all the riches of the world, brought physical incapacities, weakness of digestion—at times he could take nothing but fruit and overripe cheese—and other signs that the body had run its course. In 1551 he summoned the principal brothers to Rome and sought to resign, but all recognized the impossibility of having any other general during his lifetime. A few years later the end drew near. Ribadeneira says: "Aflame with desire to be with Christ, with many tears and violent sobs he began to pray God that it might be to His service to take His servant from this wilderness and lead him to that place of peace, where with the freedom that he longed for he might praise God and among the rest of His elect rejoice in His presence."

The summer of 1556 was full of sorrow for him, because His Catholic Majesty Philip II and Pope Paul IV were at war, and Rome was full of soldiers, and military preparations. He sought to avoid the unchristian sights and sounds by withdrawing to the little villa in the vineyard in the Aventine, but foreseeing that his end was near at hand, he returned to the house in town. He had a slight fever, and the doctors came daily, but there was no sign of serious illness. I will begin the story in Ribadeneira's words:

On July 30th (a Thursday) about the third hour before sundown, he called Father Juan de Polanco to him [Polanco had assisted him for nine full years in every sort of business in the government of the Society] and taking him apart,—Polanco had no suspicion of what he wanted— with the utmost composure of mind said: "Master Polanco, the hour of my departure from this world is at hand. Go in my behalf and kiss His Holiness's feet, and ask for his blessing, and together with it a plenary indulgence for all my sins; so that I may leave this life in greater comfort and confidence; and tell His Holiness that if I (for I trust in God's infinite mercy) shall find myself on the Holy Mount of His glory, I shall not forget to pray for His Holiness, as I have always done every time that I have felt constrained to pray for myself." At this point I will let Polanco speak for himself: "I answered, 'Father, the doctors do not regard your illness as dangerous, and for my part, I hope that God will leave your Reverence for His better service with us for several years still. Do you think that you are as ill as Lainez?' [who was seriously ill in another part of the house]. 'So sick,' he answered, 'that there is no more to do but die.' I asked if I might wait till Friday, because I had to get some letters off to Spain by the post for Genoa which was to start that same evening. He answered: 'I should like today better than tomorrow, the sooner the better. However, do what you deem best. I leave it to you.' I waited to find out if the doctors believed him in danger, and sent for the head doctor, Master Alexander, and asked him to tell me frankly what he thought, and I told him the errand I was charged with to the Pope. He answered: 'I can't say anything today; tomorrow, we'll see.' Things being in this condition, as Father Ignatius had left the decision to me, I decided—acting in all too human a way—that we could wait till Friday (the next day) to hear the opinion of the doctors. That same Thursday in the evening, about eight o'clock, Doctor

Madrid and I took supper with Father Ignatius. He ate
as usual and chatted with us, so I left his room without a
thought of any fatality. At daybreak we found our Father
on the point of death. I ran to St. Peter's; the Pope expressed great sorrow, and blessed him with all possible affection. An hour after sunrise, in the presence of Dr.
Madrid and Master André Desfreux, our Father very peace-
fully gave up his soul to his Creator.

So his life ended; is it to be judged a success, or a failure?
At the time of his death the Society, as I have said, had
colleges, houses, missions almost all over Catholic Europe,
and in India, Africa and South America. In the course
of the next two centuries its fortunes mounted, fluctuated
and fell. It was suppressed and rose from its ashes. In
1912 its colleges, houses and missions were spread wherever
Roman Catholicism extended, in England, Ireland, France,
Germany, Austria, Spain, Portugal, Italy, Canada, Mexico,
Brazil and so on. In the United States the Order numbered
twenty-three hundred members; there were six professional
schools with 4363 students, twenty-six colleges,—Holy
Cross and Boston College in Massachusetts, St. Francis
Xavier and Fordham University in New York City, Loyola
College in Baltimore, Georgetown in Washington, others
in Jersey City, Buffalo, Cincinnati, St. Louis, Chicago,
Omaha, Milwaukee, etc.—besides preparatory and high
schools. In the whole Society, everywhere, there were some
sixteen thousand five hundred members. Nevertheless, in
spite of all this record, some Protestants will think that
Loyola was a failure. They regard mediæval Christianity
as a lost cause. And, as a rule—for it is easy and comfortable to judge of merit by the event—people are inclined
to impute some wrongheadedness or deficiency to the leader
of a lost cause, if only to justify the condemnatory event,
that has saved them the trouble of a laborious investigation.
I do not feel very sure what constitutes a lost cause. A
state may crumble, witness the German Empire, or the
classical instance of Athens, or the Roman Empire itself;
but Bismarck, Pericles and Julius Cæsar are not thought of

as the standard bearers of lost causes. The history of philosophy is like a procession of evening clouds, many-hued
and impermanent; nevertheless, Plato and Plotinus are still
famous names, and modern philosophers—James, Royce,
Bergson—although they seem to set up their theories like
ninepins for newcomers to bowl down, are not therefore
considered failures, but rather valiant seekers after truth
who have lost their way. A scientific theory may be over-
thrown by new discoveries, but Hippocrates and Ptolemy
(to cite ancient instances) enjoy great renown; Darwin has
been criticised and corrected, and even Newton himself is
not beyond questioning. Πάντα ῥεῖ (all is flux); humanity
and all its causes, lost or gained, are but little particles in a
universe that is forever shifting, forever breaking up the
old in order to constitute the new. If a cause won means
immutability, all causes must be lost, or progress would be
impossible, for a cause won would block the path. And, in
truth, the words *lost cause* have little meaning. "Thou
fool, that which thou sowest is not quickened, except it die."
Every action is a seed. Defeats as well as victories are
integral factors in building the future.

Did Loyola achieve success, or did he go down to failure?
But I do not ask the question to answer it myself; I will
do no more than suggest two consequences of his life and
doctrine. The first is a deduction to be drawn from a passage in the *Life of Saint Ignatius* by Père Bartoli, S.J., the
second a deduction from a passage in *Les Relations des
Jésuites dans la Nouvelle France*. Of Bartoli's book the
judicious and reasonable Astrain says: "Although Bartoli
lived a hundred years after Saint Ignatius, nevertheless, as
he had at his disposition all the documents in the general
archives of the Society, he was able to write a biography of
the Saint that, in wealth of facts and accuracy of information, surpasses all the others written in that century."
Bartoli devotes the sixth book of his work to the miracles
wrought by Loyola's intercession or influence. Among other
stories is the following:

A priest used to preach at Arbois, in Burgundy, not far
from Dôle. This priest was invited one day to dine with

Dr. Gillabos, a good, intelligent man, who came out with
a great panegyric upon the holiness and miracles of Saint
Ignatius. The preacher did not like the panegyric; he
burst out laughing and said, with a disdainful and contemptuous air, that the Founder of the Jesuits, if he used
all his influence, might perhaps cure a toothache, but that
he could not do more. This pleasantry, quite out of place
in a priest, scandalized the company and cast a damper
on the subsequent conversation; for the family entertained
a great devotion to Saint Ignatius. This was on the Monday before mid-Lent. Out of regard for the good of the
people thereabouts, God postponed His vengeance; and
the preacher was able to finish his course of sermons. On
Easter Monday he was again invited by the same doctor.
This time he received the just reward for his improper
pleasantry. He was holding a glass of wine in his hand,
and was about to carry it to his lips, when he suddenly began to tremble and shriek that his teeth were being pulled
out and that he could not open his mouth. And in fact his
jaws were so locked that he could not utter a word; all he
could do was to roar in despair. Then came a fit of terror,
convulsions, and such transports of madness that five or
six men could hardly hold him down. All the physicians
roundabout were called in; but as the illness came from
heaven, the art of man could do nothing. The wretch lived
on for three days in these torments,—a severe lesson on
the respect due to saints. At the end of the three days he
died miserably, without being able to say a single word,
even of repentance.

To have helped produce, or render possible, such credu-
lity in Père Bartoli, or anybody else, as to believe or
tell so silly a story, is surely evidence of failure.

My second passage concerns Father Brébeuf, the Norman
gentleman whom Francis Parkman, through his book *The
Jesuits in North America*, introduced to Protestant readers.
There is enough to do honor to the Society in the mere
record of Brébeuf's hardships from the time he left Samuel
de Champlain at Quebec until reaching a village of the
Hurons,—to quote his own words—"Where poor Estienne

Brulé had been barbarously and treacherously murdered, which made me think that some day we might be treated in the same manner, and to wish that at least it might be while pursuing the glory of Our Lord." Some three years later, that day seemed close at hand. In a letter to his Superior, he writes:

Mon. R. Père, Nous sommes peut-estre sur le point de respandre notre sang, et d'immoler nos vies pour le service de nostre bon Maistre Jésus-Christ. It seems that His goodness is willing to accept this sacrifice from me in expiation of my great and numberless sins, and to crown now the past services and burning desires of all the Fathers here. . . . *En tout, sa sainte volonté soit faite; s'il veut que dès cestre heure nous mourions, ô la bonne heure pour nous!*

But the day did not come for eleven years, until almost the very time that Père Bartoli was writing the miraculous story, that I have just quoted. *Les Relations des Jésuites* for the year 1649, Chapter IV, *"De l'heureuse mort du P. Jean de Brébeuf,"* tells the story of his capture and torture by the Iroquois. It is too terrible to recount. Parkman says:

Thus died Jean de Brébeuf, the founder of the Huron mission, its truest hero and its greatest martyr. He came of a noble race,—the same, it is said, from which sprang the English Earls of Arundel; but never had the mailed barons of his line confronted a fate so appalling, with so prodigious a constancy. To the last he refused to flinch, and "his death was the astonishment of his murderers."

Heroism, scarcely if at all inferior, was shown by many another member of the Society in the endeavor to save the souls of Indians in *la Nouvelle France.* To have helped produce, or render possible, such courage in Père Brébeuf and many, many others, as to brave horrors unspeakable for the greater glory of God, is surely triumphant success.

CHAPTER XXXIV

SUCH, then, are the usual charges that are brought up by ill-informed persons who are out of sympathy with the Order of Jesus. I repeat: the doctrine that the end justifies the means was devised for use in party warfare at some period or other after Loyola's death; as a weapon of assault, it can scarcely be praised too highly, it is insulting, harmful, hard to refute and easy to remember. Perhaps no phrase ever carried more mud that sticks. It so happens, however, that the maxim, at least as a rule of conduct, is far older than the Jesuits, and has been said to obtain, now and again, with Secretaries of State, Ministers of War, or Captains of Industry, in countries which are not under Jesuit control. With establishing the Inquisition in Italy and in Portugal, Ignatius had but little to do, with establishing it in Spain, nothing.

As to the doctrine of obedience, to hear some Protestant critics you might almost suppose it to be a diabolical invention of Loyola's. It is, of course, as essential in an ecclesiastical army as on board ship, or on the parade ground, or on the football field, or in the trenches. It is said of Phillips Brooks,—"no ancient Roman, pagan or Christian, ever asserted more strongly the claim of obedience to be the highest virtue." In addition to the necessity of obedience in order to secure the united action among any body of men in the accomplishment of any purpose, it had always been the favorite mediæval method of teaching humility. You will find the simile of the dead body as the type of perfect obedience set forth with elaboration by St. Francis of Assisi. His biographers, Thomas of Celano, in both the *First* and *Second Life,* and the Three Companions, lay special emphasis upon his insistence on this point.

Some people may regard with disfavor Loyola's habit of worship, for instance his devotion to the Eucharist. He was a child of the middle ages, and passionately accepted its elementary creed. In our world of Protestantism and agnosticism we think of that mediæval creed as over and done with; but that is because we do not travel beyond the bounds of our own religious sympathies. These mediæval Christian beliefs, as we call them, still justify themselves by the service they render to individual souls. Newman and Manning are instances to prove this. The great schoolmaster, Dr. Coit, wrote:

I think the simple attendance on the Blessed Sacrament, week by week, and forming the habit of careful preparation and frequent reception, remembering into Whose presence we come, and for what we hang upon His grace, will do more for stable peace and true growth in moral strength than any other means whatever.

And Phillips Brooks speaks of this Sacrament as "the rallying-place for all the good activity and worthy hopes of man." To Ignatius partaking of the Eucharist was eating the bread of spiritual life.

In addition to these three criticisms there is a fourth, which is usually thought, but taken so much for granted as not often to be specifically directed against Ignatius; or rather it is crowded out by the more clamorous protests against "The end justifies the means" and his supposed connection with the Inquisition. This fourth criticism concerns the practice of asceticism, which Loyola enjoined and exemplified to so extreme a degree. Hunger, thirst, dirt, scourgings, an emaciated, maltreated body, scarred with welts, are not merely unattractive to us, they are odious. We are all agreed that comfort is a great good; we usually act as if it were our chief good, and when some rude force shatters it, our very bowels cry out against the sacrilege. There have always been a few men—bigots or fanatics we call them—who have felt an imperious compulsion to ill-treat the flesh. The Cynics felt this; the hermits of the

Thebaid much more so; also St. Francis and a long line of mediæval saints. The usual explanation of this disregard of what we deem our great good, is that the primitive fear of a cruel Power constrains timorous men to seek to placate it by torturing themselves. Let us not forget that this superstition is found in company with very noble human qualities. Epictetus says that the true Cynic is free from anger, envy, resentment, that his conscience and his life are pure, that he loves modesty, and is a friend worthy of the gods. St. Anthony of the Desert was pure in heart, sober in judgment, equable in spirit, full of courtesy, tender to the sorrowful; "Seek ye wisdom (he said), chastity, justice, virtue, watchfulness, care of the poor, hospitality, and a mind that overcomes anger." The charm of St. Francis's character is known to everybody. To maltreat oneself seems, in these classes of men, to be correlated with kindness to one's neighbor. But it is not on behalf of any such correlation that I wish to argue here. This compelling need of self-mortification, whether or not a relic of primitive superstitions, is still dominant with some men, and as I think, is a trait of great social value.

I will quote a French gentleman, Charles Foucauld, who died but a few years ago. After his training as an officer at Saint-Cyr, he served in Algiers as a *chasseur d'Afrique,* distinguished himself as a daring explorer in Morocco, then took to religion, plunged, as it were, into mediæval Christianity, and lived all the rest of his life in the desert, partly in Syria, mostly in Sahara, hermit, priest, missionary and scholar. His self-mortification was extreme; he fasted, he prayed, he kept vigils, he adored the Holy Sacrament, he trampled self-indulgence, bodily appetites, human affections, under his feet. He was ravished by the passion of self-sacrifice. He rejoiced in suffering. With a fervor, equal to Loyola's, he writes of parting from dearly beloved friends as a great good,

a good that gives us the chance to offer a sacrifice to the good Lord, and it is indeed the greatest good, the only real good that there is in life, one that unites us closest to our

Blessed Saviour. When one loves, what is there so sweet as to give something to Him one loves, most of all to give some dearly treasured possession, to suffer for love of Him, to give Him all one's heart's blood? . . .

And what follows is from a letter to a priest written just after Père Foucauld has visited the Colosseum with its memories of Christian martyrs:

O Father, how dearly we ought to love!   How much must we, you and I, try to love the Divine Spouse of our Souls! If our souls are able to love with passion, and they are, let us drown ourselves in love of Him! . . . Let this flower, that I enclose, picked in the Colosseum, remind you as it does me what the Saints suffered, and what we ought to wish to suffer. . . . It is our advantage over the angels! . . . At least we have tears, sufferings, perhaps even, if God please, blood to offer to Our Lord, to mingle with His tears, His sufferings, and His blood!

And in order to reinforce my suggestion that this medi-æval Christianity still contains a power of conferring permanent and abiding consolation upon poor, suffering human nature, I quote again from his diary:

How good Thou art, O God, to have broken all that I had, to have crushed and crumbled all that would have hindered me from belonging wholly to Thee! To grant me this profound sense of the vanity and unreality of a worldly life, this sense of the vast distance that separates the perfect life of the gospels from a life in the world, . . . and this tender, ever increasing love for you, Lord Jesus, this taste for prayer, this faith in your word, this assurance of the duty of charity, this desire to follow you. . . . At this moment I am in great peace. It will last as long as Jesus pleases. I have the Holy Sacrament, and love of Jesus. Others have the earth; I have God. When I am downcast, here is my recipe: I recite the glorious mysteries of the rosary, and say to myself, "What does it matter after all that I am miserable, and that no good thing I wish for comes to pass? That does not hinder my beloved Jesus who wishes the good a thousand times more than I, from being happy, eternally and infinitely happy."

Do we not utter idle words when we say that a creed which rouses a man to this pitch of passion and love, is a lost cause? But I merely refer by way of parenthesis to this union of passion with asceticism, throwing out the suggestion that any cruelty of self-mortification is more than repaid by the power of loving,—*quand on aime, qu'est-ce qu'il y a de plus doux que de souffrir pour l'amour de ce qu'on aime*—and pass on to my point, which is that we, mankind, civilization, the interests of hearth and home, need these fanatical excesses in order to counterbalance the meanness, the grossness, the bestiality that hangs about the neck of poor human nature. Aristotle's *ne quid nimis* is perhaps the wisest goal for stumbling men, but how fares the golden mean when the balance on one side is piled high, if the balance at the other end is to hang empty? Say that these fasts, living,—no, not living but sustaining life,—on a few dates or a handful of rice, as Père Foucauld did, these vigils that fill the exhausted brain with the hideous phantasms of insomnia, these macerations that slice the skin, daub it with blood, wrench the muscles and twist the bones awry, and all the abstinences, punishments, indignities and cruelties that religious fanatics have inflicted upon their bodies—say that these are monstrous, that they disgust and horrify you; then look into the slums of some great city, see the prostitutes herded together, look into opium joints and gin hells, look into the rubber forests of Peru or the Congo, look at the lynching of negroes, look at Germans, or drunken soldiers of any other nation, sacking a town, and reckon up the horrors that are heaped mountain-high, and then ask yourself, if it is not a comfort, a tonic, a source of hope and strength, to find men who treat their own flesh as others treat slaves and captives, who trample lust and appetite under foot, who rejoice in the purification of suffering? If humanity is to set before its

eyes the golden mean, it will not attain it if the lovers of
good do no more than enroll themselves in the sect of Epicurus; some may do so, but not all, or the game is lost. As
long as we have intemperance and excess at one extreme, so
long we must have intemperance and excess at the other.
Comfortable pulpits, prosperous clergymen, professors of
ethics, cannot kindle the flame that shall burn the dross out
of our hearts; there must be men like Père Foucauld to lead
a hermit's life of passionate protest against human brutality,
and like Ignatius Loyola with the courage to acquire that
spiritual strength that can only be got from self-mortification, and the will to put it to daily use in the service of
common men. At any rate that is the argument; and I
take it that the reason why Christianity is losing its influence more and more, is just because its belief in its own
tenets is too feeble to kindle the passionate conviction of a
Loyola or a Père Foucauld.

There is one thing more and I have done. We almost
always think of Loyola, or Luther, or Calvin, as a doughty
fighter for his particular creed. Let us drop, for the moment, their disagreements and divisions, and look upon them
all as striving, each in his own mistaken way, to achieve one
common end. All were at one in the conviction that religion is of the first importance for man. But before proceeding further, I suppose that I should attempt some
definition of the meaning that I attach to the word *religion*
or *religious*. I take it that religious men are at work on the
creation, or exposition, of some wide home of thought, where
imagination and hope may wander free. The function of
poets may serve to explain what I mean; and the comparison
cannot be looked upon as irreverent, for I have in mind the
spacious temple of thought built, or rather opened up and
out like a celestial canopy, by Æschylus, Plato, Dante,
Shakespeare, Milton, Shelley and the rest, in which weary
men, discouraged, vexed, sick at heart, vanquished or ship-
wrecked on the high seas of life, may wander in peace, delight and reverence, undisturbed by the consciousness of self,
with its unloveliness, its weaknesses, blemishes and inade-
quacies and all the noisy insistence of the appetites and

ambitions that animate physical life. In a similar fashion, religious men,—when wisely minded, working in unison with the poets, or, when wayward, trying to undo what poets have done,—create or reveal an ample tabernacle, a region, a heaven, of etherial substance, where ideas of goodness, beauty and love have power to compel devotion and self-dedication.

Religion, then, is the creation, or revelation, of this temple, canopy, or garden of thought. To be aware of this expanse is faith. After this uncircumscribed region has been discovered, framed, or flung toward heaven, and like a celestial sphere overarches poor human existence, comes the task of theology. That task is to give to this etherial region the semblance of reality, that is, to touch it with signs of familiarity, colors of the known, marks of the recognizable, and thereby give plausible justification to the assurances of faith. The task was difficult; it was necessary to avoid the fatal faults of abstraction, of mathematical coldness, of the nihilism of the absolute, and therefore theology has usually resorted to the device of transferring human matters up bodily into this austere and beautiful domain; and in its overeagerness, has done so too much, at least more than we today can approve, creating human deities, as with the pagans, that were grossly human, or as with Semitic peoples egotistically national, or as with the Christians, transferring thither the type of human perfection, and asserting that there humanity made perfect possesses infinite power. No doubt the task of giving a semblance of reality to the House of Hope is difficult. On one hand the grossness of human nature seems to convert the bare idea of it into irony, into a sort of Voltairian *jeu d'esprit;* on the other, the increasing knowledge, as we call it, of the stuff or energy that composes the physical universe round about us, tends to divert our minds from what men of science say are our Platonic dreams. But religion is founded on a deep laid foundation. The mystical rests upon the deepest mystery, the fact of consciousness. Matter and mind are incommensurable; and even if it should come to pass that the nature and course of matter—or whatever the generic term is that should be applied to the causes of sensation—be discovered and charted beyond a reasonable doubt, still the human mind will always be free to feel that certainty is denied to it, and therefore that nothing, not even its highest dream, is impossible, however unlikely.

This task of quickening faith was, as I say, difficult, and of course theology has made mistakes. Perhaps it should have been more discreet in talking as much as it has done about truth. But it may well be doubted whether any religious doctrine that confined itself to probabilities, or hopes, or poetry, would have been acceptable to more than a handful. We poor human beings are oppressed with the fleetingness of life, with the series of banishments from Gardens of Eden,—from youth, from health, from affection, —banishments that follow on one another's heels; we are oppressed and giddy with the changes that dance about us. A philosopher may be content to say: "There is but one reality—our present life, which carries in it its history, and is making itself," but the ordinary man cries out for something holy.

It is with this aspect of his life that I wish to take leave of Ignatius Loyola, not as a champion of Roman Catholicism, not as an enemy to pagans or a hammer of heretics, but as a husbandman in the vineyard of the true God,—as a passionate believer in holiness. His dominating purpose all his life was to save his soul, and the soul of his neighbor; and what is a man's soul, but the turning away from the base, the mean, the brutal, the bestial, the inheritance of an almost infinite animal existence, and a reaching out toward ideas of holiness. It was for this end that Jesus Christ lived his life and died, that men might believe in holiness; and Ignatius Loyola, with his faults, his inadequate comprehension, his bigotry, his blindness, strove with all his might to be a faithful servant of Christ, his Master.

I will grant that Loyola had ideas of religion, ideas of God, which time and knowledge have rendered inadequate and unsatisfactory to hungry, mystical souls today, that his conception of the Kingdom of God on earth lacks the poetry that alone makes such a Kingdom lovable, that the modes in which he sought to imitate the life of Jesus Christ have little or no resemblance to the story of the Gospels, that the means he employed were backward and mistaken; I will grant that what he did would often have been better left undone; and yet with all these concessions, there are few such heroic figures in history. He and his disciples have not conferred the benefits they meant to confer, but others that they knew not of, perhaps no whit less valuable.

> See! In the rocks of the world
> Marches the host of mankind,
> A feeble, wavering line.
> Where are they tending?—A God
> Marshall'd them, gave them their goal.—
> Ah, but the way is so long!
> Years they have been in the wild!
> Sore thirst plagues them, the rocks,
> Rising all round, overawe;
> Factions divide them, their host
> Threatens to break, to dissolve.—
> Ah, keep, keep them combined!
> Else, of the myriads who fill
> That army, not one shall arrive;
> Sole they shall stray; on the rocks
> Batter for ever in vain,
> Die one by one in the waste.
>
> Then, in such hour of need
> Of your fainting, dispirited race,
> Ye, like angels, appear,
> Radiant with ardour divine
> Beacons of hope, ye appear!
> Languor is not in your heart,
> Weakness is not in your word,
> Weariness not on your brow.
> Ye alight in our van! at your voice,
> Pain, despair, flee away.
>
> . . .
> Thou wouldst not *alone*
> Be saved, my father!

Semper immenso hominum salutis desiderio exarsit.

APPENDIX

APPENDIX

A

Sources: almost all these are published in *Monumenta Societatis Jesu*, Madrid.

Acta S. Ignatii: dictated in 1553 and 1555 by Ignatius to Father Luis Gonzalez de Camara. In volume entitled *Ignatio de Loyola, Scripta* I.

Epistola P. Lainii de S. Ignatio: written by Lainez to Polanco June 17, 1547. In volume last mentioned.

Memoriale P. Consalvii de Camara de S. Ignatio: notes and anecdotes of Gonzalez (1573). Same volume.

De Actis S. Ignatii a Ribadeneira: a collection of sayings, anecdotes, etc. Date uncertain, probably prior to 1572. Same volume.

Dicta et Facta S. Ignatii a P. Ribadeneira collecta.

De ratione S. Ignatii in gubernando, by same.

Acta quædam S. Ignatii a P. Natali.

Dictamina S. Ignatii a P. Lancicio collecta.

Memorabilia de S. Ignatio a P. Lancicio collecta: these are collections of anecdotes, memorabilia, etc. Same volume.

Vita Ignatii Loyolæ et rerum Societatis Jesu Historia; by Joannes Alphonsus de Polanco, who was Loyola's Secretary 1547-1556. Volume I, contains the life.

Vida del P. Ignacio de Loyola, fundador de la Compañia de Jesús, by Pedro de Ribadeneira, a disciple who was first acquainted with Ignatius in 1540, and very intimate from 1552 to 1555. The first edition was in Latin in 1572; the best is in a French translation by P. Ch. Clair, S.J., furnished with excellent notes. (Paris, 1891.)

Epistolæ et Instructiones: in twelve volumes, these are letters from 1536 to his death.

Epistolæ Mixtæ: in five volumes, these are letters from members of the Society to Loyola.

Litteræ quadrimestres: in four volumes, these are business letters written every four months to Loyola by provincials and others, from 1546 to 1556.

Spiritual Exercises of Saint Ignatius. I have used an English translation entitled, *The Text of the Spiritual Exercises of Saint Ignatius translated from the original Spanish,* fourth edition revised, London, 1913.

Constitutiones Societatis Jesu. I have used a copy, Latin and French, entitled *Les Constitutions des Jésuites,* Paris, 1843.

De Origine et Progressu Societatis Jesu: this is an account by Father Simon Rodriguez, one of the First Fathers (1577). Volume entitled *Epistolæ Paschasii Broëti et Aliorum.*

Memoriale Beati Petri Fabri: this is a sort of pious diary composed by Pierre Lefèvre (Favre or Faber, for his name is spelt in various ways), one of the First Fathers (1542-1546). Volume entitled *Fabri Monumenta.*

Epistolæ P. Lainii: These are letters written by Lainez, one of the First Fathers. Volume entitled *Lainii Monumenta.*

Epistolæ P. Salmeronis: These are letters written by Salmerón, also one of the First Fathers.

Epistolæ Paschasii Broëti, Claudii Jaji, Joannis Codurii et Simonis Rodericii. These are four of the First Fathers.

Fabri Monumenta: Letters and *Memoriale* of Pierre Lefèvre, one of the First Fathers.

Bobadillæ Monumenta: These are letters of Bobadilla, one of the First Fathers.

Epistolæ P. Nadal. He was one of the early disciples, having known Loyola familiarly in Paris in 1535.

Monumenta Xaveriana: Letters of Xavier's, and a life by P. Alessandro Valignano.

LATER BIOGRAPHIES

De Vita et Moribus Ignatii Loyolæ: Giovanni Pietro Maffei, S.J. (1585).

Historia Societatis Jesu, Pars Prima: Nicolaus Orlandini, S.J. (1598-1606).

Della vita e dell' Istituto di S. Ignazio: Daniele Bartoli, S.J. (1650).

Vie de Saint Ignace: Dominique Bouhours, S.J. (1679).

Acta Sanctorum, Julii, Tom VII, Die trigesima prima (1731).

Saint Ignace de Loyola: Henri Joly.

Ignatius Loyola: Stewart Rose (Caroline Erskine Stewart, Lady Buchan) (1870).

Saint Ignatius Loyola: Francis Thompson (1910).

Saint Ignace de Loyola: G. Desdevises du Dezert, *Revue Hispanique,* Vol. 34 (June, 1915).

Saint Ignatius Loyola: John Hungerford Pollen, S.J. (1922).

Storia della Compagnia di Gesù in Italia: Tacchi Venturi, S.J. (Vol. I, 1910, Vol. II, 1922).
Loyola's life is narrated in Vol. II, which contains a list of authorities, pp. xlix-lx. This work is scholarly, accurate and just.

Historia de la Compañía de Jesús en la Asistencia de España (Vol. I, 1902): Father Antonio Astrain, S.J.

This is a scholarly, moderate, and, in all respects that I can judge, excellent work, in several large volumes. The first volume is given up to a narrative of Loyola's career and of the doings of the Society in his lifetime. A very full bibliography concerning matters, both printed and not, will be found in Volume I, pp. xiii-xlv.

APPENDIX

B

Authorities for specific statements in the text, translations of passages in a foreign language, etc.

Chapter II

Chapter III

Chapter IV

Chapter X

CHAPTER XV

Chapter XVI

Chapter XVII

Chapter XVIII

CHAPTER XXX

Chapter XXXI

Chapter XXXII

Chapter XXXIII

APPENDIX

C

DATE OF LOYOLA'S BIRTH

The date almost universally accepted by Jesuit writers, although admitted not to be free from doubt, is 1491, which in imitation of Father Polanco I shall call the *Nurse's date*. Who the nurse was I have never heard. This date seems to have been fixed upon by those Fathers who were in Rome at Loyola's death, and put upon his tombstone; at that time Ribadeneira was in Flanders, Nadal in Spain, and Gonzalez in Portugal. The arguments in favor of the *Nurse's date* will be found in Astrain, Vol. I, p. 3, Note 2.

In support of the date 1495, I may refer to Father Kreiten and to *La Civiltà Cattolicà*, July, 1900, both cited in Astrain's note.

My reasons are briefly these:

(1) My proposition may be stated categorically:

    A. His conversion occurred after his wound at Pamplona, in 1521.

    B. At that time he was 26 years old.

    C. It follows that he was born in 1495.

As to A: it is clear beyond a reasonable doubt that his conversion took place during his convalescence; although the upholders of the *Nurse's date* (as they are obliged to do) try to maintain that the conversion took place five years earlier (*Acta Sanctorum Julii*, Tom. VII, p. 637). How do they explain that, under their hypothesis, he continued to be a soldier and made no change of life?

As to B: it is equally clear from the opening sentences of his *Memoirs* that he was 26 years old at the time of his conversion. His conversion was the memorable event of his life. His disciples asked him to dictate an account of his *converted* life; they did not care particularly about his boyhood. They asked: Quem ad modum *ab initio suæ conversione* illum Dominus Gubernavit? And his answer begins: Hasta los 26 annos de su edad,—i.e., he starts his narrative at the age of 26.

Acceptance of this age of 26 at the time he was wounded establishes the date 1495.

(2) Polanco at first (*Historia S. J.*, 1537, Vol. I, p. 77) accepted the *Nurse's date*, 1491, but afterwards abandoned it in favor of 1495 (*do*, p. 9). This, I submit, must have been because he had good reason to believe that he had been wrong.

(3) Ribadeneira first took 1495, but on the strength of Polanco's earlier position and of the inscription on the tombstone, shifted to 1491; he does not seem to have been aware of Polanco's change of mind.

(4) Esteben de Garibay (see Astrain's note aforesaid), although pooh-poohed by Astrain, is not, I think, a negligible witness. In 1566 he wrote a chronicle of Spain, and having come to the attack on Pamplona, makes a digression to give a summary of Loyola's life, and puts the date of birth as 1495. He was a Spaniard, and in Spain at the time, and must have had some authority, wherever he may have got it, for that date.

(5) All the chief incidents in Loyola's life accord better with the later date:

1515: It is more likely that when he took part in the carnival fracas he was nineteen years old rather than twenty-three.

1517: He left Don Juan Velazquez's household at the latter's death. It is more likely (as he was only adopted until a place in the King's court should be found for him) that, failing such a situation, he should go to his kinsman, the Duke of Najera, when he was twenty-two than when he was twenty-six. I suspect that he would have left earlier but for the approaching death of Don Juan.

1521: The emotional crisis of conversion psychologically befits the younger age better.

1526: In the inquisitorial proceedings at Alcalá, the witnesses call him a *young man,* and (except one who thinks he was the eldest) make no distinction between his age and those of his college comrades, who were probably eighteen to twenty-one, and the priest suggests his age as *twenty.* (*Scripta,* Vol. I, p. 600, line 1.)

1556: His illnesses and extreme asceticism make it remarkable that he attained the age of sixty-one; each added year makes his length of life still more surprising.

(6) I cannot but think that deference to authority, especially to the Bull of Canonization, affects Jesuit scholars, however unconscious they may be, and that they accept the *Nurse's date* as a *chose jugée.*

INDEX

Acton, Lord: on Ignatius, p. ix.
Alcalá: university of, p. 71; Loyola's stay there, p. 72; first inquisitorial proceeding, p. 73; third, p. 86.
Araoz, S. J.: goes to Spain, p. 245; his preaching, p. 246.
Aretino, Pietro, p. 163; quoted, pp. 298, 299, 303.
Arnold, Matthew: *Rugby Chapel*, quoted, p. 367.
Astrain, S. J.: *History of the Society of Jesus in Spain:* p. xii.

Barcelona: description of, p. 39; Loyola's return, p. 51; stay at, Chap. vii, p. 63.
Bartoli, S. J.: quoted, on Loyola's humility, p. 337; narrative of miracle, 356-357.
Bellay, Jean du, Cardinal: ambassador to Pope, p. 299; search for antiquities, p. 300.
Berquin, Louis de: p. 140.
Bobadilla, S. J.: introduced, p. 120; behavior in Germany, p. 122; letter to Lainez, p. 123; to Cardinal Farnese, p. 347.
Borgia, Francis, duke of Gandia, S. J.: pp. 246-7.
Brébeuf, S. J.: pp. 357-358.
Broët, Paschase, S. J.: life, p. 149; in Ireland, pp. 230-234; dying declaration, pp. 149; vote, p. 212.
Buchanan, George: on students at Sainte Barbe, p. 98.

Canisius: on Erasmus, p. 70; on Pierre Lefèvre, p. 286; on the ideals of the Society, p. 350.
Cano, Melchior: opposes Jesuits in Spain, p. 248; quarrel with Lainez, p. 265.
Capuchins: p. 302.
Caraffa, Gian Pietro, Cardinal (Paul IV): at odds with Loyola, p. 166; letter to, from Loyola, p. 167; life of, p. 168; and Order of Teatini, p. 302; and Inquisition in Italy, p. 350.

Charles V: pp. 57, 177; and Council of Trent, p. 253; and Wolsey, p. 298.
Charter: Chap. XX, p. 202.
Cisneros: his *Ejercitatorio*, p. 126.
Coduri, S. J.: life, p. 150; at death of Hoces, p. 150; his death, p. 150; vote, p. 212.
Coimbra: eccentric conduct of students there, p. 236; Loyola's letter to them, p. 240.
Colonna, Vittoria: hears of Jesuits, p. 185; inquires about them, p. 148; her poetry, p. 303.
Columbus: p. 43.
Confraternità della Carità: p. 302.
Constitution of Society: pp. 216-222.
Contarini, Gaspar, Cardinal; on Spaniards, p. 6; and *Spiritual Exercises*, p. 188; letter to say that Charter was granted, p. 204.
Contarini, Pietro: p. 166.
Council of Trent: Chap. XXV, p. 253.

Dissimulation (?): pp. 24, 346-347.
Don Quixote: comparison of Loyola to, p. 28.
Doctis, Gaspar de: in Venice, p. 166; in Rome, p. 195.
Duprat, Guillaume: Bishop of Clermont, p. 250.

Eguia, don Diego: pp. 165, 325.
Eguia, Don Esteven, p. 165.
Ejercitatorio Espiritual of Cisneros: p. 126.
Erasmistas: p. 67.
Erasmus: on Turks, p. 41; fame, p. 66; attacks on, p. 68; *Enchiridion*, p. 69.
Ercole d'Este, duke of Ferrara: pp. 185, 205.
First Fathers; see Lefèvre *et al.;* Journey from Paris to Venice, p. 179; charitable works there, p. 180; go to Rome, p. 180; see Paul III, p. 182; ordination of, p. 182; mission in Venetia, p. 183;